The European Union

The European Union

Duncan Watts

Edinburgh University Press

© Duncan Watts, 2008

Edinburgh University Press Ltd
22 George Square, Edinburgh

Typeset in 11/13pt Monotype Baskerville by
Servis Filmsetting Ltd, Manchester, and
printed and bound in Great Britain by
Antony Rowe Ltd, Chippenham, Wilts

A CIP record for this book is available from the British Library

ISBN 978 0 7486 3297 8 (hardback)
ISBN 978 0 7486 3298 5 (paperback)

Contents

Section Five: Attitudes

Boxes

Tables

Maps

Introduction

In the post-1945 era, many international bodies have been formed which enable the nations of the world to cooperate with each other, some on a global scale, some more regional in character. They have ranged from the global United Nations and the World Trade Organization, to Western gatherings such as the *Group of Eight (G8)* industrial states and the *Western European Union*.

Countries have joined with one another in search of mutual benefit. Of the coalitions in Europe, the European Union has been by far the most significant. The very fact that so many new democracies in Eastern Europe have been attracted to the idea of membership in recent years shows that they recognise that it is now an important player not just on the European stage but on the wider international scene as well.

The Union was not the first attempt at European cooperation, but it has been the boldest in conception, the most developed and the most successful. In aim, method and achievement it goes further than any other body. It is not just a customs union. It has a number of distinguishing characteristics, including a very complete set of institutions and a wide range of policy responsibilities. But what makes it especially distinctive is the fact that members have been willing to hand over powers to some *supranational authority* and be bound by its decisions and policies. Its aim is also grander: an ever closer union of European peoples. As Nugent[1] remarks: 'These characteristics do not make the EU a state, but they do make it a highly developed political system'.

Jean Monnet, one of the founding fathers of the European Union, took the view that the sovereign states of the past could no longer solve the problems of the day. They could not ensure their own progress or control their own future. He disliked the *intergovernmentalism* of some bodies created in the years immediately after 1945, for he believed them to be 'the opposite of the Community spirit'. In his view, 'mere cooperation' was not enough. Instead, he urged the creation of 'new functional authorities that superseded the sovereignty of existing nation states'.[2]

Not all European statesmen shared his outlook, although his ideas were well received in much of continental Western Europe. In Britain, from the earliest days of postwar cooperation, there were doubts about the wisdom or desirability of the closer union that Monnet favoured. British ministers of either main party disliked the spirit of *supranationalism* which pervaded the European Coal and Steel Community, the first major initiative taken by the six nations who later went on to form the European Economic Community. They preferred the idea of cooperation in appropriate areas, where nations found working together to be to their mutual benefit.

Since those postwar days, the process of *integration* in Europe has not always been easy, nor the path smooth. There have been tensions between the member states, and the conflict between national interests and the interests of Europe as a whole has posed particular difficulties for some countries. Yet the direction of movement has always been towards greater integration, a term that the *Oxford English Dictionary* defines as 'the harmonious combination of elements into a single whole'.

Integration and intergovernmentalism have been two forces at work in the evolution of the Community, as it has developed from its original form into the Union of today. At different times, both sets of ideas have gained the ascendancy, as thinkers and statesmen have pressed their particular viewpoint. The dispute is still at the heart of the controversy within the Union about the way it has developed and the future direction it should take.

One factor that emerges very clearly from any consideration of the European Union's history and present structure is that for several years the debate about Europe in Britain and some other countries has not been primarily about membership or non-membership of the Community, now Union. It has been more concerned with the sort of cooperation member states wish to have with their partners and the nature of the Europe to which they wish to belong.

About this book: themes and perspectives

The European Union is one of the world's most complex political systems and is therefore a challenge to study. To the uninitiated, its institutions seem remote, its remit unclear, its operations difficult to understand and its outputs sometimes perplexing. Moreover, it combines some attributes of a state with those of an international organisation, yet it closely resembles neither. Its development is shaped by an increasing number of players, including twenty-seven member governments, multiple common EU institutions, clusters of experts, private interests and citizen groups. All converge to influence what the EU is and what it does. My concern is to demystify the Union and make its institutions and processes more readily intelligible to all who share an interest in how the organisation functions.

As it has developed in size and scale in recent decades, the European Union has come to have a dramatic impact on government and politics in the member states. In Britain, it has assumed importance in Politics examination syllabuses both at Advanced level and in higher education. For some courses, knowledge of Britain in Europe and Europe in Britain is required. Study of these courses entails some understanding of the nature of the Union and how it works. In others, the focus is on the EU itself, how it has evolved, its institutions (including the individuals, parties and pressure groups that interact with them) and main policies. There is also a plethora of European Studies courses, in which the work involves knowledge of the development and workings of the Union.

Most books which feature Britain and Europe have some information referring to the EU, its evolution and organisation. However, texts which concentrate on the Union are markedly fewer in number. There are some good ones available – indeed, a few of very considerable merit – which perform the same task. These tend to be written at a highly specialist level, rather than in a way that might prove appropriate for someone requiring a thorough, but more accessible and less daunting analysis.

What is currently lacking is an up-to-date and comprehensive text covering key aspects – including history and developments, institutions, actors, policies and policy processes, and the role and attitudes of member states – in a way that meets the needs of a wide audience of teachers, students, practitioners and interested general readers. The challenge is to provide an authoritative account which will enable students at several levels to cope with the questions asked of them, yet to do so in a manner which enables them to grasp easily and clearly the information with which they are confronted. It is to be hoped that this book fulfils such demanding criteria and in the process also conveys some sense of the academic debate over the manner in which the EU has evolved.

This volume provides an opportunity to introduce a number of themes, problems and terms involved when studying the European Union. The use of the latter term raises an issue worth mentioning at this early stage: the difference between 'European Union' and 'European Community'. The European Community is the older term and is taken to refer to the three original communities established by the Treaty of Rome and merged in 1967. The Union, as established by the Maastricht Treaty with its defence/security and justice/home affairs pillars, is the wider of the two terms. Those of us who are citizens of member states are *de jure* citizens of the European Union. But all the institutions we think of as European, from the Commission and European Parliament to the Court of Justice, belong to the original European Community rather than to the European Union.

When the alternative terms 'Union' or 'Community' are used in this book, they both essentially refer to the same thing and should be regarded as interchangeable. The same apparently indiscriminate use of both labels is found in much of the literature produced by the EU institutions themselves. Broadly, the pattern adopted is to employ the word 'Community' in the period up to the implementation of the Maastricht Treaty and 'Union' when referring to events of roughly the last fifteen years.

With terminology out of the way, it is important to explain the structure of this volume. The material is organised in such a way that distinct sections provide comprehensive coverage of five key areas: the history and institutions of the Union, representation within it, its policies and attitudes to it in the member states. The conclusion surveys and reviews the past development, current trends and possible future directions of the EU.

This introduction is followed by some background information concerning the issues that arise later in the book, along with a list of the most commonly employed abbreviations. Advice on further reading at a basic and more demanding level is to be found at the end of the volume.

At the end of each chapter there is a glossary of the words printed in bold in the text. Italic type is occasionally used in the text for emphasis of some key points, to help imprint them on the memory.

Understanding attitudes to Europe

A century or more ago, the Austrian statesman Metternich, faced with rampant Italian nationalism, contemptuously remarked that 'Italy is no more than a geographical expression'. Yet the term 'Italian' was always rather more than merely geographical. The concept of being Italian may not have been a statement of nationality, but it did encapsulate an entire people's culture, language and way of life, even though there was no cohesive political entity called Italy at that time. So too, in the first half of the twentieth century, the term 'European' gave an indication of geographical origin and could be seen also as a statement of cultural identity. But it had very little meaning beyond that.

Today, *eurosceptics* dismiss the idea of European integration with as much contempt as Metternich showed for Italian nationalism. However, just as in spite of Metternich's dismissal of the idea, Italians overcame their internal differences and did achieve political union, so too in the years since 1945 those with a personal vision of a European identity have encouraged Europe to develop its own political and economic union. As Walter Hallstein,[3] the first president of the European Commission, said in his memoirs:

> Europe shares a sense of values: of what is good and bad; of what a man's rights should be and what are his duties; of how society should be ordered; of what is happiness and what disaster. Europe shares many things such as its memories that we call history.

Opinions about the Union that has been created range widely across its twenty-seven countries, although in several of them there is a broad range of support not only for membership but for full involvement in its operations and policies. In Britain, there are varying shades of opinion, from the fervently pro-European (i.e., the relatively few *euroenthusiasts*, some would say *eurofanatics*, who believe that Britain must become more European in outlook and work enthusiastically to make a success of British membership) to the outright hostile.

Opponents of closer ties between member states and the EU either feel that their country should never have joined or that integration has gone as far as is desirable, perhaps already too far. If eurosceptics are wary of the Union and its deeds, *europhobes* dislike intensely any institutions and policies that derive from

Brussels, the heart of the EU. In between, there are many people who recognise that outside the Union, their country would be isolated and exposed, but who nonetheless have doubts about the direction the Union is taking and about surrendering any further powers to its institutions. There are many such *euroagnostics* in Britain today.

To the casual and uninformed onlooker the impression is sometimes given that the only argument over Europe is whether Britain or any other country should ever have joined. In fact, although there always has been, and continues to be, a strong (if relatively small) anti-European body of opinion in most countries of the Union, the real arguments that have influenced development over the years, and which continue to dominate discussions, concern different views as to the nature of EU membership.

In the course of time differing perspectives have governed attitudes towards what is seen as European cooperation. These sometimes diametrically opposed approaches thread themselves through the historical development, lay constraints upon the function of European institutions and determine the degree of commitment to the *European Idea*.

Background information

Key dates in the evolution of the Union

1950 Schuman Declaration
1951 Treaty of Paris signed by the Six
1952 European Coal and Steel Community in operation
1955 Messina talks on further economic integration
1957 Treaties of Rome, establishing EEC and Euratom
1958 EEC and Euratom in operation
1962 Common Agricultural Policy agreed
1967 Merger Treaty: ECSC, EEC and Euratom combined to form
      European Community (EC)
1973 Admission of Denmark, Ireland and the United Kingdom
1975 Lomé Convention agreed and in operation
1979 European Monetary System in operation
      Direct elections to the European Parliament
1981 Admission of Greece
1985 Withdrawal of Greenland
1986 Admission of Portugal and Spain
      Signing of the Single European Act
1990 Accession of East Germany
1991 Maastricht Treaty (TEU)
1993 Ratification process of Maastricht Treaty completed: EC becomes a
      Union
1995 Accession of Austria, Finland and Sweden
1997 Amsterdam Treaty
1999 Official launch of the euro
2000 Nice Treaty
2002 The euro becomes the sole currency in the eurozone
2004 Admission of ten new countries, including eight 'new democracies'
      from Eastern Europe
2005 Rejection by French and Dutch kills prospects of implementation of
      Constitutional Treaty
2007 Admission of Bulgaria and Romania

The current member states

Country	Date of accession	Population (in millions)
Austria	1995	8.3
Belgium	1952	10.5
Bulgaria	2007	7.9
Cyprus	2004	0.8
Czech Republic	2004	10.3
Denmark	1973	5.4
Estonia	2004	1.4
Finland	1995	5.3
France	1952	63.4
Germany	1952	82.3
Greece	1981	11.1
Hungary	2004	10.1
Ireland	1973	4.2
Italy	1952	58.8
Latvia	2004	2.3
Lithuania	2004	3.4
Luxembourg	1952	0.5
Malta	2004	0.4
Netherlands	1952	16.4
Poland	2004	38.1
Portugal	1986	10.6
Romania	2007	21.6
Slovakia	2004	5.4
Slovenia	2004	2.0
Spain	1986	44.7
Sweden	1995	9.1
United Kingdom	1973	60.7
Total 27		Total 494.8

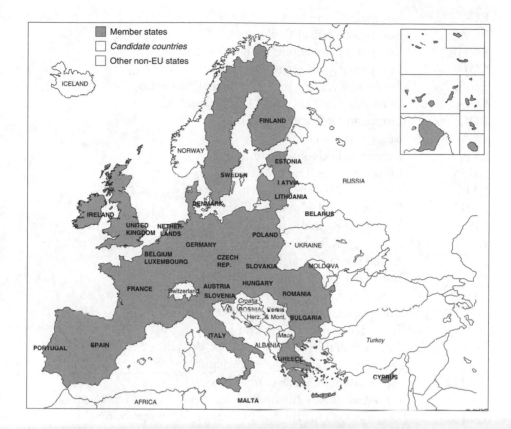

Map P.1 Current EU member states and candidate countries

Abbreviations

The European Union is littered with acronyms for its various institutions, treaties, agencies and policies. The following is a glossary of abbreviations used frequently in the text.

ACP	African, Caribbean and Pacific countries associated with the EC
BBQ	British Budgetary Question, aka the Bloody British Question
CAP	Common Agricultural Policy
CFP	Common Fisheries Policy
CFSP	Common Foreign and Security Policy
COPA	Committee of Professional Agricultural Organisations
COR	Committee of the Regions
COREPER	Committee of Permanent Representatives
DGs	Directorates-General of the Commission

EC	European Community
ECB	European Central Bank
ECHR	European Convention on Human Rights
ECJ	European Court of Justice
Ecofin	Economics and finance (Council of Ministers)
ECSC	European Coal and Steel Community
EDC	European Defence Community
EEA	European Economic Area
EEC	European Economic Community
EFTA	European Free Trade Area
EMS	European Monetary System
EMU	Economic and Monetary Union
EP	European Parliament
ERM	Exchange Rate Mechanism
ESC	Economic and Social Committee
ETUC	European Trade Union Confederation
EU	European Union
	Europol European Police Office
IGC	Intergovernmental Conference
IMF	International Monetary Fund (of the United Nations)
MEP	Member of the European Parliament
NATO	North Atlantic Treaty Organization
OECD	Organisation for Economic Co-operation and Development
OEEC	Organisation for European Economic Co-operation
PPE/ED	European People's Party (Christian Democrat) and European Democrats
PSE	Party of European Socialists
QMV	Qualified Majority Voting
SEA	Single European Act
TEU	Treaty for European Union
UKREP	United Kingdom Permanent Representation
UNICE	Union of Industries of the European Community
WEU	Western European Union, defence arm of the Council of Europe
WTO	World Trade Organization

SECTION ONE: HISTORY

Introduction

The idea of a united Europe has a long history, its origins dating back to at least the time of the **Holy Roman Empire**. Attempts were made in the last two centuries to unite the continent by force, under first Napoleon and then Hitler, but they were unsuccessful. More peaceful schemes have been advanced, with proposals for a Pan-European Union and a common market being made in 1923. However, it was the failure of the Führer's bid to dominate Europe which proved to be the inspiration for a new initiative.

World War Two was a catastrophe which discredited the old international order and for many Europeans the basic ingredient of that order: the independent nation state. Indeed, according to one commentator:

> [the] past failure and current weakness of nation states in 1945 is a prime wellspring of what was to become known as the European movement, dedicated to the broad notion of seeking to unite the states and people of Europe through some new entity . . . which might have the size and strength to avoid the calamities which had befallen the post-1919 state system.[1]

With the exceptions of Britain, Sweden and Switzerland, every European state either had witnessed the relatively violent overthrow of its constitutional arrangements or had been militarily occupied by an enemy or both.

By 1945, many people saw that it was the time to lay aside the old rivalries and create new bonds of cooperation and friendship between Germany and the other countries of the continent. In particular, it was necessary to ensure that France and Germany should live and work together in peaceful cooperation, for they had been at war three times in less than one hundred years.

There was in 1945 and the years immediately following a most unusual willingness to think in European rather than in national terms, helped by the fact that politicians such as Adenauer in West Germany, De Gasperi in Italy and Monnet and Schuman in France were, in varying degrees, internationalists. If reconstruction was their immediate goal, they also realised the need for this to be underpinned by peace in Europe. Without this, economic recovery would merely serve to fuel the engines of future war. European leaders, therefore, had to address themselves to twin tasks:

1. how to promote economic recovery and provide a decent standard of living for the people of Europe
2. how to bring about reconciliation so that old hatreds would not resurface and move forward by creating a new political stability on the continent.

In this section, we explore the way in which six nations in Western Europe tried to effect a transformation of the continent, thereby introducing a new era of peace and prosperity.

Glossary

Holy Roman Empire A mainly Germanic conglomeration of lands, created at the time of Charlemagne's coronation as emperor in 800 and lasting until 1806, during the Napoleonic Wars.

CHAPTER 1

The drive for European unity to 1973

In the years immediately following the ending of World War Two, there was a determination among some Europeans to rebuild the continent and in so doing to ensure that it would not be plagued by war again. They felt that in unity, there would be strength. A series of international bodies was created which provided for varying levels of cooperation. However, it was the signing of the Treaty of Rome in 1957 that marked the key turning point. By creating the European Economic Community, the pioneers of postwar unification were taking a step which had the potential to reorder economic and political relations among its member states.

In this chapter, we explore how and why European states which had previously jealously guarded their national independence were willing to surrender or pool their sovereignty and join an organisation whose immediate goal was to create a common market but whose longer-term aspiration was to achieve ever closer union. We then examine how the success of the enterprise led to Britain and other countries seeking membership.

In 1914, Europe was at the centre of world affairs. Thirty years later, it was in ruins and world leadership was passing into the hands of two **superpowers**, the Soviet Union and the United States of America.

World War Two had resulted in millions of deaths and physical and economic destruction across the continent. The nations of Europe were virtually bankrupt and faced the prospect of a long struggle to regain the position they had attained before hostilities. Britain, which had been the world's greatest trading nation in 1914, was now a debtor and had little chance of returning to its former glory without assistance. To get back to earlier levels of production and standards of living would need outside help from the United States' which alone had the money and resources that Europe lacked. It would also depend upon the willingness and ability of the European nations to put their own house in order and work together in a new spirit of cooperation.

Why was unity desirable after 1945?

In the early postwar era, there had been economic, political and military cooperation between the countries of Western Europe as never before in peacetime. It was encouraged by the United States and for many years stimulated by fear of the Soviet Union (USSR). Soon after World War Two, it became apparent that the main threat to Western Europe came not from Germany but from the USSR. At first, not everyone recognised the danger posed by the Soviet Union, which for more than four decades was to split the continent in half and dominate the Eastern sector via its puppet governments. However, as the tension and suspicion of the **Cold War** era developed, so too did the feeling that unity might give more security.

Initially, however, the German problem was one which had to be addressed. Any movement in the direction of unity could not preclude German involvement. If there was close cooperation in Western Europe, then this might help to contain German strength. A later British prime minister, Harold Macmillan,[1] noted this at the time:

> The most important motive behind the movement for European **integration** is the need to attach Germany permanently to Western Europe, but in such a manner that she cannot dominate it. This is as much a British as a continental interest. After all, we have fought two wars about this in one generation.

He realised the importance of Germany's position in Europe, and like other forward-looking politicians of the era recognised that it was a key barrier against the potential threat posed by the Soviet Red Army.

Beyond this tactical consideration, however, there were other factors. Above all, there was a desire to bring about a lasting peace in Europe. After 1945, there was a feeling that fighting could break out all over again. The Frenchman Jean Monnet,[2] one of the inspirational figures in those early postwar days, was later to describe the atmosphere as one in which there was an acceptance 'of a war that is thought to be inevitable'. Martin Holland[3] makes the point very clearly: 'Hindsight should not make us undervalue this preoccupation; East–West relations were confrontational; the status of Berlin remained precarious, Germany was formally divided; French economic recovery was stagnating; and the proliferation of atomic weapons had begun'.

After many wars, there tends to be a mood of idealism, a feeling that the horrors of war must never be allowed to haunt the world again. This happened after World War Two and in particular it was recognised that there was a need to bind France and Germany in an alliance of friendship, support and mutual interest. For Monnet, such an axis was the key to stability in Europe. To him and others, the developments we are about to survey were not just a series of useful steps along the road towards recovery. In their thinking, Europe was more than an economic or a political concept. It was, in Monnet's words, a moral idea. It was all about a new venture in international relations whose main objective would be peace and reconciliation. This would end the anxiety in France which continued even when the war was over. For Frenchmen, the question on many lips was: 'What's to be done about Germany?' Monnet's instinct was to end national rivalries in Western Europe once and for all. In so doing, he believed that Western nations would be taking a step towards securing a larger peace which would prevent the continent from experiencing the century's third major war.

A '**European Idea**' developed, the idea of a strong, independent, prosperous and above all peaceful Europe. There was certainly a need for cooperation to bring about renewed economic strength, for following the appalling destruction the continent was devastated, France, Germany and Italy reduced to chaos, their peoples often out of work, sometimes starving or homeless, always poor. Common action, it was believed, might help industry and agriculture to recover.

There were, then, good reasons for European nations to come together. A number of groups were formed in the years after 1945 to promote the European cause. In October 1948 they came together in the European Movement, a pro-integrationist lobby which had national organisations in twenty-nine countries and was the principal all-party pressure group committed to European integration. Its first honorary presidents included De Gasperi and Winston Churchill, in recognition of their strong support for unification.

Monnet and other continental politicians looked to Britain for a lead. Britain's commitment to the causes of freedom and parliamentary government was implicit in the way it had fought against the German dictatorship in World War Two. During the hostilities, exiled leaders from several nations had based their operations in London. The pronouncements of Prime Minister Churchill seemed encouraging. Just before the fall of France in 1940, he had – at Monnet's instigation – proposed the union of Britain and France into a single state.

Early postwar attitudes in Europe to integration: federalism v. functionalism

Among the enthusiasts for European cooperation, there were differing theories about the ways in which European unity might progress. Essentially the conflict was between the **federalists** and the **functionalists**. At different times in the postwar era, proponents of either approach have had the upper hand. Between them, however, they provided the impetus for integration.

Federalists viewed **nationalism** as the major threat to a peaceful continent. They wanted more than the creation of a series of functional economic agencies. They wanted to move swiftly towards unification, arguing that all layers of government – local, regional, national and European – should cooperate with and complement each other.

Federalists were inspired by the phraseology of Churchill[4] in his **Zurich Speech**, in which he promoted the idea that the nations of Europe should join forces and work together. Most famously, he sought to remedy a situation in which 'over wide areas a vast quivering mass of tormented, hungry, care-worn and bewildered human beings gape at the ruins of their cities and homes, and scan the dark horizons for the approach of some new peril, tyranny or terror'. He went on to point to the remedy which,

if it were generally or spontaneously adopted, would as if by miracle transform the whole scene . . . and re-create the European family, or as much of it as we can, and provide it with a structure under which it can dwell in peace, in safety and in freedom. We must build a kind of **United States of Europe**.

Functionalists believed that greater unity in Europe would develop through a more piecemeal and gradual approach of which moves towards economic union would be the first stage. The organisations which were to be formed were seen not as an end goal in themselves, but rather as steps on the way towards building a new Europe. Such an approach would involve a more gradual transfer of national sovereignty to a European level.

There were also **intergovernmentalists**, representatives of those states which wished to retain as much of their **national sovereignty** as possible. Supporters believed that governments of major states had a key role to play in the evolution of the continent. They could see the merits of cooperation in specific areas, but had no wish to see any supranational body take policy decisions in key areas of political life, such as national defence and foreign policy. In their view, such integration as might occur would only take place as a result of individual governments pursuing their national interests, interests which might on occasion overlap.

In the early days after 1945, there was much idealism in Europe. Statesmen sought to create new structures which would enable cooperation and union to flourish. In those days it was the rhetoric of the federalists which carried the day. From 1948 to 1954 their ideas inspired the bold moves that were initiated, from the Council of Europe (1949) through to the creation of the European Defence Community and the European Political Community (both 1954) which between them would look after political and military union. But already by the early fifties, concrete steps were being taken which were much more in the functionalist mould. They were more cautious in their immediate goals, but more practical and achievable. The plan to pool French and German coal and steel supplies was the first of these and this functionalist phase was to culminate in the signing of the Treaty of Rome (1957).

Box 1.1 The outlook and approach of Jean Monnet

Jean Monnet was noted for his belief in carefully coordinated planning in France. Unhampered by any concern for the faded glories of the past, he was intent on the modernisation of his country, to be achieved by coordinating the plans for individual industries and launching new ones. He placed France's need for reconstruction in a European context. As he wrote in his *Memoirs*: 'The countries of Europe must turn their national efforts into a truly European effort. This will be possible only through a "federation of the West" '.[5]

He was clear about the end target which he wished to achieve in his European project, but recognised that there was scope for disagreement on the means by which the goal might be reached. In a broad sense, he is usually described as a federalist and indeed his writings are littered with references to the term, although he rarely spelt out what this might mean in practice. The ambiguity and vagueness were deliberate, because his preferred approach was to take concrete steps towards ultimate unity.

To arrive at the ultimate goal, Monnet was concerned with what was politically possible at the time. If appropriate, it might sometimes be wise to adopt an intergovernmental approach, for progress had to reflect what was possible 'at that time and that stage in men's thinking'. Generally, he favoured a pooling of sovereignty in a particular area, for this would sublimate national rivalries and tensions. The hope was that eventually, via such closer economic integration, there might develop closer political union if the results seemed good. As he put it at the time:

> Little by little, the work of the Community will be felt . . . Then the everyday realities themselves will make it possible to form the political union which is the goal of our Community and to establish the United States of Europe . . . Political Europe will be created by human effort when the time comes on the basis of reality.[6]

Because of his commitment to a step-by-step method of building European union and his willingness to accept a variety of approaches en route towards the federal goal, some commentators find it difficult to locate Monnet firmly in the federalist camp. In particular, Burgess[7] is critical of Monnet's contribution, noting its 'contradictory and diverse principles' which were sufficiently elastic that they could embrace 'incrementalism and intergovernmentalism'. He argues that despite the language the Frenchman sometimes employed, it is unrealistic to see him as a 'champion of the federalist cause in Europe', even if some form of federation was his ultimate object. He describes him as an 'economic functionary first and only secondly as an incremental federalist'. The phrase 'incremental federalist' has some merit. Monnet was certainly not a mere economic functionalist, for there was always a political objective to which he aspired, even if it was not one which was clearly formulated and elaborated.

In an interesting essay on the contribution of Monnet to the creation of modern Europe, Duroselle[8] detects four themes in his approach:

- He was not a nationalist and wanted to see the force of nationalism in Europe set aside.
- He believed in a Europe of concrete institutions.
- He wanted an 'open Europe' in which Britain would play a leading part.
- In particular, he wanted a Europe linked with the USA. He felt the transatlantic partnership was vital and noted that American governments were keen to see the European continent get its act together.

Essentially, Monnet was a visionary, albeit a very practical one. Without being obsessed with too many details, he had a sense of mission and of history. His approach was not one which allowed much room for the expression of popular feeling. He worked with and through a small elite, taking the view that when the beneficial results of new initiatives became apparent then the public would willingly offer their support for any venture which the elite conceived. His paramount concern was to achieve a common approach between the leaders of opinion in the various countries concerned.

Early steps in European unity, to 1950

The roots of today's European Union date back to the resolution of postwar statesmen to create a new structure in Europe based on peace between nations, political cooperation, economic recovery and a growth in international trade. In making this fresh start, it was hoped that progress might follow in three broad areas: military, political and economic union.

Early military cooperation

Soon after the war ended, the Western Powers saw more danger from the USSR than from a resurgent Germany. Many statesmen saw the need to create a military framework to complement other arrangements for the rebuilding of Europe. The Soviet Union had armed forces estimated at 4.5 million and was credited with possessing 6,000 planes. This represented a massive superiority over the military resources of the West and served to confirm fears in England and France that there was a red menace in the east of the continent. It was seen as a priority to preserve Western Europe from the danger of attack.

In March 1947, France and Britain signed the *Treaty of Dunkirk*, and entered into a fifty-year year alliance, each promising assistance if either was attacked by Germany. With the accession of the **Benelux** countries, this was expanded in the following year into a *Western Union*. This time, there was provision for aid against any armed attack. The Union was targeted against the USSR, with whom France and Britain still had a legally valid military alliance.

In 1948, Britain, France and the Benelux countries signed the *Pact of Brussels*, a vague commitment to set up a joint defensive system. No surrender of independence or sovereignty was involved, this being an essentially intergovernmental step – albeit one in which the wording did speak of the purpose of encouraging the progressive integration of Europe. Yet without assistance, these early initiatives were not sufficient to enable the member nations to resist a determined communist attack. Hence the importance of a speech made by President Truman[9] which laid down the basis of postwar American policy. He spoke of the need for 'containment' of communist aggression and promised American help for 'free peoples who are resisting attempted subjugation by armed minorities or by outside pressure'.

Formation of NATO

The military significance of the Pact of Brussels was soon overshadowed by the establishment of the *North Atlantic Treaty Organization (NATO)*, in 1949. The governments of the USA, Canada and ten West European nations (Benelux, Denmark, France, Iceland, Italy, Norway, Portugal and the United Kingdom) agreed that 'an armed attack against one or more of them in Europe or North America [should] be considered an attack against them all' and consequently that they would take such action as was necessary (including the use of armed force) to cope with any such act of aggression. NATO was a mutual defence alliance, though each nation was free to decide the form of that assistance in the event of an attack.

The treaty was prompted by the urgent need to combine against the powerful Russian army which was then seeking to drive the Western allies from West Berlin. America had the vast industrial resources and a monopoly of atomic weapons which could counterbalance the military power of the Soviet Union and its satellites. Unsurprisingly, the Soviet Union interpreted developments differently. In its view, NATO was aggressive in intent, rather than defensive.

Early political cooperation

This was for a long while less marked than cooperation in the military or economic field. It was hoped that integrating countries into a closer political community would eliminate the possibility of war between member states. In 1948, supporters of the idea of a united Europe met at an unofficial congress at The Hague presided over by Winston Churchill. The Congress led to the establishment in 1949 of the *Council of Europe*. This served (and continues to serve) primarily as a forum for parliamentary opinion. Its purpose was 'to achieve a greater unity between its members for the purpose of safeguarding and realising the ideas and principles which are their common heritage'. The Council was also responsible for drawing up the 'Convention on Human Rights and Fundamental Freedoms', which imposes obligations on all signatory powers. Coming into force in 1953, the Convention obliged members to respect and promote fundamental human rights and to recognise that individuals possess them under international law.

The idea was that the consultative assembly of 147 delegates from national parliaments of the Council would act as an embryonic European Parliament, but this did not prove to be the case. Individuals such as Adenauer, De Gasperi, Monnet and Spaak of Belgium were keen that the initiative should work, but Britain was unwilling to allow it to assume any real power or influence. The British foreign secretary, Ernest Bevin, saw dangers in an effective Council: 'Once you open that Pandora's box, you'll find it full of Trojan horses'. The remark was what Hennessy[10] has called a piece of 'classic Bevanese', but it illustrated the British fear of anything more than a body of limited power, based loosely on voluntary cooperation.

Early economic cooperation

In the search for closer economic cooperation in Europe, both of the two broad approaches, intergovernmental and integrationist, were apparent. Monnet was keen to see step-by-step progress along the road to greater union. But on the other side of the debate were many statesmen (notably in Britain) who were happy to think in terms of Europe drawing closer together but shrank from any binding commitment of the sort which he favoured.

In 1944 the governments of Belgium, the Netherlands and Luxembourg had agreed on the desirability of forming a free-trade area between them; in July 1947, an agreement on a customs union was also concluded. Thereafter, they became known as the Benelux countries. The success of their venture encouraged further cooperation. What made it particularly significant was that this was an experiment in integration as opposed to the intergovernmentalism of some other initiatives. However, the first key developments in economic cooperation derived from the conception and implementation of the Marshall Plan for economic recovery.

The Marshall Plan
At the end of the war, the economies of Europe were shattered and in ruins. The United States was the only Power with a strong economy. It supported the idea of European integration as a means of setting aside old rivalries, promoting prosperity and strengthening the ability of Western Europe to resist communism. Its main instrument of policy was the Marshall Plan. In June 1947 General Marshall announced that America would 'assist in the return of normal economic health in the world'. Billions of dollars were committed to propping up the states of Western Europe, for although the aid was available to all countries on the continent the Eastern bloc was uninterested in becoming involved. Bevin thought that the Americans were giving an 'inspiring lead', whereas the response of the Communist Party newspaper in Russia (*Pravda*) was less flattering. It discerned an attempt to interfere 'in the domestic affairs of other countries'.

American motives were mixed. Altruism played a part, but so did self-interest. It was in America's economic interests to see Europe prosperous again, for a flourishing continent could afford to buy American goods. In addition, there was a political motive, for Washington understood that hunger and deprivation made for popular discontent and disillusion with the democratic process. If aid could promote recovery, then there was less likelihood of Europeans being tempted by the communist ideas which were becoming entrenched in Eastern Europe. The position of West Germany was especially crucial in this regard, for it was geographically adjacent to the Soviet bloc. It was easier to sell the idea of assisting German recovery and rehabilitation to Western governments if it was part of a wider programme of economic assistance.

Altogether, some $13.5b were made available. Of this sum, the largest share (over $3b) went to Britain, whilst France, Italy and West Germany also benefited considerably. These countries were helped by the economic boom in the United States, both in the rising demand for manufactured goods and because of heavy investment in European industry by private firms. By the early fifties, the West European economies were beginning to recover, much helped by the assistance given by the United States through the Marshall Plan.

It had been necessary to create an organisation to supervise the administration of this relief. Early in 1948 a number of countries joined together in the **Organisation for European Economic Cooperation (OEEC)**. This was a classic example of intergovernmental cooperation, valuable in itself, but quite distinct from the sort of mutual commitment favoured by the more enthusiastic federalists among European politicians. No surrender of national sovereignty was involved. Monnet[11] diagnosed what he saw as the 'intrinsic weakness' of an approach which went no further than mere cooperation between governments: 'The idea that sixteen nations will cooperate effectively is an illusion'. It was true that in such a situation, if there was no consensus there was likely to be little effective action. But this suited those who preferred to think in terms of cooperation rather than integration.

European Coal and Steel Community (ECSC)

For some time, Monnet had been looking for a way of bringing about economic integration in Europe. He was looking for a bold idea which would capture the imagination of internationalists in Western Europe. Although he was a visionary, he understood that the politicians and civil servants in his own country and other countries would only back his ideas if they were in line with their national interests and their postwar recovery programmes. In his *Memoirs*,[12] he later recalled why his fertile mind alighted on a plan for future coal and steel harmonisation:

> Coal and steel were at once the key to economic power, and the raw materials for forging the weapons of war. This double role gave them immense symbolic significance, now largely forgotten . . . To pool them across frontiers would reduce their malign prestige and turn them instead into a guarantee of peace.

Problems in the coal and steel industries
In the late 1940s, a crisis in the steel industries of Western European countries seemed likely, for there was the potential to produce vast quantities of the material. Europe appeared to be running into excess steel production. It was estimated that by 1952 production would be approximately 69m tons, and consumption plus exports only 61m – hence the danger of a cut-throat price war or some new international cartel to keep prices artificially high.

Monnet was aware that France had a clear interest in tackling the problem of excess capacity. He was conscious of Germany's economic resurgence and against this background was keen to safeguard French national interests. He wanted to ensure that his country had access to German raw materials and European markets. As he wrote in his diary in 1950: 'France's continued recovery will come to a halt unless we rapidly solve the problem of German industrial production and its competitive capacity'.[13] The problem needed to be tackled before German recovery enabled it to outstrip France and become a potential danger once again. It required new thinking and Monnet did not seek to 'solve the German problem in its present context. [We must] change the context by transforming the basic facts'.

Monnet's brainchild was to devise a plan for the harmonisation of the coal, iron and steel industries of France and Germany. The French foreign minister, Robert Schuman, was enthusiastic. Both men wanted to lay aside the age-old tensions between France and Germany, and joint action between the two countries would make this more likely. Such a scheme would have the advantage that although limited in its specific scale, it was bold in its implications.

Schuman was responsible for the political action needed to implement the initiative. With his backing, Monnet drew up proposals for a coal–steel pool in Western Europe. Instead of allowing the French and German governments to agree the development of the industries through negotiations and bargaining, the two men proposed the creation of a High Authority whose decisions would be binding on the two countries. This was **supranationalism** in action, for it meant that in a limited sphere there was a cessation of national control. It was also a realistic step, the way for Europe to make progress.

Though French prime minister Bidault was rather lukewarm about the Schuman Plan and showed little interest in its details, the approval given by the French cabinet on 9 May marked a turning point in the development of postwar Europe. Schuman[14] could go public and announce the scheme in a speech known as the Schuman Declaration. Two aspects of his pronouncement stand out:

1. The recognition of the importance of the Franco-German relationship to Europe's future. In the last paragraph quoted, there is even an implication that the two countries could initially act on their own. The pronouncement really marks the beginning of that Franco-German axis which has underpinned much of the development of the European Community, later Union. As such, this was a dramatic development in French and European affairs.
2. Schuman implicitly recognised that there would not be any swift creation of a federal Europe with its own constitution. In his view, there would be no 'single framework', but rather there must be action 'concentrated on one limited but decisive point'. In other words, this was an acceptance of progress via functional means.

Gathering support
From the beginning, Monnet and Schuman could see that the proposal would be better if more countries were involved, so that it was open to others to join. However, the Plan had matured in secrecy, and it was sprung upon the relevant nations in such a way as to cause maximum impact. This would achieve a

momentum, and get negotiations swiftly started on the right level of boldness and vision.

The French foreign minister[15] announced that 'it is no longer the moment for vain words, but for a bold act – a constructive act'. He referred to the French initiative as 'preparing the creation of a united Europe'. The German chancellor, Adenauer,[16] was surprised at the news of the French project, but welcomed it and gave his country's approval, for it was 'a magnanimous step . . . making any future conflict between France and Germany impossible. It is a step of extraordinary importance for the peace of Europe and of the entire world'. Adenauer was a shrewd politician who saw that the 'magnanimous step' was good not only for Europe, but also for West Germany. It provided him with the opportunity of rebuilding his fledgling state and giving the country enhanced respectability. To an aide[17] he observed that the plan for an ECSC was 'our breakthrough . . . our beginning'.

Agreement on the principles between France and Germany was the essential starting point, the precondition for securing assent from Italy and the Benelux countries. The French invited six countries to participate in discussions. Britain declined the offer, whereas the others accepted. They signed the Treaty of Paris in April 1951.

The idea underlying the new Community was to establish a new body to manage all coal and steel production. There would be a tariff-free market in which there would be no customs barriers to restrict trade in coal and steel across Western Europe. It began to operate in 1952, a date which marks the foundation of serious economic union in Europe.

Monnet[18] was candid about his end goal. Addressing the Common Assembly for the first time, he stated:

> We can never sufficiently emphasise that the six Community countries are the forerunners of a broader united Europe, whose bounds are set only by those who have not yet joined. Our Community is not a coal and steel producer's association; it is the beginning of Europe.

The Preamble to the Paris Treaty makes this clear, for it offers an explicit commitment to ongoing integration.

When the ECSC was formed, there was a choice of routes available. Europe could opt again for the intergovernmental approach in which national sovereignty was retained. Or it could instead take a significant new departure and over a limited area abandon any notion of national control and go for the supranational. It chose the latter. This meant that, whatever its broad sympathy, Britain was not likely to be content with the new arrangements.

The American secretary of state, Dean Acheson,[19] wrote of his reactions to Schuman's exposition of its detail. He described it as 'so breathtaking that at first I did not grasp it: [Later] we caught his enthusiasm and the breadth of his thought, the rebirth of Europe which, as an entity, had been in eclipse since the Reformation'.

Aftermath of the ECSC: a new defence community?

In August 1950, the French Chamber of Deputies voted for the Pleven Plan, named after its author, the prime minister. It proposed the creation of a European army into which German units could be integrated. In October, the French officially launched the idea of two new communities, one for defence and one for a political community. The European Defence Community (EDC) involved 'the creation, for common defence, of a European Army under the authority of the political institutions of Europe'.

In many ways, the proposal was a logical development of the neofunctional approach, for it was an expansion of cooperation sector by sector. The initiative indicated that once the momentum to closer integration had been started it was difficult to rein in. Indeed this was precisely what the British feared. They saw the ECSC as a step along a long road which, at varying speed and by different routes, would lead to the ultimate goal of a Europe united along federalist lines.

Five of the six nations ratified the twin proposals, but in August 1954 it was ironically the French who effectively scuppered the idea as a result of an adverse vote in the French Assembly. British participation might have helped to persuade the French to go ahead but this was never on the cards. Britain was prepared to work with an EDC, but not to participate in one.

Churchill[20] actually urged the Six to ratify the plan, and declared himself in favour of the immediate creation of a European army under a unified command. He offered to play 'a worthy and honourable part'. But that part was 'all support short of membership'. Churchill was aware of several factors that inclined Britain to stand aloof – its island tradition, its Commonwealth associations and its commitments to the United States. All were still important in the British psyche.

In a way, the idea of an EDC suffered by being too ambitious, for as yet the ECSC had not been given a chance to demonstrate how well close cooperation along supranational principles could work. It was remarkable that it got as near to being successful as it did. Its failure suggested that the moment was not yet right and that the pioneers of the new Europe were perhaps rushing their fences. As Desmond Dinan[21] puts it: 'It was a bridge too far for European integration'.

Failure was a setback to the dreams of the federalists and had a significant impact on the character of future cooperation. Duchêne[22] has argued that ever since then 'political federation as such has never been on the Community agenda. In fact, the federal element in all European integration plans was cut to the bone'. Europe was certainly not ready for closer political integration, which

was too far-reaching for many of those involved. Step-by-step economic integration was to be instead the chosen route to unity.

The Americans and the British had a contingency plan for a failure of the
French Assembly to ratify the EDC. They decided to widen the Brussels Treaty
of 1948 so that Italy and Germany could join in an enlarged *Western European
Union* which was created in 1955. Furthermore, it was agreed that the occupation of Germany was to be ended and Germany was to be allowed to join NATO.
This formulation was acceptable to the Americans, and the French were per-
suaded to accept it.

Further economic progress; preparations for a wider economic community

The success of the ECSC inspired the Six to extend their cooperation over the
whole area of economic activity, and at the Messina Conference in 1955 they
decided to examine the possibility of a general economic union and the development of the peaceful use of atomic energy. The intergovernmental conference
was seen as an opportunity to relaunch the European idea, and to do so by
extending the ECSC into a wider area of the economy. The countries involved
wished to see a structure develop which would increase the chances of their
achieving recovery and growth. They thought in terms of an enlarged free-trade
area. This time, the initiative came not from the Franco-German axis, but from
the Benelux countries which had shown how neighbours could work together
and harmonise their policies. The Dutch had suggested the idea of a common
market for all industrial goods back in the early part of the decade. When they
revived their idea in 1955, it met with general approval.

The leading Belgian federalist, Paul-Henri Spaak, and Monnet were the
statesmen who did much of the preparatory work for the new meeting. They
ensured that there was an achievable agenda which would enable agreement to
be reached on basic and concrete steps. The Messina Conference went well, and
its participants were convinced, in the words of the joint resolution, that 'It is
necessary to work for the establishment of a United Europe by the development
of common institutions, the progressive fusion of national economies, the creation of a common market and the progressive harmonisation of social policies'.
Spaak's draft treaty formed the basis of the intergovernmental discussions which
took place in June 1956, talks which were as much concerned with the progress
in moving towards an atomic community as they were with the creation of a free-
trade one. Yet it is the creation of the common market which is most remem-
bered about this period.

The discussions were carried out in a way which has become characteristic of
Community development, with gains for any country in one area being matched
with concessions in another. The French were keen to see the atomic community

develop along the lines they urged. The Germans were more committed to an enlarged free-trading area. Neither side would have agreed to the other proposal unless it was able to achieve what it wanted in the area of its preference. That two treaties could be signed together made a 'trade-off' possible.

In the discussions on free trade, agriculture was especially significant. For the French this was an area of enormous interest and importance (see pp. 214–15), for the sector was one which aroused strong feelings in rural France. The Germans were concerned to get a customs union covering goods, services and capital. As long as they achieved this, they were happy to allow agriculture a special position; Germany had its own farming community to appease. In those negotiations, the leading figures showed that they had learnt from the failure of the defence scheme. Federalism was still to be the end goal, but in devising the machinery of the new arrangements more concessions were made to intergovernmentalism so that national governments could always defend their country's overriding interests.

The Treaties of Rome: Euratom and the European Economic Community

In March 1957, two treaties were signed in Rome to establish two separate organizations: the *European Atomic Energy Community* (Euratom) and the *European Economic Community*. Euratom was created to research and develop nuclear energy, create a common market for nuclear fuels and supervise the nuclear industry. Again, as with coal and steel, it was understood that a common community for atomic energy would limit its potential as a means of war. However, its scope was limited, focusing as it did primarily on the peaceful uses of nuclear energy, the major concerns being issues of health and safety, supplies, security and trade. The Euratom Treaty had no grandiose ambitions of the type found in the Preamble to the Treaty of Paris, but in one respect it did continue a theme consistently expressed in the evolution of the European Community. Having stated that 'nuclear energy represents an essential resource for the development and invigoration of industry', it went on to say that the new body would 'permit the advancement of the cause of peace'.

When commentators refer to the Treaty of Rome, they usually mean the one creating the European Economic Community (EEC). Its purpose over the long term was clearly stated in its Preamble: to establish 'an ever closer union' between European peoples. However, the more tangible objective was stated in Article 2:

> The Community shall have as its task . . . to promote . . . a harmonious development of economic activities, a continuous and balanced expansion, an increase in stability, an accelerated raising of the standard of living and closer relations between the states belonging to it.

The main Rome Treaty set out major guidelines for the Six, including:

* establishing a customs union in which all internal barriers to trade would be removed, and a common external tariff applied to the outside world
* developing a common agricultural policy
* harmonising social security arrangements
* providing for the free movement of labour and capital
* developing regional and social funds to assist poorer areas of their territory to produce new products and retrain workers whose skills become obsolete.

With the fulfilment of these objectives, there would be a 'Common Market', comprising the three elements of the ECSC, the EEC and Euratom.

The treaties again contained elements of supranationalism and intergovernmentalism. Although the Preamble contains the wish to move to 'an ever closer union among the peoples of Europe', it does not specifically say that this must eventually be a federal outcome. At the time, national sensitivities were recognised, so that there was a need to balance the aspirations of pioneers of European integration with provisions for states to protect their national interests. Yet this was another defining point in postwar Europe. Although the EEC had a much wider remit than the ECSC, there was also strong continuity. Once again six nations had confirmed their determination to press ahead with integration via supranational activity, in a process that was intended to be irreversible. Again, Britain was removed from the centre stage when the momentous development took place.

The institutions were all-important, however. As with the ECSC, they contained important supranational bodies, the European Commission (the equivalent of the High Authority of the ECSC) and the Assembly (later known as the Parliament), which initially had only very limited powers. In the evolution of the Community, the decisions of the Court of Justice have also provided an important push towards integration. Again, the Economic and Social Committee, though only advisory, has provided a useful 'transnational complexion to policy-making by institutionalising the concept that European interests take precedence over national interests'.[23]

Of the supranational elements, the Commission was the most important. It was to deal with the day-to-day functioning of the EEC and had responsibility for implementing Treaty provisions and making recommendations. The national interest was again intended to be safeguarded via the Council of Ministers, which was made responsible for Community-level decision-making.

Formation of EFTA: the Inner Six v. the Outer Seven

Britain played no active part in the Messina talks and therefore had no input into the early evolution of the Community. If it had done so, the EEC and other bodies would have assumed a different character, for in the bargaining involved Britain would have stressed the importance of intergovernmentalism and sought to achieve greater safeguards for national interests.

British ministers were surprised at the pace of developments on the continent in 1955–7. They did not wish to see a trade split in Europe and had hoped to persuade the Six to join them in a wider association of countries which could then work towards customs-free trade in industrial goods. But once the details of the EEC were agreed, the British government concentrated on pressing a scheme involving all OECC members.

In 1960, Britain was instrumental in forming EFTA (European Free Trade Area), a loose free-trade association but one much demanded by industrialists in the seven OEEC countries involved. The seven nations involved in EFTA were peripheral to the continental mainland: Austria, Denmark, Norway, Portugal, Sweden, Switzerland and the United Kingdom. They agreed that over ten years (to 1970) they would remove duties on industrial goods, though there was to be no free trade in agriculture and no common external tariff. This meant that Britain could continue to import Commonwealth goods without there being any duty upon them.

Those involved in the new organisation believed that although it was a body totally distinctive from the EEC, nonetheless it could work easily alongside it. But hopes of such 'bridge-building' were a delusion, the aims and practices of the two bodies being very divergent. As Monnet[24] pointed out: 'The Community is a way of uniting peoples, and the Free Trade Area simply a commercial agreement'. EFTA was an organisation which had none of the built-in supranationalism which was a key feature of the Treaty of Rome. It was purely intergovernmental in character.

To many continental politicians, the formation of EFTA seemed to be part of an attempt to undermine the Six in their bold venture. When serious talks got underway between leaders of the two countries in 1958, they soon ran into difficulties. The coming to power of General de Gaulle in June of that year had an important impact, for he was unsympathetic to any dilution of the Community's negotiating position. The French announced to the press in November 1958 that no agreement was possible and the other five member nations acquiesced. The British attempt to secure a wider, looser agreement had failed. In the architecture of the new Europe, there were thus two rival bodies: the Inner Six and the Outer Seven. It was soon apparent that the likelihood of any agreement between them was small and that it was the now well-established and larger Common Market which was achieving such impressive results.

Map 1.1 Members of the EEC and EFTA (1960)

Progress within the EEC

Significant economic strides were quickly made within the Community which soon showed that it was a great success for its members. 'Big business' and especially large, multinational corporations benefited, and many mergers took place. In the first five years, the GNP of the Community rose 27 per cent, as compared with 15 per cent for the USA and 14 per cent for Britain. Statistics for industrial production were similarly impressive. American investment in Europe, especially in technology, soon developed, and trade within the Community was considerably expanded.

In fact, the years up until the early 1970s were good ones for the Six. During that time, industrialists benefited from the large market of about 170m people, and

Germany especially prospered via its membership. The Franco-German bond was strong and their high degree of cooperation made progress possible in some other areas. The creation of a Common Agricultural Policy (CAP) was agreed in 1962 and all customs duties between the Six were eliminated in 1968, by which time a common external tariff was being applied to goods from outside the Community. In transport, industrial and social policies, progress was less impressive. But by the late 1960s/early 1970s, discussions began on ways of moving towards political and monetary union, although they were at this stage inconclusive.

In 1965, a Fusion (Merger) Treaty was signed in Brussels. As a result, the institutions of the three independent organisations (the ECSC, EEC and Euratom) were merged in 1967, with the Commission based in Brussels, the Parliament in Strasbourg and the Court of Justice in Luxembourg. The treaties and communities remained technically separate, but from then onwards it was common to speak of one entity: the European Community (EC).

By this time, France was led by a statesman who was to dominate the Community, General de Gaulle, the first president of the recently created Fifth Republic. In fact, his return to power following the collapse of the Fourth Republic probably had more of an impact at the time than did the creation of the EEC. De Gaulle's thinking on the role of member states was in some respects more akin to that of Britain than that of his EC partners, but until his retirement in 1969 he successfully blocked British attempts to join with them in an enlarged body.

De Gaulle's attitude to European cooperation

In a world which was moving towards internationalism and interdependence, de Gaulle clung to a belief that France could fulfil its destiny as a great nation by exercising fully the traditional freedom of a nation state. He viewed moves to integration in Europe as a danger to France and disapproved of any loss of sovereignty to supranational organisations. Indeed, his record in opposition before 1958 had shown considerable antagonism to any idea of a European community, for he had opposed both the ECSC and the abortive EDC. Yet when he assumed office in 1958, his freedom of manoeuvre was restricted, for France had already signed up to the Treaty of Rome. Although he had spoken caustically in the past, now was the time for France to honour its word – and he regarded himself as a man of honour.

Stanley Henig[25] has noted that in 'the pantheon of European heroes and villains, de Gaulle is frequently condemned for rejecting supranationalism and the nascent "Community method". [He] seemed to embody a resurgence of nationalism – a counter-pose to Jean Monnet and integration'. Yet at this time France was committed to a Europe of the Six. Even if the General was unenthusiastic about schemes for closer political cooperation, he could tolerate an EEC which provided France with substantial economic opportunities.

Within the Community, de Gaulle's views soon became apparent. He believed in Europe, but his faith was grounded in the view that its only underlying realities were its states and peoples. Any plan for closer political cooperation was regarded as impractical as well as undesirable, the stuff of 'myths, fictions and Pageants'.[26] Indeed, over several years in power, he was to exploit every opportunity to thwart any moves to federalism, and instead sought to move the Community along more intergovernmental lines. Having no liking for Monnet's vision, he began to espouse his own idea of a 'union of states'. His conception was of a '**Europe des Patries**', a Europe of sovereign states who came together for their mutual advantage but who were free to act as they wished in pursuit of their own interests.

In the 1960s, de Gaulle was sympathetic to 'rapprochement' (a restoration of good relations) with West Germany, even though the Gaullist movement had never been very well disposed towards its neighbour in the past. Like Adenauer, he believed in national interests but he also saw that it was necessary to set aside the 'German problem'. Moreover, neither man had much liking for the superpowers, the USA and the USSR, and both were suspicious of the motives and behaviour of Great Britain. For the moment, it was convenient for the General to share the limelight with the German chancellor, who was a much older than he and was unlikely to be around for many years more. France would then have its chance to assume the leadership of Europe and to speak for the Six.

In January 1963 France and Germany signed a Treaty of Friendship. This was a momentous step, for the leaders of the two countries publicly stated that they renounced armed conflict as a means of resolving any disputes between them. This initiative formally signified the ending of the bitter rivalry of two historic enemies who had fought each other three times in seventy-five years.

Defence of national interests

De Gaulle was unwilling to make any concessions which would have allowed an extension of the powers of EEC institutions. He opposed any development of the European Parliament which would have given it increased powers over the EC budget. He was also markedly hostile to a strengthening of the Commission and to many of its attempts to extend its supranational powers into areas of French policy-making. The only constitutional development which he was prepared to support was the Merger Agreement.

His approach to European issues was very different from that of the other five members, even more so after the retirement of Adenauer in 1963. The rest wanted to strengthen the links between them and move towards majority voting. This was a departure from existing practice, for it had been agreed that for eight years after the Treaty of Rome the Common Market would proceed only on the basis of unanimity. In January 1966, it was due to move to a system of weighted voting, under which the three larger nations would have had more impact on the outcome of decisions than the Benelux countries. France refused to go along with majority voting and was prepared to call a halt to Community cooperation over the issue of how the EC would operate in the future. In the second half of 1965, de Gaulle prohibited his ministers from attending Council meetings (the 'empty chair' crisis).

For a while, there was a threat to the continued existence of the Six as an entity. Yet, faced by some hostility to his stance from within his own country, the General backed down and was willing for France to be represented at a meeting of foreign ministers in Luxembourg in January 1966. The outcome was a compromise, one which was to have significant results for the future course of events. Spaak drafted the Luxembourg Compromise, as it became known. Its words are worth quoting:

> Where in the case of decisions which may be taken by a majority vote on a proposal of the Commission very important interests of one or more partners are at stake, the Members of the Council will endeavour, within a reasonable time, to reach solutions which can be adopted by all the Members of the Council, while respecting their mutual interests and those of the Communities [. . .] The French delegation considers that where very important interests are at stake, the discussion must be continued until unanimous agreement is reached.

The Compromise was not produced as a formal amendment to the Rome Treaty but rather as a convention. However, the French had successfully asserted the idea of national sovereignty in decision-making. This was to be a key weapon in the armoury of negotiators for many years. They could act, except where there were explicit objections by a state or group of states to what was being proposed. Ultimately, there was a blocking mechanism which was a barrier to further progress to integration.

If integration was opposed by the French, so was enlargement of the Community. De Gaulle was determined to block its further expansion, particularly the admission of the United Kingdom.

Moves to enlarge the EEC: the British position

By the late 1950s, serious practical considerations were beginning to persuade a number of British politicians to amend their outlook on European developments. The British approach to European affairs was pragmatic rather than idealistic. It was based firmly upon a perception of British interests and was not easily swayed by the rhetoric of continental pioneers of unity such as Monnet and Schuman.

However, seriously practical considerations were to persuade a number of British politicians to amend their view. For several years, Britain had been slow to adjust to a decline in world status, and only in the late 1950s did attitudes begin to change. In world terms, the enforced withdrawal from the **Suez** zone in 1956, the loosening of Commonwealth ties as countries achieved independence and increasing doubts about the 'special relationship' with the United States high-lighted a loss of British power and influence. At home, there were balance of payments difficulties and a lacklustre 'stop-go' economy, whilst on the continent the Six benefited from their expanded market.

As the new decade loomed on the horizon, many of the reasons for British scepticism about the EEC seemed less important. Its early success helped to promote new thinking in London, for ministers could see obvious advantages in sharing in the industrial development of Europe, with its large market of over 180m people and its impressive rate of economic growth. With Britain inside the Community, there would be a population comparable in size to that of the USSR and larger than the United States. In such an arena, Britain would have a greater say in world affairs, and would deal with the USA more as a partner than as an increasingly poor relation.

Abortive British attempts to join the EEC: 1961–3 and 1967

In July 1961, the Macmillan (Conservative) government announced that Britain would pursue an application for membership of the EEC. This was a major departure in policy, signifying a change of direction in Britain's external rela-tions. Handled in a deliberately low-key manner, the initiative was presented as purely a trading matter, without political complications. There was no attempt to persuade the electorate of the merits of the European Idea. Indeed, the prime minister's rhetoric still included references to the country's important world role and its key relationship with the United States.

Similar applications were made in July 1961 by Denmark, Ireland and Norway. In October 1961, negotiations got underway. Edward Heath (the lord privy seal) led the British team. In January 1963, General de Gaulle used a press conference at Rambouillet to announce the effective ending of enlargement talks, thereby vetoing the British application. Strong nationalist that he was, he wanted the Community to have a powerful voice, preferably one with a French accent. As a member, Britain might become a rival for Community leadership.

De Gaulle claimed that Britain was not yet ready to be admitted. It was dis-tracted by its Commonwealth interests, and was too much of an Atlantic power to be truly committed to a European destiny. Certainly, there were many 'reluc-tant Europeans' in Britain for whom the driving force of our application was a fear of being left behind in a highly competitive economic race. There was little sign of a desire to think in genuine European terms.

In 1967, under the Wilson (Labour) government, Britain tried again, along with Denmark, Norway and the Irish Republic. Ministers were attracted by the potential of a large single market, arguing also that joint research and shared development costs in high-technology industries would prove beneficial to British manufacturers. It was suggested that British entry would give the Community a new dynamism and that Britain's capacity for technological innovation would be an asset.

The attempt was nonetheless again frustrated by de Gaulle, though – as previously – the application was not withdrawn. This time the French veto came before negotiations even began. No longer could Britain be said to be more concerned about Commonwealth interests and this time other members wanted Britain to join. Rather, he argued that Britain was still too subservient to the USA. Moreover, its ailing economy would be a drag on the rest of the Community.

Britain had moved some considerable way from its earlier postwar stance of detachment from Europe. Even Labour ministers (some of whom had previously been cool or even hostile to the EEC) now tended to see the Community less as a threat and more as a means of national salvation. But there was little enthusiasm within the party for European entanglements.

Third application, 1970

De Gaulle's resignation and death boosted Britain's chances of successful negotiations. The pro-European Conservative Edward Heath was prime minister, and the French president, Georges Pompidou, was personally and politically sympathetic to him. Pompidou did not have any rooted objection to British membership. Moreover, fears of growing German power and independence were developing in France. Pompidou understood that Britain might prove to be a useful counterweight within the Community.

This change of disposition across the Channel eased what were sometimes difficult discussions. In October 1971, the House of Commons accepted the principle of entry into the EEC and thereby accession to the Rome treaties. The Treaty of Accession was signed in January 1972, and Britain joined a year later, along with Denmark and Ireland as part of the First Enlargement. In a referendum, the Norwegians rejected the opportunity to join.

The British attitude to developments on the continent had been reassessed. In a Europe of 'sixes' and 'sevens', it found itself in the outer, less influential tier. Against a background of EEC success and diminishing British influence, many politicians perceived – or came to be convinced – that Britain's future was to be increasingly based on the European circle, even if the Commonwealth and Atlantic ties remained strong.

Conclusion

Important strides had been taken in the early postwar years. Six nations had cooperated to launch the ECSC. They had gone on to form the EEC, an extensive free-trade area covering six and later nine countries. The Common Agricultural Policy had been devised, the institutions of three communities (the ECSC, Euratom and the EEC) had been merged and national heads of government were beginning to develop the practice of meeting together to try and harmonise their approaches to political problems.

The unfolding story was not without division and disagreement. The failure to achieve a defence community, France's stand which eventually resulted in the Luxembourg Compromise, the French veto on enlargement and the failed negotiations to bring about political union were all indications of friction and periodic crises. But there was no difference between the six member states in the central position they attached to the EEC in the conduct of their national affairs.

By 1973, de Gaulle was no longer in power. He resigned in 1969 and was dead a year later. His successor seemed to be more in touch with the mood of the times. Along with the arrival of a new British prime minister and a new German chancellor (Willy Brandt), the scene seemed to be set for a new departure. As yet, the bonds between the countries of the EEC were economically strong, but still politically weak. A fresh injection of political will might be expected to move forward the process of integration.

Glossary

Benelux Benelux is an economic union in Western Europe comprising three neighbouring monarchies: Belgium, the Netherlands and Luxembourg. The name was created for the Benelux Customs Union signed in 1944, but is now used in a more generic way.

Cold War In 1947 the term was introduced by Americans Bernard Baruch and Walter Lippmann to describe emerging tensions between the two former wartime allies: the United States and the Soviet Union. It describes a hostile relationship characterised by mutual suspicion between countries or power blocs, but short of outright war. The Cold War was a period of conflict, tension and competition between the United States (and its allies in Western Europe, Japan and Canada) and the Soviet Union and its allies in Eastern Europe. It lasted from the mid-1940s until the early 1990s. There was never a direct military engagement, but there was a massive military build-up, espionage and political battles for support around the world.

Europe des Patries A Europe made upon of independent nation states which cooperate for purposes of mutual benefit: the Gaullist/Thatcherite vision of how Europe should develop.

European Idea The idea of a continent united by peaceful means, free, prosperous and untainted by the enmities and rivalries of the past – the dream of postwar pioneers of European unity.

Federalism/Federalists Federalism is a political system in which power and sovereignty are divided between different levels of government, usually between a central (federal) level and a sub-state (regional or provincial) level. Seen on the continent as a system in which power is decentralised, it is commonly viewed in Britain as one in which there is strong central control. The British tend to portray any accretion of power in Brussels as a step towards the creation of a federal monster superstate.

Postwar federalists wanted to see a swift movement to complete political unification in Western Europe. They were inspired by Churchill's notion of a United States of Europe. Their vision enthused the post-1945 generation of political leaders on the continent.

Functionalists Supporters of one of several theories of integration (along with federalism, neofunctionalism and intergovernmentalism), they believe that cooperation is best conducted through a sectoral approach. Nations cooperate in a limited area, perhaps agriculture, with decisions being taken by supranational high authorities under the direction of technocrats. As the habit of working together develops, so nations may begin to cooperate in further areas.

Integration The process of making a community into a whole, by strengthening the bonds between its component parts. In this case, building unity between nations on the basis that they pool their resources and take many decisions jointly, leading to a deepening of the ties that bind the EU. Nations relinquish or pool their national sovereignty, in order to maximise their collective strength.

Intergovernmentalists Those who favour cooperation between governments for their mutual advantage. They want to retain as much national sovereignty as possible, hence the Gaullist belief in a Europe des Patries. Theirs is an essentially practical rather than a visionary approach.

National sovereignty Sovereignty means 'complete power'. National sovereignty refers to the ability of a country to maintain complete control over its people and territory. In other words, nations retain their total independence.

Nationalism The desire of a nation to be recognised as a state. In the case of a country that has already achieved independent statehood, a nationalist approach is one that is super-patriotic, the primary concern being to advance national interests.

Organisation for European Economic Cooperation (OEEC) The OEEC was formed in 1948 to help administer the Marshall Plan for the reconstruction of Europe after World War Two. Later its membership was extended to non-European states. In 1961, the OEEC was replaced by a new body with a much greater geographical scope: the Organisation for Economic Cooperation and Development (OECD). All the major industrial countries of what used to be known as the 'free world' are now members, including the United States and Japan. The OECD groups thirty member countries sharing a commitment to democratic government and the market economy in a unique forum to discuss, develop and refine economic and social policies.

Suez Crisis In 1956, the Egyptian president, Colonel Nasser, nationalised the Suez Canal, which was an important shipping route for Britain. British forces intervened, but under threat of economic pressure by the United States the armed action was quickly halted. Suez shattered many illusions that Britain was still a Great Power and seriously divided the nation. Belief in the American Alliance took a hammering, for the British government felt exasperated and utterly disillusioned with what ministers saw as American indifference when backing for their deployment of troops was needed. Neither was the Commonwealth a strong ally; it was divided, with only Australia strong in its support. Many Commonwealth countries felt that British policy smacked of imperialism. Given the lack of international approval, British troops were soon withdrawn. This did nothing for national morale. To embark on a military adventure of the Suez type and then not carry it through was the worst of all possible policies. The whole episode indicated weakness and relative isolation.

Superpowers States of the first rank in the international system, possessing the ability to project power and exert major influence because of their industrial and military might. They are categorised as one step up from the ranking of 'Great Power'.

Supranationalism Literally meaning 'above states', the term refers to the transfer of some national sovereignty to a multinational organisation which acts on behalf of all the countries involved – e.g. from the United Kingdom to the EU. Supranational bodies, largely independent of national governments, make key decisions.

United States of Europe Churchill envisaged the re-creation of the 'European family' which would 'unify this Continent in a manner never known since the fall of the Roman Empire'. He was referring to a regional organisation within the United Nations that 'could give a sense of enlarged patriotism and common citizenship to the distracted peoples of this turbulent and mighty continent . . . the structure . . . If well and truly built, will be such as to make the material strength of a single state less important. Small nations will count as much as large ones and gain their honour by their contribution to the common cause' (Zurich speech; see below).

Zurich Speech Speaking at the University of Zurich on 19 September 1946, Churchill returned to a theme that he had placed before the Belgian Parliament back in 1945. He wanted to see the creation of a 'United States of Europe', believing that through a re-creation of the 'European family' Western Europe could remain secure from the threat behind the 'Iron Curtain', of which he had spoken in Fulton, Missouri in March 1946. He made it clear that his own country would heartily cheer from the sidelines if the nations of continental Europe adopted and implemented his proposal for European unity, but would not itself be part of that 'bold and noble' undertaking.

CHAPTER 2

From Community to Union, 1973–93

By the end of the Gaullist era, the European Community was an established economic success. Political progress was less obvious. However, there was a key development at the beginning of the period covered in this chapter. This was the First Enlargement, which was to be followed by two further ones within the next decade or so.

We shall see that in many respects, the 1970s were a dismal decade in the history of the Community, an era often referred to as one of **eurosclerosis**. Economic recession, the British accession and in particular the election of the Thatcher government all posed problems. But once the budgetary problems of the early 1980s were resolved, the Community was ready to move forward once again. The impact of the Delors initiatives on the process of integration was to be considerable. By the end of our period, the EC had become the European Union.

The years up until the early 1970s were good ones for the Six. Europe was peaceful and business was thriving. Since then, things have been more problematic, with periods of tension and difficulty alternating with periods of creative activity.

The period covered in this chapter begins with the First Enlargement, which took place in 1973 and increased membership of the Community from six to nine members. By the end of the period, the Union was on the verge of becoming the Fifteen.

Further enlargement

Greece had long hoped to become a member of the EEC and in the early 1960s had made an **Association Agreement**. Any chance of full membership received a serious setback in 1967 when a military junta seized power and began what became known as the Rule of the Colonels. The Community froze the Agreement for the period in which democracy was suspended. When the Colonels were brought down in 1974, the Agreement was reactivated and within a year the new government applied for full membership. Member states were keen to encourage the democratic regime. Accordingly, in 1979 Greece signed the Accession Treaty and entered the EC two years later. With this Second Enlargement, there was now a community of the Ten.

Spain and Portugal were also unacceptable as members of the Community as long as they had authoritarian regimes. Both disappeared in the mid-seventies and the EC was keen to recognise the new situation and in so doing extend its influence in the Mediterranean region. The negotiations took much longer to conclude than they had done with other countries, so that although applications were made in 1977 they were not able to become members until January 1986. This was mainly because of internal problems within the EC, which for several years in the early 1980s was preoccupied with consideration of its own budgetary arrangements.

As a result of the accession of two new members, this Third Enlargement increased the Community to twelve. There was a modest setback to the process of enlargement when Greenland, a Danish territory, voted to leave the Community in a referendum held in 1982. Greenlanders were unhappy about the application of EC fisheries policy and felt remote from the Brussels bureaucracy. The territory officially left in January 1985.

Inevitably enlargement was bound to transform the character of the Community. This made it necessary to review the methods by which it conducted its business. It was also important to ensure that measures were taken to improve the position of less developed states, so that they would not become a permanent drain upon the EC budget. Living standards varied considerably. Of the Twelve, some were clearly more economically successful than others. Luxembourg, Germany, Denmark, France, Belgium and Holland had the highest average incomes per head, then came Britain and Italy, followed by Spain, with Ireland, Greece and Portugal at the bottom.

Division and stagnation

The widening of membership in the First Enlargement coincided with the energy crisis and a developing recession in the Western world. In October 1973, the Organization of the Petroleum Exporting Countries (OPEC) quadrupled the price of crude oil. The EEC, which imported 63 per cent of its energy requirements, was badly hit. In its reaction to the oil crisis, it was torn by schism, as individual countries began to make separate deals with Arab states. There was little sense of a Community interest, but rather a situation in which members thought primarily in terms of defending their national position. This was to be the pattern of the 1970s and early 1980s, which saw a number of internal disagreements.

The late 1970s and early 1980s were a period of stagnation and disappointment for those anxious to promote closer European cooperation. There was little sign of progress towards integration, so that in 1983, in a sceptical analysis of European decision-making, Paul Taylor[1] could write that 'the challenges to sovereignty were successfully resisted, and the central institutions failed to obtain the qualities of supranationalism'. *The Economist* was gloomier, its cover for an edition in March 1982 showing a tombstone on which were inscribed the words: 'EEC born March 25th, 1957, moribund March 25th, 1982, capax imperii nisi imperasset' ('It seemed capable of power until it tried to wield it').[2]

Budgetary problems

A new Conservative government took over in Britain in 1979, led by Margaret Thatcher. The question of Britain's contribution to the European budget arose at her first European Council meeting (Dublin, November 1979) and thereafter dominated discussions in the Council for five years, much to the despair of the

Commission and its British president, Roy Jenkins, and of the other members of the EEC. The issue was known in Brussels as 'the BBQ' which, according to Jenkins,[3] meant 'the British Budgetary Question', but was more usually referred to as 'the Bloody British Question'.

The point was that, despite economic difficulties, Britain was making net contributions to Community funds quite as large as those being paid by Germany. Overall, it was paying into the EC vastly more than it got out of it. At the time, nearly three-quarters of the EC budget was being used to support agriculture. Britain did not greatly benefit from this, for its agriculture was smaller and more efficient than that in most of Europe. Payments to Britain out of CAP funds were comparatively so low that British taxpayers were heavily subsidising inefficient farmers in France. To make matters worse, EEC rules forced Britain, which imported more food from outside the Community than the others, to pay a much higher import levy than they did. What would have helped Britain was assistance for its ailing regions and for the modernisation of traditional industries. But compared to the 74 per cent of the Community budget spent on farming, only 4 per cent was spent on the Regional Fund whose purpose was to make grants to areas of low income, chronic unemployment or declining population.

Mrs Thatcher presented her demand for a £1m reduction in the British contribution to the Dublin Summit. She rejected the offer of one-third of that sum out of hand. At this point she succeeded in shocking both her European colleagues and her own advisers, with constant demands for what she called 'her money'. She made it clear that the sum she wanted was not negotiable and she would do no deals. She accused other European states of the outright theft of British money, an accusation that horrified Foreign Office advisers who knew the rules of the European game. Under those 'rules', negotiations would improve on the £350m offered by a potential deal on oil, or fishing rights, or the price of lamb. However, there was to be no deal. Experienced negotiators were lost in what for them was an unprecedented situation.

Among Britain's partners there were many who, while originally sympathetic, were subsequently alienated by the prime minister's behaviour. As Jenkins[4] said, 'on the merits Mrs Thatcher had right broadly on her side although she showed little sense of proportion, some of her favourite arguments were invalid and her tactical sense was as weak as her courage was strong'. Thatcher continued to demand her money throughout dinner and after. The Europeans retaliated: Giscard ignored her, Schmidt pretended that he was asleep and Jorgensen, the Danish prime minister, shouted insults. The complete breakdown of the Council was only prevented by postponing a decision on the BBQ until the next year. That Dublin meeting set the tone for Britain's relationship with Europe throughout the Thatcher years. Her behaviour was deplored by the other Community members and indeed, at one point led French prime minister Jacques Chirac to call for Britain's expulsion from the Community.

The issue dragged on over several Council meetings, against a background of much behind-the-scenes work by Foreign Office officials. Eventually, it was resolved at the *Fontainebleau Summit* (June 1984). An eleventh-hour agreement was reached, by which Britain would receive a permanent rebate worth 66 per cent of the difference between what it paid into the Community and the amount it got back. The same agreement increased Community resources by raising the levy on VAT from 1 per cent to 1.4 per cent. The matter was finally settled after five years; Britain could be said to have 'won' and indeed was said to have 'obtained much more than was reasonable'.[5] The agreement, however, was only achieved at considerable cost to future relations between Britain and Europe. The insistent demands made by Mrs Thatcher, and her domineering and insulting treatment of her supposed partners, had at times almost turned Britain into a pariah in European circles.

The disagreement over the 'budgetary imbalance' used up an enormous amount of EC time, being endlessly discussed in gatherings of the Council of Ministers and in the European Council. Everything else assumed secondary importance, so that the questions of enlargement and of the future shape of the Community never received the attention which many statesmen wished to give them.

Progress to integration: 1. new initiatives

The 1970s and early 1980s were in many respects a dismal era for the Community, because of the combination of economic stagnation and the preoccupation with Britain's budgetary difficulties. Yet this period was not without positive initiatives. One of the first was the signing in 1975 of the Lomé Agreement, which introduced a programme of development assistance and trade preferences for many African, Caribbean and Pacific (ACP) countries.

In 1976, the Belgian Leo Tindemans[6] produced a report entitled *The High Road to European Union*, in which he argued for a common foreign policy; moves to develop a monetary and economic policy; and reform of the institutions including a provision for direct elections to the European Parliament. The proposals had little immediate effect, for in the mid-1970s European leaders were preoccupied with the aftermath of the oil crisis and this had prevented any creative thinking about the future. The one important change that occurred in line with the Tindemans paper was the introduction of direct elections to the Strasbourg Parliament in 1979, a move towards greater democracy in a Community not known for carrying the peoples of Europe along with it.

In other respects too, 1979 was a significant year for the Community. As we have seen, it saw the return of the Thatcher administration which was to have a major impact on relations between Britain and Europe. Also in that year, the European Monetary System (EMS) came into operation. With an **Exchange**

Rate Mechanism intended to regulate currency fluctuations at its core, the formation of the EMS represented the first step in a process intended to lead to a single currency and economic and monetary union.

Within a couple of years of the first direct elections, Parliament established a Committee on Institutional Questions with the purpose of drafting proposals for a European Union. It was chaired by Altiero Spinelli, the longtime federalist and past commissioner. He was keen to see definite progress to closer integration. The European Parliament accepted his report and in February 1984 voted overwhelmingly in favour of the Draft Treaty establishing the European Union.

In the early 1980s, Community enthusiasts in the Commission and the most supportive member states were also beginning to contemplate bold initiatives. Inevitably there were divergent views as to how the EC should develop. The Germans and the Italians were especially active in devising plans to carry the EC forward into a closer union with more distinctive political objectives. The attempt to do so at a rapid pace had received a setback with the failure of the EDC, and thereafter it was apparent to most politicians and diplomats involved that progress would be made via economic cooperation. Yet whenever there was the opportunity to advance the cause of integration there were some statesmen only too willing to seize their chance. This could be done by extending the powers of the European Parliament in the budgetary area, as had happened in 1970 and 1975. However, there were plans afoot for more substantial changes.

By the middle of the 1980s, the future of the Community was under serious consideration. After nearly a decade and a half of stagnation (eurosclerosis), the issues of monetary, economic and political union came once more to the fore. The breakthrough came with the assumption of the presidency of the Commission by Jacques Delors and the agreement on the content of a Single European Act in the second half of 1985. The Delors presidency and the SEA between them generated momentum not only for the creation of the internal market but also for the moves to closer cooperation to be resolved at Maastricht in December 1991.

Progress to integration: 2. the Single European Act (SEA) and its aftermath

The original concept of the European Economic Community was that there should be a common market: a free-trade area without any restraints to trade. The idea of a unitary market governed by a single set of rules was set out in Article 2 of the Treaty of Rome, which read:

> The Community shall have as its task, by establishing a common market and progressively approximating the economic policies of the Member States, to promote

throughout the Community a harmonious development of economic activities, a continuous and balanced expansion, an increase in stability, an accelerated raising of the standard of living and closer relations between the States belonging to it.

The language employed in Article 2 illustrates the high expectations of the benefits that might flow from such a common approach. Yet by the early 1980s, there remained some regulations and barriers that had never been eliminated and others had developed as the Community expanded.

By the mid-1980s, discussion of the merits of a single internal market had been in the air for a few years. The idea had strong support from many businessmen and from some national political leaders and members of the Commission. The driving force who gave the proposal a higher priority was Jacques Delors. He recognised that the Community was in need of a bold and imaginative idea which would focus its energies and impart a new sense of direction.

Under Delors' leadership, the Commission produced a White Paper in 1985 on the completion of the single market, written by the new commissioner for trade, Lord Cockfield, a Thatcherite appointee. Cockfield and his team were given the task of working out what measures would be needed to enable the single market to be ready for the date for its introduction set by the European Council. He identified nearly 300 legislative measures that would be necessary if physical barriers (e.g. concerned with frontiers), technical barriers (concerned with product standards) and fiscal barriers (concerned with differing rates of duty and VAT) were to be overcome.

Cockfield was never in doubt about the political importance of the single market. As was explained in the concluding section of the White Paper:

> Europe stands at the crossroads. We either go ahead – with resolution and determination – or we drop back into mediocrity. We can now either resolve to complete the integration of the economies of Europe; or, through a lack of political will to face the immense problems involved, we can simply allow Europe to develop into no more than a free trade area.

Importance of the SEA

The changes urged by the White Paper were embodied in the Single European Act. Before it could be implemented, the SEA required the agreement of each member country and had to be formally ratified in all of the national legislatures, because it amended the Treaty of Rome. Margaret Thatcher felt able to go along with the measure, for her Conservative government had a very market-oriented approach to economic policy. Her ministers had worked for open trading conditions and had since 1979 allowed the free movement of currency into and out of Britain. There was some opposition in Parliament to the measure, not least among the Labour Party, which had yet to embrace the European cause with any enthusiasm. There was an initial threat of a rebellion in the House of Lords, for as in other countries, there was some unease about the loss of sovereignty involved. Because of these constitutional implications, Denmark and Ireland held referendums prior to ratification.

The passage of the SEA greatly extended the scope of the Community. The Act provided for the completion of the single market by the end of 1992. What this meant was that all technical, physical and fiscal barriers to intra-Community trade were to be eliminated, as were all barriers to the free provision of professional and other services. The Act became effective from mid-1987.

In signing the Single European Act, the Twelve committed themselves to move towards monetary union, a goal to be progressively realised. The phrase is to be found in the Preamble, rather than in the main legally binding clauses of the Act. As part of the main text, there was – in addition to details of the operation of the single market – a commitment to lessen disparities between the richer and poorer areas of the Community (known as the policy of '**cohesion**'); an obligation to allocate more resources to the '**structural funds**' for regional and social expenditure; provision for closer cooperation in the area of foreign policy and security; and an acknowledgement of the need to work for environmental improvement.

Box 2.1 The Single European Act and the single market

The purpose of the Single European Act was to create a single internal market among the Twelve by the end of 1992. This would fulfil the original version of a tariff-free trading area without obstacles to the free movement of goods, services and capital.

Among other things, this involved:

1. the creation of a single market for services such as banking, insurance, credit and securities
2. the creation of a single legal framework for business
3. the standardisation of differing national technical requirements for products
4. the gradual harmonisation of indirect taxes so as to remove the need for tax adjustments at the border
5. the easing of restrictions on living and working in another member state, with mutually recognised qualifications and diplomas.

The Objectives and Principles of the Treaty of Rome were amended by the new Act. The Preamble agreed by the High Contracting Parties set out the new version:

Determined to lay the foundations of an ever closer union among the peoples of Europe. Resolved to ensure the economic and social progress of their countries.

Four main innovations in Community procedure were agreed:

1. The extent of majority voting was widened so that unanimity was required only for sensitive issues on which there were strong national interests.
2. Matters concerning aspects of energy, environmental, research/technological and social policy were brought within the authority of the EC.
3. A new decision-making procedure was introduced. For matters concerned with the single market there was in future to be a 'cooperation procedure' which would allow the Parliament a greater say in the development of policy.
4. Parliament gained two important new rights – to give or withhold assent when asked by the Council for its view on the entry of new members into the Community and when agreements were made for association status with the EC.

The single-market programme was a success. The target date was met, business and commercial leaders responding positively to the challenge of gearing their operations to fulfil the new requirements. As countries prepared for the implementation of the 1992 arrangements, the Community attained a high level of popularity. As Bomberg and Stubb[7] put it, '1992 unleashed a wave of Europhoria'.

Work left undone
There was inevitably disappointment with the SEA among those Europeans who wanted to hasten the pace to integration, for it was a compromise. Some member states were not too keen to see any further moves, whilst others wanted to see faster progress. All could agree on the desirability of this one measure, but there was doubt about what would follow. Enthusiasts for a more federal Europe were keen to see the Community develop more boldly, and for a combination of reasons, both internal and external, the period from the mid-1980s onwards was to witness a burst of euro-activity along the lines they wished to see.

Several issues had not been finally resolved by the new Act, although some partial steps had been taken. In the Preamble, there was the reference to economic and monetary union as a desirable goal. Several integrationists felt that such a policy – and in particular a single European currency – would be a useful adjunct to a single market and would allow it to work more effectively. There was mention (in a new Article 102a made part of the Treaty of Rome) of the possibility of a new intergovernmental conference to achieve any necessary changes in this field. Such a possibility was also mentioned in Article 30(12), a part of the Act dealing with political union.

Others were more concerned with the possible side effects of deregulation. In a free market, the weakest peoples and the weakest countries might suffer – hence the need for cohesion to protect the interests of the ailing regions. But what about the peoples of Europe whose livelihood could be adversely affected by the absence of controls? Did not the SEA need to be accompanied by social measures to protect the living and working standards of the member states?

Again, there was the worrying question about the possibility – if frontier controls were abolished on travellers – that 'undesirables' might be able to move freely throughout the Community. Drug-trafficking, international crime and terrorism were potential growth areas and in addition there was the fear of an influx of Eastern European migrants entering into the EC who might then find a safe haven in one of the member states.

Institutional reform had not been addressed, with many issues in need of attention. The role of the Parliament had been enhanced, but other than increasing the powers of an elected body nothing had been done to tackle the 'democratic deficit' in the decision-making process. Lack of accountability was seen as a major weakness, and both supporters and critics of the EC could agree that there was an absence of effective democratic control over the work of the Commission.

Outside the Community, the face of Europe was undergoing dramatic change by the late 1980s. The fall of the Berlin Wall and the subsequent reunification of Germany created a country of such a size and potential strength that it could dominate the continent if it was not fully 'locked in' to the EC. To the East, communism was collapsing in many countries of the old Soviet bloc. By 1991, the USSR itself was to be no longer in existence.

An expanding Community

The fall of the Berlin Wall in 1989 brought about an increase in the size of the Community, but not an increase in the number of countries which belonged to it. Within a year, the two halves of Germany, very different in their economic and political characteristics, were united. What had been the separate state of East Germany had ceased to exist. It could have been granted an Association Agreement or become a thirteenth state within the EC. Instead, it decided to join with the Federal Republic, and as it was incorporated into a member country there was no legal alteration in Community membership. This addition was not technically an enlargement, for there was no treaty of accession. If it had been an entry following the usual negotiations, more specific provision would have been made to cope with the particular difficulties involved in integrating the less-developed economy of the old German Democratic Republic into the more advanced West.

There was a need to consider carefully the implications for the Community of the transition to democracy in Eastern Europe, for some of the countries once dominated by Moscow would be keen to align themselves more closely with the West, now that they were free to do so. In particular, as the Cold War came to an end, the security policies which had been based on the Cold War needed to be re-examined. The whole role and strategy of NATO – effectively an anti-communist alliance – was in need of serious rethinking.

Some EFTA members were also queuing up to join the Community and for EFTA as a whole there was the prospect of developing closer ties with the EC by the formation of a *European Economic Area* (the EEA). The EEA was a free-trade area covering the nineteen states that belonged to either EFTA or the EC. In effect, it extended many of the benefits of the SEA to the EFTA countries, so that over a vast section of the continent there was free movement of capital, goods, services and workers. To ensure compliance with rules and regulations, EFTA countries agreed to abide by around 80 per cent of the Community's rules on the single market. Switzerland rejected the opportunity to join the EEA in a referendum. In fact, much of the significance of the new body was shortly to be diminished, for three EFTA countries (Austria, Finland and Sweden) were keen to enter the EC as full members.

These were all weighty questions ripe for consideration. Once the passage of the SEA had been completed and work was in hand to achieve the single market by the end of 1992, there was a chance to reassess the position of the Community in changing circumstances. It was on the verge of possible – indeed likely – enlargement. Before this could happen, the prevailing view in some member countries was that there must be a deepening of Community bonds to prevent any dilution once membership increased.

In the 'widening or deepening' debate, there were many in the British government who came down firmly in favour of widening first, in the hope that this might make any deepening impossible. In the late Thatcher/Major years, there was a growing coolness within the Conservative Party about all things European. On most of the issues which arose for discussion from the passage of the SEA onwards, the majority of British ministers seemed to be seeking to stem the tide of European advance. They wanted to limit Community **competence** as much as possible, and keep to the idea of a common market with, maybe, a little inter-governmental cooperation tacked on, where this seemed appropriate. Such an attitude was far removed from what the makers of the European Community had always had in mind.

It was during the presidency of Jacques Delors (1985–94) that the Commission began to develop policies designed to bring about a closer union extending well beyond anything achieved since the signing of the Treaty of Rome.

The Delors programme

Jacques Delors was an energetic and activist president of the Commission. In that capacity, he had unveiled the proposals for a single market to the European Parliament in 1992. Two years later, he presented a new programme in which he dealt with the challenges created by the steps already taken – the prospect of moving onwards towards closer union, via increased cooperation on economic and monetary policy, and on matters of foreign policy. In addition, he saw a need to re-examine Community finances and review the workings of the Common Agricultural Policy. He then began work on a plan for economic and monetary union which the European Council had asked a committee chaired by him to devise.

In June 1989, the Delors Report was presented to the Council of Ministers. It envisaged a three-stage progression to its ultimate goal of full monetary union, of which a common currency would be an important element. For Delors and Chancellor Kohl of Germany, economic and monetary union (EMU) was justifiable not only on economic grounds. They viewed it as a further step towards the creation of political unity in Europe. President Mitterrand of France took a similar view. By a majority vote, the decision was taken that there should be an intergovernmental conference to examine EMU and other issues more thoroughly. Delors believed that the EC was more than a common market. It was 'an organised space governed by commonly agreed rules that [will] ensure economic and social cohesion, and equality of opportunity'.[8] In other words, there was a social dimension to the market, which involved the protection of individual rights so that the Community worked for the benefit of all its citizens.

In May 1989, the Commission produced a draft Charter of Fundamental Social Rights in connection with terms of employment. This was the Social Charter, later to become the Social Chapter. It was a bold document, but largely as a result of pressure from the British government it was much watered down in its next version. Even this was unacceptable to the British, who alone refused to go along with the proposals.

Approach to Maastricht

Two intergovernmental conferences were convened in 1990. One concerned EMU, the other political union. The key decisions were reserved for the meeting of the European Council to be held at Maastricht in December 1991. In the months leading up to the summit, issues such as the Social Charter, the common currency and the democratic deficit were much argued over by politicians and in the press. There was to be a settlement of a number of European matters, with a view to signing a treaty which would, among other things, set out the target dates for achieving the next stages of the Delors Plan.

Many British Conservatives expressed strong hostility to the author of these suggestions, for they realised that he wished to see a massive transfer of power to Brussels and away from individual governments. His comment back in 1988 that he expected to see 80 per cent of all legislation in member countries coming from Brussels within ten years convinced many of his critics that the implications of any proposals from him needed to be carefully studied.

Maastricht Treaty

The Maastricht Summit (December 1991) was an important step in the process of moving towards a united Europe. It laid the foundations for more radical moves towards a federal-style union which would follow later in the decade. At British insistence, the 'f' word (federal) was excluded from the agreement, but the commitment remained to work towards an ever closer union of the peoples of Europe.

The most important agreement was to fix a definite date for the achievement of economic and monetary union (EMU), 1999 at the latest, or 1997 if seven members met the necessary criteria. The French government, backed by the Germans, was determined to set an irreversible date for the introduction of a single currency. Leaders in both countries understood that shifts in public attitudes could lead to a questioning of the idea, especially as the German people realised that their familiar D-Mark could disappear. Tying the community to a fixed date would, it was hoped, preempt the emergence of any such doubts. The commitment made to achieve union was strong even in countries such as Italy and Spain, for whom achieving convergence looked a more daunting task.

As a quid pro quo (a 'something for something' bargain), the French backed the German desire for a powerful central bank which would be free from political interference. The Germans also gained their wish that there should be tough rules governing entry into EMU, involving strict criteria on budget deficits, interest rates and inflation. The effect of such conditions would be that countries with high inflation and low productivity would need to improve their performance, or become depressed areas of the Community.

In certain major areas, the Parliament was to have new powers of co-decision with the Council of Ministers, allowing it to reject a proposal if agreement could not be reached. This applied particularly to areas where the Council could decide matters on the basis of majority voting. Co-decision-making covered issues relating to the internal market, and common policies for research and development, training and consumer affairs, among other things.

The Parliament could also request the Commission to draw up proposals where it decided, by a majority vote, that new EC legislation was needed. In addition, the Commission and its president would be subject to Parliamentary approval at the beginning of their mandate.

Some progress was made towards a common foreign and security policy. In foreign policy, the principles would have to be agreed unanimously, but it could be unanimously agreed to use weighted majority voting for their implementation. NATO was accorded the key role, but defence arrangements might be gradually Europeanised, with the WEU becoming the vehicle for implementing EC policies. For those eleven nations which were signatories to it, the Social Chapter (formerly the Social Charter) meant that they could embark on new measures as soon as they were agreed. No longer would they need to fear a British veto when they were seeking significant improvements in workers' rights.

Box 2.2 The three pillars of the Maastricht Treaty

The concrete result was agreement on the text of a Treaty of European Union. In the words of the Preamble, it was designed to achieve 'an ever closer union among the peoples of Europe where decisions are taken as closely as possible to the citizens'.

The agreement marked a new phase in the life of the Community, establishing a Union based on three separate sections, or 'pillars'.

1. First Pillar: the new European Community

The First Pillar, built on the existing EC treaty, was a development of what was already occurring. In many ways, it formalised the Community's commitment to what happened in practice. In addition, it extended its scope to cover such matters as economic and monetary union and the growth in power of the European Parliament.

Maastricht took the SEA further. Internal frontiers were already due to be abolished by January 1993, and the new Treaty decreed that citizens of member states would automatically become members of the European Union. As such, they could live and work in any member state, stand for municipal office or for the European Parliament wherever they lived, and vote in the country of residence.

The key clauses were concerned with the irrevocable path to economic and monetary union. Other important developments were that:

- The Council of Ministers would be able to act on a qualified majority vote, in some new policy areas, effectively removing the national veto.
- The Parliament was to acquire greater powers.
- A Parliamentary Ombudsman was to be established.

2. The other two pillars

The other two pillars were based on intergovernmental cooperation, outside the scope of the existing treaties. In both cases, provision was made for reporting to the Council and Parliament.

Second Pillar

The new arrangements on foreign and security policy were important. In the SEA, there had been a formal mention of European Political Cooperation, a process which was already in existence and which referred to the search for a Common Foreign and Security Policy (CFSP). At Maastricht, this term was used and the cooperation involved was strengthened.

The Second Pillar was intended 'to assert the Community's identity on the international scene'. It covered all aspects of European security, and included provisions for the eventual framing of a common defence policy and perhaps a common defence force. Decision-making would generally be through unanimity, though the governments could decide to take implementing decisions by majority voting. Policy-making was to be through the WEU, but it was agreed that it not conflict with NATO obligations.

Third Pillar
This was concerned with policing and immigration control, and dealt with matters ranging from asylum and illegal immigration to the fight against drug-trafficking and terrorism. The intention was to agree a common asylum policy by the beginning of 1993, and to develop police cooperation to combat drug-trafficking and organised crime through EUROPOL, the new international police unit.

The three pillars, as described in Box 2.2, were set out in Title 1 of the Treaty of Maastricht. Title 2, the longer section of more than 100 pages, was concerned with the complex but necessary legal amendments to the Rome Treaty. In addition to the main document, there were seventeen protocols and thirty-three declarations attached to the Maastricht Treaty. One important protocol was that on social policy, which was designed to improve working conditions and industrial employment practices. This is better known as the Social Chapter.

The texts, much criticised for their obscurity and complexity, were subject to ratification by all twelve national parliaments of the member states.

Initial reactions in Europe

The Germans were pleased to see a start made towards a common foreign policy, though progress towards political union and in the strengthening of the European Parliament was less than they would have liked. Above all, they welcomed the moves towards currency integration, and were pleased that the Central Bank was to be modelled on German lines.

For the French, the most significant step was the timetable towards monetary union, with the deadline for the single currency. They did not get the commitments on majority voting for the Council on matters of foreign policy which they favoured, nor the development of a defence policy more independent of the USA.

Spain, Portugal and Greece obtained the concession of more funds for the poorer countries of the Community, and Greece was to be allowed to enter negotiations with a view to joining the WEU, the future defence arm of the Twelve, in 1993.

The Netherlands, in its presidency of the Council, had brokered an agreement, despite the odds. The fact was that everyone wanted an agreement, so that concessions were made all round. The text was designed to ensure that there was something for everyone, for each national leader obtained some trophies to take back home so that he could claim some national benefit and Community progress.

There was disappointment and irritation about special treatment for the British. As the Dutch premier[9] put it: 'The United Kingdom is very much the same, except that this Prime Minister does not have a handbag'. Progress was less than some would have liked, with the British again seeming to have applied the brakes. But the majority could comfort themselves with the thought that, in the end, those nations which initially lag behind in their commitments do usually eventually catch up with the others.

Position of the United Kingdom

British tactics at Maastricht had been influenced by short-term considerations, such as not upsetting the Tory Right. Most Conservatives were highly relieved by the outcome of the summit, for after all of the interparty strife which led up to it the result was one which many of them could accept. A damage limitation exercise was needed, and they felt that, by a deft performance, John Major had secured a negotiating triumph and won 'game, set and match'. British national interests had been protected, for many of the things they feared most had been omitted from the Treaty. Majority voting on key issues of foreign policy had not been approved, so that Britain still retained a theoretical right to act alone if it so wished. The 'f' word had been dropped, so Conservatives could reassure themselves that they were no longer on a conveyor belt to a federal future. Above all, no irrevocable decision had been made to join a single currency (Britain could 'opt in' at a later date). In addition, the government did not sign up for the much-despised Social Chapter.

The long and difficult road to ratification

As we have seen, the immediate outcome of the Maastricht Summit was a feeling of satisfaction among many of the European leaders who took part. Each had come away with something which could be displayed to the electorate at home as a personal triumph of skilful negotiation. Public reactions initially seemed modestly encouraging, although there was little evidence of widespread popular enthusiasm. Such europhobia as there was among certain groups was to be much tested prior to ratification and in the years which followed as steps were taken towards the achievement of economic and monetary union.

Growing doubts in Denmark and France

For the Maastricht Treaty to come into force, it had to be ratified by the parliaments of all the member states. The target date for ratification was given as 1 January 1993, so that the Treaty could be operative from 1994, with the title European Union then replacing that of European Community.

The process soon ran into difficulties, though the Treaty was approved by the European Parliament early in 1992. By the spring, it was becoming apparent that there were growing misgivings in several countries. In Denmark the Treaty was approved by a strong majority in the Folketing, but in a referendum in June 1992, the Danish people narrowly rejected it. Although there were only 48,000 votes between the two sides, the verdict caused a political earthquake. The effect was to kill the Treaty unless there was to be another vote which reversed the stand taken, for the Treaty had to be ratified by all member countries. This suggested that either there must be renegotiation to allay Danish fears, or the other eleven must go ahead on their own.

Meanwhile, other countries pressed ahead with their own ratification. In Ireland, later in the same month, the electorate voted strongly in favour of the Treaty. The Yes vote exceeded expectations, and this gave a boost to the process of ratification after the shock of the Danish setback. Given the strongly agrarian and backward nature of their labour force, the Irish were net beneficiaries from the EC. They had a strong reason to favour the further development of the Community.

However, the mood of many people in France was becoming more sceptical, with opposition to Maastricht particularly strong on the far left and far right. The situation was worsened by growing discontent with changes to the CAP (see p. 217) which upset the farming vote and helped to fuel anti-EC feeling. In September, the voters gave a very narrow (50.5 per cent to 49.5 per cent) endorsement to Maastricht. For the French to stagger over the hurdle so perilously was in some respects a surprise, for they had always been in the forefront of the mow towards European integration. Nonetheless, that they did so at all created a huge sense of relief in other EC capitals.

Solving the Danish Problem

Attention turned to attempts to resolve the Danish problem. The Danish voters needed to be assured that, among other things, the EC would develop in a more 'user-friendly' and decentralised manner, so that the drift of power from national states to Brussels could be reversed (see the note on **subsidiarity** in Box 2.3). There were cautious hopes that a formula could be found to enable the Danish government to go back to the voters with a reasonable prospect of them giving approval to the Treaty.

The Danish issue was examined at the Edinburgh Summit in December 1992, along with a series of budgetary issues. The 'Loose ends' of the Maastricht Treaty were finally tidied up. This was a settlement which all the twelve members of the Community badly needed. Several problems were resolved, and each country gained something suitable. The British were finally able to ratify the Maastricht Treaty in August 1993. However, a legal challenge in Germany threatened to derail the ratification process, for some opponents argued that the Treaty fundamentally altered the German Constitution. This last-minute move failed. As a result there were no further obstacles to negotiate. Ratification was completed in all member states, and on 1 November 1993 the new European Union came into force.

Box 2.3 A note on subsidiarity

The doctrine of subsidiarity was first put forward by Pope Pius XI in 1931. For him, it meant 'government at the lowest possible level'. At the Edinburgh Summit, the British government placed much emphasis on the idea, for it seemed to be useful ammunition against those Tory rightwingers who feared that a 'federal superstate' was being created on the foundations of Maastricht. Subsidiarity could help to tame the so-called 'Brussels Monster' and bring about a decentralisation of decision-making.

Subsidiarity was already written into the Maastricht Treaty, which insisted that decisions should be taken 'as closely as possible to the citizen'. In Article 3b, it was spelt out that:

In areas which do not fall within its exclusive competence, the Community shall take action, in accordance with the principle of subsidiarity, only if and in so far as the objectives for the proposed action cannot be sufficiently achieved by the Member States and can therefore, by reason of the scale or effects of the proposed action, be better achieved by the Community. Any action by the Community shall not go beyond what is necessary to achieve the objectives of this Treaty.

Douglas Hurd,[10] the then British foreign secretary, spoke in July 1992 about subsidiarity in this way:

In the wide areas outside the exclusive competence, the Community should ask two questions: Is it necessary for the Community to act: If so, to what extent? Even in the areas where national governments have by treaty given the Community exclusive competence, the institutions of the Community should ask to what extent do we need to act to secure the full objectives of the Treaties, bearing in mind that excessive intrusion is one of the accusations most often brought against it.

Jacques Delors tried to reassure the British and others, by stressing that under the principle, matters such as internal security, justice, planning, education, culture and health should remain the responsibility of member states. Some continental MEPs expressed the concern that subsidiarity could be used as an excuse to weaken integration. They feared that the cloak of subsidiarity was being used to enable the British government to kill off environmental and social directives in which Britain lagged behind.

At Edinburgh, new procedures were agreed to 'fill out' the doctrine which only had much meaning when applied to particular policies. In future, national power was to be the rule and EC power the exception. The EC was to act only when member states could not achieve the desired goal as well themselves.

There was no question of challenging the existing powers of the Community. However, the Commission agreed to withdraw or amend twenty-one pieces of actual and draft legislation, as opposed to the seventy-two favoured by Britain. They include matters such as the treatment of animals in zoos, the harmonisation of gambling regulations and certain food labelling directives.

See also p. 282, for a discussion of subsidiarity and its relationship to federalism.

Conclusion

After several years of relative slumber following the First Enlargement, the drive towards unity in Europe received a new impetus from the mid-1980s onwards. The passage of the Single European Act; the creation of the single market; the development of a European Union; and the extension of EU into new areas such as the environment, justice and home affairs, and foreign and security policy – all these from the point of view of euroenthusiasts were positive moves. Moreover, the EU was on the verge of further expansion.

No one could be sure of exactly where the Maastricht Agreement would lead, or that the necessary convergence of the European economies in preparation for EMU would come about. However, most member states were intent on strengthening and uniting the new Union. In an uncertain Europe, where the East was in confusion and in France and Germany there was the possibility of a rightwing backlash, the wish of many Europeans was to see irreversible progress towards their ultimate goal.

The future looked uncertain. There was talk of a major world recession, with the most important economies of the postwar years, Germany, Japan and the United States, all beset by difficulty. Whether the preparations for EMU could survive a sustained recession could not be predicted, but a downturn in the world economy was a threat to the Maastricht initiatives.

Box 2.4 A note on Jacques Delors

Delors is French, a Catholic, a socialist and a federalist, and three of these made him a 'bête noire' to Mrs Thatcher. Despite British misgivings about his attitudes and role, John Major supported an extension of his presidency, so that he served a further two years, after two four-year terms.

During his ten years, he was an active and interventionist president who intellectually dominated his colleagues. He was driven forwards by a single-minded vision of European integration. His work to promote the single market, economic and monetary union and the Social Chapter, and his package of anti-unemployment measures (**Delors II**) entitle him to be considered one of the architects of the drive towards European unity.

He was much involved in the Maastricht negotiations and believed it was the best treaty that could be obtained in the circumstances – faced as the participants were by British 'intransigence'. But it was not the outcome that he personally wanted. He saw it as a mixture of obscure, technocratic and sometimes undemocratic elements which bore only the vaguest and most muted echo of the federalist ideals which had long inspired the goal of European union. In particular, he disliked the incomprehensibility of a treaty which had three separate decision-making 'pillars' built into it. Yet the alternative to ratification was, he feared, a retreat to an inward-looking, impotent Europe plagued by the dangers of economic nationalism.

Glossary

Association Agreement An agreements concerning the relationship of a country outside the EU to the Union itself. Candidate countries for entry have often made 'association agreements', the first being the one between Greece and the EC in 1961. There have subsequently been fourteen such agreements. Romania was the first country of Central and Eastern Europe to have official relations with the European Community. In 1974, a treaty had included Romania in the Community's Generalized System of Preferences. Its associate status was agreed in 1993.

Cohesion Action to reduce regional differences within the EU, brought about by the use of structural funds designed to boost living conditions. A Cohesion Fund was established in 1993 as part of the Delors II package, at the Edinburgh Council (December 1992). It provides specific financial assistance for projects in the least prosperous areas of the Community, at that time Greece, Ireland, Portugal and Spain.

Competence An area within the EU's sphere of responsibility. The term is used when examining the extent of the Union's power and influence in relation to that of member states.

Delors II A budget package advanced in February 1992 to secure the financing of the EU over the medium term. Budget resources were increased, particularly with the intention of making cohesion affordable. The package was agreed at the Edinburgh Summit (December 1992) and provided for an increase in 'own resources' of the Community to 1.27 per cent of GDP from 1999 onwards.

Eurosclerosis A period of stagnation and disappointment, when the Community/Union seems mired in difficulties. The term is generally applied to the 1970s, when there was little movement towards integration.

Exchange Rate Mechanism (ERM) A central component of the European Monetary System, the ERM was a mechanism devised to reduce currency speculation among member states and therefore promote financial stability. Each participating currency was given an exchange rate set in relation to the ECU (the currency an accounting unit employed prior to the adoption of the euro), there being some scope for fluctuation. Britain initially declined to join the ERM, but eventually did so in October 1990 at a time when the system was becoming more rigid. Uncertainty in the currency markets in the summer of 1992, accompanied by a rash of speculation against ERM currencies, led to British withdrawal in September 1992, on 'Black Wednesday'.

Structural funds These are the principal means via which aid is directed towards the least developed areas of the Union. There are four structural funds: the European Regional Development Fund, the European Social Fund, the European Agricultural Guidance and Guarantee Fund and the Financial Instrument for Fisheries Guidance.

Subsidiarity A description of a political system in which the functions of government are carried out at the lowest appropriate level for efficient administration; the idea that each level of government has its suitable geographical level. Subsidiarity is believed to enhance democracy. Germans would portray it as the very essence of federalism, but Majorite Conservatives saw it as a means of fending off a more deeply integrated Europe.

CHAPTER 3

Consolidating the European Union, 1993 to the present day

The period since the ratification of the Maastricht Treaty has been an eventful one in the history of the EU. It includes two treaties, three further enlargements and the creation of the eurozone. However, the abortive effort to gain approval for a Constitutional Treaty and foreign policy divisions over Iraq have created difficulties for those who attempt to chart its path. In this chapter, we examine the events between the Fourth and most recent enlargements, to see how effectively the Community has been transformed into a Union.

The background to the latest period in the evolution of postwar Europe was the ending of the Cold War. The threatening might of the Soviet Union had provided strong motivation for the countries to the west of the continent to cooperate and unite. The breakup of the USSR and the collapse of Soviet rule in Eastern Europe arguably changed the situation in important respects. It reduced the need for the United States to remain as involved in European affairs as once it had been; it might no longer wish to police every trouble spot. It left a power vacuum to the east, with European leaders uncertain as to how political life in Russia and its neighbouring states would develop. Russia itself had the potential to become again a key player on the continent. But in the former satellites governments varied from the strongly nationalist to the vaguely reformist and it was unclear what path they would pursue.

As for the European Community, which had just become a Union, one of the justifications for closer integration had been removed, a point noted by the Thatcherites in Britain. They claimed that integration was becoming obsolete. It had been originally conceived as a means of fending off the Soviet threat. Now that this had been removed, there was a case for a wider and much looser Europe. This might well be realised, for the Union was attractive to the 'new democracies' of Central and Eastern Europe which viewed it as an area of peace and stability. They wanted to join and in Britain their membership was seen as particularly welcome. The countries of the 'New Europe' could become a counterpart to those of 'Old Europe', particularly the dominant Franco-German axis.

Pressure for expansion: the Fourth Enlargement

In the 1990s, the process of enlargement seemed to be accelerating. An increasing number of countries were queuing up to join the new Union, carrying the potential membership to between twenty-five and thirty. This was a very different situation from the first twenty-eight years, which is how long it took for membership to increase from six to twelve.

After the accession of Spain and Portugal in 1986 the movement towards enlargement gathered additional momentum, until there were three groups of would-be members:

- The first group consisted of Turkey, which applied in 1987, and the islands of Malta and Cyprus, both of which applied in 1990. In December 1989 the Commission advised the Council of Ministers to reject the Turkish application, partly because of doubts over human-rights violations. The applications of Cyprus and Malta remained on the table but were elbowed to one side by other developments.
- The second group of aspirants to membership were former members of the Soviet bloc, most of whom negotiated '**Europe Agreements**' with the EU giving them favourable trade terms. The countries most enthusiastic for membership were the Czech Republic, Hungary and Poland.
- The third group consisted of former EFTA countries which, concerned at the implications of the single market and freed from fears for their neutrality by the end of the Cold War, applied first for associate status and then for full membership. The applicants were Austria, Finland, Norway, Sweden and Switzerland, who initially joined the single market to form a European Economic Area (EEA). Britain was very keen on these five applicants because:
  1. Enlargement might help to dilute the federalist tendencies within the Union.
  2. All five countries were wealthy and potential net contributors to the Community budget, easing the strain for existing ones.

In June 1993, the European Council offered the prospect of membership to all Central and Eastern European countries which either had agreed or were on the verge of concluding the Europe Agreements referred to above. It also set out a formal statement of requirements for membership that would have to be met by would-be entrants. These **Copenhagen Criteria** declared that applicants should be fully democratic, have a functioning market economy and be willing to adopt the *acquis communautaire*.

Meanwhile, as a result of a referendum in December 1992, Switzerland had already withdrawn its application to join both the EEA and EU. However, Austria, Sweden and Finland, three traditionally non-aligned states, had pressed ahead and opened negotiations in February 1993, with Norway following in April. Negotiations were rapid. All issues were resolved by early March 1994 and accession for the four countries was planned for 1 January 1995. But the applicant countries still had to seek the approval of their own citizens. Referendums in Austria, Finland and Sweden approved the accession agreements, although by very small majorities in the latter two cases. Then, in November, the people of Norway voted against membership, as they had done in 1972. Norway joined Switzerland, Liechtenstein and Iceland in being the only Western European countries not belonging to the EU, retaining the trading benefits of EEA membership but lacking any power to influence decisions of that body.

Norway is often cited by eurosceptics as an example of a country that manages to reap the trading benefits of EEA membership without the adverse factors of EU membership. The suggestion is sometimes made that such an arrangement would provide an ideal solution for the UK. However, as Hugo Young[1] has pointed out, the idea that Norway has all the advantages of membership without any of the disadvantages is the reverse of the truth:

> The entire apparatus of EU rules on immigration, transport, manufacture and trade in goods and services applies in Norway. Norway's courts and companies live under law as interpreted by the European Court in Luxembourg. This is the precondition for Norway's trade with the EU, unmediated, however, by the presence of any Norwegian ministers at the political table.

Appointment of the Santer Commission

The main business of the European Council held on the island of Corfu in June 1994 was the election of a new president of the Commission to succeed Jacques Delors. According to tradition the presidency of the Commission is held alternately by someone coming from a large member country and someone from a small country, by someone on the left and someone on the right. As the Commission had been headed by a French socialist from a large country, it therefore followed that the new president should be a centre-right politician from one of the Benelux countries.

The most obvious candidates were Dutch prime minister Ruud Lubbers and Jean-Luc Dehaene, prime minister of Belgium. However, there were strong differences of opinion among member states about their respective merits and therefore a compromise candidate was chosen. The name of Jacques Santer, prime minister of Luxembourg, was put forward and the new Parliament elected in June 1994 exercised its right, granted by the Maastricht Treaty, to vote on whether to accept the nominee. Santer was accepted by a mere twenty-two votes.

Within four years of his assumption of that position, his presidency was in tatters. In March 1999, he and all his fellow commissioners had been forced to resign, amid allegations of fraud and mismanagement (see p. 83). Santer's successor, Romano Prodi, set about producing and implementing a reform programme to improve the image of the Commission.

A change of government in Britain: New Labour in office

The European Union became an important issue in the 1997 general election. The debate on Europe was initiated by eurosceptics in the Conservative Party and encouraged by the tabloid press. Later, Labour introduced the topic, knowing that a mere mention of Europe provoked a Tory response that was both self-destructive and self-defeating. Discussions on the subject were almost exclusively about the single currency, about which the general public had no firm opinion.

Labour won the election handsomely. Thereafter, the re-establishment of Britain's position in Europe was one of the first priorities of the Blair government. Within days of assuming office, the British government committed itself to signing the Social Chapter and agreed to extensions of majority voting. Doug Henderson was appointed as the first specifically European minister at the Foreign Office and it was made clear that in future intergovernmental talks Britain would be represented by Henderson as a minister, rather than by a civil servant as had been the case under the Conservatives – thus bringing UK procedures into line with other member states. Within a month Robin Cook had gone further than any British minister had gone before by appointing an MEP as his European parliamentary private secretary to handle liaison with the EP.

These concessions, together with a willingness to negotiate and accept compromises rather than seek confrontation, sent out hints to Europe that Britain would henceforth be far less obstructionist than had been the case in recent years. This change in relations between Britain and the EU may to some extent have been more a difference of style and attitude than of substance, but it proved acceptable to the other members.

On becoming leader, Tony Blair soon made it clear that he wished Britain to play a constructive role in Europe. He had not always been so enthusiastic, but by the time he became leader in 1994 he was describing himself as a passionate European. He wanted to see the country 'at the centre of Europe', fulfilling its destiny on the continent and its 'historical role in the world'. Without being active within the Union, Britain would forfeit any chance of global influence; Europe must be 'our base'.

Amsterdam Treaty 1997 and *Agenda 2000*

In negotiations to draw up the Amsterdam Treaty the new mood of give and take meant that other member states were disposed to accommodate British positions on contentious issues. The Amsterdam Council was hailed as a triumph for Tony Blair and his government in that, without surrendering a tough negotiating stance, the Blair team showed a willingness to listen to the arguments, an ability to compromise when required and a reluctance to employ the British veto.

At the intergovernmental conference in Amsterdam:

- Agreement was reached on a range of internal security measures, including freedom of movement, immigration, political asylum and harmonisation of civil laws such as divorce.

- Britain gave up its solitary opt-out on the Social Chapter.
- Strong measures were introduced against discrimination on the grounds of gender, race, religion, sexual orientation or age.
- Policing remained with national governments but a supranational Europol was inaugurated.
- Britain and Ireland, as island members with a terrorist problem, were allowed to retain their external border control.
- Plans by France and Germany to make the Western European Union into the defence arm of the European Union were blocked by Britain, Finland, Sweden and Ireland, leaving NATO as the safeguard of European defence.
- New anti-unemployment measures were introduced across Europe. The European Investment Bank was to make £700 million available to underwrite pan-European job creation schemes and an employment chapter written into the revised Treaty for European Union.

Institutional reform was a contentious issue, with its implications for representation on key bodies and voting rights in an enlarged Union. The Amsterdam Council failed to agree on new constitutional structures, preferring to leave the issue to be resolved in a new IGC in 2000 and form the basis of a new Treaty of Nice. In fact, the overall outcome of the meeting was a rather bland treaty that left unresolved quite a few of the issues carried forward from Maastricht.

To continue the examination of these unresolved issues, Jacques Santer went before the EP in July 1997 to outline the Commission's strategy for strengthening and widening the Union in the early years of the twenty-first century. The document submitted by the Commission, known as *Agenda 2000*, was 1,300 pages long and made a detailed assessment of what needed to be done in the wake of the Maastricht and Amsterdam treaties. It stressed the need to concentrate on five broad aspects:

1. enlargement of the union through the accession of new member states, initially there being five serious contenders
2. a more proactive role in foreign affairs
3. further institutional and constitutional reform
4. effective action to create employment and reduce unemployment
5. further reform of the Common Agricultural Policy.

Treaty of Nice, June 2000

At Nice, the assembled heads of government were concerned to achieve the changes required for the next enlargement. It was agreed that the institutional and policy foundations of a Union of fifteen would be inadequate when the EU had perhaps another ten members. In the event, the major governments won the important arguments and confirmed their unassailable dominance.

The summiteers seemed more concerned with national interests than the cause of integration. The Treaty:

- capped the size of the Commission and the number of seats in Parliament; larger countries would each lose one commissioner to accommodate representatives of the new entrants
- (as a quid pro quo) gave those larger countries a favourable reweighting of votes in the Council of Ministers, ensuring that the interests of the main players in the Union would be preserved as majority voting became more common
- continued the movement towards qualified majority voting (QMV), permitting it in some twenty-three policy areas
- allowed for the establishment of a Rapid Reaction Force (see p. 237).

The Treaty was signed in 2001 and ratified following a second Irish referendum in October 2002 (after the voters in the first one had rejected the agreement).

Recent developments: the beginnings of the twenty-first century

In the twenty-first century, there have been four other significant developments within the European Union: the issue of the single currency; a further stage in the process of enlargement; the divisive issue of policy towards the Iraqi regime of Saddam Hussein; and the attempt to reach agreement over a constitution for Europe.

Eurozone

In 1995, EU heads of government had agreed that the proposed single currency should be called the euro, rather than the European Currency Unit (ECU) as previously planned. In May 1998, it was decided that all member states other than Greece could be deemed to have met the Maastricht convergence criteria, necessary for entry into a new eurozone. Three countries – Britain, Denmark and Sweden – decided against membership, so that when euroland was created in January 1999 there were eleven participants. The national currencies of members of the eurozone disappeared in January 2002, banknotes and coins of the single currency becoming the sole basis of all transactions. At that time, Greece was allowed to join with the other eleven countries, leaving three countries outside.

Of the twenty-first-century entrants, Slovenia qualified in 2006 and was admitted on 1 January 2007, bringing total eurozone membership to over 316m people and thirteen member states. Cyprus and Malta plan to join in January 2008, Slovakia in 2009. Other states of the Fifth Enlargement parts i and ii are gearing themselves to join within a few years. Monaco, San Marino and Vatican

City also use the euro, although they are not officially euro members or members of the European Union.

Further enlargement

In 1995, the EU had become an organisation of fifteen members in what was the fourth enlargement to the original six-member Community. But by then its leaders were already having to grapple with the unexpected and unprecedented opportunity to extend European integration into the countries of Central and Eastern Europe that were formerly members of the Soviet Union. In the aftermath of the collapse of the Berlin Wall in 1989, several 'new democracies' had been created. At first they had association agreements with the EU, but at the Copenhagen meeting of the European Council in December 2002, it was agreed that ten more countries should accede to the Union in May 2004 (the **Fifth Enlargement** (Central and Eastern part i)). A prolonged process of preparation and negotiation culminated in the entry of the Baltic states of Estonia, Latvia and Lithuania, Hungary, Poland, Slovakia, Slovenia, the Czech Republic and the two Mediterranean islands of Malta and Cyprus. The process of enlargement was taken further in 2007, with the accession of Bulgaria and Romania at the same time.

The new member states are unlikely to favour any irksome interference from Brussels. They mostly believe in open markets, but are less enthusiastic about state intervention and undue central interference. Their entry is likely to bolster the EU's liberal economic credentials and affirm support for the idea that the EU

Table 3.1 The growth of the European Union: a summary

Enlargement	Date	Countries joining
First	1973	Britain, Denmark and Ireland
Second	1981	Greece
Third	1986	Portugal, Spain
Fourth	1995	Austria, Finland, Sweden
Fifth (Central and Eastern part i)	2004	Cyprus, Czech Republic, Estonia, Hungary, Latvia, Lithuania, Malta, Poland, Slovakia, Slovenia
Fifth (Central and Eastern part ii)	2007	Bulgaria, Romania

should be an association of nation states rather than evolve into a giant super-state of the type feared by many British Conservatives. The model they favour is not the traditional Franco-German integrationist project. Rather, shunning the idea of any monolithic entity, they are nearer to the pragmatic British and Scandinavians, in their preference for a looser, more varied and multi-speed European Union.

Policy over Iraq

The idea that the European Union should speak with one voice in world affairs is a long-standing one, almost as old as the postwar process towards greater unity itself. However, despite repeated attempts to galvanise the issue, the EU has made much less progress in forging a common foreign and security policy than it has in creating a single market and a single currency.

The difficulties of achieving any breakthrough were highlighted by the deep divisions among EU member states in early 2003 over whether or not the United Nations Security Council should authorise the American-led war on Iraq (see p. 236). In the event, the British government gave strong endorsement to the US position and thus reaffirmed its traditional transatlantic ties. It had the backing of Spain and some of the countries then awaiting entry into an enlarged Union, but found itself on the opposite side of the fence to France and Germany. As one of the permanent members, France would not support the war in the Security Council and had the backing of Russia for the stance it adopted. EU member governments once again found it difficult to reconcile the cause of Union solidarity with their own national preferences.

A constitution for the EU?

Meanwhile, a Convention on the Future of Europe chaired by former French president Giscard d'Estaing was engaged in devising a constitution for the enlarged European Union. Set up in late 2001, its task was not so much to revise the existing constitutional structure of the European Union, but more to clarify and modernise it. The most visible achievement of the Convention was the merging of all previous treaties (with the exception of the Euratom Treaty) into a single text which formed the basis of further negotiation in an intergovernmental conference which first met in October 2003. There were contentious issues to resolve, particularly over voting rights in the Council of Ministers.

The proposed Constitutional Treaty

At the Brussels European Council (June 2004), agreement on the contents of a new Constitutional Treaty was finally reached. Its main aims were to replace the overlapping set of existing treaties that compose the Union's current informal Constitution, to codify human rights throughout the EU and to streamline decision-making in what had just become a twenty-five-member organisation. It was hoped that this would provide a clearer structure and focus to the Union, providing it with a simpler and more accessible set of rules.

To its supporters, it was essentialy a codifying-up exercise that clarified and elaborated existing practice. However, it contained new features that included:

- The replacement of the six-monthly rotating EU presidency with the new post of EU President which it was anticipated would provide a greater sense of coherence and continuity to Union affairs. The President would be elected for thirty months by the elected heads of government of member states.
- The creation of a new EU Minister for Foreign Affairs who would replace the European Commissioner for External Relations and the High Representative for CFSP and thereby give the Union a more distinctive international identity.
- Incorporation of the EU Charter of Fundamental Rights.
- Removal of the national veto in some areas such as asylum and immigration policy, though not on budgetary, tax, welfare, and defence and foreign policy.
- A fairer distribution of votes in the Council of Ministers, ensuring that a QMV would need the support of fifteen member states and a minimum of 65 per cent of the population.

The treaty was signed in Rome by representatives of the member states in October 2004 and was in the process of ratification by the members states when, in 2005, the French and Dutch voters rejected it in referendums. The failure to win popular support in these two original member countries of the ECSC/EEC led to other countries postponing or abandoning their ratification procedures. The Constitution now had a highly uncertain future. Had it been ratified, it would have come into force on 1 November 2006.

An amending or mini treaty?
The Barroso Commission was forced to admit that the Constitution was effectively dead. Yet of the present twenty-seven states, eighteen ratified it, several of which were keen to see it resurrected in some form. When Germany took over the rotating EU Presidency in January 2007, the Merkel administration declared the period of reflection over. It urged progress on a new treaty to be in place before the 2009 elections, a position agreed by the member states in the Berlin Declaration which marked the fiftieth anniversary of the signing of the Treaty of Rome.

There were different priorities among those who gathered at the European summit in June to agree on the way forward. The Germans wanted to salvage as much as possible from the dead constitution, the French favoured a mini-treaty, Britain an amending treaty and the Czech, Dutch and Polish representatives a document that would give national parliaments the power to block EU legislation. After hard bargaining, agreement on the text of an amending treaty was achieved in October 2007.

The new 'Reform Treaty' is intended to keep most of the institutional innovations that were agreed upon in the European Constitution, such as a permanent EU president, foreign minister (renamed 'High Representative of the
Union for Foreign Affairs and Security Policy'), the same distribution of parliamentary seats, a reduced number of commissioners, a clause on withdrawal from
the EU and a full legal personality (currently held only by the European
Community) allowing it to sign international agreements. It was agreed to drop
most of the state-like features such as the name 'constitution', as well as a reference to EU symbols (flag, anthem, motto) that had been subject to major controversy in some member states. Also, new names for various types of EU
legislation, in particular the proposal to rename EU regulations and directives to
be EU 'laws', were dropped.

The Reform Treaty became better known as the Lisbon Treaty after it was
signed at a special ceremony in Lisbon in December 2007. If successfully ratified by all twenty-seven states, it is due to become operative from January 2009.

Box 3.1 A new President of the Commission

Also under discussion in Brussels (December 2003) was the question of a successor to Romano Prodi, widely seen as a lacklustre president of the
Commission. The preferred choice of France and Germany was Guy Verhofstadt,
the Belgian federalist who had the additional disadvantage in British ministerial
eyes of being anti-American in his rhetoric. British ministers had hopes that its
outgoing Conservative commissioner might be chosen, but the French were
equally unwilling to accept their candidate. Out of the stalemate emerged a compromise choice, the Portuguese prime minister, José Manuel Durão Barroso.

As a free marketeer, moderniser and pro-American who backed the war in
Iraq, Barroso was acceptable to the British government, which hoped that his
appointment might prove helpful in its bid to influence the orientation of the
future Union. He was confirmed as the new president at the special summit in
Brussels at the end of June 2004.

Though consensus is the preferred route to nomination, a formal vote in the
Council of Ministers still has to be taken. Barroso was chosen by a clear majority in the QMV. Should they have tried to block him, France or Germany would
have risked an embarrassing defeat in the newly enlarged Europe.

The Union today

With the admission of Bulgaria and Romania, the European Union has now
become a community of twenty-seven states. All but four of the Western
European countries are now members. In two of those – Iceland and
Switzerland – some politicians continue to express interest in joining.

- Iceland's close trading connections with the EU make membership at some point seem likely, though application is not on its current political agenda.
- In Switzerland, serious doubts remain among the voters, who rejected the Union in a referendum held in March 2001 by a margin of more than 3:1.
- Liechtenstein is unlikely to join unless Switzerland does. If it were to do so, it would become the smallest country in the Union.
- Norway has applied four times already, its people rejecting the opportunity to join on two occasions. As inhabitants of the richest countries in the world on a per capita basis, Norwegians are aware that they have much to lose and little to gain via membership. Having a small agrarian sector and few undeveloped areas, Norway would benefit little from income from the Union. It would be a substantial net contributor and would also lose full control over the fish, gas and oil resources in its territorial waters.

Three out of four Europeans now live within the European Union. Those who inhabit other countries that at present seem far from membership may still find themselves becoming members at some point in the future, for the EU has a powerful attraction for small states. In addition to the Russians, the peoples who are not members include the Albanians, Croats, Moldovans, Norwegians, Serbians and Swiss, all of whom constitute relatively small populations. An exception in terms of size is Turkey, whose possible membership raises questions of European identity, as well as other issues. If Russia and Turkey are viewed as constituting the eastern limits of the European continent, then at present twenty-seven of its thirty-eight countries now belong to the Union.

The European Union has tended to enlarge along regional lines, adding groups of nearby nations, the accession of Greece being the notable exception. Currently, it is very interested in the integration of the Balkan states. Of Eastern Europe Heather Grabbe[2] of the Centre for European Reform has observed that 'Belarus is too authoritarian, Moldova too poor, Ukraine too large, and Russia too scary for the EU to contemplate offering membership any time soon'.

The Union has become the world's largest trading power, fifteen of its members now sharing a single currency. Merely to state that indicates just how far Europe has travelled since the early postwar years described in Chapter 1. The six countries who took that first step of forming a coal and steel community have become twenty-seven in a process of enlargement that has gathered pace over the last decade and a half. In that time, there have been a series of what Henig[3] refers to as 'defining moments', including the signing of the Treaty of Rome which launched the European Economic Community, agreement on and implementation of the Single European Act, the signing of the Maastricht Treaty which created the present Union, the creation of a single market and the adoption of the euro.

Conclusion

The Union itself has undergone different stages of development. At some times, it has seemed to be stuck in a groove of stagnation and introspection; at others (usually when the economic outlook has seemed more promising) there have been prospects for a further move forwards. In the periods of stagnation, little is heard of the long-term possibilities and the dreams of ever closer union.

In the formation and evolution of the Community into the Union, two forces have been at work: intergovernmentalism and integration. At different times over the last forty years, one set of ideas has gained the ascendancy, as different thinkers and statesmen have pressed their particular viewpoint. The dispute is still at the heart of the controversy within the Union about the way it has developed and the future direction it should take. These twin forces making for integration are more fully examined in Chapter 4.

Glossary

Acquis communautaire The rights and obligations deriving from the accumulated laws currently in force that must apply in every state if the EU is to function property as a legally regulated community. Laws include treaties, directives and regulations, as well as the case law of the Court of Justice.

Copenhagen Criteria A set of criteria laid down at the Copenhagen Council (June 1993) against which the applications for membership of the Union of states from Central and Eastern Europe should be assessed.

Europe Agreements Agreements via which the EU has undertaken to provide applicant countries with specific economic and political assistance, prior to full membership. Following the ending of the Cold War, eight of the Central and Eastern European states that have sought membership of the Union have concluded such agreements, the first being Hungary and Poland.

Fifth Enlargement The latest enlargement is being viewed as the completion of the Fifth (Central and Eastern) Enlargement, rather than as a sixth one, so the Fifth Enlargement is referred to as having two stages: parts i and ii. Between March 1994 and January 1996, ten Central and Eastern European Countries (CEECs) applied to join, but Bulgaria and Romania were slower than the others to implement the necessary political and economic reforms, and so were deemed not ready for membership in part i (2004). In fact it is rather misleading to think of the 2004 entrants as all being CEECs, for Cyprus and Malta do not fit the description. This is why Nugent[4] labels the 2007 enlargement as the 10 + 2 round.

CHAPTER 4

The movement to integration: a theoretical perspective

Since the ending of World War Two, several moves have been made towards unification in Europe. They have culminated in the creation of the European Union, as a result of the implementation of the Maastricht Treaty. A union can imply relatively loose cooperation between member states designed for their mutual advantage or a much closer degree of unity in which key decisions are made by supranational institutions. The term 'integration' refers to the process via which this unification has come about, a process in which for more than fifty years sovereign states have relinquished or 'pooled' some of their national sovereignty in order to maximise their collective strength. The various steps along the road to greater unity – economic, military and political – are seen as moves in the direction of closer integration.

Integration theory refers to the views advanced in a considerable amount of literature to explain the manner in which the EU has evolved and the factors involved in its evolution. As we shall see, none of them provides a complete picture. In this chapter, we examine the main perspectives that writers have adopted, in particular the key division between intergovernmentalists and supranationalists.

In Chapter 1, we referred to the different theories relevant to an understanding of the development of postwar integration: federalism, functionalism and intergovernmentalism. Monnet felt that intergovernmentalism was not enough, but as to whether he was himself a federalist or a functionalist is a matter of disagreement.

The same difficulty has afflicted those commentators who have attempted to provide a theoretical explanation of the dynamics of integration, in other words to explain how and why it has come about. The difficulty is all the greater because at different periods the Union has exhibited different tendencies, sometimes seeming to progress more by intergovernmental agreement, at others because of the inspiration of those who have urged a federalist agenda.

Theories of integration: why it has come about

In the postwar era, national leaders in several countries have seen the merits of closer unity in Europe. Various theories have been advanced to explain the transformation of Europe that has resulted from the steps they have taken:

- Some writers emphasise the long-standing enterprise of articulating the 'idea of Europe'. They see the events of the late 1940s as the fulfilment of a dream of European unity which has deep roots. Unity is therefore an expression of, or a search for, a clear identity and a distinctive set of European values. In this view, Europe is seen as the 'cradle of civilisation' and postwar cooperation as an attempt to restore the continent to its former importance and glory.

- Others see postwar cooperation as the outcome of the hostilities of World War Two. War shattered the economies of the main participants and made them aware of the need first to prevent such a catastrophe from ever happening again and secondly to unite in a common bid to restore prosperity. Such motives were particularly strong in the early years after 1945. For many writers they provided the inspiration behind postwar integration. The historian Alan Milward[1] has argued that pursuit of economic interests was the prime motivation for integration. But in his view national governments were only willing to pool their sovereignty as far as was necessary to tackle problems that otherwise threatened to undermine their national well-being.

- A third explanation stresses that in the postwar world there has been a growing move towards interdependence, with the progressive integration achieved by the European Union as a particularly good example of this trend. States have cooperated out of necessity, because the problems they face increasingly require a response that goes beyond traditional national boundaries. Environmental problems, for instance, do not recognise traditional frontiers. Similarly, many difficulties in the financial markets require a coordinated response.

- Other writers have stressed the role of the United States as being the key factor in the process of integration. In the early years after 1945, the American government championed the cause of unification on the European continent, seeing it as the best means of securing reconciliation between France and Germany, the old enemies whose rivalry had been at the root of so much conflict. A peaceful and prosperous Western Europe was likely to be politically stable and provide a strong barrier against communist incursion. The chosen instrument of American policy was initially the Marshall Plan. But over subsequent decades, several US politicians were supportive of and keen to promote greater European unity. Successive administrations wanted to see Britain join the EEC, recognising that the **special relationship** might offer the Americans a foothold on the continent. Britain could act as a useful bridge between the continental powers and the USA. Indeed, as we have seen, one reason for Gaullist reluctance about British membership of the EEC was the thought that its transatlantic ties were seen as its main national priority in external affairs.

    If US thinking was broadly supportive of closer European cooperation, at times a motivation of continental politicians for greater unity has been their desire to see a strong Europe which would be powerful enough to resist American dominance. The Gaullists had such a vision, but more recently others have argued that only a large, strong and united EU can be to some degree independent of the leading industrial and military power in the world.

- Sometimes it is argued that the origins and inspiration of the movement towards unity in Europe were to be found in the many now largely

forgotten organisations which were active in campaigning for the unification of Europe. As individual bodies, their impact was insignificant, but
when they combined to form the European Movement in 1947 they
were creating a platform on which sympathetic statesmen could express
their ideas. Certainly, the leading pioneers of postwar integration belonged
to the Movement, but this does not prove that this outlet for their enthusiasm had a key impact on early developments on the continent. Milward is
particularly unimpressed by the contribution of such 'ill-matched movements', concluding that 'the European Unity Movement . . . appears to
have had practically no influence on the negotiations for the Treaty of
Paris'.

- Finally, there are those who stress the importance of national interests. They
  feel that for all the grandiose talk of the merits of cooperation and the dreams
  of the founding fathers, the main reasons for cooperation have derived from
  individual states pursuing their own advantage. On occasion – in fact on the
  continent, rather often – there has been obvious value in nations working
  together. France and Germany had their own distinctive reasons for wanting
  a coal and steel community. Some French men and women still see the EU
  as a good means of ensuring that France's past rival and now powerful ally is
  locked firmly into a European entity strong enough to contain its power. In
  the same way, smaller states such as Belgium, Ireland and Luxembourg have
  sound reasons for wishing to see closer ties in Europe, for as members of an
  economic and political community they carry more clout in European affairs
  than would otherwise be possible. For many British politicians, the perceived
  advantages of close union have often been less apparent – hence their wish
  to pursue such a degree of intergovernmental cooperation as is appropriate
  for the task in hand. Andrew Moravcsik[2] is perhaps the foremost proponent
  of the view that national governments have controlled the timing, pace and
  extent of integration.

Idealism and pragmatism have both been prominent features of the postwar era.
For many countries in Europe, the two impulses have gone hand in hand. Such
countries have wanted to see integration develop for the reasons we have
reviewed. For Britain – and at times other nations – the advantages of cooperation have often seemed less self-evident. Britain, Denmark (on occasion) and
France (under de Gaulle) have detected more merit in the intergovernmental
approach in which states work together as seems necessary and desirable. They
favour a *Europe des Patries*, whereas most countries have been inspired by the early
visionaries and attracted by a more federal future.

Such differing approaches have led Nugent[3] to conclude that there has been
no 'common and coherent integrationist force at work in Western Europe. Far
from the states being bound together in the pursuit of a shared visionary mission,

relations between them have frequently been extremely uncomfortable and uneasy. Even in the EC, which has been at the integrationist core, the course of the integration process has varied considerably'.

How the drive towards integration has been accomplished

In the years after 1945, federalists wished to see a rapid movement towards their grand design: complete political unification as implied by the term 'a United States of Europe'. Their vision inspired some pioneers of unity in the postwar generation. But at no time was the adopted approach to unification one that would quickly implement a federal Europe. Outright federalists were relatively few, more practical advocates of unity being functionalists who wanted to see step-by-step cooperation. However, in varying degrees and at different speeds, federalists and functionalists wanted to see movement towards closer union and ultimately arrive at some form of federal outcome. Others, the intergovernmentalists, have been more wary of powers being transferred from the national to the Union level. They have sought to slow down the pace of change and limit cooperation to the search for mutual benefit.

In explaining the dynamics of integration in the postwar era, three theories are worth examining in detail: functionalism, neofunctionalism and intergovernmentalism.

Functionalism

Several of the early attempts to explain the development of the Community reflected the functionalist theories which began to flourish back in the interwar years. David Mitrany[4] put forward an approach based on the idea of the 'common index of need'. There are many areas where the needs of governments overlap, and for him the best way of resolving them was to act in a way that cuts across national boundaries.

In Mitrany's words, it was 'not a matter of surrendering sovereignty but merely of pooling so much of it as may be needed for the joint performance of the particular task'. There would be a shared agency run by technocrats which would have supranational authority over the specific policies included within its orbit. Mitrany was thinking in terms of a number of such international agencies, not because he saw supranationalism as in any way preferable to the idea of the independent state but because he thought it was the better way of running services and fulfilling needs which cut across national boundaries. He did not envisage one supranational agency which could preside over several sectors. The schemes put forward after 1945 went beyond what he was contemplating, for they were not merely a series of complementary functional agencies. They had an end goal in view, and this was a federal one – what Martin Holland[5] has called functionalist principles with a political objective.

Functional theory has recognised that once you go down the route of allowing the creation of a number of independent bodies in which several members participate, this has an effect on relations between those countries, which find themselves becoming increasingly dependent on each other. Mitrany saw great merit in providing the opportunity for different nations to work together, for he believed that their experience of cooperation would help to counter the dangers of nationalism. Moreover, the leaders and peoples of the nations involved become used to a situation in which cooperation extends across frontiers. As Pentland[6] put it: 'They are weaned away from their allegedly irrational nationalistic impulses toward a self-reinforcing ethos of cooperation'. Functionalism therefore accustoms people to a new way of thinking, and thereby helps to bring about attitudinal change.

Neofunctionalism

Later writers, who saw the way in which postwar Europe was developing, perceived deficiencies in the functionalist approach as a way of explaining what was happening on the continent. In the early stages of integration in the 1950s and early 1960s, Americans such as Ernst Haas[7] and Leon Lindberg[8] advanced their theory of **neofunctionalism**, which seemed to offer a convincing insight into the way in which the European Community was operating at the time.

Neofunctionalists accepted that there should be institutions with supranational authority over several areas of policy, particularly economic ones. But in their view, greater political unity would develop as a result of the processes involved in achieving cooperation. This closer integration would evolve as a result of 'spillover'. The more cooperation there was in one area, so there would be a spillover effect into other areas, for few policies operate in isolation. Decisions in one area have repercussions elsewhere.

In the neofunctionalist perspective, integration would be achieved by essentially secretive means. Haas was not unduly concerned with creating a change in popular attitudes, for he believed that the move to integration would come about as a result of leadership from an elite. Popular backing would come later, when the beneficial results of the policies were widely apparent.

Haas' theory is widely seen as having validity for the period through to the mid-1960s but for the next two decades there was little sign of spillover or steps towards integration. Indeed, what was happening was that there was an assertion of national self-interest, as was indicated by France's 'empty chair' position in the dispute over voting procedures in the Council (see p. 24). Moreover, attempts by the Commission to extend the area of central decision-making ran into national opposition which had to be resolved by mediation between the competing states. Harrison's[9] work reflected this sombre view of the prospects of step-by-step integration, suggesting that there was 'no evidence . . . of the beguiling automaticity . . . of economic integration leading eventually to political integration'.

This more cautious view reflected the experience of the period until the 1980s, but then the pace of change accelerated and new development came about. Keohane and Hoffmann[10] have concluded that the Haas approach is about right, and that what we have now is a supranational style of decision-making in which member states 'seek to attain agreement by means of compromises' rather than by vetoing proposals unconditionally. In their view, such a bargaining process (as each side seeks to view its national interests in the light of the common interests of the Union) is a prerequisite to spillover. The more agreement that can be reached, the greater the chances of spillover occurring.

At the heart of this approach is intergovernmental cooperation. Keohane and Hoffman point out that change often results less from a burst of 'heady idealism', and more because of 'a convergence of national interests'. Discussion at conferences where disputes are ironed out can help to promote a consensus, and as a result the process of integration can move forward. Spillover is not enough to explain the process of integration; it requires among other things what Holland[11] calls 'the bargaining process characteristic of intergovernmentalism'.

Neofunctionalism was a theory specifically designed to explain the evolution of the European Community. If the Haas approach seemed inadequate to explain what was happening in the 1960s and 1970s, it again had some relevance when applied to the new impetus towards integration that occurred in the two following decades. Alisdair Blair[12] makes the point that 'it is possible to argue that the desire to create Economic and Monetary Union was directly the result of the spillover pressure from the single market programme'. It is significant too that Keohane and Hoffman were reviving the concept in the 1980s.

Holland has concluded that neofunctionalism as an explanation for the way the Union operates is useful in that it stresses three highly relevant features:

1. It suggests that there is a connection between the processes of economic and political integration, with the former being a key factor in helping to promote the latter – 'although the precise form of political union is left intentionally ill-defined'.
2. The process of spillover provides 'the necessary but not automatic link between economics and politics'.
3. It acknowledges that via the institutions of the union, the individual states have an important part to play at intergovernmental level in promoting integration, when it seems conducive to their interests.

Intergovernmentalism
The main alternative to functional and neofunctional theory is provided by those who support intergovernmentalism as the means of explaining integration. This approach emphasises the role played by nation states rather than supranational actors. As we saw above, Keohane and Hoffman have stressed

the role of national governments, regarding spillover alone as an inadequate explanation.

To intergovernmentalists, idealism is not enough to explain the process of integration. In their 'realist' perspective, national governments take a hard-headed view of the problems confronting them. Their decisions are based on their perception of their national interests. In several areas of policy, integration might be entirely acceptable, for the national interests of one country might be similar to those of other countries. This is unlikely in areas such as defence and foreign affairs, where crucial considerations of national security are at stake.

Intergovernmentalism involves keeping supranational institutions to a minimum and is therefore the opposite of federalism. Its model is more that of a confederal Europe, the *Europe des Patries* in which states cooperate where it is to their mutual advantage. Moravcsik[13] has been the foremost exponent of inter-governmentalist theory. Drawing upon case studies from the 1950s onwards, he detects regular evidence of the importance of national interests. In his view, this applies even to the era usually portrayed as one in which idealism was tri-umphant over pragmatism. For instance, in analysing the origins of the Coal and Steel Community, he notes the high-flown rhetoric of the Schuman Declaration about the desirability of laying aside old enmities and taking the first step towards the creation of a new Europe. But he draws attention to Monnet's concern to protect and advance French national interests. He was aware of the German wish to increase substantially its output of steel. Rather than seek to block Germany's ambitions, he preferred to launch a European initiative. Such a plan suited Adenauer as well, for it offered his country the chance to achieve respectability on the European scene.

Most international organisations are intergovernmental. Intergovernmen-talism enables nation states to decide on the extent and nature of cooperation, cooperating if and when it suits them, but defending national interests on any occasion where they are seen to be under threat. The approach is one that finds enthusiastic support from those who wish to defend national sovereignty. Within the European Union, there is plenty of evidence of intergovernmentalism at work, ranging from the 'empty chair' episode to the creation of the second and third pillars of the Maastricht Treaty. In many key areas of policy today, deci-sions are still taken at the national level; decisions on the broad direction and pri-orities of the EU are taken by the Council; and even where QMV is employed there is an attempt to achieve consensus. This is an approach that suits British politicians well. Within the EU, they have always been keen to retain certain sensitive EU policy areas such as immigration and national security firmly within the ambit of the Council of Ministers, where they can employ their right of veto.

The varying pace of integration

Whatever the dynamics which promote the development of the European Union, it is clear that it moves in phases. Sometimes there appears to be a period of stagnation, at others one of great movement. Suddenly the circumstances are right and the opportunity presents itself for new momentum and a drive onwards. When such opportunities arise, theory must always take second place. In the words of Jean Monnet:

> The unification of Europe, like all peaceful revolutions, takes time – time to persuade people, time to change men's minds, time to adjust to the need for major transformations. But sometimes circumstances hasten the process and new opportunities arise. Must they be missed simply because they were not expected so soon?[14]

Such a view expresses the pragmatism of the man often referred to as the 'founder of modern Europe'. As we have seen, historians differ in how they label his approach to integration, for whereas some literature labels him as a federalist – because he shared the ultimate federal vision – other writings (such as that quoted below) place him in the functional camp, because he preferred a gradual, sector by sector, transfer of sovereignty to Community level. The description of him as a neofunctionalist recognises the final destination which he favoured and the approach which he thought best geared to achieving that long-term aim.

Differing approaches to integration

Among the twenty-seven member states, there are differing degrees of enthusiasm for the long-term goal of closer union in Europe. Those who adopt the intergovernmental approach appreciate that there are benefits to be gained from cooperation, but wish to limit Union competence and go no further along the road to integration.

States have their own reasons for wishing to speed, delay or reverse the process, and this is related to the perceived advantages which membership brings. Those countries which have gained most out of the Union are more often willing to surrender sovereignty to it – especially if they are small countries which would count for little on their own.

- Belgium, Holland and Luxembourg have less to lose for it is many years since they played a leading role in European affairs, even if they once had greater continental prestige. They are willing to embrace supranationalism and have not spent time in anguished debate on the question of a surrender of national independence. Such states (and indeed the majority of the others who currently make up the European Union) have been keen to see progress on several fronts. They are willing to push forward at greater speed towards an ever closer union.

- Some large and powerful nations such as Germany and France have been strongly integrationist members. Both have found that they could reconcile national and European interests.
- A minority, and sometimes a minority of one or two, has been anxious about the pace of development, and wishes to call a halt to further integration. They believe in the nation state as the preferred means of protecting their national interests. They can see merit and perhaps necessity in developing cooperation of an intergovernmental type, but any loss of national sovereignty and independence is to them quite unacceptable. Britain and sometimes Denmark have adopted this approach.

Klaus-Dieter Borchardt[15] has attempted to distinguish between the two camps by labelling them as the confederalists and the federalists, the former favouring interstate cooperation and the latter integration:

> Essentially the confederalist approach means that countries agree to cooperate with each other without ceding any of their national sovereignty . . . The . . . principle underlies what are known as the second and third pillars of the European Union . . . [this] does not rule out the possibility of progress towards closer integration in these areas at some stage in the future.
>
> The federalist aims to dissolve the traditional distinctions between nation states . . . The result is a European federation in which the common destiny of its peoples is guided and their future assured by common (federal) authorities.

Box 4.1 Approaches to integration: a summary

Federalists
Their bold ideas were a powerful influence upon the pioneers of European integration. Despairing of the nation state as the basis for international relations, they wished to see a new constitution for Europe which would have involved the swift transfer of power to new supranational institutions. They were inspired by the notion of a United States of Europe. Spinelli was an enthusiastic federalist.

Functionalists
More cautious in their approach, they preferred to work for unification sector by sector, as seemed necessary and appropriate. They favoured practical cooperation for the more efficient working of different economic and state functions and would hand over power to a supranational body where this was the best way forward. However, national governments would retain their traditional authority, for integrated decision-making would only apply in a limited number of sectors. As Henig[16] explains the difference between federalists and functionalists: 'Federalism, if not directly aimed at the subordination of the nation state, does firmly place it in a reduced and less influential position. Functionalism is, rather,

the hand-maiden to the nation state: it facilitates its strengthening'. It may be a way of progressing towards a federal outcome, but it still leaves the nation states as the major international players.

Neofunctionalists
They expected integration to come about as a result of 'spillover', which may eventually bring it about almost by stealth. Intergovernmental meetings can sometimes provide a push towards greater cooperation, via the bargaining process. Monnet could be placed in this school, for he was always committed to a federal outcome, though he was often vague on detail – hence the description of him as an 'incremental federalist'. He took the view that economic integration in selected areas would eventually bring about political integration.

Intergovernmentalists
They favoured cooperation between governments for their mutual advantage, an essentially pragmatic rather than visionary approach. It is reflected in the habit of member states sending representatives to participate in intergovernmental conferences (IGCs) in which all member states need to be in agreement with the final treaty or communiqué. Individual national leaders bargain amongst themselves on many of their negotiating positions, making compromises in one place in order to secure concessions in another. As Moravscsik[17] explains the process: 'governments first define a set of interests, then bargain among themselves to realise those interests'. The preferences and inclinations of national government can result in important breakthroughs, such as those agreed at Maastricht.

Conclusion

In postwar Europe, the main arguments over political cooperation have reflected the intergovernmental–supranational debate. Most continentals, be they outright federalists, functionalists or neofunctionalists, have seen the merits of closer union. For many of them, there has been the prospect that this may in time lead to some form of federal outcome. Others, the intergovernmentalists, have been wary of powers being transferred from the national to the Union level. They have sought to preserve national interests and limit cooperation to those situations in which it serves some national purpose. Where necessary, they have slowed down the pace of change.

Whereas in the early years of the European Community, neofunctionalist ideas found favour as a means of interpreting European integration, in recent decades explanations have tended to focus on intergovernmental explanations.

Glossary

Neofunctionalism The view that economic integration in a limited number of sectors will inevitably lead to further integration in others. Economic integration can similarly lead to political integration. As such, the term neofunctionalism describes the way in which functionalist techniques can be used to secure federalist objectives. Such movement towards integration is brought about by the process of spillover.

Special relationship The phrase often used to characterise the generally warm political, diplomatic and cultural relations between the United States and the United Kingdom.

SECTION TWO: INSTITUTIONS

Introduction

The organisational structure of the European Community was formally established by the Treaty of Rome in 1957, but the basic framework was already there
in the machinery of the ECSC. Outwardly, these institutions have changed very
little over fifty years of existence, despite the mutation of the Assembly into the
European Parliament (EP). But behind the apparently unchanging facade, their
underlying nature and functions have been subject to a fundamental process of
amendment that continues still. In addition, new institutions have emerged over
the last twenty years, such as the European Court of Auditors, the European
Investment Bank, the European Ombudsman, the Committee of the Regions
and the European Central Bank.

One aim of the Maastricht Summit was supposed to be the redefinition of the
institutions of the EU in the light of these organisational changes, formalising
the resulting amendments by incorporation in the Treaty. However, in the event,
it was not possible to complete a full review of the institutions at Maastricht and,
like other aspects of the Treaty, this was one of the tasks passed to the IGC which
reported at Amsterdam in 1997. And even then it was not completed. At Nice
(2000), various changes were made to prepare for enlargement, although the
issue of voting rights in the EU Council still remained unresolved. At the Brussels
summit to discuss the draft constitution in December 2003, no agreement could
be reached, for Germany and Poland were locked in deadlock. The Irish
taoiseach Bertie Ahern brokered a compromise over the issue at the Brussels
Summit six months later, during the talks on the proposed constitution. But of
course the Constitutional Treaty never came into effect.

The impact of the various treaty revisions upon the main institutions is con-
veniently summarised on p. 91.

Two constitutional problems influence the restructuring of the EU's institutions:

1. the so-called '**democratic deficit**' of those institutions
2. the vexed question of the rights belonging to individual member states.

Glossary

Democratic deficit A situation in which there is a deficiency in the democratic
process, usually where a governing body is insufficiently accountable to an elected
institution. Intergovernmental organisations have a special problem in achieving the
legitimacy that direct election confers. The term is often applied to the alleged lack of
democracy and accountability in the decision-making processes of the European
Union and to the obscurity and inaccessibility of its difficult legal texts.

CHAPTER 5

Institutions of the European Union

The Treaty of Rome established four main institutions to give effect to the provisions of the treaty: the Commission, the Parliament, the Court of Justice and the Council of Ministers. In the 1970s, European Council meetings became a regular feature. These Community institutions continue to function in the European Union. In addition, there are a number of other bodies which have less prominence but nonetheless perform useful work. At Maastricht, some powers were acquired that are not subject to the institutions of the EC. Instead, they are dealt with on an intergovernmental basis.

Institutions can seem dull, but their activities and proposals for their reform often provoke much controversy. In this chapter, we explore the composition, role and powers of these various bodies, showing how they have developed, how they interact with each other and why they are of interest and importance.

Of the five main institutions, three are more supranational in character and two more intergovernmental. In each case, we will examine their membership and formal powers, before giving consideration to any issues surrounding their workings. We will then more briefly describe the main details associated with the other institutions. We begin our coverage with the institutions that are supranational.

The Commission

The Commission is the executive arm of the European Union. Some portray it as the 'government' of the Community, while others see it as the 'civil service'. In fact, it is neither. In policy-making decisions the Commission differs from a civil service in that it formulates statements of policy but, unlike a government, it is powerless to control the vote on acceptance or rejection of that policy. In reality, the Commission is a unique institution, somewhere between an executive and an administrative machine. The very term 'Commission' is itself a misnomer, for the body's organisation embraces these two distinctive aspects. The executive responsibilities are carried out by the College of Commissioners (in effect, the political arm of the Commission) and the administrative ones by the bureaucracy.

College of Commissioners

Until 2004, larger countries such as France, Germany and the United Kingdom each had two commissioners. Since the creation of the new College of Commissioners in November of that year, there has been one representative for every EU country. At Nice, it was agreed that the Commission will have a maximum of twenty-seven members, with a rotation system that is fair to all countries to be introduced once EU membership exceeds twenty-seven states. This was confirmed in the new constitutional arrangements agreed at Brussels, as a step to ensure that the institution does not become too unwieldy. (If the Treaty establishing a Constitution for Europe had been adopted, member states would have taken it in turns to nominate commissioners, with any given state making a nomination on two out of every three occasions that a new Commission was to be appointed.)

In theory, according to the Treaty of Rome, appointment to the Commission is a collective decision of all member governments. In fact, the appointments are usually the result of nominations by individual countries. Since January 1995 commissioners have been appointed to serve for five years, instead of the original four. This five-year term now coincides with the life of the European Parliament, although the commissioners take office in January, six months after the June parliamentary elections. This delay is designed to allow time for the commissioners-designate to be vetted by the new Parliament before they take office.

The people nominated to be commissioners are experienced politicians, often having held ministerial office in their home countries before going to Brussels. Because the Commission is a supranational body, those appointed must forget their national origins and serve only the Union. Newly appointed commissioners swear an oath of independence, undertaking that they shall 'neither seek nor take instructions from any government or from any other body'.[1] While it is only natural that commissioners maintain links with former colleagues at home and remain sympathetic to their own country's interests, the Commission cannot function if its members are too preoccupied with national loyalties.

On the whole, commissioners are community-minded, often to the despair of the governments that appointed them. Margaret Thatcher chided her commissioners for their failure to represent the viewpoint of her administrations. As a former British commissioner, Sir Leon Brittan,[2] said: 'I may be a British Conservative but I do not agree with the Conservative government on many European questions'.

Commissioners are given a portfolio, placing them in charge of some aspect of the Commission's work such as Health and Consumer Protection or Development and Humanitarian Aid. In that respect they are rather like government ministers, although with greater freedom. As Brittan is quoted as saying in the article referred to above: 'Commissioners do have somewhat greater personal political autonomy than a cabinet minister – you do not have to clear things with the top'.

To assist them, commissioners have a small group of aides or advisers known as a *cabinet*. The word here is used in its French sense and would be better translated into English as 'private office'. The members of a *cabinet* are mostly civil servants who have been seconded, either from the commissioner's own national civil service or from another part of the Community's bureaucracy. Members of the *cabinet* are often fellow-nationals of the commissioner, although convention expects at least one to be from another member state.

As a collective body, commissioners form the powerhouse of the Commission, meeting weekly to formulate and develop proposals.

President of the Commission

Nomination

Before Maastricht the original rules stated that a new president should be chosen from the ranks of the existing commissioners. This was never a practical possibility since the office is so important that member governments need to spend a long time in consideration of the choice. It would be impossible to wait until an entirely new Commission was in place before beginning the selection process. As it is, the process of lobbying and negotiation begins well over a year in advance of appointment, the nominee traditionally being announced at the European Council held in the June prior to the January appointment.

A convention has grown up over the years under which the office of president alternates between citizens of large and small countries, and between representatives of the right and left. Normally the appointment is tacitly agreed between the member states before the European Council meets to announce the appointment, but such preliminary agreement is not always reached. Most recently, in 2004 Britain made it clear that it would not accept the preferred French and German choice, the Belgian prime minister, Guy Verhofstadt, who withdrew from the race. France responded by taking the same view of the existing British commissioner, Chris Patten, whose name had been under discussion. José Manuel Durão Barroso was proposed as a consensus candidate.

The president is appointed by the European Council, but during the process of bargaining the heads of government will be made aware of the views of the Parliament on the candidates for nomination. Since ratification of the Maastricht Treaty, Parliament has had to approve the choice of the president and the Commission en bloc. The Santer Commission was the first to be endorsed in this way and the same procedures applied when the Prodi and Barroso Commissions began their work. Parliament endorsed Barroso by 413 votes to 251.

Powers

Although possessing limited powers, the president of the Commission is the nearest thing the EU currently has to a head of government. Probably the true head is the president of the European Council but, since that post circulates on a six-monthly rota, the president of the Commission is a more clearly identifiable figurehead for the Community as a whole. Barroso occupies a prestigious and potentially influential position.

The more easily identified duties of the president of the Commission are:

Table 5.1 Five most recent presidents of the Commission		
President	**Nationality**	**Dates in office**
Jacques Delors	French	1985–95
Jacques Santer	Luxembourgian	1995–9
Manuel Marin	Spanish	1999 (Interim)
Romano Prodi	Italian	1999–2005
José Barroso	Portuguese	2005–

- to allocate portfolios at the start of a new Commission, a process that requires all the president's skills of negotiation and political judgment for there are fewer important portfolios than there are available personnel
- to chair weekly meetings of the College of Commissioners at which proposals are adopted, policies finalised and decisions taken
- to coordinate the work of the various commissioners, an even more arduous task than it might appear since they often have partisan interests and ideological positions at variance with those of the president
- to represent the Commission with other institutions of the EU, including giving an annual State of the Union address to the European Parliament, and attending and participating in meetings of the European Council; at these meetings the president has the same status as other heads of government
- to represent the European Union at international gatherings such as the **G8** economic summits
- to give a sense of direction to the supranational development of the EU.

The definition of the president's role is sufficiently vague as to allow a strong personality to dictate his own agenda. Delors imparted a real impetus to policy initiatives. The Delors Plan led eventually to the implementation of the single market, monetary union and the Maastricht Treaty. When he took over, Prodi aimed to create a quasi-prime ministerial role for himself, heading a cabinet-style administration in which he had the powers to fire or reshuffle individual members of the College of Commissioners.[3]

The administrative Commission: the bureaucracy

About half the staff employed by the EU serve with the Commission. Despite the public perception of a massive bureaucracy, the Commission's staff of about 25,000 people[4] is actually remarkably small, being no larger than the average government ministry in one of the member states or the administrative staff of a large municipal authority such as Barcelona.[5] Only around 4,000 personnel are involved in policy-making positions. Some 3,000 are involved in the work of translation and interpretation. Although the Commission's working languages are French and English, there are larger meetings where interpreters are required and, of course, documents of record must be issued in all the twenty-three official languages of the Union.

The Commission is divided into twenty-three policy units, similar to government ministries, each headed by a director general. These directorates general are not known by their area of responsibility but by a Roman numeral preceded by DG: hence DGVI for agriculture, DGXVI for regional policy, and so on. Each director general is answerable to a commissioner but there is no precise match between the areas of responsibility given to the directorates general and the portfolios given to commissioners. The style and attitude of directorates can vary enormously and can change over time according to the nationality and personality of the director general.[6] Liaison between the College of Commissioners and the directorates-general is through the officials forming each individual commissioner's *cabinet*.

Apart from the directorates-general there is quite a sizeable section of Commission staff that is organised into a dozen or so specialised service units such as the translation and interpreting services mentioned above.

Tasks and duties of the Commission
The most important duty carried out by the Commission is the drafting of policy documents for discussion and decision by the Council of Ministers, its remit being to initiate and formulate those policies that will promote the aims for which the European Communities were founded. The Commission is not the only source of policy to be presented to the Council, but the majority of issues discussed in the latter can only be accepted if they have been framed by the former.

Apart from this task, the Commission:

- has an executive role after policy decisions have been made. It issues the regulations, directives and instructions by which Community decisions are executed in the member states. The Commission issues some 5,000 of these legislative instruments each year, although most deal with relatively minor matters such as price levels for a single commodity in the CAP.
- is responsible for preparing the Union's annual budget and for the management of Community finances, including the various structural funds
- monitors the actions of member states in obeying and carrying out Community law. In the event of non-compliance or deliberate law-breaking, it is up to the Commission to demand obedience or, if the offence continues, prosecute the country or organisation through the European Court of Justice.

- has the ability to determine policies and actions in some areas. As a result of certain clauses in the Maastricht Treaty, there are areas of responsibility such as competition, agriculture and trade policy over which the Commission is autonomous and able to take decisions without consulting the Council of Ministers.
- sends commissioners and senior Commission staff to meetings of the European Parliament and its committees. Commissioners must answer questions from MEPs as well as attending and participating in debates which deal with the subject of their portfolio.
- is represented and participates in the work of various international bodies such as the United Nations, the Council of Europe and the OECD
- deals on behalf of the EU with diplomatic missions from over 125 foreign countries accredited to the EU. The Commission itself maintains diplomatic relations with nearly a hundred non-member states. Via the Lomé Convention, it regulates relations between the EU and the developing countries of Africa, the Caribbean and the Pacific.
- acts as the first check on new applications for membership of the EU, conducting an enquiry into all the implications of the bid for entry. Negotiations can only begin with the Commission's approval.

In pursuance of its tasks, the Commission held some 44 meetings in 2001, presenting some 456 directives, regulations and decisions for adoption by the Council of Ministers. In addition, it presented 297 Communications and reports on EU activities and produced 4 White and 6 Green Papers.[7]

The European Parliament

Until 1979 the European Parliament was composed of delegates nominated by their national governments in the same proportions as the various parties were represented in their national parliaments; many members had 'dual mandate' membership of both European and national parliaments. At the European Council in Paris (1974), it was decided to bring into force the provision for direct elections that had been written into the Treaty of Rome. The first ones were held in 1979.

Direct elections may have increased the legitimacy of the Parliament but they did not immediately produce any strengthening of its powers. Indeed, throughout its life, via discussions in the Council of Ministers and the European Council, member states have sought to hold back the powers of Parliament, because of their fear that strengthening it would weaken the sovereignty of national parliaments.

There are currently 785 MEPs. They spend one week of every month in plenary session in Strasbourg and between one and two weeks in every month on committee work in Brussels. The rest of the time is spent working within the political group to which they belong, travelling with an EP delegation on a fact-finding mission or consulting with EP officials in Luxembourg. Some MEPs, including the British, also do a certain amount of constituency work. (See pp. 146–50 for further discussion of the role and duties of MEPs.)

In the Strasbourg chamber, commissioners deliver reports, debates take place and there is also a question time; plenary sessions quite often vote, using electronic means to do so. Yet there seems to be little interest in the proceedings. The perpetual language problem means that speeches are deprived of oratory or humour, the sessions being invariably dull as a result. Much of the important work is done in committee, each MEP being assigned either to one of the twenty or so standing committees or to an ad hoc specialised committee. These have an important input into the legislative process, because committee members draft reports on proposed legislation and put forward amendments.

Powers of the European Parliament

Parliament has several functions, the powers being supervisory (control), legislative and budgetary. In all of these areas, the powers have increased, in some more than others. Key responsibilities include:

- the right to vote on the accession of new member states
- the right to be consulted by the Council of Ministers on the granting of associate status to other countries
- the power to reject or amend Council decisions on matters relating to the single market, a move that can only be reversed by a unanimous vote of the Council if a proposal is rejected, or by qualified majority if it is amended
- (most importantly) the ability to reject the Union's budget in its entirety or to amend any part of the budget that does not relate to a provision required by treaty.

The Commission must report to the EP every month and the EP has the ultimate weapon of being able to dismiss the entire Commission (although it cannot dismiss individual commissioners) on a two-thirds majority. The TEU also gave the EP the right to pass a vote of confidence or no confidence in an incoming Commission. These rights were exercised to the full during the controversy surrounding the Santer Commission in 1999 (see Box 5.1).

Parliament makes the most of its limited powers. It is much derided for its weakness, critics often being disparaging about its status as a 'talking shop'. In comparison with many national parliaments, it is a powerless body, having originally been only a consultative assembly. But every recent treaty change (see the table on p. 91) has enlarged its role in EU decision-making and in several areas it shares equal power with the Council in formulating legislation. Even in the 1980s before it had the power of **co-decision**, it was able to employ procedural devices to exert greater influence than it actually possessed. Parliament has proved skilful in extracting maximum influence from limited formal powers.

The introduction of direct elections marked a significant step towards reducing Parliament's democratic deficit, but an important contributory factor to that deficit remains – the apathy of the public in several member states. Europeans seem uninterested in the workings of the EP and are in most cases ignorant as to the function and identity of MEPs. Moreover, with the exception of those countries such as Belgium where voting is compulsory, turnout in European elections is pitifully small, while the issues on which people vote have more to do with national rather than with European factors: 'This places the EP in a legitimacy bind: it claims to represent the people of Europe, but the people of Europe demonstrate little interest in its activities'.[8]

Box 5.1 The Santer Commission

The Santer Commission was that headed by Jacques Santer, holding office from 1995 until March 1999. During that time, there were mounting allegations of fraud and corruption within the organisation, particularly concerning the French-appointed Edith Cresson. The President defended his commissioners from serious charges but eventually conceded that a culture of favouritism had prevailed and that there were cases involving conflicting interests. Cresson refused to step down, on the basis that other commissioners were involved in the same kind of favouritism that had prevailed within her area of operations.

Parliament conducted an investigation into the allegations, carried out by an independent group of 'wise men'. Their report was scathing about the behaviour of Edith Cresson, but also highly critical of the failure of Santer to impose order on the Commission. It absolved other commissioners of direct involvement, but noted that their claims to be unaware of 'undoubted instances of fraud and corruption' were a serious admission of failure. On publication of the report there were immediate calls for their resignations, the more serious because the majority socialist group added its voice to the criticism.

The outcome was that the Commission decided to resign en masse, the first time a Commission had ever resigned. Parliamentary pressure had helped to bring about its downfall. Parliament has the power to censure the Commission and – on the basis of a two-thirds majority – to force the resignation of the entire Commission from office. This power has never actually been used but it was threatened to the Santer Commission, who subsequently resigned of their own accord. Manuel Martin, a vice president of the Santer Commission, became interim president, head of an interim team of commissioners.

European Court of Justice

The Court of Justice, based in Luxembourg, is not to be confused with the European Court of Human Rights, which meets in Strasbourg and is part of the machinery of the Council of Europe. The latter has nothing to do with the EU, even though all twenty-seven member states of the EU have signed the European Convention on Human Rights. The Court of Justice is exclusively concerned with the administration of Community law.

The Court is made up of twenty-seven judges appointed for a renewable term of six years. Judges are nominated for appointment by the member states, those nominated being individuals whose independence is beyond doubt and who have usually either held high judicial office in their own countries or who are international jurists of known competence. The judges choose one of their members to act as president of the Court, with a three-year term of office. The presiding judge administers the work of the Court, in particular assigning cases to specific panels of judges and appointing the individual judge-rapporteurs who will be in charge of those panels.

Eight advocates general are nominated as of right by the five largest member states of the European Union: Germany, France, the United Kingdom, Italy and Spain. The other three positions rotate in alphabetical order between the twenty smaller member states. These are currently (2007) Slovenia, Slovakia and Portugal. Being only a little smaller than Spain, Poland has repeatedly requested a permanent representative. Advocates general are in charge of collecting documentary and other evidence for presentation to the judges, together with their own conclusions and legal judgments.

Because of the pressure of business as the Community grew, a second court, the Court of First Instance, was introduced in September 1989 in order to deal with the consequences of the Single European Act and specifically to protect individual interests. This innovation allowed the Court of Justice to concentrate on the interpretation of Community law. The Court of First Instance also has twenty-seven judges as members, but does not have advocates general, one of the judges acting in the capacity of advocate if required.

Cases can be brought before the Court by the institutions of the Community or by member states. Possibly the most frequent are cases brought by the Commission against member states for non-compliance with Community directives or regulations. Cases can, however, be brought by individuals or organisations who feel that their national governments are penalising them in breach of Community law, although these are usually held before the Court of First Instance. Many cases are referred to the European Court after they have failed on appeal in the national courts, but the Luxembourg judges emphasise that they are not a court of appeal. The only valid basis for appeal against a member state's national courts is in situations where there has been a misinterpretation of Community law by those courts.

Actual court actions, however, only form part of the Court's duties. More than half the work done by the Court arises from requests by member states for clarification or interpretation of some aspect of Community law.

Only the most important cases, involving the Community institutions or member states, are heard before a full plenary Court, for which the quorum is seven judges. Most cases are heard in chambers before a panel of three, five for more complex matters.

Since the Court began as an institution of the ECSC in 1954, it has heard well over 9,000 cases and delivered more than 4,000 judgments. However, for the average individual or small business the Court of Justice is far too expensive (legal aid is not available) and the process is far too slow, even urgent cases taking two years to reach judgment.

Council of Ministers (aka Council of the European Union, post-Maastricht)

The twenty-seven-strong Council of Ministers is the decision-making body of the European Community. It has a crucial role in the legislative process, although the Maastricht Treaty increased the role of Parliament through the co-decision procedure. However, to use the term 'Council of Ministers' as though there is only one institution of that name is misleading. The treaties refer to one Council, but there are more than twenty, because the type of minister present varies according to the subject matter of the meeting. Transport ministers will meet to discuss transport policy, energy ministers to discuss energy, and so on.

If there is such a thing as the definitive Council of Ministers, it is the General Affairs Council which is made up of foreign ministers from the member countries. It has the widest brief, dealing with general policy issues rather than foreign affairs. Another important council is the Ecofin Council which is made up of the economic and finance ministers and deals with matters such as developments

Table 5.2 The rotating presidency of the Council of Ministers, 2007–12		
Year	January–June	July–December
2007	Germany	Portugal
2008	Slovenia	France
2009	Czech Republic	Sweden
2010	Spain	Belgium
2011	Hungary	Poland
2012	Denmark	Cyprus

within the eurozone. The other councils – transport, energy, etc. – are known generically as technical councils. In each case, there is one representative from each member state.

There are Council meetings throughout the year. They are normally convened in Brussels, although meetings are held in Luxembourg during April, June and October. As an example of how busy the programme can be, there were eighty-four formal ministerial meetings in the year 2001, the General Affairs, Ecofin and Agricultural Ministers' Councils collectively accounting for thirty-eight of them. Whereas they meet at least monthly, some of the minor technical councils may not meet more than once or twice a year. Of course, advisory groups and working parties continue to operate between meetings and some groups, especially the foreign and finance ministers, will meet informally outside Brussels, perhaps within the context of a social weekend.

Leadership of the Council is determined on a rotating basis among member states, each of which holds the responsibility for a period of six months. During their tenure, ministers of the country holding the presidency can call Council meetings, decide the agenda, introduce initiatives and take the chair for all Council meetings. The position of president is a key one in the affairs of the EU, for as Martin Westlake[9] observes: 'the modern presidency is at one and the same time, manager, promoter of political initiatives, package broker, representative to and from the other Community institutions, spokesperson for the Council and for the Union, and an international actor'.

The Secretariat and COREPER

There is a vast bureaucratic input into Council meetings from a number of sources, including the 2,000 members of the General Secretariat. Headed by the secretary general, they have an important role in brokering deals and crafting compromises. Their duties in servicing the Council involve, among other things:

- preparing for meetings
- keeping records and giving advice
- providing all the services that might be looked for in civil servants
- providing some services peculiar to the European situation, such as the need to translate working documents into all twenty-three official languages.

COREPER (the Council of Permanent Representatives of Member States) is of considerable importance in the policy and decision-making processes of the Community. It was recognised as an official organ of the Community by the Merger Treaty of 1965: 'A committee consisting of the Permanent Representatives of the Member States shall be responsible for preparing the work of the Council and for carrying out the tasks assigned to it by the Council'.[10] The committee is not only a vital part of the legislative process but is the principal channel of communication between the institutions of the Community and national governments.

The permanent representatives are the Brussels-based ambassadors of the member states. In the case of Britain, while civil servants seconded to the Commission must forget their national loyalties and civil servants accompanying ministers to Council meetings are transient, the senior British diplomat sent to Brussels as permanent representative (UKREP) ensures the continuous representation of British national interests at all times. The permanent representative has a large staff including a delegation of up to forty officials, most drawn from the Foreign Office but with other policy areas also represented.

COREPER has developed into one of the most powerful groups of officials in the world. Over the years the committee has begun to devolve some of its duties to specialists and, as a result, now comprises literally hundreds of officials, splitting for convenience in 1962 into two bodies: COREPER I and II. The two committees into which COREPER is divided are responsible for:

- keeping the EU's institutions and the governments and bureaucracies of the member states informed of each other's work
- ensuring that national and European policy are not at loggerheads
- finding compromises so as not to undermine core national positions.

In practice these different functions are difficult to separate and merge into a more general aim of keeping the Union working smoothly.[11]

Westlake's analysis of the Council at work suggests that 80 per cent of its business is conducted in working parties, 10 per cent in COREPER, 5 per cent in the Council and 5 per cent in corridors. The corridors are a hive of activity and the location of much bargaining and compromise. They make it possible for the formal Council meetings to reach agreed decisions more easily. COREPER and the vast number of working groups therefore account for the bulk of the background, preparatory work.[12]

Voting in the Council

There are three ways in which the Council of Ministers can vote to take a decision: by unanimous vote, by simple majority or by qualified majority. Originally, decisions of the Council needed to be unanimous, in effect giving a dissenting state the veto, a fact exploited by de Gaulle in the 1960s. The Luxembourg Compromise of 1966 reduced the need for unanimity, extending the number of issues that could be settled by qualified majority. Since then there has been a steady extension of qualified majority voting (QMV), most significantly as a result of the Single European Act.

In pillar one of the TEU, unanimity is still required for:

- all new policies
- amendments to the policy issues of taxation and industry
- matters relating to regional and social funds

- where the Council wishes to agree or amend a policy against the wishes of the Commission.

Since Luxembourg in 1966 the member states have additionally insisted on retaining the right to veto any decision they can claim is against their national interests. However, the veto is usually regarded as being like a nuclear deterrent, held in reserve but never used. The Major government nonetheless decided that its use was justified as a result of the impasse reached over BSE.

For the other two pillars created by the Maastricht Treaty – foreign and security policy (pillar two) and justice and home affairs (pillar three) – the Council was given the sole right to act as decision-maker and unanimity was the rule. (Since then, policy on asylum, immigration and visas has been transferred to the First Pillar, signalling a shift towards more supranational decision-making in these areas.)

QMV is the most contentious of the voting methods, since it is directly related to the question of states' rights and the comparative strengths of small and large states within the Community. Under QMV the member states are given so many votes each, with a token acknowledgement of the comparative size of the member states. From the start it was agreed that for a decision to be passed it would require in the region of 70 per cent of the votes, representing something like 60 per cent of the population of the Community. The votes are distributed in such a way that the large countries acting together cannot outvote the smaller, needing the combination of two major countries and at least one more to block the decision-making process.

The weighting given to individual states is of critical importance, and has been a matter of fierce debate in every enlargement. It has proved a vexed topic in a series of IGCs and was a major issue to be resolved before the latest increases in membership in 2004 and 2007. Under the arrangements painfully negotiated at Nice and amended to take account of the latest enlargement, the revised figures are as given in the table below. A 'triple lock' operates under which any decision requires that three criteria be fulfilled:

- a QMV decision must have 73.9 per cent of the votes
- QMV must be supported by a majority of the member states
- any individual member state may require confirmation of a 'demographic test', namely that the QMV represents at least 62 per cent of the total EU population.

In the 1990s, majority voting was very seldom used by the Council of Ministers, even in areas where it was permitted. It remains the case that any member state can call for its use, but the Council prefers to seek agreement on its policies. Members are aware that a formal vote can be divisive and a cause of resentment. This may make it more difficult to work together in the future. Yet every new treaty has expanded the policy areas in which QMV operates, both Nice and the

Table 5.3 QMV in the Union of twenty-seven states

Countries	Number of votes
France, Germany, Italy, UK	29
Poland, Spain	27
Romania	14
Netherlands	13
Belgium, Czech Republic, Greece, Hungary, Portugal	12
Austria, Bulgaria, Sweden	10
Denmark, Finland, Ireland, Lithuania, Slovakia	7
Cyprus, Estonia, Latvia, Luxembourg, Slovenia	4
Malta	3

NB To be approved, a policy decided under QMV requires 255 votes. In effect, therefore, there is now a blocking minority of 90/345 votes. These Nice voting rules will remain in place until 2014 when – should the Lisbon Treaty be ratified – there will be a phased transition to new arrangements.

abortive new constitution each adding some thirty additional issues subject to its provisions. Today, it can be applied on around three quarters of all legislation and is regarded as the norm in matters concerned with the single market and any issues related to the clarification and implementation of existing law and policies.

Simple majority voting, with each state allowed one vote, is not permitted on policy or legislative proposals. Its use is mainly confined to procedural matters.

European Council

Throughout the 1960s the heads of government of the member states of the Common Market met from time to time in what were largely unofficial and informal summits. In the early 1970s, however, after the First Enlargement, a feeling grew that there was a lack of leadership. The institutions of the Community coped well enough with detailed policy but there was no focus of authority to give direction and purpose to future developments. It was agreed at the Paris Summit in 1974 that the occasional summit meetings should be formally institutionalised.

The term 'European Council' first appeared in the Single European Act of 1986, but clarification of its functions only came with the implementation of the Maastricht and Amsterdam treaties in 1993 and 1999, respectively. However, since the European Union became established through these treaties, the European Council gained a particular importance as the sole body which links, coordinates and integrates the three separate pillars of the EU. Article D of the Treaty of Maastricht sets out its role as being to 'provide the Union with the necessary impetus for its development and define the general political guidelines thereof'.

The Council still does not form part of the legal framework of the EU. It cannot legislate unless it transforms itself for the purpose into an extraordinary meeting of the Council of Ministers. Moreover, decisions of the European Council are not subject to the jurisdiction of the Court of Justice. It is a political body, whose role has dramatically grown in importance. In many recent meetings, the assembled heads of state and government have resolved issues left undecided elsewhere and provided real leadership. It sets the agenda for future developments, the major initiatives on Treaty reform, direct elections, monetary union and the creation of a rapid reaction force having been set in motion at this level.

Much valuable work of the European Council takes place outside the meeting room. Some of the most important contacts take the form of informal head-to-head meetings between individual leaders, popularly known as 'fireside chats'. Most of the preparation, however, is accomplished by the officials of the presiding country working alongside officials from the various national delegations. There is always far too much on the agenda for the participants to debate at length. In the months preceding the Council, teams of officials will have drawn up papers which they feel will be agreed by the members of the Council. If they are successful, it is only the finer points of detail that need to be discussed in the meeting.

In the past, the European Council has met at least twice a year, a meeting usually being held in the final month of each six-month presidency and hosted by the country holding the rotating presidency at that time. The meetings of the European Council have therefore come to represent a public statement on the performance of the presiding country during its half-year tenure. Under the Lisbon Treaty, if ratified, the intention is to separate the position of president of the European Council from that of president of the Council of Ministers. The presidency of the European Council will become an elected position, held for thirty months. Election will be conducted between the elected heads of government of member states.

Other EU machinery

Court of Auditors

The European Court of Auditors is an important institution set up to scrutinise the Union's budget and financial accounts. It has been in existence since 1977 and has increased its visibility and enhanced its reputation over the last decade. Its powers were strengthened at Maastricht, in answer to calls for greater 'transparency' in the EU.

Table 5.4 The treaties and institutional change: a summary

Treaty	European Council	Council of Ministers	Commission	Parliament	Court of Justice
Rome	N/A: non-existent	Granted powers to pass legislation, appoint Commission and agree budget	Able to propose legislation, draft budget, act as guardian of Treaty	Right to be consulted on legislation and to dismiss Commission en bloc	Guardian of EC treaties and of EC law
SEA	Acquired legal status	Use of QMV in areas related to single market	Granted right of initiative in new areas, re. single market	Cooperative procedure introduced, extending legislative authority	Court of First Instance created
Maastricht	Granted responsibility for determining general guidelines of Community	Extensions to QMV: able to propose legislation under Second and Third Pillars	Increased powers in relation to EMU and foreign policy	Co-decision introduced in limited range of policy areas: stronger role re. appointment of Commission	Granted powers to impose fines on member states, but not in Second and Third Pillars
Amsterdam	Confirmed role in EMU and strengthened its position re CSFP	Extensions to QMV and powers of co-decision with Parliament	President's role strengthened	Extensions to co-decision. Granted rights of approval over choice of president and Commission	Granted jurisdiction over Third Pillar, justice and home affairs
Nice	Location moved to Brussels	Extensions of QMV, plus reweighting of votes to the advantage of larger states	President's role strengthened: changes to size of Commission, to cater for enlargement from 2005	Extensions to co-decision, plus right to place matters before Court on same basis as Council and Commission	Further sharing of tasks with Court of First Instance; more chambers created to improve judicial capacity in larger EU

Adapted from Table 3.1 in E. Bomberg and A. Stubb, *The European Union: How Does it Work?*, Oxford University Press, 2003

The Court has twenty-seven members – one for each member state – all of them suitably qualified and often being members of an official audit body in their own country. Nominees have to be approved by the Council of Ministers and the European Parliament. Appointment is initially for six years, after which time the appointment can be renewed. From among their number the Court elects one member to act as president for three years.

The duties of the Court of Auditors are quite obviously related to auditing the Community's annual budget and validating the Commission's efficiency in administering that budget. There are groups within the Court of Auditors that deal with specific budgetary questions such as the CAP or the Regional Fund. Since being revised at Maastricht, the Court has extended its activities away from mere concern over financial rectitude and is more involved in questions of policy effectiveness. To that extent the Court both checks that the legal regulations laid down by the Community are observed and ensures that the Union is getting value for money.

European Investment Bank
Set up under the terms of the Treaty of Rome, the European Investment Bank (EIB) provides long-term loans for capital investment and is controlled by a board representing all twenty-seven member states. Administering a vast loan budget, the EIB is devoted to strengthening the economies of EU member states. To this end it has two principal areas of operation:

- underpinning regional development in the Union
- financing trans-European networks (TENs), large-scale and long-term projects in the fields of transport, telecommunications and energy.

Although the EIB is principally concerned with lending within the Union, it also assists with the EU's financial involvement with non-member states. The Bank operates in more than a hundred countries, supporting development projects.

Economic and Social Committee
The Economic and Social Committee (ESC) was written into the Treaty of Rome because it was felt that the then Assembly would not represent fairly the various sectional interests of the Community. The resulting committee has two main functions within the EU. It acts as:

- a forum for special interest groups in the exchange of views and ideas
- a body with a minor but integral place in the policy/decision-making process.

Originally the ESC was seen purely as a consultative body for the Council and Commission but successive treaties have extended the range of mandatory issues that must be referred to it. Also, the Amsterdam Treaty allows for the ESC to be consulted by the European Parliament as part of the decision-making process.

The 344 members of the ESC are appointed by their national governments for a renewable four-year term of office, membership being roughly proportional to the size of the member state. Membership of the national delegations can be divided into three broad socio-economic groups:

- employers – of which about half represent industry, the other half being from commercial bodies or services in the public sector
- workers – which basically means representatives of trade unions
- other interests – about half represent protectionist groups in areas of importance to the Community such as agriculture and transport, the other half representing special interest groups such as the environment or consumer affairs.

Box 5.2 Membership of the ESC

- Germany, France, Italy and the United Kingdom (24 members each)
- Spain and Poland (21)
- Romania (15)
- Belgium, Greece, the Netherlands, Portugal, Austria, Sweden, Czech Republic and Hungary and Bulgaria (12)
- Denmark, Ireland, Finland Lithuania and Slovakia (9)
- Estonia, Latvia and Slovenia (7)
- Luxembourg and Cyprus (6)
- Malta (5)

Members serve as part-time representatives. The ESC meets in plenary session about ten times each year. Most of its work is in subcommittee, drawing up opinions and producing advisory documents which are often well researched but liable to be ignored.

Committee of the Regions

The Committee of the Regions (COR) is one of the newer Community institutions, set up in the aftermath of Maastricht in order to facilitate the doctrine of subsidiarity; it met for the first time in March 1994. It was established as part of an attempt to bridge the gap between Brussels and citizens of the Union, although anti-federalists claimed that its creation was part of a Brussels plan to undermine the nation state.

The existence of the Committee reflects the growing importance of the regions in many member countries and, indeed, of the new relationships encouraged by cross-border regions such as the Rhine–Meuse (created from parts of Belgium, Germany and the Netherlands) and the Atlantic Islands Council (created by the UK, Republic of Ireland, Scottish Parliament, Welsh Assembly and the Isle of Man).

The COR must be consulted during the legislative process on any matter which it is felt has regional implications, the key issues being identified as trans-European networks, health, education, culture and economic and social cohesion. There are those who would like to see the COR become a directly elected body and form a second chamber in an enlarged and strengthened European Parliament.

Like the ESC, the COR also has 344 members, provided by member states in exactly the same proportions and appointed for a four-year term. The criteria for appointment to the COR differ between member states, largely depending on their degree of decentralisation. As a federal state, Germany is represented by members of the Länder governments. Belgium is also virtually a federation of the Flemish and Walloon communities. Other countries such as Italy and Spain are highly regionalised into semi-autonomous regional administrations and these countries draw most of their COR members from the regional governments. More centralised states such as Britain have traditionally appointed COR members from the ranks of mayors of cities or chairmen of county councils. However, the devolved legislatures (the Scottish Parliament, and the Northern Irish and Welsh Assemblies) are also represented.

The COR meets in Brussels for five plenary sessions a year. Again, much of its work is done through a structure of seven standing committees, covering areas such as:

- regional policy, structural funds, cross-border and inter-regional cooperation
- agriculture, rural development, fisheries
- urban issues, energy, environment.

As with the ESC, members are keen to belong to it, but often lament its lack of influence. Its internal divisions and the nature of its membership (deriving, as it does, from large, autonomous bodies but also smaller local councils) combine to mean that as yet it has not fulfilled all of the high hopes of those who devised it. But it remains a useful channel of communication between the various units of government across the Union.

Ombudsman

The idea of appointing an ombudsman for the EU was first mooted at Maastricht but, because of 'procedural delays', no appointment was made until 1995. The ombudsman's purpose is to reconcile the interests of EU citizens and EU institutions by providing for a thorough investigation of any accusation of maladministration on the part of any EU institution other than the Court of Justice. The appointee has wide-ranging powers of inquiry, the Community institutions being required to hand over all the documents and other evidence that he or she might demand of them. If maladministration is discovered the ombudsman:

- reports in full to the institution concerned and makes recommendations for correcting the fault
- can also refer the case to the European Parliament for further action.

In the first year of operation the ombudsman and his staff dealt with nearly 700 complaints, the largest number of which came from Britain. Most, however, were ruled to be inadmissible. The number of complaints received has increased steadily year by year since the office was established. In 2004, the total was 3,726, 195 of them from the United Kingdom. Spain has the highest proportion of complaints (482), although on a complaints to population basis Malta has the highest percentage, the UK the lowest.

European Central Bank

The European Central Bank (ECB) was instituted as of July 1998, at a meeting of the Ecofin council in Brussels. Prior to that date work on monetary union had been carried out by the European Monetary Institute (EMI) supported by the combined forces of the central banks of all Community members, the European System of Central Banks (ESCB).

Based in Frankfurt, the ECB is intended to serve as a normal central bank for those countries able and willing to participate in monetary union. As such the bank has three main areas of responsibility:

- the printing, minting, issue and administration of the new euro notes and coins, together with the ultimate withdrawal of the old currencies after the transition to a single currency, which came about in July 2002
- the determination of fiscal policy, including the setting of interest rates, for all countries in the 'eurozone'
- maintaining a watching brief on the suitability for entry of countries currently outside EMU.

The ECB has an executive board and governing council that should be composed solely of representatives from those member states participating in stage three of EMU. But the European Council can give special associate membership to non-participating states, the UK being keen to maintain observer status. At the head of the ECB is a president who is appointed for eight years.

Foreign affairs, defence and internal security

The institutions described in this chapter have all been first and foremost institutions of the European Community, which is only one of the three pillars of the European Union, the other two pillars being a common foreign and security policy and a common policy relating to justice, home affairs and internal security. The only institution common to all pillars of the EU is the European Council. For the two created at Maastricht, the TEU had to create new institutions, or rather to rationalise existing ad hoc institutions within a frame-work of intergovernmental cooperation.

Conclusion

Institutions may seem dull and complex, but they are important to an under-standing of the EU, providing the starting point for any understanding of how the Union operates, its policy processes and the direction in which it is moving. By achieving a clear idea of how they function and the way in which power is shared between them, we can better comprehend that the EU is an international body that is distinctive, still evolving and seeking to adjust to its enlarged membership.

Opinions vary as to where power lies within the Union. Supranationalists argue that the supranational institutions, the Commission, Parliament and Court of Justice, are a driving force behind the process of integration, for they are autonomous, being able to take decisions that are binding on member states. Intergovernmentalists stress the role of national governments (via the European Council and Council of Ministers) in making key decisions, leaving them in control of the direction of Union affairs.

Supranationalists can show that the introduction of QMV and co-decision, along with the growing importance of the European Parliament, all point to a loss in the influence of member states over decision-making. Intergovernmentalists can point to the ability of individual countries to opt out of policies they cannot accept as evidence that supranationalism is being held in check. Moreover, the ability of the European Council to shape the future direction of Europe reflects a broader trend in which the role of member states has been increasing in recent years, at the expense of the supranational Commission. The Council has played a leading role in the shaping of European integration and the resolution of contentious issues.

The way in which the Union moves forward is not on the basis of conflict between the various institutions, but via an attempt to achieve consensus which ensures that decisions are acceptable to as many countries as possible.

Glossary

Co-decision A procedure introduced by the Maastricht Treaty that enhances the role of Parliament in the legislative process. Ultimately, parliament can in many areas veto a measure put forward by the Council of Ministers.
G8 – Group of Eight An international forum for the governments of the original G7 advanced industrial countries (Canada, France, Germany, Italy, Japan, the United Kingdom and the United States), plus Russia, which achieved full status in 2002. Together, the eight countries represent about 65 per cent of the world economy. The G7/8 Summit deals with macroeconomic management, international trade and relations with developing countries. The group's activities include year-round conferences and policy research, culminating in the annual gathering attended by the heads of government of the member states.

CHAPTER 6

Policy-making and law-making processes

The Union's responsibilities ('competences') have significantly developed in recent decades, so that today EU policies and laws have a considerable impact at national and sometimes international and subnational levels as well.

Here we examine the sources of policy, the various procedures by which the EU takes decisions on policy issues and how it makes laws.

Origins of EU policy

Proposals for and decisions on Union action come about in various ways, the impetus sometimes deriving from within the Community's institutions (the Community method) and at others resulting from the expressed wishes of the member states who give a strong lead (the intergovernmental method). On occasions, EU powers are exercised jointly by Union institutions and national governments or national policies are coordinated at the Union level (the coordination method).

There is, then, no fixed process by which policies emerge. At times in EU history, national governments have been actively involved in pushing forward new initiatives, but in other phases of the Union's development there has been a greater interest in supranational policy-making. Of course, there is an overlap between the two fields of activity. Some of the same personnel can be involved in national political life and in EU politics. Ministers from each country – and the officials who advise them – meet together periodically in the Council of Ministers, but much of their time is spent in the domestic arena. Even MEPs, members of the supranational Parliament, spend varying amounts of their time 'back home'. In other words, 'European' and 'national' politics are not entirely distinct from each other.

Moreover, the bargaining that is part of EU policy-making is not always a matter of the potential conflict between EU and national interests. There will be negotiations and sometimes clashes in the home country between different government departments over how a particular issue should be handled. As Bomberg and Stubb[1] explain: 'Perhaps naturally, environment ministers often find agreement easier among themselves in Brussels than agreement with their "own" industry ministries'.

Three sources

The *Community method* applies where treaties have granted specific powers to the EU. In these circumstances, the initiative in policy-making usually comes from the Commission, which tables a formal proposal. As we see on pp. 104–7, the

Council then takes the final decision via one of three law-making procedures, of which co-decision is the most common. The Court of Justice resolves any conflicts and enforces the resulting laws.

This was the traditional approach to policy-making as the Community evolved from its earliest days. In various areas, national governments had granted specific responsibilities to the EC to be handled by the machinery in Brussels and to a lesser extent in Strasbourg. The emphasis was on supranational institutions agreeing common policies, the CAP being an obvious example. In this case, Parliament had only modest involvement, whereas on matters affecting the internal market it exercises much greater influence. Even the Council of Ministers, usually portrayed as the defender of national interests, was involved in the bargaining process, for instance helping to make the deals which made the CAP possible.

The *intergovernmental method* covers policy areas over which national governments have control. In these circumstances, the supranational bodies – the Commission, Parliament and the Court – play only a very limited role. Ever since the formation of the Community, there have always been issues which have been handled primarily by member states within the European Council and Council of Ministers. National representatives engage in frank discussions and prolonged bargaining, as they seek to achieve a compromise position which they can sell to their ministerial colleagues and to the public in their own countries.

Some of the issues resolved in this way concern matters that are fundamental to the national interests of member states, such as tax harmonisation and defence and foreign policy. In these cases, cooperation between states may be desirable if it can be achieved, but for politicians of some countries – particularly those less known for their *communautaire* approach – they wish to retain the chance to determine the future outcome of policy areas that affect vital national interests.

On policies decided primarily at intergovernmental level, the bulk of the work will be done by the Council of Ministers and the national delegations and working groups that service it. Individual ministers will seek support from others around the negotiating table who share at least some of their outlook and priorities, creating coalitions of support around particular issues. Where necessary, the summits of the European Council can provide a sense of direction and urgency to the process of reaching agreement.

There are obvious difficulties in achieving any consensus on 'sensitive matters' affecting national interests, which is why the Maastricht negotiators excluded national security (the CFSP) and justice and home affairs (JHA) from supranational decision-making. Whereas the Commission and Parliament are active within the First Pillar, they are much more distantly associated with these second- and third-pillar topics. But even on JHA-related policy, there has been considerable progress in developing a common approach to matters affecting asylum, migration and terrorism, illustrating how intergovernmental cooperation can have a role in progress towards integration within the European Union.

The *coordination method* has developed in recent years, most obviously in the area of JHA, where – as we have seen – there is a trend towards the adoption of a common approach. On employment policy too, there has been a trend towards member states working more closely together either to agree on non-binding policy recommendations or to examine the practice of those countries which are having greater success in combating the problems, with a view to learning from their experiences. In this process, experts are called in to assess the value of initiatives taken in individual countries and make recommendations. The Commission has an input, facilitating the contribution from outside specialists and examining national policies. So too does Parliament, whose specialist committees can be involved in monitoring new initiatives and suggesting future action.

Policy-making: a reflection

What is apparent from this brief description of how policy emerges is that both the traditional Community and intergovernmental approaches can contribute to the evolution of European integration. Supranational institutions can drive and often have driven the Union forward, but so too the actions of national governments can provide a momentum of their won. Sometimes, as a result of intergovernmentalism in action – as with JHA – there are clear signs that the close and regular interaction between member states can create the conditions that lead the Union forward into greater cooperation.

Whatever the method of policy-making, there is a constant search for agreement and – if possible – consensus. It is recognised that member states have their own national priorities and difficulties. If it is possible to accommodate them, then the emphasis is on compromise, doing deals with which politicians and the public in each country can live. Discussions at summit gatherings where disputes are ironed out can help to promote the agreement that drives integration forward. It sometimes requires what Holland[2] calls 'the bargaining process characteristic of intergovernmentalism'.

Bomberg and Stubb[3] have also noted this tendency towards seeking an outcome satisfactory to all players:

> Competition is fierce but so, too, is the search for consensus. Enormous efforts go into forging agreements acceptable to most. The overall trajectory of the integration process is thus a result of to-ing and fro-ing between a wide variety of actors and external pressures . . . the pendulum swinging sometimes towards intergovernmental solutions and sometimes towards supranational solutions, but not always in equal measure.

EU law

By whatever means policy decisions emerge, when they are made they are in many cases then turned into law. EU law accounts for approximately half of all the legislation enacted within the member states.

There are two categories of law in the European Union:

- *Primary legislation* involves the body of law established by the founding treaties of the Communities, together with all later amendments and protocols attached to those treaties.
- *Secondary legislation* encompasses all laws passed by the institutions of the Communities in order to fulfil the aims and purposes of the treaties.

Primary legislation

Community law in this respect is provided by the three treaties, with the various annexes and protocols attached to them, and their later additions and amendments: these are the founding acts . . . Because the law contained in the treaties was created directly by the Member States themselves, it is known as primary Community legislation. This founding charter is mainly confined to setting out the objectives of the Community, establishing its mechanisms and setting up institutions with the task of filling out the constitutional skeleton and conferring on them legislative and administrative powers to do so.[4]

Primary law is therefore constitutional law, dealing largely with the relationship of the member states, both with Community institutions and with each other. It is the basis on which the European Court of Justice makes its judgments and, as in any legal system, the decisions made by judges and the precedents set by them form the basis for case law. And case law can apply to individual citizens, firms and organisations.

EU law v. national law

Over the forty years or so that the European Communities have been in existence there have been a succession of judgments, by both the European Court of Justice and the various national courts, that have helped to build up a formidable corpus of case law concerning the relationship between Community and national law. It is now established that:

- Member states have transferred sovereign rights to a Community created by themselves. They cannot reverse this process by means of unilateral measures inconsistent with the general interests of the Community.
- No member state may call into question the status of Community law as being a system uniformly and generally applicable throughout the Community.
- Community law, enacted in accordance with the treaties, has priority over any conflicting law of the member states.

• Community law is not only stronger than earlier national law but has a limiting effect on laws adopted subsequently.[5]

The primacy of Community law over national law has long been established. But it was the Factortame judgment that most clearly set out the position should there be any conflict between Community law and national law: 'Under the terms of the 1972 Act, it has always been clear that it was the duty of a United Kingdom Court to override any rule of national law found to be in conflict with any directly enforceable rule of European law.'

Box 6.1 The Factortame case

The subordination of national law in member states to Brussels was underlined in an important legal judgment involving the United Kingdom in 1991. The European Court of Justice gave its verdict in *Factortame* v. *Secretary of State for Transport*.

In 1988, the Thatcher government passed the Merchant Shipping Act, designed to deal with the problem of quota-hopping by Spanish and other fishermen who were registering their vessels under the British flag and using the UK's fishing quotas, much to the dismay of British trawlermen. The Act provided that UK-registered boats must be 75 per cent British owned and have 75 per cent of their crew resident in Britain.

In the Factortame judgment, the Merchant Shipping Act of 1988 was ruled invalid and therefore effectively quashed by the Court of Justice. The position was made very clear. The Act contradicted EC law because it was discriminatory in a Community committed to freedom of movement. It was therefore invalid. In the words of one journal, 'this is a historic judgement . . . it overturns the English ruling that no injunction can be granted against the Crown . . . the Europeans are rewriting our constitution'.[6]

At the time, senior judge Lord Bridges[7] observed that the verdict was only a reaffirmation of the supremacy of Community law, as had been recognised since 1973. But it has come to be seen as a major test of the constitutional position. In the Maastricht debates, Margaret Thatcher invoked it as evidence that 'European law will prevail more and more'.

Even more important for the individual are the judgments referring to what is called 'direct applicability'. This means that the rules laid down in the foundation treaties are not only applicable to the member states and institutions of the Community but directly impose obligations and confer rights on the citizens of the member countries – without those rules having to be adopted and amended by national law.

The first important judgment on this issue concerned Article 12 of the Treaty of Rome, limiting the ability of states belonging to the Common Market to impose or raise customs duties on goods circulating between members of the Common Market. Van Gend and Loos, a Dutch transport firm that imported chemical products from West Germany, went to court in the Netherlands in 1962 protesting that Dutch customs had increased customs duties on the goods they handled, in clear breach of Article 12 of the EEC Treaty. At that time it was believed that laws contained in the Treaty applied only to states and institutions, and could apply to firms and individuals only if adopted by national law. Now the Dutch court was being asked to rule that the Treaty of Rome conferred rights on individuals within member states.

Feeling that it was not competent to rule on Community law, the Dutch court referred the case to the Court of Justice. Naturally, any such decision had major implications for national sovereignty and many member states made representations to the Court. However, judgment was given in favour of the firm, the judges stating: 'Community law not only imposes obligations on individuals but is also intended to confer upon them rights'.[8] This judgment was taken as the criterion for direct applicability and the case law thus established set a precedent for all subsequent cases of this nature.

We can therefore summarise the situation concerning the importance of primary law in the EU as follows:

- Primary law, as established in the Treaties, has primacy over national law and, in these matters, the European Court of Justice has primacy over national courts.
- Its provisions are as binding on the citizens of member states as they are upon the states themselves.
- The foundation laws of the Community are to be enforced by the national courts of the member states in exactly the same way as they apply national law.

Secondary legislation

'Secondary legislation' refers to all those legal instruments devised and issued by the Community in order to administer policies laid down by the Community and achieve such aims and objectives of the Community as were established under primary legislation.

Decisions made by institutions of the Community are passed to national governments for acceptance and implementation in the form of one of five different classes of legal instrument: regulations, directives, decisions, recommendations and opinions.

1. *Regulations* Once issued, regulations become immediately effective as law within the member states without the need for any national legislation to endorse them. For the UK, the European Communities Act of 1972 gives authority for all subsequent EC regulations to have the same effect as UK

domestic law approved by Parliament. Although regulations become law in the form that was agreed in Brussels, sometimes additional legislation is required in the member countries to make them more effective.

2. *Directives* These are not as complete and detailed as regulations, but consist more of policy objectives. The results to be achieved are communicated to national governments and those objectives are binding on the governments. But the form and method in or by which those results are transposed is left to the discretion of the national governments. Usually, up to two years are allowed for this transposition, providing them with sufficient latitude to cater for their individual circumstances in a way that may overcome initial reservations.

3. *Decisions* Unlike regulations and directives, decisions are not directed at all member states but are specifically directed at one country or a firm, organisation or individual within it. Because these decisions are specific they are often administrative rather than legislative acts.

4. and 5. *Recommendations* and *opinions* These are little more than suggestions or tentative proposals put out by the Council or Commission and are not binding on the member states in any way. Strictly speaking, they do not constitute Community legislation but are included here under secondary legislation because they may be taken into consideration by the Court of Justice when making a judgment about some other matter. In addition, the Commission may also state its views via official *Communications*, the Council may proclaim *Declarations* and Parliament can issue *Resolutions*.

In any one year, several thousand legal instruments are issued. The number has declined in recent years given the completion of the drive towards the single market and an attempt to simplify and streamline EU procedures. The majority of these instruments are non-political, being routine administration and dealing with matters such as price levels in the CAP. Of those instruments that could be considered legislative, Commission figures indicate that of those enacted in 2004 822 were regulations, 512 decisions and 107 directives. There were also 49 recommendations.

There are basically two sources of Community legislation:

1. *Commission legislation* is made directly by the Commission and enacted under powers delegated by the Council. This legislation is largely made up of technical, trivial or routine administrative detail arising from legislation already agreed by the Council. However, the Commission can legislate without reference to the Council in certain areas, such as the granting of financial support from public funds.

2. *Council legislation* is described more fully below and involves consideration and consultation by the Council and European Parliament of proposals formulated by the Commission.

Legislative process within the Union

Broadly, this has been the general pattern of what happens, although there are significant variations at stages 2 and 3:

1. The Commission proposes new legislation.
2. The Council consults on the proposal with the Parliament which scrutinises (and may suggest amendments) and with the Economic and Social Committee which advises.
3. The Council decides whether to go ahead.
4. The Commission implements the proposal.
5. The Court of Justice arbitrates on any infringement of the law and resolves any disputes.

In 1970, Lindberg and Scheingold[9] wrote of policy-making in the following terms:

> It is no exaggeration to view the whole policy-making process in the Community as a dialogue between the Council, representing national cabinets, and the Commission, appointed originally by the governments but acting autonomously in terms of its own view of the 'interests' of the Community as a whole.

Since then, the policy-making process has moved on. The Commission remains the starting point of the decision-making process. However, with the passage of the SEA, the TEU and subsequent treaties, the powers of the Parliament have been increased, so that what was a dialogue between two institutions has become more of a partnership between three of them. Finally, the use of qualified majority voting in the Council has been extended into new areas.

Most administrative or regulatory legislation coming from Brussels takes the form of Commission legislation, drafted by the relevant directorate general with the assistance of an advisory or management committee. With such routine measures there is little need for scrutiny of decisions by ministers, commissioners or national officials. On the other hand, when the regulations or directives to be issued are felt to be important or are likely to set a precedent or establish principles, then they are thought to need examination through the full Council legislative process.

There are four main procedures, other than that for handling budgetary matters.

Consultation procedure

The consultation procedure involves Parliament giving an opinion on Commission proposals. Use of this method of policy-making has gradually been reduced with the introduction of the cooperation and co-decision procedures, but it still covers important fields such as the CAP, taxation and certain aspects of economic and monetary union.

How a proposal develops

Much of the work of the Commission is concerned with the implementation of policies approved by the Council, but new initiatives are continually being suggested by the Commission. These may derive from suggestions of one or more of the member states, or from the discussions which are regularly held with leading interest groups with which the Commission has a strong association. They may result from thinking within the Commission itself.

Once conceived, the idea will be formulated into a draft proposal by the appropriate directorates general which may be in the form of a **Green Paper**, a consultative document setting out possible ways forward. This early version will be sent to any organisation which might be thought to have a valid input to make. Such outlets include national governments, interest groups, committees of the Parliament, the Economic and Social Committee and – depending on its relevance – the Committee of the Regions. Once any suggestions have been considered (and rejected, incorporated or refined), then a **White Paper** is published. It is sent to the Council and other institutions, perhaps including the Committee. At this stage, the pressure groups will be involved in active lobbying of the institutions and their personnel.

The Council will refer the proposal to one of its study groups which comprise civil servants from the various states. These officials will consult with national parliaments and groups, and then send an analysis of their findings and views to COREPER. COREPER will seek to establish common ground on the proposal, via consultation with the member states and with the Commission. At this stage, procedure varies, depending on the article in the various treaties from which the legislation derives, but usually the Council then discusses the proposal and the advice it has received having taken into consideration the views of the EP, ESC and, maybe, of the COR. It makes a decision, which it is then the task of the Commission to implement.

Cooperative procedure

The passage of the Single European Act extended the role of the Parliament although the Council still has the final say. In the TEU, cooperation was taken further, and now only covers some limited aspects of EMU.

Again, the Commission initiates a proposal, as described in the section above. However, under this procedure, rather than being allowed merely consultation (the first reading), it acquired more of a legislative role; it was given a second opportunity to examine any proposal. The agreed position of the Council was to be submitted to it for scrutiny during a second 'reading'. For up to three months – or four if the period is extended by the Council – Parliament can discuss the proposal.

Parliament has a number of options. It can:

1. *Accept the proposal*, or do nothing about it. In this case, the Council can go ahead and adopt it without further delay.

2. *Amend it*. If the Parliament decides (on a majority basis) to modify the proposal, then within three months the Council must either accept Parliament's modifications, accept the amended version of the Commission, or amend the revised version from the Commission.
3. *Reject it*. If this happens, the Council can override the objection of the Parliament, but only on the basis of a unanimous vote.

Assent procedure

The SEA also introduced another device: the assent procedure. On any proposed enlargement of the EC or on any association agreements, the assent of Parliament is needed.

Parliament may give or withhold its agreement on the proposal laid before it, but it has no power to amend it. Assent covers any international agreements as already mentioned, but in the TEU (Article 228) it now covers other items such as policies with important budgetary implications for the Union as a whole, and matters connected with citizenship or reform of the structural or cohesion funds. In its analysis of the workings of the TEU (May 1995), the Commission identified thirty-two proposals which had been adopted under the assent procedure, twenty of which were before the ratification of the Maastricht Treaty. In seven cases, the procedure had been completed, five concerning international agreements, one the accession of a new member and the other on a piece of legislation concerned with the Cohesion Fund.

This is not a legislative procedure but is nevertheless an important part of EU decision-making. The requirement that the assent of the EP was needed for any proposed enlargement of the Union was extended under Article 228 of the Maastricht Treaty to include such other constitutional matters as association agreements with third world countries, the organisation and objectives of the Structural and Cohesion Funds and the tasks and powers of the European Central Bank.

Co-decision procedure

Article 189b of the Maastricht Treaty introduced a further legislative procedure, that of co-decision. This covers some matters previously dealt with under the cooperation procedure and certain issues concerned with the workings of the single market.

Under the co-decision procedure, Parliament and the Council adopt legislative initiatives on the basis of joint agreement. Parliament has an absolute right of veto if it rejects the approved position of the Council, though in a conciliation stage a committee made up of representatives from the Parliament and the Commission can look for a compromise satisfactory to both institutions. The conciliation procedure can also be utilised if Parliament wishes to amend a Council proposal covered by co-decision in a way which the Council cannot accept. In the absence of agreement, the policy initiative fails.

Although there were fears about the likely time and complexity of co-decision-making, it has worked well and enabled decisions to be taken reasonably quickly on a number of issues. The Commission document referred to above suggests that the average time involved in the procedure is less than 300 days, although as to whether this will remain true is difficult to say for there is as yet little evidence to go on. It only identified two occasions where the procedure failed to produce a decision.

Much EU legislation falls within the co-decision procedure. Originally, the procedure was used in decision-making on consumer protection, culture, education, free movement of workers, health, freedom to provide services, the single market and the adoption of guidelines or programmes covering trans-European network, research and the environment. At Amsterdam, its use was extended to cover such items as discrimination on grounds of nationality, environment policy and the fight against fraud. At Nice, further extensions covered asylum and immigration, economic and social cohesion and judicial cooperation on civil matters. Had the Constitutional Treaty been ratified, co-decision would have become the usual legislative procedure, covering most aspects of EU law.

When the proposal has been approved under whichever of the four procedures is relevant, it is then introduced in the form of a regulation, directive or decision.

Comment on the decision-making procedure

In preparation for the Intergovernmental Conference prior to Maastricht, the Commission[10] itself concluded that there were three main deficiencies in the decision-making process:

1. *Continuing divergence between legislative procedure and budget procedure* Parliament tends to push through measures under the budgetary procedure which more appropriately come under the auspices of the legislative procedure. The converse is that the Council tends to use the legislative procedure to introduce its financial plans when they should really come under the budgetary procedure, on which Parliament has greater power.
2. *Complexity of the legislative procedure* There was a time when decision-making followed a simple pattern but this has not been the case since the introduction of changes in the budget procedure in the 1970s. The introduction of cooperation, assent and co-decision, as well as special arrangements for EMU, CFSP and JHA at Maastricht all added to the confusion.

   The addition of new layers of responsibility since then has led to a growth in procedures and there are many variations in existence. Sometimes there is delay while discussion occurs as to which procedures should be employed.

Some procedures are particularly complex and this only adds to the difficulty of understanding. Procedures need to be clearer and more precise for those not actively involved in the process; this would provide for greater openness and transparency.

3. *Lack of logic in the application of procedures* Different procedures apply in three equally important sectors: agriculture (consultation), transport (cooperation) and the internal market (co-decision). Sometimes, several procedures may apply in one area such as cohesion and the environment.

Decision-making is now unacceptably complex. This suggests the need for a radical transformation of the legislative processes, so that there is a clear hierarchy of issues, and an appropriate procedure to deal with each layer. The range of procedures in use at present could be reduced. At the IGC, the Commission itself envisaged only three main forms in the future: the assent procedure, a simplified co-decision procedure and consultation. Simplification of decision-making in budgetary matters (see pp. 110–12) was also seen as desirable, to ensure that the institutions cooperate in a more genuinely interinstitutional manner.

Criticism also focuses on other aspects of the policy-making process, however.

Search for agreement in the Council
It remains the fact that one of the major barriers to any reform is the sturdy (some would say stubborn) defence of national interests offered by some member states which are unwilling to compromise. Agricultural reform is an area where the French are particularly unwilling to make any concessions, for fear of the outcry which it will provoke in the national agricultural lobby. As a way of getting round this problem, the Commission has favoured an extension of qualified majority voting, seeing it as an 'effective tool' in the decision-making process. Since Maastricht, QMV now covers new fields of activity, including consumer protection, public health, visas and vocational training, among other things. It also applies to some areas of EMU and to the environment and social policy. Where it is difficult to reach agreement, an extra push can sometimes be provided by a meeting of the European Council. This may then enable agreement to be reached within the Council of Ministers.

The decision-making process is not only concerned to achieve agreement between representatives of the national governments. The procedure in all cases is designed to achieve consensus – agreement between the institutions involved. Of course, this may result in an ineffective policy, for compromise may be on the basis of the lowest common denominator. Pleasing everybody may mean actually doing very little, and in the area of common transport policy or especially reform of the Common Agricultural Policy it has been particularly difficult to achieve substantial change.

Implementation

Even where the policy is agreed, much depends on the political will to implement it. Some countries have a notably poor record at doing so. In many areas, Britain has a good rate of compliance, though less so on environmental matters including water safety. In some countries, EU regulations and directives are regularly flouted. Implementing measures is the responsibility of the Commission, in partnership with national government departments, and, where the law is concerned, of the Court.

Table 6.1 Transposition into national law of internal market rules, pre the Fifth Enlargement

Member state	Number and % of directives not implemented	
Greece	80	5.1
Italy	71	4.5
Luxembourg	67	4.2
Belgium	54	3.4
Portugal	51	3.2
France	50	3.2
Germany	40	2.5
United Kingdom	40	2.5
Ireland	38	2.4
Finland	37	2.3
Denmark	36	2.3
Austria	33	2.1
Sweden	32	2.0
Netherlands	31	2.0
Spain	21	1.3
EU average	45.4	3.6

Adapted from A. Blair, *Companion to the European Union*, Routledge, 2006; based upon figures provided by the European Commission, covering the period to 15.11.2004.

Lack of transparency and democracy

The Union's decision-making rules and procedures should also serve to make the institutions more democratic and help them to operate effectively. Central to the criticisms which are often made of the way the Union operates is the lack of **transparency** and democracy in its working arrangements.

NB For further discussion of the lack of democracy in EU institutions and procedures, see the following chapter.

EU budgetary process

The EU budget is a contentious issue that has, on occasion, been the cause of considerable debate and conflict among the member states. Because of the controversies of the early 1980s (see in particular pp. 31–3), it was agreed at the 1988 Brussels Summit that it would be better if there was agreement between the institutions on the overall size and structure of the Union's income and expenditure for a period of five or seven years ahead. In the *Interinstitutional Agreement on Budgetary Discipline and Improvement of the Budgetary Procedure*, it was accepted that there should be a financial framework for the immediate years ahead. This became known as the **financial perspective (FP)** and it covered the period 1988–92 (Delors I). Subsequently, the other financial perspectives have been fixed for 1993–9 (Delors II), 2000–6 and 2007–13.

Financial perspective

The financial perspective is a multi-annual financial planning framework which sets limits on European Union expenditure. It is compulsory in the sense that the financial perspective ceilings must be respected in the annual budgetary procedure. It is agreed by the European Parliament, the Council and the Commission and lays down maximum amounts by major heading of expenditure within which the annual budget must be established over the period in question. Effectively, it translates into financial terms the priorities set for the Union's policies and is at the same time an instrument of budgetary discipline and planning, and determines the limits on the financing of the EU budget.

The financial perspective is, then, an interinstitutional agreement between three elements, but it is the European Council which decides by unanimity on the figures, on the basis of a Commission proposal. The European Parliament must give its consent. Parliament approved the current FP by simple majority.

The financial perspectives are a cause of major controversy, each settlement usually requiring the allocation of much time and effort at more than one Council meeting. In particular, there was much controversy over the adoption of the 2007–13 FP, for it revived a number of issues on which strong national positions had in the past been taken up – most obviously, the agricultural reform which Britain was urging and the curtailment or removal of Britain's budgetary rebate in which the other twenty-four countries had an interest (see pp. 201–2, below). Some long-standing member states were worried about the burdens they were bearing as net contributors to the Community and wanted to see action to reduce their outgoings. In addition, the states about to join in the Fifth Enlargement (Central and Eastern part i) were looking for more generous treatment than that which they believed they had received under the terms of the previous perspective.

Whatever the heat they generate, the setting of these perspectives has clear advantages. They do ensure that strict budgetary discipline is imposed, by setting limits to expenditure in any one area of EU spending, and they allow for medium-term planning of EU funding and policies. They also have the benefit of limiting the full-scale rows to once every few years, rather than having them arise every time the annual budget is discussed.

2007–13 financial perspective (%)

Farm and rural support	42.8
Cohesion aid	35.4
Competitiveness	8.3
Foreign policy	5.8
Administration	5.8
Justice and security	1.2
Other	0.7

Devising the annual budget

The establishment of these broad outlines has done much to ease the path of negotiations over the preparation of the annual budget. The phrase 'budgetary discipline' denotes the broad constraints under which it is drawn up, ensuring that there is a balance of revenue and expenditure.

The budget is covered by a special procedure, with Parliament and the Council together forming the budgetary authority. The Maastricht Treaty set out the framework via which the annual budget is prepared. However, each year's budget is different, there sometimes being particular necessities and problems that have to be handled. There is therefore no typical format for the determination of the budget. But it is possible to detect a standard pattern for the process.

It begins with the estimates of expenditure being sent to Directorate General XIX of the Commission, which has responsibility for formulating the budget. These estimates arrive in the summer of the year prior to which the budget will apply. The likely revenue for the coming year is then calculated. The budget is drafted in a preliminary form by the Commission before the first day of September, and submitted to the Council in the form of a Preliminary Draft Budget (PDB). The Council considers this document – acting by qualified majority – and sends its own revised version (the 'draft budget') to the European Parliament by 5 October. Parliament has forty-five days to debate the amended budget and propose its own amendments, before returning it to the Council.

The proposals go back and forth between the Council and the Parliament, the two institutions that together form the budget authority. In the case of 'compulsory' expenditure (mainly the money spent on the CAP), the Council has the final word. In the case of other 'non-compulsory' expenditure (e.g. the size of the Social Fund), Parliament has the final say and can modify expenditure according to conditions laid down in the Treaties. It must not increase the overall budgetary expenditure beyond the ceiling devised by the Council.

There can be much conflict between the Council and the Parliament, who experience what Nicoll and Salmon[11] call an 'uneasy partnership'. The procedure can be slow, so that on occasions there is no settlement by the end of the year. In this case, the Union is allowed to spend each month one-twelfth of the provision made in the previous year's budget, so that the machinery of the EU may continue to function.

After difficulties over the budget in 1980, an attempt was made in the following year to improve the machinery. A Trilogue was created, comprising the president of the Budget Council, the president of the Commission (maybe with the relevant commissioner) and the president of the Parliament (maybe with the president of the Committee on Budgets). In 1988, it managed to bring about an agreement after a period of deadlock.

It is Parliament that ultimately adopts the budget and it has used its budgetary powers to the full in order to influence Union policies. This determination, together with the long-running threat that the Union budget might be stifled by a ceiling on 'own resources', explains why the budget procedure has often sparked off disputes between Parliament and the Council.

Overall, the influence of Parliament is uneven. It has almost no say over the sources of revenue and on key issues such as agricultural spending it is the Council which has the final say. On the other hand, the budget is only finally approved when the president of Parliament appends his signature to it. Moreover, the fact that pressure-group spokespersons lobby parliament so much at the time when the settlement is being negotiated suggests that lobbyists recognise that on some spending areas including the regions and social policy its influence is considerable.

Monitoring the budget

To ensure that money has been spent as was intended, Parliament's Committee on Budget Control conducts an annual assessment of the management of the budget before giving – on the basis of the Annual Report of the Court of Auditors (ECA) – a 'full discharge'. Because of the complexity of the Community budget, individual members of the Committee specialise in particular Community policies and prepare the EP's response to ECA special reports in their field, often in the form of working papers for the guidance of the general rapporteur on the discharge.

All matters relating to the budget will have been closely scrutinised by the ECA, within which there are groups dealing with specific budgetary questions such as the CAP or the Regional Fund. Since Maastricht the Court of Auditors has extended its activities from concern over financial rectitude to a wider monitoring of policy effectiveness. The Court not only checks that both revenue and expenditure observe legal regulations but also ensures that the Community is getting value for money by checking how far financial objectives have been met.

Conclusion

The Community has an established and complex procedure for the determination of policy-making and legislation in which national representatives can take part and which involves all the institutions of the Community. Provisions of the SEA, TEU and Amsterdam Treaty are leading to a reduction in the democratic deficit through increased powers for the European Parliament in an extended legislative process.

Broadly, in those areas where there has been a transfer of responsibility from national governments to the EU, its institutions – and especially the Commission – are deeply involved in the creation of policy. Where the competence of the EU is more modest – as in education and health – most of what happens is decided in the member states and the Union has little involvement. Yet circumstances can change. As we have seen with the JHA policy sector, the participation of the EU has increased. At first, EU activity on JHA-related matters was mainly of the intergovernmental kind, but it is now in some respects supranational in character.

For those areas of policy that fall within the competence of the EU, there is no typical process of policy-making or decision-making. The situation is complicated, the procedure varying according to the issue being discussed. As Nugent[12] observes: 'A host of actors, operating within the context of numerous EU and national-level institutions, interact with one another on the basis of an array of different decision-making rules and procedures'.

The range and complexity of EU policy- and decision-making processes is remarkable, twenty-eight having been identified by the Constitutional Convention. The involvement of the various institutions differs according to the area in question. Where the Community method applies – broadly those areas that fall within the First Pillar – decisions are taken according to the interaction of three institutions: the Council of Ministers, the Commission and the European Parliament. But the role that each plays is dependent on what is being discussed. On most issues other than agriculture, JHA and trade, the role of Parliament is now extensive, because they are subject to co-decision; EMU is not, for decisions in this area are taken largely by the Council of Ministers and the officials who serve it and the European Central Bank. For pillars two and three, which are intergovernmental in character, the Council remains the main player, the roles of the Commission and Parliament being subordinate. Sometimes, the momentum for decision-making is provided at gatherings of the European Council.

Glossary

Financial perspective The financial perspective is an agreement on the key priority tasks of EU budget expenditure for multi-annual periods. It lays down the basic framework of the EU policies in the following years. Multi-annual interinstitutional agreements on budgetary discipline were first introduced in 1988 to give stability to annual budgets and better support EU priorities. They provide for an adequate level of resources, strong budgetary discipline and an enhanced focus on EU priorities.

Green Paper A set of proposals put forward by the Commission as a basis for discussion in a given policy area.

Transparency A mode of institutional operation in which nearly all decision-making is carried out publicly. All draft documents, all arguments for and against a proposal, the decisions about the decision-making process itself and all final decisions, are made publicly and remain publicly archived.

White Paper An official set of proposals from the Commission in a given policy area. They may follow publication of a Green Paper. A notable example was the 1985 White Paper drawn up by Lord Cockfield outlining proposals for action to bring about the completion of the single market by 1992.

CHAPTER 7

Democracy and the European Union

The EU's alleged democratic deficit is subject to much debate. Arguments against the democratic shortcomings of the Union are varied and come from many quarters, but there is general agreement among many observers that the EU's ruling elites have become increasingly out of touch with its citizens.

In this chapter, we present a synthesis of the main arguments that have been advanced. Having analysed some of the apparent problems of legitimacy and democracy within the EU, we then explore possible ways of overcoming them.

The word 'democracy' derives from two Greek terms: 'demos' meaning people and 'kratia' signifying rule of or by. Many people therefore see democracy as meaning 'people power', with government resting on the consent of the governed. A democratic political system is one in which public policies are made, on a majority basis, by representatives subject to effective popular control at periodic elections which are conducted on the principle of political equality and under conditions of political freedom.

The European Union has often been criticised for its lack of democratic institutions and for the way in which they operate. In a speech in 1994, Sir Leon Brittan,[1] a former British commissioner, identified 'a widespread sense of unease about Brussels and what it stands for'. He drew attention to:

- the feeling that Brussels was interfering where it should not do so
- the absence of knowledge of what was going on in the central decision-making bodies
- the belief that Brussels lacked sufficient democratic legitimacy.

By way of a solution, Brittan urged devolution of decision-making (subsidiarity – see p. 48), transparency (more open and accessible decision-making) and more democracy (to overcome the democratic deficit).

Former French president Valéry Giscard d'Estaing[2] has gone as far as to suggest that 'if the EU itself applied to join the EU as a member, it would be rejected for being insufficiently democratic . . . The Community cannot continue to be governed according to procedures which are contrary to the imperative requirements it formulates itself in relation to countries which are candidates for membership'.

A draft document prepared for the Laeken Summit (December 2001) also suggested that the European Union was out of touch with its citizens and had failed to placate its critics. It argued that the Union was facing an identity crisis, with a serious gulf opening up between the people and Brussels. The Laeken Declaration implicitly recognised these concerns. In launching the constitution-drafting process, it observed that 'citizens are calling for a clear, open, effective, democratically controlled Community approach, developing a Europe which points the way ahead for the world'.

Democratic deficit

The term 'democratic deficit' has been attributed to a British MEP, Bill Newton-Dunn,[3] who used the phrase in a pamphlet back in the 1980s. He was referring to the widely held belief that there was a lack of democratic control and accountability within the European Union. These deficiencies were said to prevent its institutions from acquiring political legitimacy and widespread recognition and acceptance.

Such a democratic deficit is not unique to EU machinery, for in many countries there are problems with establishing effective democratic control, associated with:

* falling turnouts in elections
* declining membership of political parties
* a lack of interest in and a distrust of politics and politicians
* a feeling of disengagement and alienation from the political process.

In other words, there is a developing gap between those who are governed and those who seek to govern them.

Box 7.1 Academic debate surrounding the democratic deficit

In recent decades, there has been a plethora of books and articles on the democratic deficit. However, the contributions of two major academics, Majone[4] and Moravcsik,[5] have opposed the general trend and argued in effect that the EU is as democratic as it can or should be. This has sparked off a scholarly controversy.

The broad line of argument of both writers is to suggest that because of the nature of its functions, there is no reason to force democratic mechanisms upon the Union. The Italian academic Giandomenico Majone argues that as the EU is primarily a regulatory body – in this respect not unlike an independent central bank – it should be insulated from democratic pressures. In his view, it is unreasonable to apply the same democratic criteria to, say, the Bank of England as we would to any national system of government. He also suggests that the absence of any real sense of European identity, in which people feel themselves to be citizens of Europe, does in any case make a democratic system difficult to operate.

Andrew Moravcsik has expressed similar views, again arguing that concern about the 'deficit' is misplaced. He suggests that 'when judged by the practices of existing nation states, there is little evidence that the EU suffers from a fundamental democratic deficit'. He makes the point that most critics compare the Union to an ideal plebiscitary or parliamentary democracy, standing alone, rather than to the actual functioning of national democracies adjusted for its multilevel context.

In an interesting rejoinder, Andreas Follesdal and Simon Hix[6] accept a number of the points made by Majone and Moravcsik, but disagree over a key element. They take the view that in a truly democratic polity, there must be a contest for political leadership and public argument over the direction of the policy agenda. They suggest that it is these criteria that distinguish democracies from enlightened authoritarian regimes. They find the EU wanting and did not see the contents of the Constitutional Treaty (see pp. 56–7), as proposed, as providing an adequate answer to the problem they detected. They saw some benefits in what it included, but felt that an opportunity was missed to allow the majority in the European Parliament to nominate the Commission president instead of the European Council. This, in their view, would have established a clearer link between the outcome of European elections and the formation of government at the EU level.

Fundamental to their critique is the belief that although EU policy might be in the interests of the citizens of Europe when first agreed, without electoral competition there are few incentives for the Commission or national governments to change their policies in response to changes in citizen preferences: 'Political competition is an essential vehicle for opinion formation. It fosters political debate which in turn promotes the formation of public opinion on different policy options'. This could help bring about the informed demos or citizenry the absence of which Majone laments.

How the Union evolved

In the case of the European Union, the gap between those who are governed and those who seek to govern them is much concerned with the way in which the Community and then the Union emerged. Jean Monnet and his co-founders of the ECSC and the EEC were not primarily concerned with the issue of democratic legitimacy. Their urgent desire was to create the Communities at the earliest opportunity and to ensure that effective supranational practices were in place. Some commentators have spoken of 'rule by technocracy' in the early days. Today, this approach is reinforced by the way in which decisions are agreed in a secretive Council, in the search for agreement and compromise.

In his *Memoirs*, Monnet[7] claimed that he did always envisage a move towards democratisation. He wrote of how 'the pragmatic method we had adopted would also lead to a federation validated by the people's vote'. But Monnet and others like him had a tendency towards elitism, a belief that they understood best what was good for the continent and its inhabitants. Martin Holland[8] has shown how 'Europe was being constructed by a cohesive and remarkably small elite; while public support was welcomed, it was never a prerequisite for Monnet's Europe'.

Europe has developed in a rather open-ended way. The original pioneers were federalists, some being advocates of an immediate federal solution, others being incrementalists who felt that federalism would be achieved by an onwards, step-by-step march towards ever closer integration. No clear boundaries or limits have been set down to this notion of an 'ever closer union', the term having more far-reaching implications than federalism itself, for it implies a never-ending journey in which member states ultimately seek to merge their identities. Whatever the vision, some national politicians have been less than frank in explaining the journey on which the pioneers were embarking. In the United Kingdom, many of those who voted in the 1975 referendum had good reason to be unclear about the nature of the Community, the joining of which was then portrayed as an issue of primarily economic debate.

Shortcomings related to EU elections

The transformation of Parliament into an elected assembly in 1979 was an undoubted step forward in making the EU more democratic. It remains the only elected body within the Union. However, the five-yearly European elections (see Chapter 5) are frequently criticised, some casting doubt on whether they really are a meaningful way of allowing European voters to register their preferences. Among the common criticisms:

1. A study conducted by Karlheinz Reif and Hermann Schmitt[9] in 1980 concluded that they vote primarily on national issues and do not use the mechanism to make a judgment on the performance of the EU and its players.
2. Many studies since then have suggested that the elections are of the '**second order**' category, with voters opting for smaller and sometimes extremist parties as a means of registering a protest against their domestic governments, safe in the knowledge that such voting will not precipitate the downfall of the administration and bring about another general election.
3. Average turnout figures across the Union have declined over the six elections held.
4. The lack of genuine transnational political parties competing across the EU raises issues about the representativeness of elections.

In offering support to these observations, Max Kohnstamm[10] argues that the 2004 elections were an example of 'the illness which threatens the progress, and if not looked after, the existence of the Union itself . . . they widened the deficit. Not because the participation in general was low, but because there was nothing European about them'.

We have seen that the alleged lack of democracy within the Union has many causes, some of which we have identified: the limitations of elections as a means of registering popular opinion about the EU; the way in which an elite imposed its vision of a united Europe upon the people and the way it evolved; the lack of knowledge about and low public interest in European developments; and poor levels of popular participation. Yet the criticism is deeper. It is much concerned with:

- the way in which institutions operate
- the lack of democratic control over those who have the power to make decisions.

A Union detached from its citizens

EU institutions are frequently criticised for their remoteness from ordinary citizens. This is in part a matter of geography. The transfer of competences to Brussels means that many issues are taken further away from inhabitants of the member states. Just as the Scots and Welsh used remoteness from the location of decision-making as part of their arguments for greater control over their own affairs, so too it is unsurprising that many European voters – particularly those on the periphery of the core six states who founded the ECSC/EEC – see EU institutions as distant and lacking in knowledge or understanding of what matters to them.

The criticism is not just about geographical distance. The suggestion has often been advanced that complex EU legislative procedures and policies are technical and difficult to understand, factors which discourage popular interest or engagement. More seriously, decision-making machinery operates in a secretive way, out of the public gaze. This is said to cause further resentment and alienation among European citizens. In this respect, the main target has been the Council of Ministers.

Attempts have been made to open up EU decision-making and to make information about procedures and policies more widely available to those who wish to access it. At Maastricht, it was agreed that the new Union should act transparently and in a way that people can understand. Since the TEU was signed, the Council has changed its rules of procedure, so that although debates and votes are held in secret, there is now more information available about the way member states reacted, along with some explanation of the events leading to the final outcome. Some open debates have been held in countries occupying the presidency, and the Commission has produced more consultative White and Green Papers, establishing areas for reflection and discussion. In addition, there has been some attempt to open up access to European documentation.

Complaints are still made about the seclusion in which the Council (and COREPER in particular) makes its decisions, it being one of the few legislative bodies in the democratic world to do so. This may facilitate the process of reaching a consensual agreement, but it does nothing to reassure commentators and members of the public who are sometimes suspicious of the way in which deals are done.

Lack of democratic control over decision-makers

Executive dominance

Whatever the limitations of parliamentary control in the domestic politics of member states, legislatures can scrutinise the behaviour of government ministers and ultimately hire and fire the cabinet. However, the transfer of several competences to the European Union enhances executive power at the expense of that of legislatures. As the EU has increased the areas of policy in which it has a say and as the EU's institutions are disproportionately controlled by national governments (directly in the Council and indirectly through the nomination of Commission members), there has been a shift in power away from national parliaments.

The shift has not been adequately compensated for by the European Parliament because of its limited powers. So too, serious difficulties are experienced by national parliamentary bodies in exercising any real controls on decisions it makes. In the words of Ronald Holzhacker:

> The national parliaments of the member states of the European Union (EU) have been losing power. Decisions that parliaments traditionally had the right and power to decide are increasingly being made either within the institutions of the EU or by the national executives of the member states. Increasingly, the law-making powers of national parliaments in important areas of policy are tightly circumscribed by the EU.[11]

In his rejoinder to criticism concerning the lack of democracy in the EU (see pp. 116–17) Moravcsik argues that the EU has actually made executives more accountable to their citizens. He notes that the actions of government ministers are no longer scrutinised simply at home but in a wider European context, and that ministers are now held to account not solely for their domestic record but for their performance in Brussels. He cites the volume of domestic criticism received by Tony Blair after concessions made over the UK rebate in 2005.

Lack of popular control

Moravcsik's opinion is not widely shared. It is more common to lament the lack of democratic legitimacy of EU institutions, the third point made in Brittan's 1994 contribution to the debate. Philip Norton[12] too has referred to the democratic deficit as 'the limited input into the law-making processes of the European Community by directly elected representatives of the people'. To these and other analysts, it is a worrying feature that there is still no very credible system of democratic control within the Union. There is no effective accountability of the Council or Commission to either the national Parliament or the European one.

It has been suggested that in addition to electing the Parliament every five years, voters might elect the national commissioner in each country or the president.

Choice of the Commission and its president: possible changes

The Commission could be democratised by making it more responsible to Parliament. A start was made at Maastricht, in the provision that the Commission's appointment should be subject to Parliamentary approval. This was a useful step, but more could be done to enhance its credibility and popular support. There are two ways in which this could be achieved:

1. Parliament could be responsible for the initial choice of the Commission, so that it would no longer comprise nominees of the individual states. Instead, it would be an executive chosen to reflect the particular balance of the assembly. In this way, elections to the Parliament would also, in effect, become elections to choose the body which initiates legislation.

2. A different route to the one just outlined would be to allow the public to vote for the Union's commissioners rather than allowing them to be appointed by the national governments subject to the Parliament's approval, perhaps on the same day as the European elections. Such direct election would provide the Commission with a powerful popular base and enable it to share power with the Council. Under this scheme, the Commission and Parliament would then represent the European electorate, whilst the Council would represent the electorate via the elections organised in the member states.

3. A variation would be to allow Parliament to choose the Commission but for the public to vote for its president, on the basis of the transnational party groupings described on pp. 158–64.

The point of these options is that there would be a contest for the election of key players in the EU, enabling the public to determine the makeup of government and to have a direct impact on policy outcomes. They would introduce an element of accountability in Union proceedings.

Strengthening control by the legislatures

Norton has suggested three possible approaches to the problem:

1. strengthening the powers of the European Parliament
2. creating a new EU institution comprising elected representatives from national parliaments
3. strengthening the role of national parliaments in the law-making process.

At different times, all three suggestions have been contemplated and they each have their advocates and detractors.

Strengthening the European Parliament

As regards the European Parliament, the key step forward was taken in 1979, with the onset of direct elections. We have examined their alleged shortcomings.

There is a case to be made in favour of equipping Parliament with more powers, given its status as the only directly elected institution. Indeed in the SEA, at Maastricht and subsequently, it is a body whose power and influence have grown (see pp. 82–3). No longer is it a mere talking shop, although, in Norton's phrase, it is 'still only on the edge of constituting a legislature'. It does have limited powers to exercise supervision or control over the Council, so that – for instance – its assent is required before the Council can approve the accession of new members. It has more powers over the Commission, having to approve the Council's nominee for the presidency, appoint (or not) the whole Commission and sack the entire body in a vote of censure. (It played a role in bringing about the resignation of the Santer Commission in 1999 and used its power to veto the Commission line-up proposed by Barroso.) But it has relatively little control over areas of policy such as the CAP, justice and home affairs, and security policy.

Those who strongly criticise the democratic deficit are often the very same people who are most reluctant to make Parliament a more effective watchdog, British governments often being particularly keen to ensure that control is firmly maintained in Westminster hands. Any extension of its current role is therefore highly contentious.

Creating a new EU institution

The creation of a new institution comprising elected representatives from national parliaments is an approach that was urged by Brittan,[13] who believed that 'if voters felt their local MPs were lending a hand to the process of Euro-legislation, it would greatly strengthen the EU's democracy and enhance its credibility'. One way of achieving this goal would be the creation of an upper house or senate, made up of people from either chamber in their national state. One of the problems is that this would create a rival body to the existing European Parliament, which is still seeking to establish a greater role for itself. Any such move might be seen as diluting the position and importance of the existing body. The outcome might be two relatively weak bodies, instead of an increasingly effective single one.

As British foreign secretary until 2003, Robin Cook[14] was concerned about the separation of European institutions from the people they are meant to represent: 'Our Parliament needs to be part of the project rather than outside of it . . . The European Parliament does a very useful job, but the missing link is tying the national parliaments with the work of Europe'. He advanced an idea to remedy the problem, by involving MPs directly in the running of the Union. He proposed the creation of a second chamber in Europe, made up of MPs from national parliaments, to curb the power of Brussels. The chamber would sift through decisions made in Brussels and block any that meddle in the minutiae of British life.

As we have seen, others take a different view, claiming that the body that should hold this European executive to account is the European Parliament. If directly elected MEPs had genuine powers of scrutiny, this would erase the democratic deficit at an instant. But Cook felt that the problem was that the European Parliament lacks public esteem, that it is national parliaments that are respected. This may be true, but of course if MEPs were given political muscle, voters might then learn to take them more seriously.

Control via national parliaments

Norton[15] notes the view taken by the Danish government a few years ago: 'It must be recognised that a considerable part of what is known as the democratic shortfall is attributable to the fact that apparently not all national parliaments have an adequate say in the decisions at community level'. The Danish chamber, the Folketing, is better placed than others in this respect. It has the reputation of keeping a watchful eye over any European initiatives. In general, the Nordic states have been successful in devising effective scrutiny and control of the Union, via their domestic legislatures.

From the 1980s onwards, most legislatures have made greater provision for dealing with European legislation and have given their MPs or deputies more opportunities to acquire specialised information. In Britain, apart from the committees which have been established in the two chambers of Parliament (e.g. the House of Lords European Union Committee), there are rare occasions when MEPs are invited to meet with their national colleagues in party committee meetings and informally. Yet keeping up with the burden of work coming from Brussels is a difficult task for the British Parliament, and one that has grown with the preparation for and implementation of the single market. If eventually much foreign and security policy – as well as immigration and policing – are handled in Brussels, the task will be even more daunting.

Alternative means of dealing with the deficit

In most democracies, it is of course via political parties that effective links are established between citizens and their governments. Single-party or coalition governments are formed from political parties that compete with one another in periodic general elections. These parties provide a channel of communication through which voters are kept in touch with those who make decisions, for ultimately the electorate has the power to 'throw the rascals out'. Governments have an incentive to carry popular opinion with them, for fear of losing the next election if they become remote from popular aspirations and out of touch.

As yet, there is no developed European party system with Europe-wide parties contesting elections, and it is unlikely that any genuinely European parties will emerge in the foreseeable future. If they existed, and had truly transnational membership and programmes, then this would encourage

Table 7.1 Examples of referendums held on EU-related matters

Country	Date	Issue	Outcome
Norway	1972	Whether to join the EC	Against membership
UK	1975	Whether to remain in the EC	In favour of staying in
Finland	1994	Whether to join the EC	In favour of membership
Norway	1994	Whether to join the EC	Against membership
Ireland	2001	Vote to ratify Nice Treaty	Rejection of Treaty
Ireland	2002	Vote to ratify Nice Treaty	Acceptance of Treaty
Malta	2003	Whether to join the EC	In favour of membership
Slovenia	2003	Whether to join the EC	In favour of membership
France	2005	Whether to ratify Constitutional Treaty	Rejection of Treaty
Luxembourg	2005	Whether to ratify Constitutional Treaty	Acceptance of Treaty

debate on European issues by an EU-wide electorate and provide a clearer link between individuals and those who make decisions. But there is little likelihood that the decision-making machinery of the Union will have cause to respond directly to voters' needs and wishes on an EU basis in the foreseeable future.

One other channel of communication is via the use of referendums. These have been employed in some countries as a means of claiming popular backing for treaty developments. The problem here is that they only allow the voters to express their views about isolated constitutional issues. Even then, the outcome of any vote on a single issue may owe more to the standing of the government than to the merits of the case. The issue can become blurred with other factors. In any case, as some countries make little use of referendums under any circumstances or have no provision for them, it is unlikely that we shall see anything like a Europe-wide referendum as a means of ascertaining popular feeling. Hence the view expressed by Follesdal and Hix: 'Referendums are . . . ineffective mechanisms for promoting day-to-day competition, contestation among policy platforms, articulation and opposition in the EU policy processes'.[16]

Box 7.2   The Reform (Lisbon) Treaty and the democratic deficit: rival claims

Supporters claim that it would have helped to reduce the democratic deficit, in that it would have:

- extended the power of co-decision to virtually all policy areas, effectively making Parliament an equal legislative partner with the Council in most EU decision-making
- required the Council to meet in public when legislating
- ensured that national parliaments receive information about EU legislative proposals in sufficient time to mandate ministers on how to vote in the Council
- given national parliaments a new power to refer back to the Commission any proposal thought to lie outside EU competence
- confirmed the principle of subsidiarity, keeping decision-making at the lowest level possible
- created a new right of citizens' initiative, obliging the Commission to consider any proposal for legislation that had the backing of 1m EU citizens.

Opponents argue that:

- the appointed Commission would have remained the sole initiator of legislative proposals, with Parliament, the Council and EU citizens only being able to require it to consider ideas for a proposal
- similarly, national parliaments would have acquired the right to refer a proposal back to the Commission for further thought, but there was no requirement for the Commission to make changes as a result
- the idea that EU laws ('and the Constitution itself') supersede national laws would not have been amended, so that directives and regulations from Brussels could still have been imposed on member states.

Conclusion

Some EU policy-making institutions are rather more open than their national counterparts in their mode of operation, not least the Commission, which has been very willing to consult with lobbyists in recent years (see chapter 10). But they are not perceived in that way. People detect a large gap between the elites who live in Brussels and elsewhere, and the peoples whose interests they purport to represent. The more they see it this way, the less likely they are to feel inspired to vote.

Bomberg[17] points out that 'supranational systems of governance like the EU pose a dilemma for their citizens, as gains in performance may be at the cost of losses in democratic legitimacy'. She quotes the theorist of democracy, Robert Dahl,[18] who notes a problem affecting large organisations:

> In very small political systems, a citizen may be able to participate extensively in decisions that do not matter much, but cannot participate much in decisions that

really matter a great deal; whereas very large systems may be able to cope with problems that matter more to a citizen, but the opportunities for the citizen to participate in and greatly influence decisions are vastly reduced.

The comment fairly describes a problem with large organisations. But it is worth reflecting on the alternative, for the implication appears to be that if there were no European Union the distance problem and the lack of effective democratic controls would be overcome; competences would be returned to national level and decisions made closer to the citizenry. But if Britain and other states were not members of the EU, there would still be pressures to create or belong to some international body or make ad hoc agreements, at the very least for the better coordination of trade. Decisions taken in this way would also be taken under circumstances where they are removed from and not subject to popular control.

There is a difficulty. Some issues are too big for individual countries to resolve on their own. European integration may be considered necessary to enable effective solutions to be applied to common problems. On the other hand, the problems of remoteness of decision-making and lack of accountability are greater in vast international bodies.

Glossary

Second-order elections Second-order elections are contests other than general elections. Local and regional elections are almost always considered second-order elections. As voters take the view that second-order elections are less important than first-order ones, they may take the opportunity to punish the current governing parties. Their protest may be registered by abstention or voting for different (often minor) parties. In the EU, elections to the European Parliament are considered to be second-order national elections, in that voters use their choices for representatives to the supranational body to send signals to their national governments.

SECTION THREE: REPRESENTATION

Introduction

European integration has proved to be a difficult issue for governments in many countries. Political leaders make deals, but in some member states the public seems markedly unenthusiastic. As Geddes[1] explains, 'the intensity of elite level debates about European integration within the political parties and in Parliament has not been matched by a similar fascination about European integration and its implications amongst the general public'. Many voters claim not to know about, not to understand and not to trust the EU and its workings. In Britain and some other countries, there is a high degree of scepticism about what is being done on their behalf.

Common policies have resulted in a situation in which important powers have been transferred from member states to Brussels. Individual citizens are therefore much influenced by the decisions made by EU machinery. But their opportunities to influence the making of those decisions are limited. Integration has developed more effectively than has the process of making the Union accountable to its citizens. The Commission is not accountable, the Council of Ministers meets behind closed doors and only Parliament is elected – but as we have seen in Chapter 5, it has traditionally lacked teeth.

In this section we explore the opportunities for groups and individuals to make known their views about the way in which the Union is evolving. How are they enabled to participate in its political life and have direct or indirect links with those who make decisions?

There are four main channels through which the peoples of Europe can influence the policies pursued by those who have the power to make decisions: via elections, referendums, political parties and pressure groups.

CHAPTER 8

Elections to the European Parliament

European elections have been held every five years since 1979. They operate over a huge area of the continent. However, the campaigns for them are largely national ones, decided on national rather than European issues. The role of transnational political parties remains limited and media interest is low. The outcome provides inconclusive evidence of Europe-wide trends, for losses for one party in one country are often compensated for by gains for a similar party in another.

In this chapter, we examine the way in which elections are conducted in member states, with particular emphasis on the choice of electoral system. We note problems of turnout and the difficulty of engaging the electorates of many countries. Finally, we examine the role of referendums within the Union.

The European Parliament is the only EU institution to be directly elected by the peoples of the twenty-seven member countries. The first elections were held in 1979, thereafter to occur every five years. They currently operate under Article 1 of the European Elections Act agreed by the Council of Ministers in 1976, although there have been some subsequent modifications.

Euro-elections are the world's only international elections, involving an electorate of some 265m at the time of the Fourth Enlargement and just under 350m when membership of the EU rose to twenty-five countries. They were designed to provide Parliament with a new legitimacy and to introduce an element of democracy into the Community. It was felt that a supranational elected assembly would act as a more effective brake on the intergovernmental Council of Ministers than an appointed one. In addition, the onset of elections might be expected to contribute to an emerging sense of European identity.

The introduction of direct elections was a step along the integrationist road, for inevitably the elected body – with some success – has consistently sought to acquire further powers since 1979, giving it a greater role in the procedures of the Union. Yet many commentators are sceptical about the extent to which elections have made Parliament a key player on the European scene. They tend to deride the elections as at best not very significant, at worst pointless, for they are of little concern or interest to the majority of inhabitants of the member states. As yet, there is little sign of a distinct European identity and the elections themselves have so far been not one European contest but rather twenty-five different national contests reflecting the differing concerns and priorities of EU countries.

The way in which voters use euro-elections often has little to do with what they feel about matters European. Campaigning has not stimulated a major political debate about Union policies and the future direction that the organisation should take; the engagement of some national politicians is half-hearted; the levels of interest and understanding of voters in several countries are strictly limited; and the media do little to encourage any kind of election fever, preferring as they do

the more familiar domestic stories of party schisms, personal lapses and governmental problems. Indeed, elections reveal what Curtice and Steed[1] identify
as the usual characteristics of second-order elections: 'low turnout, an anti-
government swing and a relatively high level of support for small parties'.
Second-order elections do not change governments and so less is at stake for the
voters, who can decide not to vote or to flirt with small or new parties that would
be highly unlikely to win a general election.

If it is easy to deride the lack of interest in euro-elections and their failure to
engage the public in a genuine discussion of European affairs, they do not lack
significance in the political life of the member states.

- For the voters, they are a chance to register their protest over what they see
  as governmental failures or more broadly about the general direction in
  which the ruling party is travelling.
- For the party in power, they are a useful means of discerning trends in public
  opinion. They provide a chance to measure ministerial popularity or
  unpopularity, their findings possibly leading to a cabinet reshuffle or even a
  change of leader.
- For established parties long in opposition, they can test the extent of their
  recovery and demonstrate to the voters that they are proceeding on the right
  lines.
- For small parties, particularly those with a keen interest in European developments and policy, there is an opportunity to hit the headlines and make
  some kind of breakthrough. Various far-right, anti-immigration and
  eurosceptic parties performed strongly in 2004. As Geddes[2] points out: 'the
  votes cast at a European election may be more expressive, or from the heart.
  A vote for UKIP may represent anti-EU sentiment rather than a hard-
  headed decision that a UKIP government would actually be a good idea'.

European integration has become an issue in the national politics of some states.
It might not rank highly as a general election issue; in the 2005 general election
in the United Kingdom, it was barely mentioned by the established parties, only
UKIP and Veritas making it a key theme. But in the previous two elections, it
had featured more strongly, in 1997 proving particularly divisive and damaging
for the British Conservatives.

Anti-government swings and support for small parties

In second-order elections, voters are influenced much more by what they think
about the performance of the national government of the day than by any other
issue. Broadly, parties that gain success in national contests may expect to do well
in European ones held within a short period of time, whereas government parties
that are experiencing a bout of mid-term unpopularity can expect to fare badly.

The elections present an opportunity to register discontent with the ruling party, even though they are supposed to be a means of choosing a parliament dealing with different issues to those that dominate the domestic political scene. Voters are more preoccupied with their concerns about the state of their national education or health service, or what is happening to pensions, matters which are not determined by the European Parliament.

Yet if elections are dominated by national issues, nonetheless some consideration is given by the parties to European issues. The European party federations adopt common manifestos and produce brochures and material which address contentious topics concerning the future direction of the Union. In the last three elections, national parties have made increased use of the federation material. But the attempt to sway voters on European issues is a half-hearted one. In Britain, European coverage by the main parties is often more related to the desirability of fending off Brussels interference, hence the Conservative slogan in 1999: 'In Europe, but not run by Europe'.

The third feature which Curtice and Steed pinpoint as a characteristic of second-order elections has traditionally had less application in Britain, for the electoral system was not favourable to small parties. Now that there is a greater choice of parties and a situation in which they have a realistic chance of securing representation, voters have responded by awarding them their votes in greater numbers – in 2004, 35.8 per cent (20/78 seats) did not go to the three main parties. In particular, UKIP performed particularly well, securing more votes than the Liberal Democrats and an equal number of seats (twelve each).

In Europe as a whole, some small or new parties fared well, particularly eurosceptic groupings such as the Swedish Junelist, which gained three seats, and the League of Polish Families. But the present Parliament contains a highly diverse collection of representatives of many persuasions, ranging from far rightists to unreconstructed communists, from nationalists to populists.

Turnout and apathy

The disappointing level of voter participation in European elections has always attracted a great deal of attention. In three countries, Belgium, Luxembourg and Greece, voting is compulsory and their turnout figures can be regarded as respectable. Belgium and Luxembourg regularly manage a turnout of just above and just below 90 per cent respectively, while in six elections Greece averages out at just over 74 per cent. In Italy, where voting is not compulsory but is regarded as a civic duty, there has always been has a turnout of at least 70 per cent, usually considerably better.

In most other countries of the Union, the turnout is little more than 50 per cent, recently rather less. It can, of course, be affected by the timing of other elections. Holding a national and a European election on the same day yields a higher figure. On the other hand, if a European election is held soon after a general one, it may be influenced by voter fatigue (the UK in 1979 registered figures of 76.0 per cent and 32.2 per cent in the general and European elections respectively). Such factors cast doubt on the validity of any comparison between the five-yearly figures within and between member states.

There has always been a Europe-wide apathy towards the European elections, with turnouts in the past ranging from a high of 62.5 per cent in 1979 to a low of 56.8 per cent in 1994. In 1999, however, the figure fell significantly to 49.4 per cent, meaning that less than half the EU electorate felt ready to vote for the European Parliament, despite the increased powers it had been given. Five years later, it had deteriorated further, down to 45.5 per cent. Whilst in 1999 five countries had turnouts of no more than 40 per cent of the electorate (in Britain, the figure was a mere 24 per cent), five years later the position across the continent was considerably worse, with eleven countries – admittedly in a substantially larger Union – falling below that level. Six of these were from among the ten most recent entrants, Slovakia managing only 17 per cent. The expansion of the EU has clearly not created Europe-wide or national interest in the outcome of elections.

Turnout in European elections is low compared to national elections, although it was for several years relatively high compared with US presidential and congressional ones. In 1994, it was an overall 56.8 per cent, compared with 55 per cent for the presidency in 1992 and 38.7 per cent for Congress two years later. In 2004, the 45.5 per cent represents a considerably lower figure than for the presidential and congressional elections of November that same year (59.4 per cent). Whereas the US trend is upwards, the European one is going down.

Many explanations are given for the disappointing figures across the European Union:

1. Unlike the situation in 'first-order' general elections, there is no prospect of a change of administration; polling therefore does not generate excitement or interest, for the outcome will not greatly impact upon people's everyday lives.
2. Campaigns are essentially national contests, 'but of a secondary sort . . . [having] little coherence or coordination',[3] and not arousing media interest.

Table 8.1 Trend in average turnout across the European Union since 1979 (%)					
1979	1984	1989	1994	1999	2004
63.0	61.0	58.5	56.8	49.8	45.5

3. Many voters across the Union have little or inadequate knowledge about the European Parliament and what it does – or indeed, about the European Union in general. Some do not care about an international body that seems remote from their experience. Of those who do have an understanding of the EU and the way in which it operates, some would conclude that as it has modest powers it does not merit a journey to the polling stations.
4. The politicians who approach national campaigns with enthusiasm do not exhibit the same tendency in European ones. Often, the 'big names' whose presence might arouse a response from the voters play a relatively minor part in campaigning. This may be because they wish to play down mid-term protest results that are often disappointing for those in power.
5. There is the more general consideration that voting in all elections and across the whole continent is becoming less fashionable than was once the case. There may be many explanations for this general drop in turnout, but among them are a feeling of disillusionment with political parties and the politicians who represent them; the narrowing of differences between the major parties; the disappearance of some of the leading postwar issues, such as capitalism v. communism and the introduction of contentious welfare policies; and the preference of many young voters interested in environmental and global issues for pressure-group campaigning.

Low turnout means that the EU faces a problem of legitimacy in that it has been saying for years that something must be done to correct the democratic deficit – only to find that when something is done about it the outcome is spurned by the electorate.

Yet the broad decline in public involvement in recent European elections as illustrated in Table 8.1 has not been matched by perceptions of its importance. EU polls taken during the 2004 campaign were indicating that 54 per cent of European citizens trusted the European Parliament, 46 per cent thought it had more power than their own national parliament and 66 per cent felt the European elections were 'very important'.

Box 8.1 Turnout in Britain for elections to the European Parliament

1979 31.6%   1984 32.6%   1989 36.2%   1994 36.4%
1999 24.0%   2004 38.8%

Turnout in British euro-elections has traditionally been low, perhaps a reflection of geographical insularity from the continent and a consequent feeling of remoteness from European institutions. It may also reflect the doubts of the British people about the value of the European enterprise or more specifically the ambivalence of governmental attitudes to Britain's position in the EU and the lack of leadership on the issue. Certainly, the issues surrounding the EU and its future have failed to arouse the British electorate. In 1999, there was a general decline in popular participation a cross the Union, but in Britain the lack of interest was startling. The turnout was the lowest ever recorded in a euro-election in any country: just under 24.0%. Many commentators were forecasting an even worse figure in 2004, assuming that disillusion with the government and the European Union had both significantly increased over the last few years. Contrary to expectations, the turnout was higher than before. It averaged out at 38.8%, but varied across the regions from 36.0% in the West Midlands to an impressive 51.7% in Northern Ireland.

Great Britain, as opposed to Northern Ireland, has always had a poor turnout record for anything other than Westminster elections, the level of voting in European elections being very much in line with the turnout for local ones. Large elements of the British public do not understand the European Parliament, do not see that it has any relevance to their lives, and therefore see no reason why they should vote for it.

Thanks to the indifference of the British electorate to European elections, the people who ought to be working hard to overcome that apathy – the politicians, parties and the media – are equally indifferent. The media are only interested in what interests their readers, listeners or viewers and therefore display only limited interest in what apparently leaves the public cold. The parties are not going to devote precious funds to European politics when their resources are already limited for the more important field of national politics. And, with a few notable exceptions, politicians of ability and public appeal are not going to become involved in an activity so far removed from influence and power in the national arena.

Varying features of the European elections in member states

Although the Council of Ministers was forced to concede direct elections to the European Parliament in 1979, the Council proved unwilling to grant the other provisions laid down in the Treaty of Rome that were meant to create a uniform procedure in all member states.

To exercise the right to vote in European elections, people must be 18 or over and citizens of one of the member states. However, beyond these two basic considerations, there is no uniformity about the conduct of elections:

- Since the implementation of the Maastricht Treaty, European citizens can vote and stand for election in their country of residence rather than their home country, but the interpretation of residence is different across the Union. For instance, in Austria, Denmark and the UK – among others – they must be registered on the electoral roll; in Belgium, Germany and some other states, they must customarily reside there; and in Luxembourg, which has a very high proportion of non-nationals in its resident population, they must prove a minimum period of five years' residence.

- There is no common eligibility for candidature as an MEP, the age qualification in the various member countries ranging from 18 to 25. In countries such as Germany, Spain, the Scandinavian states and most of the new entrants, 18 is the qualifying age, but it is 21 in Belgium, Greece and the UK, 23 in France and 25 in Italy.
- Some countries allow the dual mandate – enabling politicians to be members of their national parliament and the European Parliament – whilst others do not. Prior to 1979, MEPs were chosen from among the representatives of their national legislatures. Nowadays, the practice is officially discouraged and has been prohibited under national law in a number of EU countries, Belgium, Germany and most recently Italy among them. Despite this, a small and dwindling number of members do hold a dual mandate.

  The British Labour Party does not allow its MPs to stand for the EP. The Conservatives have no members of the House of Commons holding the dual mandates but in 1999 and again in 2004 three Conservative peers were elected as MEPs, as were two Liberal Democrats. Ian Paisley once held the 'triple mandate' of MEP, MP (in the House of Commons) and MLA ('Member of Legislative Assembly' in the Northern Ireland Assembly) at the same time. In its favour, the dual mandate does encourage and facilitate dialogue between national parliaments and the EP and allow prominent national figures to participate in EU affairs.
- There is not even agreement on the day on which European elections should be held. The UK chooses to stick with Thursday, the day normally used for Westminster or local/devolved elections. This practice has been followed by other countries including Denmark, Ireland and the Netherlands. Most European countries, however, vote on Sundays, in both national and European elections. Since election results are declared simultaneously in all member countries, this divided practice means that voters in those countries which vote on Thursday have to wait until Sunday evening to find out whom they have elected, while officials have to ensure that ballot papers are securely locked away for the best part of three days.
- More seriously, there are not equal electoral districts. There is a significant variation in the populations represented by MEPs in the various states. Seats are allocated between countries as much for political reasons as for considerations of strict proportionality. Smaller states are over-represented in an attempt to prevent them from being overwhelmed by the larger states in the decision-making process. Malta, the smallest state, has far more MEPs per head of population than Germany, the largest one. (See the table on pp. 145–6.)

However, the most serious failure in standardising the procedure for European elections concerns the choice of electoral system to be used.

Electoral systems

In the Treaty of Paris, it was envisaged that the ECSC should be elected on the basis of a uniform electoral procedure. Similarly, Article 138 of the Rome Treaty included the following provision: 'The Assembly shall draw up proposals for elections by direct universal suffrage in accordance with a uniform procedure in all Member States'. The Assembly approved such proposals as early as 1960, but found itself frustrated by yet another requirement of Article 138 which gave the deciding voice to the Council of Ministers with the words: 'The Council shall, acting unanimously, lay down the appropriate provisions . . .' The idea reappeared once more in Article 7 of the 1976 European Elections Act.

Yet elections are still held on the basis of different states making their own national arrangements. A small but significant change had been made to Article 138 in the Treaty of Amsterdam, for after the words 'uniform procedure', it now read 'in accordance with principles common to all Member States'. The European Parliament endorsed this procedure based on 'common principles' in July 1998, and the Council of Ministers laid down the appropriate provisions, thereby revising the Rome Treaty; Article 138 became the new 190.4. The only common principle underlying the choice of system is that all countries employ one of the variants of proportional representation.

From the description given above, it can be seen that it was always the intention that the Community should have its own democratically elected parliament. For twenty-two years, this objective was thwarted by the more intergovernmental members of the Council of Ministers, originally those representing France but thereafter those representing Britain and Denmark. The reason for these delaying tactics was the knowledge that direct elections would give increased legitimacy and credibility to the deliberations of the European Parliament; that such increased legitimacy would confer an improved status and authority on the EP; and that such an improvement could only be at the expense of the stature and authority of national parliaments. Those who valued parliamentary sovereignty wanted to ensure that the Parliament could be dismissed as being no more than an empty discussion chamber with no constitutional purpose, legitimacy or authority.

It was originally envisaged that all member countries would use the same electoral system, based on some form of proportional representation (PR). However, the UK resisted the arguments and insisted on retaining the British 'first-past-the-post' electoral system for constituencies in Great Britain, the system remaining in use from 1979 until the elections of 1994. The Blair government, on assuming power in 1997, promised that, in line with other constitutional reforms, they would have a proportional system in place by the time of the 1999 elections. In accordance with that promise, the European Parliamentary Elections Act of January 1999 established an electoral system based on regional lists that was first used in the elections of June 1999.

With the introduction of proportional voting, the UK still does not have a uniform system. Back in 1979, even the most diehard supporters of first-past-the-post recognised that the sectarian nature of Northern Ireland politics would cause considerable problems if a majority system of voting failed to give representation to the Catholic minority. Because of this, a single three-member constituency was established to cover the whole province, its three representatives to

Table 8.2 Electoral systems currently in use within the European Union		
National lists	**Regional lists**	**Single transferable vote**
Austria*	Belgium*	Irish Republic
Cyprus	Germany	Malta
Czech Republic	France	United Kingdom: N Ireland(3)
Denmark*	Italy*	
Estonia	Poland	
Finland*	United Kingdom (75)	
Greece		
Hungary		
Latvia		
Lithuania		
Luxembourg*		
Netherlands*		
Portugal		
Slovakia		
Slovenia		
Spain		
Sweden*		

NB* These states employ an open list system, allowing for preferential voting, often referred to as voter choice.

be elected under the single transferable vote system of proportional representation. That variation has continued in force despite the 1999 act.

All member states are now united in using a proportional system of voting of some kind. Yet, because the UK set a precedent by breaking ranks in 1979, there has been a consequent general failure among the other states to agree on a common system of PR. Most countries use straightforward list systems but others have a preferential vote element. The Republic of Ireland, like Northern Ireland and Malta, uses the single transferable vote and Luxembourg, with six MEPs, has a system whereby each voter is entitled to six votes that can be split between the candidates as they wish. In a number of countries employing a list system of proportional representation, there is a threshold – usually 5 per cent of the votes cast – that parties have to reach before they are granted representation.

Box 8.2 The British system adopted for the 1999 and 2004 elections: closed lists

There were strongly differing views over the type of electoral system that should be put into place for Great Britain when proportional representation was finally introduced. Some commentators and politicians supported the single transferable vote because it was used in Northern Ireland. Others wanted a suitable variation on the additional member system, similar to that used for elections to the Scottish Parliament. However, Labour ministers decided that the closed list system generally used in the European Union – for instance, in France, Germany, Greece, Portugal and Spain – was preferable. It was suggested by some critics that electors should be allowed to indicate preferences on the lists of candidates (the 'open list' system, as used in Austria, Belgium, Denmark, Finland, Italy, Sweden and the Netherlands) rather than simply vote for the list as a whole. The case for this was debated hard and long but was finally rejected, enabling the doubters to say that the European elections did nothing to reduce the Community's democratic deficit but represented yet another example of the party leader's patronage at work.

The provisions of its European Parliamentary Elections Act are that:

- The United Kingdom is divided into electoral regions, England having nine, whilst Scotland, Wales and Northern Ireland each constitute a single region.
- There are 78 MEPs elected in the United Kingdom, of whom 64 are for England, 7 for Scotland, 4 for Wales and 3 for Northern Ireland.
- The electoral regions in England and the number of MEPs elected for each are: North East (3), North West (9), Yorkshire and the Humber (6), West Midlands (7), East Midlands (6), Eastern (7), South West (7), South East (10) and London (9).
- Electors vote for a party list of candidates rather than an individual candidate (the 'closed list' system).
- Seats are divided between parties according to the proportion of the vote each has gained in the electoral region and are allocated to individuals according to their placing on the party list.

The case for and against the British 'closed list' system

The ministerial case as advanced by the then home secretary, Jack Straw,[4] was that the closed list system was widely used on the continent and that if employed in Britain, then some 70 per cent of Union MEPs would be elected in this way, a move towards uniformity in the voting system. He also claimed that the method was a 'simple, straightforward system which takes individual candidates and allows the public to vote for particular parties. It still asks the electorate to put a single cross on the ballot paper'. Above all, it was the best means of promoting gender equality and getting ethnic minority candidates on the list. He made the point that prior to the 1999 elections, there were 'no women north of the Humber and in areas with quite a high ethnic minority concentration there are no ethnic minority members'.

'Closed lists' are regarded as undemocratic because there is no element of voter choice. Not only is the choice of candidates for the list entirely the responsibility of the party hierarchy, but the very same people also choose the order in which candidates' names are listed on the ballot paper, thus influencing the chances that named candidates have of being elected or not being elected. In other words the party has complete control of the process, allowing not even party grassroots workers to have a say, let alone the electors.

In the case of the Liberal Democrats, they do allow party members to determine the composition of their list. Labour does not and in spite of the strong denial of such considerations, there has been a widely held view that the New Labour leadership (particularly under Tony Blair) wants to exercise strong control over the Labour list. An open list would enable the voters to express a preference that might be for candidates who are on the left of the party and unsympathetic to the Blair/Brown approach. At the very least, it was certainly an attraction for the former prime minister that closed lists have provided an opportunity to reform and modernise the Labour contingent in Strasbourg. He felt that many Labour members before 1999 were out of touch with prevalent thinking in the country and party.

As for gender representation, the use of proportional voting systems by all member countries has contributed to a better level representation of women at Strasbourg than is true of those legislatures that do not use such systems. Between 1994 and 1999, 27 per cent of MEPs were women and between 1999 and 2004 30 per cent. Sweden and Finland both have high levels of female representation in the Parliament, just as they do in their national parliaments. Overall, Protestant countries with a culture that is sympathetic to gender equality fare well, whereas Catholic and Eastern Orthodox countries where the prevailing view of the female role is more traditional (France, Greece and Italy) have the lowest proportions. The House of Commons elected in 2005 under a first-past-the-post system has 19.8 per cent women, but of the 78 MEPs the current figure is significantly higher at 25.6 per cent.

After the experience of the 1999 elections, some opponents of proportional representation made the point that the low turnout might be interpreted as evidence that voters did not understand or favour the new proportional system. Yet 'fair voting' is often seen by proponents of PR as a stimulus to voter turnout, because it means that all votes actually count towards the outcome.

Euro-elections 2004: a case study

The 2004 election was widely billed in the press as the world's first continental election. Nearly 349m adults in twenty-five countries stretching from the Atlantic to the border of Russia, from the Mediterranean Sea to Lapland, had the right to place their cross on a ballot form. The sixth direct elections to the European Parliament were second in scale only to those in India.

In all, 14,670 candidates – of whom one third were women – were contesting 732 seats. Among the candidates was the usual diverse array of colourful individualists: a Nobel Prize winner, an Oscar winner, a Eurovision song contest winner, a supermodel, a porn star, assorted TV celebrities and *Big Brother* finalists. Among the more serious candidates, there were six former prime ministers. Some of the politicians were trying to begin new political careers, others to revive flagging ones.

Despite the repeated pleas from Brussels, in virtually no country were the elections fought primarily on European issues. In most cases, they descended into little more than a referendum on the government of the day. Voters had the chance to cast a protest vote against those in office and to a lesser extent against the EU in general. In several contests, much of the running during the campaign was made by eurosceptic candidates and parties, noticeably in Denmark, Poland, the Czech Republic and the Netherlands.

Turnout on polling day was generally low, with 45.5 per cent turning out to vote, over 4 per cent less than in the 1999 elections. Across the continent, the mood of the voters seemed to range from apathy to resentment. The findings of Professor Rose of the Swedish think tank IDEA[5] suggested that the gap between people voting in national and in European elections stood at 21.9 per cent in the fifteen pre-2004 member states and 29.1 per cent in the ten new member countries. The latest recruits to the Union whose voters might have been expected to be flushed with enthusiasm for their new common European home had, in fact, the lowest turnouts in the election.

The outcome

Seven political groupings were initially represented in the 2004 Parliament. Their respective strengths in each member country are illustrated in Table 8.3.

The elections revealed a pan-European anti-incumbency trend. Incumbent governments of the centre left suffered (as in Germany's Social Democratic and Britain's Labour parties), as did those of the right (France's UMP and Italy's Forza Italia). In all, in twenty-three out of the twenty-five member countries, the largest party in the national government saw its share of the vote slump. The two governments that escaped the trend, the Greek New Democracy party of the centre right and the Spanish Socialists, were still enjoying something of a honeymoon, having only recently been elected into office.

Table 8.3 European elections in 2004: the results

Country	EUL/ NGL	Greens	PES	ELDR	EPP	UEN	EDD	No affiliation	Total seats
Germany	7	13	23	7	49				99
Britain		5	19	12	28*		12	2	78
France	3	6	31		28			10	78
Italy	7	2	15	9	28	9		8	78
Poland			8	4	18	7		17	54
Spain	1	5	24	1	23				54
Netherlands	2	2	7	5	7		2	2	27
Belgium		2	7	5	7			3	24
Czech Republic	6		2		11			5	24
Hungary			9	2	13				24
Greece	4	0	8	0	11			1	24
Portugal	2		12		7	2		1	24
Sweden	2	1	5	3	5			3	19
Austria		2	7		6			3	18
Denmark	2		5	4	1	1	1		14
Finland	1	1	3	5	4				14
Slovakia			3		8			3	14
Ireland		1	2		4	4		2	13
Lithuania			2	3	3			5	13
Latvia		1		1	3	4			9
Slovenia			1	2	4				7
Cyprus	2			1	2			1	6
Estonia			3	2	1				6

Country	EUL/ NGL	Greens	PES	ELDR	EPP	UEN	EDD	No affiliation	Total seats
Luxembourg		1		1	1	3			6
Malta			3		2				5
Total in EU	39	42	200	67	276	27	15	66	732

NB Figures based on those provided by the European Parliament. * Conservative total includes one Ulster Unionist.

Although most votes appear to have been cast on national lines, they had European consequences. The election confirmed the centre right as the largest group in the European Parliament, followed by the Socialists, a new Liberal and centrist group based on the ELDR and the Greens. All four groups included many committed federalists within their ranks and those parties traditionally in favour of closer European integration formed the largest block in the Parliament.

However, there was also a pan-European trend towards increased support for eurosceptic parties, most obviously in Britain, but also in Austria, Sweden and the Netherlands. In Sweden, a new party, the Junelist, took 14.4 per cent of the vote and won three seats. In Britain, UKIP did even better. However, not all eurosceptic groups fared as well, for the Danish variety lost two seats and the French *souverainistes*, who have long campaigned against the transfer of powers to Brussels, suffered a sharp decline in their popular vote. The populist anti-European Polish Selfdefence party that had been tipped to top the polls came fourth, although a Eurosceptic League of Polish Families came second. Where the far right was in power, it did as badly as the left did in Germany and Poland.

Nonetheless, if some anti or lukewarm Europeans did less well than anticipated, it remained the fact that there was a larger 'awkward' squad in the new Parliament, with broadly eurosceptic parties comprising 10 per cent of all MEPs. The number who opposed the proposed constitution or whose rallying point in the campaign was corruption within the Union constituted a much larger group. Rose estimated the number of 'euro-awkwards' to be around 200. They are a diverse collection of people of many persuasions, including British Conservatives and Swedish Greens, far rightists and unreconstructed communists, nationalists and populists.

Table 8.4 The UK outcome of the 2004 euro-election

Party	% votes	% seats	No. of seats	+ or − % votes relative to 1999
Conservatives	26.7	36.0	27	−9.0
Labour	22.6	25.3	19	−5.4
UKIP	16.1	16.0	12	+9.2
Lib Dems	14.9	16.0	12	+2.3
Green	6.3	2.7	2	0.0
BNP	4.9	0.0	0	+3.9
Respect	1.5	0.0	0	+1.5

NB In addition to the above parties, the Scottish Nationalists won two seats, and Plaid Cymru, the Democratic Unionists, the Ulster Unionists and Sinn Fein one each.

Representation of member states in the European Parliament

MEPs are largely distributed between the member states on the basis of population, meaning that some countries have far more than others. However, when the number of electors per MP is taken into consideration, it becomes apparent that there are huge discrepancies which cast doubt on the democratic basis of euro-elections. 75,000 voters in Luxembourg qualify for an MEP, whereas 833,100 in Germany only get the same level of representation. Small states are the winners in this imbalance.

Before 1994 Germany had the same number of MEPs (eighty-one) as France, Italy and the UK, despite having a much larger population. As from 1994, when the rise in population caused by German reunification made an increase in the number of EP seats necessary, the new distribution of seats meant that larger member states had one MEP for each 500,000 electors. At the other end of the scale, the smaller member states are proportionately over-represented in an attempt to prevent them being overwhelmed by the larger states in the decision-making process, in what Nicoll and Salmon[6] have termed 'a genuflection towards the sovereign status of all'. Further changes were made to cater for the expansion of the Union in 2004. As a result, the United Kingdom lost nine seats and now has seventy-eight.

The division of MEPs remains heavily weighted towards the smaller states under the new distribution and is destined to continue to do so, as the figures in Table 8.5 illustrate.

Table 8.5 Representation of member states in the European Parliament

Member state	No. of MEPs to 2004	No. of MEPs from 2007	Current population per MEP
Austria	21	18	450,900
Belgium	25	24	429,900
Bulgaria	n/a	18	416,700
Cyprus	n/a	6	133,700
Czech Republic	n/a	24	426,500
Denmark	16	14	383,100
Estonia	n/a	6	220,500
Finland	16	14	371,900
France	87	78	771,100
Germany	99	99	833,100
Greece	25	24	457,300
Hungary	n/a	24	411,500
Ireland	15	13	304,300
Italy	87	78	736,200
Latvia	n/a	9	256,300
Lithuania	n/a	13	264,900
Luxembourg	6	6	75,500
Malta	n/a	5	78,800
Netherlands	31	27	598,100
Poland	n/a	54	714,600

Table 8.5 (continued)			
Member state	No. of MEPs to 2004	No. of MEPs from 2007	Current population per MEP
Portugal	25	24	419,300
Romania	n/a	35	628,600
Slovakia	n/a	14	385,900
Slovenia	n/a	7	283,400
Spain	64	54	760,400
Sweden	22	19	467,200
United Kingdom	87	78	759,600
Total	626	785	

NB As the population figures are rounded to the nearest decimal point, the figure in the last column is inevitably slightly inaccurate.

Role of elected representatives: MEPs

Among the many aspects of the European Parliament that are unknown to the average European citizen is any conception of what an MEP actually does. As is the case with national parliaments, one obvious assumption is that members spend most of their time in the debating chamber. But if this is far from the case at the British House of Commons or other legislatures, it is even less true of Strasbourg or Brussels. Even when commissioners are summoned before Parliament to answer for their area of responsibility or to make a policy statement, very few turn up to listen or question them. An interesting example of this is provided by Matthew Engel's[7] description of Sir Leon Brittan's appearance before the Parliament in 1994 to announce the new world trade agreement that would replace GATT:

> In the whole vast near-circular debating chamber there were, officials and flunkeys aside, only a dozen people. The press gallery was almost empty . . . This was not a particular comment on Sir Leon or his subject . . . It is always like this. No one goes to debates, except to speak. No one listens except the interpreters.

The point about interpreters is important, as there are twenty-three official languages in the Union. It is very hard to make an impact with a speech when one's words cannot be understood directly by most of the people present; even the finest speech-making cannot survive the neutral intermediary of an interpreter. As Engel says, 'oratory, rhetoric and invective all fall flat'.

Few of the British MEPs are known to their electorates. They are, in the words of *The Economist*, 'unloved and obscure'.[8] However, its researchers noted that just a few had managed to attract media coverage. Labour's Glenys Kinnock, the Liberal Democrat Chris Huhne and the Greens' Caroline Lucas achieved more than 100 mentions in the national quality press in the five years of the 1999–2004 Parliament. According to the database search, the vast majority received less than half that number and more than a quarter managed only single figures, two scoring zero.

Such a survey is inevitably flawed, not least because MEPs in remoter parts of Scotland and Wales find it easier to obtain a mention in local papers than in London-based broadsheets. But the impression remains that some members are indolent and the work they perform is too specialised or uninteresting to capture the interest of journalists and therefore of their readerships. Several MEPs have been known to complain that even in discussions of the work concerning life in the Strasbourg Parliament, the media prefer to feature Westminster MPs than its representatives.

Daily life as an MEP

Being an MEP is a full-time job. One week in each month is taken up with the Parliament's session in Strasbourg, and much of the remaining three weeks by committee, Group, or full Parliament meetings in Brussels.

On top of all this is the need to keep in touch with constituents at home. The problems of having to travel frequently between Parliament and constituency, familiar to most national MPs, are compounded in the case of MEPs because the distances are much greater. Parliamentary affairs leave only a couple of days each week for MEPs to spend in their constituencies, during which time they must deal with individual constituents, local organisations, local and national politicians, businesses, trade unions, and so on. Because of these pressures, many MEPs have a substantial staff to help them.

Many MEPs choose to make their family residence in Brussels rather than in their home country, to avoid family obligations competing with other pressures in the limited time that members are able to spend in their constituency.

The example provided in box 8.3 indicates the way in which MEPs might spend a typical day.

Pay and conditions of the elected representatives (MEPs)

MEPs are paid the same salary as members of their own national parliaments, although they can choose the currency and country in which to receive that salary.

Box 8.3 'A day in the life of a Member of the European Parliament'

A teacher by training, Jean has not found it difficult to adjust to the hectic lifestyle of an MEP since her election in June 1999. However, since her re-election in June 2004, it seems that her work has increased significantly. Jean usually arrives in the office around 8a.m., addressing the matters that need her urgent attention.

Today Jean arrives in her Brussels office straight from the Eurostar terminal, collects her weekly agenda and then has a meeting with the shadow-rapporteurs and other MEPs about her Report on Asylum. Jean then speaks at an event organised by her office on the human rights situation in India and chairs the subsequent debate on caste discrimination and what can be done at EU level. Often Jean does not have time for lunch and has to grab a sandwich between meetings. Today she has a working lunch meeting on the Working Time Directive with a group of trade union representatives.

After lunch Jean goes to the Employment and Social Affairs Committee, which will last the whole afternoon. These meetings take place in Committee rooms specially equipped with microphones and headsets so that the team of translators who sit in the fishtank-like booths around the side of the main room can simultaneously translate the discussion into the Community languages. It is quite something to behold.

Once the meeting has finished, Jean returns to the office to check if there are any urgent messages or emails. She jots down a few notes for her speech at the seminar she has to attend tomorrow and then runs out again to meet representatives from AGE Concern at a reception for the launch of the Inter-group on Ageing (of which she is co-president).

When Jean finally arrives back at her small flat situated close to the European Parliament she retires with a detective novel, her preferred literature, for some well-needed relaxation.

Although this has been a busy day for Jean, it is quite a typical day for her and while going to receptions or dinners may seem glamorous, it is the ideal place to meet NGOs, lobbyists and MEPs from other political groups and to exchange views in a more informal setting.

Jean divides her time between her London constituency where she frequently attends weekend events, and the Parliament either in Brussels or Strasbourg.

'No politician I know works 9–5, Monday to Friday,' she reflects; 'as an elected person you are a public figure who is always in demand. It's just frustrating that there isn't time to pursue every issue raised by the people who voted you in.' Despite the hectic lifestyle, the constant travelling and the separation from her family, it is clear from Jean's animated enthusiasm that she relishes even the more challenging aspects of the job. 'I can't think of any other occupation with more possibilities for somebody who wants to influence real social and political change.'

Extract taken from the website of Jean Lambert, MEP

These salaries are constantly changing but the lowest-paid representatives at the time of the Fifth Enlargement (Central and Eastern part i) were the Finns and the Spanish, who received less than one-third of the salary paid to the Italians (just under £100,000), by far the best-rewarded contingent. East European members earned significantly less than their Western counterparts. British MEPs came more or less exactly in the middle, those elected in 2004 having at that time a salary of £55,000. MPs enjoying the dual mandate as a member of a national parliament as well as the EP receive their normal parliamentary salary (£60,675 in 2007–8) for their work at home, plus one-third of that salary for their work as an MEP. Because there are such wide variations in salary between MEPs of different nationalities, the Amsterdam Treaty laid down the aim of moving towards a common statute for all MEPs in order to remove disparities.

Expenses and allowances are the same for all MEPs and are often very much better than national allowances. Subsistence and travel allowances are particularly favourable since they have to cater for the considerable amount of travelling MEPs must do, not only between Brussels, Strasbourg and Luxembourg but also between the EP and their home country. The figures agreed as of 1 January 2004 are:

- general expenditure (office and communication costs, etc.): (€3,700 per month
- travel allowance: €.67 per km for the first 500km and €.268 per km thereafter – for journeys to EP meetings within the Union
- travel allowance (including hotel costs) for travel throughout the world when on parliamentary business: maximum of €3,652
- subsistence allowance: £262 for attending meetings within Union (covers both accommodation and meals); £131 per day on top of actual bed and breakfast costs for attending meetings outside the Union
- secretarial assistance: maximum of £12,576 per month.

There are frequent complaints about the amount of money paid out to MEPs and the comfortable lifestyle they are said to enjoy, the tabloids making great play of the 'Brussels gravy-train'. The pressure of complaints led to the introduction of sanctions by which MEPs may have their allowances cut by half if they do not attend at least 50 per cent of plenary sittings of the EP. Despite any such sanctions, however, it has been claimed that a perfectly honest MEP can, without fiddling the system, bank a six-figure sum for every session he or she spends as a member of the EP.

Much of the adverse comment has come from three traditionally eurosceptic countries: Denmark, Sweden and the United Kingdom. It has centred on the amount paid to MEPs as expenses and the manner in which it is paid. The alleged profligacy derives primarily from the generous flat-rate travel allowance that bears no relation to the expenses incurred in travelling to Brussels or Strasbourg. The price paid is for economy travel, not first class, but nevertheless this value often amounts to significantly more than the actual price of travel with one of the many budget airlines that serve the two centres. A further area of concern is the fact that MEPs' accounts are currently audited on a spot-check basis, not a universal one. Feeling this to be insufficient, some members voluntarily submit their accounts for a full independent audit annually.

Aware of the need to shed the gravy-train image, members bowed to public pressure on the issue and in December 2003 voted to abolish the lax expenses regime. Under the terms of the proposed deal, they would have had to provide receipts and their salaries would have been liable for national tax on top of a special low rate of EU tax. As a quid pro quo for accepting tougher limits on the perks, MEPs were to receive a hoist in salaries that in future were to be standardised across the Union. The standardisation would have granted a British member a 30 per cent rise to around £72,000 a year. However, although Parliament had supported the deal, the last word rested with member states' foreign ministers who in January 2004 baulked at picking up the tab for salary reforms, thus blocking moves to crack down on abuses of expenses. A resolution was adopted in 2005 to equalise salary differences. This is due to come into force in the next Parliament, elected in 2009.

For all the complaints and accusations, it has to be said that the costs of the European Parliament, even with its heavy expenditure on interpreters and translation, are less than half of what is spent in the USA on the House of Representatives. In 2006, the budget allocated for total EP expenditure, including office costs, staffing, buildings and MEPs pay, travel allowances and expenses was €1322m.

One area where some suspicion lingers after the corruption scandals in the Brussels Commission, as well as in various national parliaments, concerns the extent of payments that are made to MEPs by lobbyists and interest groups. In order to counter this there is a register of interests on the British pattern that is supposedly completed by MEPs, copies of which are kept in Brussels and Luxembourg. But the register is not kept very assiduously and very few MEPs are particularly scrupulous in declaring their interests. Only the Dutch and British representatives seem to make any serious attempt to declare all their external earnings and allowances.

Use of referendums

Representative democracy is not the only form used in connection with the European Union. The holding of referendums related to EU membership or initiatives is now a major reason for direct democracy on the continent, second only to constitutional matters. The votes have usually been to decide whether or not to join the Union or whether or not to accept some new EU initiative or treaty.

In Western Europe, most of the single-issue votes have been ad hoc ones, used to resolve particularly difficult issues which may divide mainstream parties and therefore raise the possibility of fissure or cut across party lines. They may touch on the constitution or on national sovereignty, as on topics such as membership of the euro. The UK's sudden decision in 2004 to hold a referendum on the proposed constitution for the Union falls into this category, announced as it was during the 2004 European election campaign in order to lessen the impact of 'difficult' European issues being discussed.

In several member states, including Austria, Denmark, Estonia, Ireland and Slovakia, it is a requirement of the constitution that constitutional changes should be put to the people in a referendum. Denmark and Ireland referred the question of accession to the EC in 1972, 71 per cent of the Irish voting 'yes' to entry, and a massive 90 per cent of the Danes doing likewise. Twenty years later, both countries held referendums on ratification of the Maastricht Treaty, the Danes most famously having to hold a second referendum in May 1993, after having voted 'no' the first time. Denmark and Sweden both held a referendum to decide the issue of membership of the eurozone, in both cases the votes saying 'no'. Since then, there have been several other referendums, either to ratify a new treaty initiative or in the case of new countries, to approve their decision to join the Union (e.g. the Austrian and Finnish ones at the time of the Fourth Enlargement). Most of the recent batch of entrants held referendums to confirm their decisions (e.g. Hungary and Poland).

Conclusion

Despite the growing democratic powers of the European Parliament, the elections of 2004, just like those of ten years earlier, seem to show that the people of the Union as a whole are less enthusiastic about Europe than many of their leaders. Turnout in European elections has always been poor in the UK and reached an all-time low in 1999. However, five years later voters turned out in much greater numbers and the discrepancy between the British and other European figures was markedly less than on previous occasions.

Overall in 2004, the figures for turnout were unimpressive, with clear evidence of a serious decline in the long-established member states and even worse performances in the countries that joined the Union in the Fifth Enlargement (Central and Eastern part i). Even when people do vote they are hardly acting out of any sense of belonging to Europe, but rather tending to vote on domestic rather than European issues, mostly in order to show their displeasure with national governing parties.

The electorates of the Union tend to show more interest in referendums than in elections for the European Parliament, perhaps precisely because they are being asked to respond to specific questions that they see as more important in their lives than the abstraction of a distant parliament.

CHAPTER 9

Political parties and the European Union

Political parties are usually viewed as national organisations which have local and regional branches. However, they may also have an international and/or transnational dimension. Given its immense size, the EU provides opportunities for like-minded parties to cooperate in pursuit of their aims. It also has a considerable impact upon party politics in the member states, providing a whole new set of issues with which politicians have to deal.

As the Union developed, so commentators began to look for signs that national parties were becoming more 'European' in their outlook, in reflection of the general move towards a more integrationist approach. To what extent is a uniquely European party system likely to develop, linked to but distinct from the party systems prevalent in member countries? Or can European party politics only be interpreted in terms of the impact on the fortunes of national parties in the various states?

There is a wide spectrum of political parties across Europe. Over recent years, there has been a decline of far-left organisations, with the diminution in support for **eurocommunism** from its heyday of the 1970s in Western Europe and the breakdown of the Soviet empire in the East. Today, social democracy is the main ideology of the left and this is a moderate form of socialism. In most cases, it combines support for governmental provision of services with a greater interest in self-reliance than was prevalent in the past. On the right, Christian Democrat parties are active in most continental countries. They share a greater interest in social issues than has been traditional in the British Conservative Party, seeing welfarism as the best means of avoiding tension within society. These two positions dominate party politics within the member states and the European Union.

At present, national political parties of whatever persuasion are involved in the affairs of the European Union in three ways:

- at the transnational level
- via the transnational political groupings in the European Parliament
- via their activities back home, where the agenda they pursue has become increasingly 'Europeanised', as developments within the Union create a whole new battleground and set of issues with which to contend.

Transnational parties

The establishment of European institutions as part of the ECSC, EEC and other bodies encouraged the growth of **transnational** confederations of political parties. They are loose associations which bring together broadly like-minded parties from member states in one organisation. Their development was given further impetus as a consequence of the introduction of direct elections to the

European Parliament. Their arrival on the European political scene was recognised in the Maastricht Treaty. A new Article 138a was written into the Treaty of Rome: 'Political parties at European level are important as a factor for integration within the Union. They contribute to forming a European awareness and to expressing the political will of the citizens of the Union'.

Since then, transnational parties have been identified as having an increasingly important role in EU affairs. The Nice Treaty authorised the Council to lay down 'regulations governing political parties and in particular rules governing their financing' at European level. In order that recognition and resources should be limited to bodies that were genuinely transnational in character, the Party Statute of the EU (2003)[1] narrowed their definition to parties which were

> represented in at least one quarter of Member States by Members of the European Parliament, members of national parliaments, or members of regional parliaments or assemblies or have received in at least one quarter of Member States at least three per cent of the vote in those Member states in the most recent European elections.

The statute gave formal shape to European parties and represented a considerable boost to their significance.

These parties have become increasingly important players in the politics of the European Union over recent years. They have one or more members in most of the member and associated states. They are actively engaged at all levels in the major institutions of the EU. They have a close working relationship with the party groupings of the European Parliament.

Transnational parties operate in much the same way as do their member parties. A congress of delegates decides on the political programme; an executive committee deals with current issues and day-to-day business; a chairman (supported by a party presidium or board) speaks for the party and represents it; a secretary general (supported by a secretariat) is in charge of internal communication and the technical and organisational work necessary to ensure that party bodies can operate properly. There are often associations for certain categories of members, such as women and young people.

Existing parties

The three main transnational parties are the rightwing European People's Party (EPP), the leftwing Party of European Socialists (PES) and the more centrist European Liberal Democrat and Reform Party (ELDR).

1. *The European People's Party (EPP)* was the first transnational party to be formed at European level and remains the largest political force on the continent, with sixty-nine member parties from thirty-seven countries. It is a family of the political centre right, which has pioneered the European project from its inception. It is committed to a federal Europe, based on the principle of

---

Box 9.1 Current transnational party federations, as registered under the Party Statute of the EU, 2006

Party family	Party federation
Moderate left (social democrats)	Party of European Socialists
Moderate right (Christian democrats)	European People's Party
Liberal democrats/centrists	European Liberal Democrats
Greens	European Green Party
Traditional left: socialists and communists	Party of the European Left
Pro-regionalists/devolutionists	European Free Alliance
Eurosceptics and nationalists	Alliance for a Europe of the Nations
Centrists, pro-integration	European Democratic Party
Conservative nationalists and eurosceptics*	Alliance of Independent Democrats in Europe
Eurosceptics and EU reformists of the centre, centre left	EU Democrats

* EU critics who reject the Treaty establishing a constitution for Europe and oppose all forms of centralisation.

---

subsidiarity. It exists to advance the goal of a more competitive and democratic Europe, closer to its citizens.

The EPP is open to individuals, via the mechanism of 'supporting members'.

2. *The Party of European Socialists* (PES) was founded in The Hague (1992) to succeed the Confederation of Socialist Parties of the European Community. It is an associated organisation of the Socialist International. Its membership includes thirty-three social democratic, socialist and labour parties of the European Union member states, as well as others from Bulgaria, Romania and Norway.

Like the EPP, there are no fully involved members, but the PES is accessible to individuals via the mechanism of 'PES activists'. Some 5,000 of these activists can exchange their views on the PES website, organise meetings within their countries and take part in Europe-wide campaigns.

3. *The European Liberal Democrat and Reform Party* (ELDR) brings together political parties with common liberal, democratic and reform ideals from more than thirty European countries. It sees its role as to strengthen the Liberal Democrat movement in the EU and throughout Europe; assist Liberal Democrat politicians across Europe to become better acquainted to define a common political vision; and draw up and adopt a common manifesto for the European elections.

If these three main transnational groups are only loosely coordinated, the smaller ones which have emerged have in the past suffered even more seriously from the disadvantages of fragmentation and limited resources. Two of the more prominent ones have been the European Federation of Green Parties and the Party of the European Left.

4. *The European Green Party* was created in 2004, as a replacement for the Federation, underlining the objective of a deeper cooperation. European Greens stand for 'the sustainable development of humanity on planet Earth, a mode of development respectful of human rights and built upon the values of environmental responsibility, freedom, justice, diversity and non-violence'. It currently has thirty-three member parties in twenty-nine states, ranging from Ireland to Georgia, from Malta to Norway.

5. *The Party of the European Left* wants to see a different kind of Europe that is anti-war; redistributes wealth, power and influence; resists capitalist globalisation; and is fully democratic and accountable. Its seventeen member parties from fifteen countries are of various shades, socialist, communist, red-green among them.

Uses and weaknesses

Transnational parties are described as confederations rather than federations, for the bonds which unite them are not strong and there has traditionally been little central direction or leadership. However, the politicians involved in them see mutual benefit in cooperation and the exchange of information. They provide an opportunity for the coordination of activities and ideas at the European level, enabling them to present common propaganda and to fight elections on a common platform. As we see below, they have in recent years coordinated campaigns for the five-yearly European elections. They have other uses. There has been a developing tendency for various national leaders within a political family to meet together prior to European summit meetings, to enable them to agree a broad stance in preparation for the main sessions. For instance, centre-right politicians might seek to coordinate their policies on business deregulation and liberal trade policies.

There are some indications that transnational parties might develop more in the future. But at present, other than organising and attending meetings and producing election literature, their role is modest. Nugent[2] explains their weakness in this way:

> because the confederations have no institutional focus (such as Westminster or the European Parliament) they are not involved in day-to-day political activities. They cannot develop attachments and loyalties. From this, other weaknesses flow; low status; limited resources and loose organisational structures.

Moreover, there are additional factors which make it difficult for them to achieve greater significance, one of which is the divergence of national interest between member parties. There are occasions when national leaders have to take a stand in Council to defend or advance their domestic interest, irrespective of whether this may conflict with their broad ideological inclinations. In recent years, Dutch and Swedish representatives have often aligned themselves with the British position in favour of reform of the CAP, whereas their French and German counterparts have been on the other side. The interests of significant groups within their populations have been a greater priority than any transnational party loyalty, so that the Third Way, centre-left premiers in the United Kingdom and Germany found themselves at odds over the issue. In the same way, a coalition based on national interest allowed Tony Blair to work with the Spanish centre-right prime minister in advancing the agenda of deregulation.

There are other difficulties. National political parties often find themselves having to adapt to decentralisation within their own country and devote more time to safeguarding their party organisation at home rather than working on any joint European initiatives. Moreover, lacking as they do in many cases a sound financial basis, they cannot afford to divert many of their monetary and personnel resources to transnational and European Parliamentary activity.

Finally, there is a difficulty in communication between the European and national levels which affects their political effectiveness and the possibilities for organisational development. Jansen points out:

> The number of politicians and officials working at European level is still fairly small. National party headquarters have many more times the personnel, operational capacity and financial resources available to the European party secretariats. Inadequate equipment makes regularly supplying comprehensive information and communication with member parties in the various languages impossible. As for spreading the word to the wider public, this is not yet feasible.[3]

At present, there is no clear idea how individual memberships should best be constituted. National parties have already had to confront a similar issue in the context of regional devolution. This led to the creation of specifically 'regional' parties, linked to their political family at the national level, but with a considerable degree of autonomy, as happens in Scotland and Catalonia. It may be that individual members joining parties which are simultaneously active at the regional, national and European levels could enjoy specified rights at all levels.

Present strength and future prospects: differing views

Opinions concerning the present and likely future state of any European party system based on transnational parties are highly diverse. At present the tendency among many commentators is to see them as facilitating bodies which are necessary to make the elections for and workings of the European Parliament more effective, bodies via which the conflict of ideas and tendencies among MEPs can be recognised and organised. For others, they are more just machinery via which the electoral battle can be fought and around which Parliament can be made to function. They add an extra dimension, providing a genuine European feel to party battle, having an appeal and reach that the national parties cannot attain. Finally, there are those who believe that the present parties will evolve into key agencies via which elections are contested, with individuals being able not only to join but to play an active part in their proceedings and in the evolution of their policies and ideas. Under this scenario, voters might come to see themselves as supporters of a national party for domestic issues and a transnational party for European issues.

Those who are dismissive of the party federations tend to view them as political parties at the European level. They lack mass membership and do not have a direct relationship with European electorates. It follows that they cannot be anything more than pseudo-parties. Those who see them as something altogether more significant perceive them as being European or at least European Union parties.

The *Tsatsos Report* (1996)[4] of the European Parliament which dealt with the financing of euro-parties saw them as important in advancing integration, for they contributed to a 'developing European awareness and were a means of expressing the political will of the citizens'. They must not be 'created with the purpose of attracting Community funds: rather, they must pursue long-term policies'. It suggested that for them to be recognised as such, they would need to have 'various features derived from the image of the political parties in the Member States and transferred – *mutatis mutandis* – to the level of the European Union'. According to Jansen, these include:

1. internal structures which resemble those of national parties
2. official recognition of their role in resourcing similar functions to these carried out by conventional political parties
3. some mechanism for agreeing programmes and manifestos
4. an agreement by the national parties that, to some extent, their authority should be limited in favour of the euro-parties.

In assessing the claims of party federations to be genuinely European parties, Jansen finds that to some degree they do meet these criteria. For instance, dealing with each of them in order, he makes the following observations:

1. The typical structure of Euro-parties is comparable to that of a national party (see above, p. 153). Moreover, some three-quarters of MEPs come from national parties committed by their membership of euro-parties to joining a corresponding group in the EP and some of these parties do provide for individual membership.
2. Since the Statute, parties are officially recognised and funded, via the Union budget.
3. Euro-parties have over recent elections agreed manifestos for European elections; their ideas on policy, as reflected in their party texts, are fed through into meetings in Council and in gatherings of MEPs.

4. The Statutes of the EPP, PES and ELDR allow party positions to be decided by majority vote, so that over some areas of policy national parties are willing to cede some decision-making to the euro-parties.

There are some similarities between national and euro-parties, but they are as yet undeveloped. Few would argue that euro-parties form a meaningful link between European citizens and their elected representatives. When voters go to the polls in European elections, they are not choosing between the candidates of euro-parties. They are voting for candidates of national parties which belong or are affiliated to euro-parties. Very few voters would identify themselves as supporters of the EPP or PES.

Bale[5] speculates that what may happen in the future is that transnational parties 'will adopt a kind of "franchising" model, whereby (like many fast-food chains) the component parties of the organisation will be allowed a great deal of autonomy as long as they use and promote the basic brand: this less hierarchical structure might facilitate within parties the kind of multilevel governance they are having to adjust to both at home and in Europe'. Others have higher aspirations. Wilfried Martens,[6] the president of the EPP, shares the view that European political parties are crucial to building up new awareness and wants to see voters 'electing the President of the Commission in a real European political campaign' for which the euro-parties nominate the candidate.

Transnational party groupings in the European Parliament

Better known than the transnational federations are the party blocs which have developed in the European Parliament and which in many cases share the same name as the bodies already described. Their activities have a specific focus – the assembly itself – and they can and do play an important role in its organisation and operations. These party groupings at Strasbourg are then a part of the wider transnational parties, but because they have a more definite role they are much more significant. Box 9.2 illustrates the organisation of the European People's Party at both levels.

The organisation of the European Parliament emphasises its supranational leanings. Members do not sit or associate as national groups but as members of a variety of political groupings based on an approximation of ideological similarity. The largest of these groupings provide mutual assistance at election time, creating propaganda and campaigning material based on an agreed manifesto. None of the main federations and few of the other groups have the cohesiveness or discipline of national political parties, but there is a feeling of common interest. The groups have more influence than individuals or small national groupings would have and they receive financial support from the Parliament for administrative and research purposes, dependent on their size. They are a recognised feature of the workings of the assembly, and they influence the drafting of the agenda and the allocation of committee chairmanships, speaking rights, and other duties and facilities.

Party groups and the 2004–9 Parliament

According to the EP rules of procedure adopted in 1999, a group must have a membership drawn from more than one member state. It requires a minimum of twenty-three MEPs if the members come from just two states, eighteen if they come from three, and fourteen if they come from four or more. There are usually between seven and ten groups, but their names are liable to change from Parliament to Parliament as members regroup to take account of the latest election results.

The latest regrouping has involved the creation of a far-right but ideologically loose entity, known as Identity, Tradition, Sovereignty. It has been described as 'anti-immigration, anti-EU Constitution and anti-Turkish membership'. The largest component of the group is the French National Front, but it has a membership drawn from seven countries. Previous attempts at creating such a body had been thwarted by the requirement that groups had to be of a certain minimum size and drawn from 20 per cent of the member states. Enlargement has made it easier to surmount such an obstacle. Indeed, the use of proportional representation across the Union means that several diverse traditions in the national life of countries can secure some representation. Nugent[7] calculates that there have never been less than sixty different national parties represented in the European Parliament. The number has increased in recent years. In the 1999–2004 Parliament there were 122; in the 2004–9 Parliament there were 175.

Reflecting the major expansion of the Union to include ten politically and economically diverse states, the composition of the sixth parliament is considerably more heterogeneous than in the past. The respective strengths of the groupings are illustrated in Table 9.1.

Two major groupings or party federations dominate the European Parliament, those of the centre left and the centre right. Voting is therefore dependent on the way in which their members and the third centrist party react. On many issues they have traditionally formed a strongly pro-integrationist 'grand coalition', and in the discussion of many policies and initiatives this remains the case today.

Advantages and difficulties of party groupings

The organisational stress on supranational rather than national interests has helped to create a sense of European identity in the Parliament. Many members do recognise a responsibility to examine issues on the basis of what is good for Europe rather than purely on the basis of what is good for their own country.

Table 9.1 Composition of the European Parliament (August 2007)

Grouping	Characteristics	Component parties	Seats
European People's Party– European Democrats (EPP–ED)	Centre-right, became the largest party in 1999 and remains so today. The direct heir to the tradition established in the 1950s by Schuman, Adenauer and de Gasperi. (See also Box 9.2)	European People's Party (EPP) European Democrats (ED)	277
Group of the Party of European Socialists	For a long while, more ideologically cohesive than the EPP. Members range widely from predominantly moderate Social Democrats to a few ex-communists and traditional left state interventionists.	Party of European Socialists (PES)	218
Alliance of Liberals and Democrats for Europe (ALDE)	Comprises members of the former ELDR. In spite of presence of British Liberals with more leftist tendencies, mainland Liberals are more rooted in laissez-faire values.	European Liberal Democrat and Reform Party (ELDR) European Democratic Party (EDP) + 2 unaffiliated national parties	106
Union for Europe of the Nations (UEN)	An assortment of convinced nationalists who are reluctant to join with one of the more established and electorally successful parties. Opposed Maastricht and any moves towards a federal Europe. Belongs to Alliance for Europe of the Nations organisation.	Alliance for Europe Nations (AEN) Some EU Democrats (EUD) + 3 unaffiliated national parties	44
European Greens– European Free Alliance (Greens–EFA)	Formed in 1999, as an alliance of two distinct European parties, the EFA (supporters of regional autonomy, centre-left) and the Greens, most of whom are located on the left. Campaigns for social-justice-related issues.	European Green Party (EGP) European Free Alliance (EFA) + 1 unaffiliated national party	42
European United Left–	Firmly on the left of the EUP, mainly socialist and communist	Party of the European Left	41

Table 9.1 (continued)

Grouping	Characteristics	Component parties	Seats
Nordic Green Left (GUE–NGL)	membership.	Nordic Green Left Alliance (NGLA) + 5 unaffiliated national parties	
Independence and Democracy (IND/DEM)	Recent grouping, formed after 2004 elections. Opposes centralising tendencies within EU and is broadly critical of Union initiatives. Includes UKIP.	Alliance of Independent Democrats in Europe (AIDE) Some EU Democrats (EUD) + 3 unaffiliated national parties	23
Identity, Tradition, Sovereignty (ITS)	Far-right, anti-immigration, anti-Turkish membership. Includes Le Pen's French National Front.	Euronationalists of 7 countries + 5 unaffiliated national parties	20
Non-affiliated (NI)		n/a	14

Box 9.2 The case of the European People's Party

The EPP is both a transnational political party and a political group in the European Parliament.

A transnational party

The EPP organisation is a transnational party, a confederation of Christian Democrat and other centre-right parties from member states. Founded in 1976 in time to prepare for the first direct elections to the EP, it aims to promote closer liaison between the Christian Democratic parties of the Union.

The EPP operates at the governmental and parliamentary levels. Heads of government whose parties belong to the EPP organisation meet prior to summit gatherings. Members of the European Commission with mainstream centre-right leanings have regular weekly meetings.

In recent years, membership has been widened beyond the CD movement. The accession of new members has brought non-CD parties into the fold, and it is now a much broader umbrella than was once the case. Neither the British Conservative Party nor its MEPs are members of the EPP organisation; nor have they applied to join.

A political group of the European Parliament

MEPs from national parties belonging to the EPP organisation automatically sit in the EP as members of the Group of the European People's Party. The EPP contingent contains some MEPs who do not actually belong to the EPP, but who are affiliated to it.

Full members accept the EPP organisation's political platform and programmes. Allied members do not. They accept the 'basic policies' of the Parliamentary grouping, not necessarily those of the wider EPP party organisation.

Box 9.3 Relationship of British parties to transnational organisations

The three main political parties in Britain each belong to, are affiliated with or have links to the appropriate transnational confederations.

UK Conservatives and the sole Ulster Unionist MEP are not members of the EPP. They have been loosely associated with it, in the sense that their leader is invited regularly by the EPP president to the EPP summit meetings of heads of government and leaders of the opposition that precede gatherings of the European Council. All previous leaders have attended, but not as yet David Cameron.

Members of the Conservative Party have not wanted membership or close ties, for they find the strongly pro-federal approach of the party hard to accept. After the June 1999 elections there were weeks of negotiations before the Conservatives announced that they would only join the EPP on the basis of a deal which had been arranged whereby it would drop all federalist references from its constitution, replacing the word 'federalism' with the words 'decentralisation and subsidiarity' wherever it appears. The EPP also added the name of the European Democratic group to its own. Until 1992 this had been a group of almost exclusively British Conservative MEPs, together with two anti-Europe Danish MEPs. It was only after the departure of Mrs Thatcher in 1990 that the Conservatives felt able to link up with the EPP, finally affiliating in May 1992.

As 'allied' or 'aligned' members of the EPP–ED group, the Conservatives are an important part of the EPP, the third largest component. They have had many advantages deriving from membership of a wider centre-right body, but are not bound by its policy statements. The Conservatives are more rightwing than many who belong to, or are associated with, the EPP. It was considered on both sides that there were sufficient similar values and ideas between them for the British to be at least partially integrated into the group.

There are still deep reservations in the minds of many British Conservatives over the merits of membership.

Labour

Labour belongs to the Party of European Socialists, its MEPs sitting with the bloc in the European Parliament. The Labour chair has a seat on the Presidency, the highest body of the PES. Labour MPs and ministers regularly participate in PES working groups and party officials regularly meet with the coordination team to discuss the planning, preparation and follow-through of PES activities.

Liberal Democrats

The Liberal Democrats are members of the ELDR and sit in the ALDE group in the European Parliament. A Lib Dem MEP acts as the leader of the parliamentary body.

Box 9.4 Party cohesion in the European Parliament

Many studies have been conducted concerning how MEPs vote within the European Parliament, but the research by Hix et al.[8] has been notably thorough and wide-ranging. In a major study of the 12,000 or so divisions held over the first five parliaments to 2004, their main conclusions were that over the twenty-five years:

1. MEPs became increasingly influenced by party rather than national loyalties.
2. Parties became more cohesive in their voting.
3. Left–right divisions increased, with the broad integrationist coalition of the EPP and PES losing some of its impact.
4. The EP was becoming more like national parliaments, more and more dominated by political parties and left–right politics.

Enlargement has had a significant impact on composition, for the representation of member states, the number of MEPs and the number of national parties represented have all increased. Moreover, in economic interests, social values, cultures and institutions, the ten new members are markedly different from the membership that existed until May 2005. Hix[9] has taken his study further, updating the work by making preliminary judgments about voting based on some 1,300 votes in the first eighteen months of the sixth parliament. His findings were that:

1. Voting behaviour is little different than in previous parliaments, with most MEPs still voting mainly along transnational lines.
2. The cohesion of groups has been little affected, remaining high.
3. Voting on national lines has remained low.
4. Left–right divisions still predominate when members vote. The main exception to this pattern is in the behaviour of ALDE. Whereas the ELDP voted approximately the same number of times with the PES as with the EPP between 2004 and 2009, ALDE has voted more with the EPP in the present parliament, perhaps a reflection of the more rightish leanings of several of its new member parties brought about by some defections from the EPP.

After all, they share a broad similarity of outlook, and because of these common values they have a distinctive way of approaching European issues.

Within any such grouping, there are inevitably difficulties in bringing about a united approach. These can be reflected in the voting patterns of MEPs, although often members show unity in division (see Box 9.4).

Sometimes, particularly within the two larger groupings, there are differences of doctrinal interpretation. Within the EPP–ED, there is some divergence over the commitment to integration, the Christian Democrats being markedly more sympathetic than the British Conservatives. In other cases, members who share the same broad political principles may nevertheless find themselves much affected by considerations of national self-interest – for instance, within the PES, French socialists tend to differ from many British Labour MEPs over the issue of reform of the CAP.

Such divisions inevitably mean that policy on key issues is sometimes fudged, and statements are often little more than vague platitudes. In particular, differences over the pace of European integration and methods of tackling racism on the continent tend to bring about less predictable alliances. This can be true of other policy areas, as well. It is not uncommon for members of one bloc to share an affinity of outlook on key issues with members of another. Often the matters discussed do not easily fit into an ideological left–right battle between the supporters of Christian Democracy and those of Social Democracy.

Internal division can be influenced by factors other than ideology or national interest. MEPs are much lobbied by various pressure groups representing differing interests in Europe. They often belong to Intergroups which cross the boundaries of the different groupings and espouse diverse causes. Finally, they often lack money and resources.

National parties

It is national parties which select the candidates who stand in European elections, and who run the campaigns designed to bring about their victory. They may increasingly use the literature of the transnational groupings, but they fight primarily on national rather than European issues and they interpret the outcome very much in terms of what it means for their standing in domestic politics.

Party politicians attend EU gatherings as national figures, advancing their countries' interests. They will be influenced by their position on the political spectrum, those who are left-inclined being more concerned with social justice, protecting employment and supporting stronger environmental action and those on the right being more concerned with deregulation of business, free markets and open trading policies. But these ideological leanings usually take second place to arguments based on national interest and the leaders' perceptions of the demands of the political situation 'back home'.

National parties have their own priorities, and use a range of policy issues in euro-elections. Yet although they tend to see them as another opportunity to rally the faithful and inflict a defeat on their main rivals, nonetheless Europe is a key question with which they have to deal. Most leading European parties have to some extent incorporated Europe into their policy thinking and ideas. They cannot afford not to. The topic has the potential to create tensions (see Box 9.3), but events on the European stage mean that engagement is essential. European developments occur with remarkable frequency, whether because of the desire of some continental politicians to devise a European constitution or to create a common currency. National politicians have no option but to respond to such initiatives.

As a broad trend, parties of the moderate left have adapted to a more pro-European position over the last two or three decades. This trend has partly reflected the parties' realisation that coordinated continental action often makes good sense and can be more effective in the pursuit of their goals than national action alone. Also, it recognises that national and international action are today more closely connected than they were in the distant past, as the ability of countries to pursue a purely independent line has been reduced. Accordingly, moderate-left politicians in Europe perceived that the European Union could develop in a way that was to the advantage of those elements that supported them. In particular, the pro-business, free-market Community of the 1980s has become the EU which now has a social dimension as a result of the Delors initiatives of the late 1980s. This allows for the possibility of interventionist policies to correct market failures and protect and enhance workers' rights.

Green parties from several countries have also learned to live with the European Union, whatever doubts they had about its early direction. It can be a force for effective action in the environmental arena, providing the opportunity to introduce stiffer regulations on anything from the emissions caused by air travel to the cleanliness of water supplies. Growing representation of the Green element in the European Parliament enables it to highlight green concerns and associated areas of policy. The situation created by euro-elections has made it highly desirable for Green parties to become involved, even in a country such as the United Kingdom where the changeover to a party list electoral system has enabled the Green Party to gain representation.

The trend has been for the main parties in most member states to adopt a broadly pro-European stance. Accordingly, the European Parliament has always had an integrationist majority. But even within the PES and EPP there have been disagreements about the pace, direction and extent of integration. At the national level, those disagreements have been echoed, the more so as parties come to realise the growing doubts of many voters about the European project. Most mainstream parties accept the fact and desirability of membership, but think more carefully today about the extent of their commitment to the political goals of the postwar pioneers of an 'ever closer union of the peoples of Europe'.

Recent European elections have revealed the growing extent of euroscepticism among the electorates of several member states. Anti-EU parties of the far right have made significant headway. They received some encouragement from the results in 1999 and 2004, which indicated a loss of enthusiasm for and interest in the EU and its works, and increased support for parties such as UKIP which question the whole direction of Union policy and 'want out'.

British political parties and their reactions to the European Union: a case study

The issue of Britain's relationship with Europe, and particularly with the European Union, has been a difficult one for the two main parties. Towards the end of the twentieth century, the Conservatives found the issue seriously divisive, whereas previously it was the Labour Party which suffered internal ructions because of it.

Initially, the dispute over Europe concerned membership of the European Community. For a long while this has not been the case, although some politicians and observers do make occasional calls for withdrawal. In recent years, the questions for the parties have concerned the form the Union should take, and how to react to the initiatives and policies espoused by leading figures in other EU countries.

Labour

In the early decades after 1945, Labour was sceptical of any moves in the direction of a unified Europe. Though a few individuals were well disposed, the bulk of the party was unsympathetic to the rhetoric of Monnet and some of the other enthusiasts. They wanted nothing to do with integration, even though fellow-socialists on the other side of the Channel were much involved in the early moves. Prime Minister Attlee showed an insular approach when he wrote in 1948: 'The Labour Party is a characteristically British production, differing widely from continental socialist parties'.

The party never displayed any real interest in joining what it portrayed as a 'rich man's club', and there was great scepticism about any benefits which might accrue. In office, it made an abortive attempt to join the Union in 1967, but thereafter the question of membership proved highly divisive. These divisions were apparent in the 1975 referendum in which some ministers were allowed to campaign against continued British membership of the Community.

After Labour lost the 1987 election, policy towards Europe was reassessed at the time of the *Policy Review*. As leader, Neil Kinnock had come to admire European socialist leaders, of whom several were in office in charge of leftwing governments. They wanted to see Britain more committed to membership. Kinnock himself appreciated that having been in the Community for fifteen years there were difficulties and dangers which made it undesirable to leave. Moreover, Europe had begun to seriously divide the Conservative government. There was possible party advantage to be gained in striking a more positive note.

Above all, however, it was the visit of Jacques Delors which was the catalyst for a change in Labour thinking. When he spoke of the social dimension of the EC, Labour found itself warming to the theme. After years in which many remnants of socialism were killed off under Margaret Thatcher, Labour realised that a version of it still survived on the continent. Via the Social Charter (as it was then known), there was a chance for the labour movement as a whole to reverse the tide. After this, there was a wider recognition that democratic socialists had a role to play in the development of the Community, and the Kinnock leadership wanted to play its part.

By the early to mid-1990s, Labour was urging that Britain should play a more active role in developing European institutions and in making membership work to Britain's advantage. It was the accession to the leadership and in 1997 to the premiership of Tony Blair that finally convinced many European leaders that the party was now firmly committed to the European cause. From the beginning, Blair was keen to sound positive on Europe. Thereafter, his rhetoric and actions established him as one of the very few actively pro-European British prime ministers.

Labour has had six broad positions on Europe since the war. Cool or hostile up until the late sixties, it advocated entry in 1967, became lukewarm again in opposition after 1970, supported membership in the referendum, was sharply critical in the early 1980s and became committed to membership later in the decade. This is how it portrays itself today. Labour is now in a broadly pro-European phase, committed to making membership work to Britain's advantage.

The Conservatives

After the war, Winston Churchill's Zurich Speech and his involvement in organisations such as the United Europe Committee combined to give the impression that he was sympathetic to political and economic union. Yet despite the language, his ideas were vague and he never seriously envisaged that Britain would be a member of a united Europe. However, it was the Conservative government of Harold Macmillan which first (unsuccessfully) applied to join the Community.

Edward Heath – the man responsible for the first set of negotiations – was committed to the European cause and saw the attempt to join as something of a crusade. As prime minister, he signed the Treaty of Accession in 1972, seeing it as an historic turning point in Britain's fortunes. His Conservative successor, Margaret Thatcher, never shared his degree of commitment. She adopted a more mimimalist position. She could see the economic benefits of membership and wanted Britain to stay in the Community. However, her outlook was more of a Gaullist one for she favoured a 'Europe des Patries'. For her, the EC was what she called in her Bruges Speech 'a partnership of nation-states each retaining the right to protect its vital interests, but practising more effectively than at present the habit of working together'.

To many members of the party, her approach was seen as determined – if sometimes strident – and there was some admiration for the way she defended her country's interests as she saw them. Party critics exhibited much irritation and resentment about her manner in dealing with European leaders, which could be carping and hectoring. Ultimately, Mrs Thatcher's attitude towards Europe was her undoing, for the divisions within her party, more especially within her government, proved difficult to contain. After 1986, several of her ministers left the cabinet directly or indirectly because of policy towards the EC.

John Major appeared to be a cool pragmatist on Europe. Soon after becoming leader, he made it clear that he wished to place Britain 'at the heart of Europe', but he was aware of the potential for division inherent in the issue. His immediate task was to keep the party together in the run-up to the 1992 election. He showed some skill in terms of party management, although pro-Europeans thought that this was at the expense of giving a clear lead to the country about the direction in which he wished to see the Community develop. After the election, he had a particularly difficult course to navigate. At the same time as he was trying to convince other members of the European Council that he was a 'good European', he was also concerned to assure his own right wing that he was rolling back the influence of the EC. He courted the eurosceptics and the jingoistic vote in the country by a series of 'tough' stances towards Britain's European partners, and by so doing he sacrificed some support from pro-European Conservatives (particularly the more pro-federal MEPs) who were dismayed by his policy and approach post-Maastricht. Europe proved a seriously damaging issue for the Conservatives in the run-up to the 1997 election.

Since the electoral debacle of that year, the party has become more united over Europe around a broadly eurosceptic approach. It has supported British membership, whilst seeming lukewarm or hostile to any initiatives taken in Brussels to move the Union forward. It still supports a Europe of sovereign states and resists what it portrays as any move towards a European superstate (see pp. 284–6).

The Liberals/Alliance/Liberal Democrats

The Liberals supported closer integration and British participation in Europe long before the two main parties were prepared to take this route. Inevitably, theirs was a minority voice, and the absence of coalition politics at Westminster meant that it was rarely advanced at the top table. They supported the attempts to join the EC made by the Macmillan and Wilson governments. Later, they gave solid backing to Edward Heath in the debates over accession in the early 1970s and joined him on the pro-European side in the Referendum campaign in 1975.

Now operating as the Liberal Democrats, the party maintains the traditional Liberal support for European cooperation. The bulk of the party has retained a pro-federalist line, though there are individuals who are uneasy about the commitment to political unity exhibited by the leadership. The pro-European rhetoric was toned down by Charles Kennedy.

United Kingdom Independence Party

The United Kingdom Independence Party was formed in 1993 but only began to make a significant impact in the 2004 elections. It was the only party to campaign primarily on European issues. It stressed that it was not anti-European, but was opposed to membership of the EU which – bureaucratic and corrupt – 'stifles our initiative and threatens our freedom' and is a drain on UK resources. It had a clear, unambiguous message: withdrawal from the Union, which made it a natural vehicle for eurosceptics and voters wishing to lodge a protest vote without changing the government.

Impact of the European issue on the parties

In no other country have the parties and politicians found the European issue so difficult to handle. Just as Home Rule for Ireland was a divisive question in the 1880s and Tariff Reform was in the first decade of the twentieth century, so Europe has been in postwar years. The issue of integration has divided both parties for more than forty years, ever since the Attlee government declined to take part in the negotiations leading to the Treaty of Paris and the creation of the ECSC.

What has been remarkable about the splits within each party is not so much their longevity but rather their intensity. At various times, Europe has constituted the fault line within each party, offering the prospect of breaking it asunder. As they have had to contend with these internal divisions, the temptation for party leaders has been to adopt short-term policies which have got them off the hook until the next election was safely out of the way.

If Labour's disunity was over the actual fact of membership, the issue for the Conservatives has been different. Few felt that Britain could survive outside the Community/Union, but many were uncertain as to the sort of future they wanted inside it. Most politicians and writers agree that there is little to be gained from espousing an anti-European viewpoint today; the debate has moved on, and there is no going back. All three parties are officially in favour of 'Britain in Europe'.

Conclusion

Political parties in Europe have had to adapt to the demands of their countries' membership of the European Union. The issue has the capacity to create internal party tensions, influence domestic election outcomes and foment discussion about the degree of commitment of member states and anxieties about the pace of integration, particularly every five years when euro-elections are due to be held.

Noting the way in which previously lukewarm or even hostile parties have adapted to membership of the Union, Bomberg[10] concludes that: 'Parties need not simply lie back and "let Europe happen to them": they can [and often do] actively engage and exploit European structures for their own party political gain'.

What is emerging, in a limited way, is a European party system mainly based on the series of transnational groupings at Strasbourg. These blocs adopt common manifestos and produce brochures which set out their policies and programmes, a development which has been apparent over the last four elections and inevitably means that more attention is paid to European issues and to the debate on the future of European integration. The political groups – in cooperation with national leaderships – have been able to influence the agenda of the European Council and have built up a foundation for European political parties. As yet, the transnational parties cannot be comparable in importance or strength to national parties in the member states. But with the help now received from the European budget, they can use their funds to organise support for their positions among the inhabitants of the Union. In the long run, they might be the basis for a stronger and more inflluential European party system.

It remains the case that the overwhelming majority of MEPs are politicians from one of the national parties in their country of election. They and their parties have stood for election and campaigned as national party candidates on national – rather than European – issues. Within the blocs of the European Parliament, they often sit and act as a national contingent.

Despite repeated pleas from Brussels, in virtually no country were the last European elections fought primarily on European issues. In most cases, they descended into little more than a referendum on the government of the day. Voters had the chance to cast a protest vote against those in office and to a lesser extent against the EU in general. In several contests, much of the running during the campaign was made by eurosceptic candidates and parties, noticeably in Denmark, Poland, the Czech Republic and the Netherlands.

Glossary

Eurocommunism The name applied to a variety of communism developed by some Western European communist parties, most evidently in France, Italy and Spain. They were seeking to develop a theory and practice of social transformation that was more attuned to Western democracies and which would appeal more broadly than the Soviet-based approach.

Transnational parties Federal associations of national or regional parties from several member states of the European Union whose members are committed to permanent cooperation on the basis of an agreed political programme. In terms of their structure and *modus operandi*, as well as their ambitions and field of operations, they are transnational. As Jansen explains: 'Their terrain is the political system of the Union and their deputies belong to the same groups in the European Parliament'.[11]

CHAPTER 10

Pressure groups and the European Union

For many years, pressure groups in Europe operated at or below the level of the state. However, they have been active in the EU since its formation, playing a significant role in its political development and policy-making. In recent decades increasing interest has been shown in this 'European' dimension of their activity. As Mazey and Richardson[1] concluded: 'It is no longer possible to understand the policy process in . . . the member states of the EU . . . and especially the role of pressure groups in that process without taking account of the shift of power to Brussels'.

In this chapter, we examine some of the interest groups, promotional groups and **New Social Movements** that operate at the European level and some of the trends in group activity.

Growth of lobbying in the European Union

In recent years, pressure groups across the member states have needed to modify their traditional methods of – and targets for – lobbying, in order to cater for their closer involvement in the European Union. They recognise that Europe has played an increasing role in national politics, especially since the passing of the Single European Act. The Maastricht Agreement and the completion of the internal market moved the Union further along the route of closer integration. Today, much decision-making power has passed to Brussels. The EU is active in a range of areas well beyond those concerned with the initial creation of a tariff-free trading area.

As countries have ceded a considerable degree of decision-making power to European institutions, it is not surprising that many groups feel the need to protect and promote their interests in Brussels and Strasbourg. Many of the measures introduced over the last decade and a half have concerned the implementation of the SEA. Designed to eliminate the technical, physical and fiscal barriers to intra-Community trade, and the barriers to the free provision of professional and other services, they were and remain particularly relevant to group activity.

It is very difficult to assess how many bodies are involved in contacts with EU machinery, but all estimates suggest that the number has increased hugely in recent decades. Recent research by Gray[2] and Wessels[3] suggests that there are around 2,000 trade associations, interest groups, regions, national associations, **think tanks**, consultants and lawyers engaged in lobbying the Union. Partly this is a reflection of the growth of EU responsibilities ('competences') and the impact of the SEA and the Maastricht Treaty. But other factors include:

- *a growing understanding by groups of the importance of the European dimension and of the opportunities that exist for lobbying*. In the early years of membership, the full implications are not always appreciated, particularly by some cause groups. Moreover, activists were faced with unfamiliar decision-making machinery and it took some time for them to find their way around the European institutions and to understand their relative powers. As they acquired knowledge and experience of the EU's decision-making processes, they were able to take more advantage of lobbying opportunities.

- *the greater accessibility and receptivity of institutions such as the Commission to lobbyists.* In part, this is because the expansion of Union responsibilities under the SEA and the Maastricht Treaty means that bodies such as the Commission find that they require the knowledge, understanding and expertise that well-informed groups can provide. As a result, the Commission keeps itself open to influence. It maintains a large register of interested bodies that it will regularly consult on matters of policy development.

- *the introduction of qualified majority voting in a growing number of areas* has meant that groups wishing to exercise an influence on policy matters need to do so at an early stage in policy development. They need to gain concessions to their viewpoint as the policy is being developed, for they cannot have as much impact when it has been formulated into a directive that Britain must adopt. They have to ensure that policies they regard as hostile are defeated or modified, for once a policy is agreed by an appropriate majority there is no national veto to stop it being introduced.

- *the escalation of regional lobbying by local and state governments* (a reflection of the increased importance attached to ending regional disparities within the EU)

- *increasing lobbying by individual firms* (some of them American corporations determined that their companies should not be excluded from the single market), think tanks (often pushing their own ideas for constitutional reform) and **professional lobbyists**

- *increased interest by the media* (both in lobbying on their own behalf and in reporting on events in the Union).

Today's European Union is a larger and more high-profile organisation than it was back in the 1970s. As such, it is an obvious magnet for lobbyists.

A good example of pressure groups and their involvement is provided by the area of animal welfare and its related subjects. Some sixty EC directives in connection with the SEA had animal-health and veterinary-control implications. Others affected the veterinary profession, having implications for such things as the freedom of movement and rights of establishment of veterinary surgeons. In Britain, the British Veterinary Association and the Royal College of Veterinary Surgeons were inevitably going to be interested in such initiatives, whilst others were of relevance to the RSPCA, the NFU and the Eurogroup for Animal Welfare, now known as the Eurogroup for Animals.

Range of groups

Six main categories of pressure group that operate in the Union can be distinguished:

1. *Manufacturing groups*, ranging from large powerful pan-European **eurogroups** such as the Union of Industrial and Employers' Confederations (UNICE) to less well-known bodies such as the Hearing Aid Association, from associations with influential members such as those operating in the chemical industry to ones of growing importance in the food and drink sectors. In addition, leading multinational companies are now lobbying strongly on their own behalf, some 250 having established a base in Brussels. Many firms in the motoring industry – not just European ones – are active in lobbying the Commission. So too are companies such as GlaxoSmithKlein, IBM and Philips.

2. *Labour groups*, ranging from the European Trades Union Confederation (ETUC), an influential eurogroup, to major national umbrella groups such as the British Trades Union Congress, as well as individual trade unions such as the Transport and General Workers Union. At a time when trade unions in several countries have found the climate hostile, the EU has provided them with a useful outlet in which they can seek to slow down or even reverse what they see as excessive deregulation of labour markets and punitive anti-union legislation.

3. *Agricultural groups*, ranging from the powerful eurogroup, the Committee of Professional Agricultural Organisations (COPA), to groups representing specialised sectors such as organic farmers (e.g. the Soil Association in Britain).

4. *Professional groups*, including eurogroups representing national law, medical and veterinary associations, as well as individual law firms. Bodies such as the British Medical Association (BMA) and the Law Society are much involved in lobbying the Commission and to a lesser extent Parliament. They are in the business of defending the interests of their members and have come to recognise that these can be advanced in Brussels. The Law Society has many members who work in the Union. The BMA has established committees to monitor developments there. In both cases, the Single European Act was relevant to their operations, especially in relation to the harmonisation of professional qualifications across the EU.

5. *Public interest groups*, ranging from think tanks such as the European Policy Centre to organisations such as the European Blind Union, from environmental bodies such as Greenpeace and the World Wide Fund for Nature (WWF) to organisations such as Human Rights Watch and the European Youth Forum. The EU decision-making processes provide greater access to a

number of promotional **outsider groups** that normally lack influence in the inner circle of Whitehall.

6. *Governmental organisations*, including more than 160 accredited non-EU embassies and delegations (e.g. the United States Embassy), as well as regional governments (e.g. the German Länder) and local authorities, some of which are very active on the European scene (e.g. Birmingham).

Targets for pressure-group campaigners

Pressure groups in any member state can adopt either of two strategies:

1. They can choose the national route, lobbying their own national government in the hope that it will take a stand on their behalf in the Council of Ministers. For some groups this is the most effective form of lobbying, because:
   - it is less expensive for any group than lobbying directly in Europe on their own; and
   - if they belong to a eurogroup they may find that their counterparts from other countries do not share their viewpoint.
2. They can pursue the European route. This European strategy may involve working through a eurogroup which represents national pressure groups from across the member states. Or it may involve making contact directly with the personnel who work in EU institutions such as the Commission and Parliament. More than a thousand lobbying groups have their own office in Brussels from which they can more closely monitor developments and policies emanating from the Union machinery.

Many groups take advantage of both the national and European routes.

EU access points

In some policy areas, member states have ceded a considerable degree of decision-making power to Brussels, whereas in others there has been a strong desire to retain national responsibility. Groups go to the seat of power, but the location of that power varies according to the issue being discussed. On agricultural and environmental matters, there is every point in lobbying EU machinery. On economic and defence policy, there is much more to be gained from lobbying in the national capitals.

Whatever the strategy adopted, the targets for lobbyists in the EU machinery are many and diverse, not just the obvious bodies such as the Commission, Council and Parliament. Decision-making in the Union is 'a complex, **multi-level** process',[4] so that lobbyists need to be prepared to seek influence at more than one level. They have to decide where they think power resides in the resolution of particular types of issue.

Lobbying the EU can be carried out at several **access points**, including the:

- Council of Ministers and COREPER
- Commission (commissioners and especially the Commission officials)
- Parliament (and its committees and party groupings)
- Economic and Social Committee
- Court of Justice.

Target institutions for lobbyists

Although the *Council of Ministers* is the most powerful institution within the Union, it is not the usual focus for most pressure groups. They find it difficult to obtain access to its members when they are assembled and it usually operates in a secretive manner. Any group wishing to influence its proceedings normally does so via pressure at the national level (in the British case, in Whitehall) or through permanent groups in Brussels such as COREPER or UKREP. An alternative approach, in the days of QMV, is for members of a national group to persuade their counterparts in a eurogroup to place pressure on their national government representative in the Council, the hope being that this will create a blocking minority to thwart a proposal they dislike.

Usually, the *Commission* is the prime target for pressure-group activists. As a relatively open bureaucracy it welcomes approaches from interested parties. It maintains a list of several hundred bodies whose spokespersons it automatically consults on matters relating to technical legislation. In particular, it has dealings with several eurogroups that are favoured because they represent a wide span of opinion. Under-resourced itself, the Commission values the specialist knowledge and expertise that groups can provide. Its regard for such consultation is evident from a passage in its 2001 White Paper *Governance* which suggests a strengthening of the partnership between itself and civil society, comprising as it does nowadays a myriad of voluntary associations and activist groups.

The role of the Commission is paramount, for it proposes Union policy and legislation, and then it implements decisions when they are taken by the Council. It also supervises the day-to-day execution of EU policy and manages the Common Agricultural Policy. It does not conceal the fact that initiatives are being planned and considered, rather it welcomes an input from pressure groups at an early stage since they can explain what is necessary and feasible. Such consultation provides the Commission with a response, however unconvincing, to the charge that there is a serious democratic deficit within the European Union. It can claim that the views of groups representing a large section of European electorates are being taken on board.

Much of the contact with the Commission involves routine meetings with officials or discussions on the phone. Some directorates general are particularly receptive to representations. Commission officials are an obvious target for group activity, for this is the institution from which many proposals emerge. Communication with individual commissioners is relatively infrequent and may be less useful than regular dialogue with the officials engaged in the development of policy. However, commissioners have a small cabinet of officials serving them and lobbying can be done with the 'chefs de cabinet' who meet prior to the weekly meetings of the Commission.

Commission officials in the directorates general are in great demand. Most are willing to meet representatives of various groups, although they have to balance the consultative aspect of their work with the need to complete other tasks. Bomberg and Stubb[5] quote one official who observed:

> Sometimes people want to see the new text [of a proposal] every time a comma is changed in a draft directive. That is unrealistic. The one big problem with consultation is that it lengthens the process. You need to balance efficiency with respect for democratic values . . . If we can get the consultation structured and put draft documents on the Internet, then everyone should benefit. It is also important that other organisations should be able to see who is in contact with the Commission.

Once agreement has been reached in the Council, the legal validity of regulations and directives can still be challenged in the *Court of Justice*. The Court is of growing significance to lobbyists, given its role of interpreting and enforcing Union legislation. British environmental groups have in the past lobbied its members in connection with the quality of drinking water. Women's groups have used it to win supportive rulings on equal pay, as in 1998 when several thousand British NHS female employees gained a decision in their favour. Trade unions benefited from a Court of Justice judgment against governmental policy on the Working Time Directive. As a result of the decision, some 4m British workers gained extra holiday benefits. Other recent examples of the involvement of the ECJ include the use made of it by lesbian and gay rights groups.

In recent years, euro and other groups have begun to attach more importance to the *European Parliament* and its committees. Its influence and legislative powers have increased considerably as a result of recent treaties such as the SEA and Maastricht, thereby enhancing its attractiveness to pressure groups. Although still much less significant than the Commission, groups representing animal-welfare interests, environmentalists and consumers have come to recognise its developing importance. They actively lobby one of the most powerful of Parliament's twenty standing committees: the one covering the Environment, Public Health and Consumer Protection. Parliament is the obvious focus for those who lack the ready access to the Commission enjoyed by many influential business groups.

Members of the European Parliament expect to be lobbied, whether they are meeting for plenary sessions in Strasbourg, in the Brussels committees or within their constituencies back home. Grant[6] has pointed out that MEPs belonging to **Intergroups** are much lobbied by groups representing a wide variety of interests. Intergroups operate across the boundaries of the different party groupings and member states, and espouse a range of diverse causes. There are some sixty of them, 'covering subjects such as financial services, pharmaceuticals, defence industries and small and medium-sized enterprises'. Other examples range from the Federalist Intergroup for European Union and the Friends of Israel to the Animal Welfare Group and the Media Intergroup.

Some groups use a number of different avenues when lobbying Europe. They may use a professional agency (see p. 183), tackle their own national officials and ministers, and also adopt a Brussels/Strasbourg/Luxembourg strategy. From the above, it can be seen that Brussels is the main seat of influence, for this is where the Commission has its headquarters. The committees of the European Parliament and meetings of party groups also take place there. However, Strasbourg, the seat of Parliament, has become another significant location.

Lobbying of the EU in Brussels and Strasbourg tends to be lower key and more discreet and informal than it is in Washington or many other capital cities, where it can be aggressive and visible. Lobbyists need to be sensitive to a wide range of languages, the more so since the Fifth Enlargement (Central and Eastern part i). They also need to be able to argue a powerful case. This will impress, for the EU's institutions are often lacking in the resources available to their closest equivalents in other major national capitals. The combination of public institutions desperate to acquire expertise and fewer providers of such information means that lobbyists have a real opportunity to influence policy decisions. By gathering, processing and disseminating reliable material, they can open many doors in Brussels and Strasbourg.

Direct action is less apparent as a means of persuading the European Union to adjust its policies than it is in member states. There may be spasmodic protests at meetings of the European Council, but generally speaking groups protest against the government back home even if there is an EU connection with what is being discussed. Many protests against the EU are not carried out by the new social movements who feature in much of today's national and international protest action. Often, they are organised by occupational interest groups such as farmers and fishermen who feel that their livelihoods are being threatened by EU-instigated policies.

Eurogroups

As we have seen, eurogroups are federations of national pressure groups. They started to spring up as soon as the original European Economic Community was created. Today, there are in excess of 700, mostly based in Brussels, though some are centred in other continental cities such as Cologne and Paris. The best-organised and largest sector represents the interests of employers. Many represent agriculture and food interests, with others dealing with such issues as

Box 10.1 A dual strategy for lobbying the EU: the RSPCA at work

Since the 1970s, much of the legislation on animal protection in the United Kingdom has been enacted by the European Community/Union. Examples include regulations concerning the transport of wild, farm and laboratory animals. This is a trading activity carried out in several countries and across borders. It involves other industries such as farming, slaughter, scientific research and the sale of animals as pets or public zoo exhibits. As a result of successive EU treaties, the Union's capacity to deal with issues such as these has been increased. Nearly all of the legislation on farm animals derives from the Union. So too, the Union has tackled issues of the protection of native wild animals and their habitats.

Not surprisingly, the EU is an extremely important part of RSPCA campaigning. It lobbies at several levels:

- the Council of Ministers and the permanent representatives in COREPER and UKREP; influence with the Council is often secured via meetings with the relevant British ministers in Whitehall
- the Commission and – at times – the British commissioner
- the Parliament, its committees and sympathetic MEPs
- the Eurogroup for Animals.

The RSPCA now has an office in Brussels, run by the umbrella Eurogroup for Animals, a federation of national pressure groups in the field of animal welfare. The group has important contacts with the Commission Secretariat and with relevant directorates general. Liaison with DG VI (agriculture) and DG XI (environment) is ongoing, but periodically approaches have been made to the DGs responsible for enlargement, enterprise, fisheries, health and consumer protection, regional policy, and research and trade.

Via its office, the RSPCA has been particularly active over recent years in seeking to improve, apply and enforce animal welfare standards in the newly enlarged European Union of twenty-seven countries, aware as it is that standards of care have varied considerably in the more recently admitted member states. In preparation for the Fifth Enlargements parts i and ii, the Eurogroup for Animals drew up an accession action programme that led to the establishment of links with national animal protection organisations and governments in the candidate countries, and monitoring of the accession negotiations between the candidates and the European institutions.

consumerism, environmentalism and labour matters. In the early 1990s, Baggott[7] found that three-quarters of the British groups surveyed belonged to such eurogroups.

These eurogroups can be used in several ways:

- to strengthen the case a group wishes to promote
- to put pressure on the government of another EU country to modify its own position

- to influence counterpart organisations in other countries, so that they might lobby their own government and collectively lobby the Commission.

Eurogroups are vital two-way channels of communication between the Union machinery and national groups. On the one hand, they keep the national groups informed of Union proposals. On the other, they represent these groups to the Union. For instance, the Commission provides the European Environment Agency (EEA) with legitimacy and recognition, as well as information that member groups can use in their campaigns. Via the EEA, groups can put across their messages, offering specialist information, including details of inadequate compliance or even non-compliance with EU legislation in member states. The Commission is the main focus of attention for eurogroups, although in as much as resources permit such groups also seek to influence the Parliament and ESC.

Some eurogroups are umbrella organisations, covering companies in a vast sector such as agriculture (the Committee of Professional Agricultural Organisations). Others represent specific business groups such as the Organisation of Pasta Manufacturers of the European Union and the European Starch Producers. To illustrate what eurogroups can achieve, Grant[8] has quoted the example of the British Spice Trade Association which, via the ESA, was able to gain special exemptions for herbs and spices from amendments to the Unit Pricing Directive.

The effectiveness of eurogroups can be influenced by:

- the lack of resources, of which staffing is but one problem. Many eurogroups are small-scale operations with only a handful of permanent staff and become more active only when an issue of relevance to them assumes importance. Very few have the resources to campaign over a long period; Butt Philip[9] identified only 5/500 which had ten or more permanent staff.
- problems of communication, which – given their diverse membership – can be time-consuming and costly for those with meagre funding
- the diversity of their membership. It can be difficult for large umbrella organisations to maintain internal cohesion and present a common front. COPA has had particular problems in managing the various groups that make up the agricultural lobbies of member states, most obviously because of the differing viewpoints they adopt towards the desirability or otherwise of the CAP. ETUC, the trade union eurogroup, has sometimes experienced problems in reconciling the divergent views of Christian, communist and socialist trade unions. The temptation for such broad groups is to water down proposals so that they command as wide an area of agreement as possible. In the process, their effectiveness can be compromised. The task is much easier for more narrowly focused eurogroups, for instance those dealing with a specific industry such as the ESA (above), the European Cocoa Association and the Savings Bank Group.

Box 10.2 Three eurogroups at work

Eurogroup for Animals

A non-governmental organisation that identifies areas of concern in the treatment of animals and lobbies for the introduction and enforcement of legislation in the European Union. It provides advice and expertise on animal welfare to the main European institutions, particularly the Council of Ministers, the European Parliament and the European Commission, and seeks to ensure that animal welfare is taken into account in all relevant European policy areas and that European laws designed to protect animals are adopted and enforced.

For more than twenty-five years it has represented the leading animal welfare organisations of the EU, speaking for them and for people in Europe who are concerned about the way animals are treated. Its close cooperation with the Commission and Parliament has led to a number of important achievements which have contributed to the development and adoption of some of the highest legal standards of animal protection in the world. It helped to secure the inclusion of a protocol on animal welfare in the Amsterdam Treaty.

Eurogroup for Animals has been closely following the enlargement negotiations of recent years and working to ensure that the *acquis communautaire* on animal welfare is properly transposed, implemented and enforced in the new and applicant member states.

The Federation of Veterinarians of Europe (FVE)

An umbrella organisation for forty-four national veterinary bodies located across thirty-four European countries. Two UK groups belong to it: the British Veterinary Association and the Royal College of Veterinary Surgeons. There is a central office in Brussels, comprising five people of whom three are veterinarians involved in work on lobbying files and two are administrative staff.

The FVE aims to inform its members of what is happening within Union organisations and also does lobbying work on behalf of the profession. For instance, when new legislation on veterinary inspectors is drafted, headquarters circulates the proposal to member organisations, forms an ad hoc working group of experts, prepares and adopts a position paper and then begins lobbying the Commission, Parliament and the Council. In particular, with the Commission, work begins as soon as possible. Often, it invites the FVE's opinion in advance of releasing its draft proposals for legislation.

Currently, the main preoccupations of the FVE are:

- veterinary education and professional recognition
- animal health and welfare
- food safety
- good veterinary practice
- enlargement of the Union and its implications.

The Union of Industrial and Employers' Confederations of Europe (UNICE)

A Brussels-based European association of industries and employers founded in 1958 to drive the creation of the European Union as a free-trade zone. Together with the Federation of European Employers and the European Round Table of

Industrialists, UNICE has been one of the principal advocates of EU treaties prior to their negotiation and one of the major backers of the international European movement.

UNICE's purpose is:

- to keep abreast of issues that interest its members by maintaining permanent contacts with all the European institutions
- to provide a framework which enables industry and employers to examine European policies and proposed legislation, and to prepare joint positions
- to promote its policies and positions at Community and national level, and persuade the European legislators to take them into account.

UNICE operates via seven main policy committees, dealing with issues such as Economic and Financial Affairs, Industrial Affairs, Social Affairs and International Relations. Working groups – comprising experts nominated by the member federations – debate proposed EU legislation and come to a consensus view of the impact on enterprise of particular proposals. The views are issued as official UNICE positions in 100 or so papers every Bold denotes glossary entry

Box 10.3 Why the European Union is important to ETUC

The European Trade Union Confederation (ETUC) was set up in 1973 to promote the interests of working people at European level and to represent them in the EU institutions. It is one of the European social partners and is recognised by the European Union, the Council of Europe and EFTA as the only representative cross-sectoral trade union organisation at European level.

'The process of European integration, with the euro, the European Constitution, and the growing impact of EU legislation on daily life, has changed the setting in which trade unions operate. To defend and bargain for their members effectively at national level, they must coordinate activities and policies across Europe. To influence the economy and society at large, they need to speak with a single voice and act collectively at European level. This is the challenge that the European Trade Union Confederation has taken up. The ETUC's objective is an EU with a strong social dimension that safeguards the wellbeing of all its citizens. Committed to building a unified European trade union movement, it already had a large number of new trade union affiliates in Central and Eastern Europe before EU enlargement in May 2004'.

Extract from ETUC website

Many eurogroups draw their membership from only a few states, which can undermine their claims to be representative of European opinion. By contrast, large umbrella groups cover the whole Union, some having a membership that is not EU-specific. UNICE's membership extends to thirty-nine national organisations from across thirty-three countries, enabling it to claim to be 'the voice of

European Business and Industry'. This scale of support across the continent is beneficial in that it enables such bodies to draw upon the experience and backing of business or labour across a wide front. But it makes it even more difficult to reach an acceptable common position. There is the additional risk that in operating on a wider scale, such groups' focus on EU institutions is weakened.

Recent trends in EU lobbying

The most obvious trend has been the growth in the number and influence of organised interests operating within the Union, as already outlined. Bomberg and Stubb[10] have noted that 'different types of interests have congregated in Brussels in a series of waves', reflecting 'the deepening and widening of the European Union itself'. In the 1960s, the dominant actors represented commercial interests and agriculture. Employer – and later labour and consumer – interests followed and by the 1980s more public-interest organisations had European representation. Trade associations and remaining professional associations became more active in Europe after the passage of the SEA with the prospect of a single market. Some large companies also began to open their own offices in Brussels and take an interest in its decisions.

Particularly significant in recent years has been the increase in the lobbying carried out by regional and local governments, ranging from the German Länder to the Scottish and Northern Irish Executives and the Welsh Assembly. The development of cohesion (a policy concerned to reduce regional economic disparities) under the SEA and the formation of the Committee of the Regions under the Maastricht Treaty both pointed to increased EU concern for Europe's regional diversity and discrepancies. Representatives of such authorities have their eyes firmly set on the prospect of special funding for their pet regional and social projects, but they are also interested in environmental policies and EU programmes for social inclusion, support for business and cultural and tourism activities. The Brussels delegations of regional and local authorities maintain close links with all institutions, collaborating with appropriate commissioners or staff of the directorates-general, and with sympathetic MEPs. The Committee of the Regions has estimated their number at around 190.

Think tanks have also multiplied, although their numbers are more modest and their resources more limited than many of those operating in Washington DC, London or several other capital cities. Other areas of growth include environmental, animal rights, public health and human rights groups, the increase reflecting growing EU interest and responsibilities in these areas.

The various groups have in recent years extended their lobbying to institutions other than the European Commission, which was always the primary target of their activities. The European Parliament has gained additional powers, giving it a more significant role in policy-making (e.g. via co-decision). The Court of Justice has been used to resolve a number of issues: in Britain, the National Union of Mineworkers and the Law Society have taken up causes such as pit closures and legal aid; and individual firms in the airline and car industries have taken cases to Luxembourg in protest against regulations that adversely affected their interests. In addition, the Committee of the Regions, the Economic and Social Committee and some other bodies have provided further access points to the Union.

As lobbyists have acquired more knowledge and experience of the decision-making processes and the role of key institutions, so they see the advantage of making contact with the personnel who work in them. Those who work within policy networks can also be identified. Policy networks have come to play an important part in sectors such as agriculture, chemicals, pharmaceuticals and technology. More often than not, they are wide and loose issue networks, rather than smaller policy communities in which relationships are close and continuous. The impact of any group may vary from time to time and issue to issue, partly depending on the expertise it possesses. Peterson[11] points out that as the EU has become a more important tier of governance in Europe, so 'EU policy networks have become a more important link between states and societies. A considerable amount of EU decision-making now occurs within policy networks'. This development is associated with the vagueness of some intergovernmental agreements that left the Commission and the groups with whom it had dealings a role in 'filling in the gaps'.

The other main development over the last decade has been the increased professionalisation of lobbying. As Bomberg and Stubb point out:

> the art of lobbying has come a long way in the EU. In the view of one heavily lobbied MEP: 'Now, we have far higher skills and standards in the lobbying industry. You very rarely get the utter fool you would have encountered some years ago'.[12]

The Commission values well-presented, highly specialised information and lobbyists need to demonstrate their expertise and carefully tailor their data and advice. Increasingly, they make links with other like-minded lobbyists, and establish alliances and networks across institutions and nationalities. E-mail has been used to develop and sustain dialogue with Commission officials and parliamentarians. It is used extensively by eurogroups, as they seek to maintain contact with their wide and highly dispersed membership.

'Professionalisation' does not refer only to improvements in the techniques of lobbying and the more skilful presentation of information. It also refers to the marked growth in the employment of professional lobbyists at the EU level. For a substantial fee, lobbying firms will monitor developments on particular areas of policy, arrange meetings and help groups prepare impressive presentations. Such lobbyists usually have access to key personnel within the institutions. Many groups are content to pay them generously for the opportunities of increased influence that these contacts provide.

Box 10.4 Policy communities and issue networks

The concept of policy networks has attracted much attention in recent years. They describe the different kinds of relationships between groups and government. The term is a generic one denoting a continuum from close and stable policy communities to looser, more open and discontinuous policy or issue networks.

Policy communities were characterised by close, mutually supportive ties, based on a stable relationship between participants and a high degree of contact. They have begun to decay in most democracies as other players have become involved in discussion of a policy area, including research institutes and the media. Commentators now often speak of issue networks. These are wider and looser, and are characterised by a more open style of policy-making.

Policy communities and issue networks in the EU

As a means of organising the policy-making process, policy communities and issue networks are just as useful within the Union as they are in individual countries. But Martin Smith[13] points to the paradox that the very characteristics they possess that make them an asset in the EU can make them harder to create. They are useful because Union policy-making is complex and multi-level; they are difficult to establish because of:

- the huge variety of conflicting interests that come from a wider range of countries
- the relative smallness of the Brussels bureaucracy compared to national bureaucracies
- the degree of openness of European institutions such as the Commission.

Such networks exist in almost every policy area. The best known policy community coves agricultural policy; this has tended to be a closed policy community in which farmers' groups work closely with DG VI of the Commission. They have traditionally placed the emphasis on production, often at the expense of consumer and environmental considerations. The same domination extends to chemical and technology policy-making. In other policy areas such as the environment, issue networks operate, characterised as they are by numerous players, constantly changing membership and conflictual rather than consensual relationships. Such issue networks became more important from the late 1980s onwards, as the Union enlarged its area of competence.

Influence of pressure groups within the EU

What distinguishes the Union from most national governments are the apparent openness of its institutions to those promoting sectional interests and the willingness of officials to talk to any lobbyist beyond just a few favoured groups. As Mazey and Richardson[14] observe: 'The very willingness of officials to talk to groups and individual firms means that the market for policy ideas is much more broad and fluid than in the UK'.

Lobbyists from well-resourced groups who are armed with an expert brief are likely to be more effective than those who represent underfunded organisations. Mark Aspinwall[15] has lamented this unequal distribution of resources and argued that it is damaging to EU policy-making if wealthy private interests are at an advantage over smaller, public bodies that cannot afford to employ professional agencies or commit extensive funding to their activities. Steven McGiffen[16] has expressed similar views, in his case stressing how the huge lobbying efforts of large industrial concerns have been directed to watering down any measures that impose high standards. Such lobbies point to the over-restrictive nature of regulations that would be expensive to implement and might endanger employment. McGiffen is particularly concerned at the way in which well-funded multinational organisations have sought to use their substantial influence to persuade MEPs to allow experimentation with genetically modified crops and to avoid introducing punitive environmental restrictions:

> Although the environmentalist lobby in Brussels is highly active and well-organised, it cannot compete with the massively funded disinformation machine employed by corporations. For **NGOs** which form the umbrella European Environmental Bureau, success might bring good publicity and help to recruit members or boost fundraising. For a corporation, the success or failure of an amendment to a directive can mean millions of euros.

But against this viewpoint, others claim that at least the Union provides another channel through which lobbying may be conducted. Organisations that do not have much access to decision-makers on the national scene may find that the European outlet offers alternative scope. Studies by Wallace and Young[17] and Peterson[18] have both suggested that lobbyists concerned with environmentalism, consumerism and women's rights have all had more opportunity to pursue their cause at the European level, perhaps by forging informal alliances with members of the Commission, Parliament or Court. Similarly, British trade-union leaders who found themselves excluded from the corridors of power in the Thatcher/Major years 1979–97 turned to Brussels as a means of achieving the measures of worker protection to which they were committed.

Inevitably, in any discussion of pressure groups, there is an assessment of their merits or otherwise, the question being asked whether they are a hindrance or a help to the workings of the democratic system. Whatever the verdict, their growth in number and range in Europe was inevitable, the more so as the Union expanded its area of competence. It is inconceivable that there can be any return to the days before lobbying took root on such a vast scale, for a myriad of national and eurogroups see the EU as an arena in which to exert their influence and/or proclaim their views.

Against the lobbyists, critics stress the imbalances referred to above, with some groups more powerful than others, the voice of producers often proving more influential than that of consumers – most obviously in the agrarian sphere. They also point to the time taken up by meetings between officials and group representatives, a problem that develops with the proliferation of campaigning bodies and with successive enlargements. Either the meetings become shorter and less valuable or there is less time for officials to spend on the development, administration and implementation of EU policies.

In their favour, lobbyists provide specialist information to those who develop Union policy. There are now few topics within the Union's area of responsibility on which expert advice and data are not available. As a result, the views of the European peoples are conveyed to the policy-makers, allowing a healthy channel of communication between the voters – many of whom feel 'left out' and alienated from Union institutions – and ensuring that policies that finally emerge are broadly in step with popular opinion. This may seem a healthy antidote to the elitism that characterised the early growth of the European Community, when decisions were made 'top-down' rather than 'bottom-up'.

Conclusion

More and more pressure groups are operating at the European as well as the domestic level, a recognition of the importance of multi-level governance to many countries today. Interest groups within the member states have played an important role in the processes of the European Union ever since its foundation. Agricultural and business interests were later joined by consumer and labour ones. More recently, cause groups and NSMs have recognised opportunities at the European level.

The intensification of group activity came about as a result of the passage of the Single European Act, which greatly extended the scope of policy-making by the Community and changed the nature of decision-making in ways that provided more opportunities for lobbyists to conduct their operations. Today, some groups take the national route, others the European route. Most target the Commission, but the Council of Ministers, Parliament and Court of Justice are all useful access points for lobbyists seeking to convey their concerns and opinions. The choice of target largely depends upon the nature of the organisation and the institution that seems most appropriate for the particular issue involved.

Glossary

Access points Those parts of the governmental structure which are accessible to pressure-group influence.
Direct action Any action beyond the usual constitutional and legal framework, such as obstructing access to a building or impeding the construction of a motorway; terrorism is an extreme form. Essentially, it is an attempt to coerce those in authority into doing something they would not otherwise do.

Eurogroups Federations of national pressure groups that represent sectoral interests within several, if not all, the member states of the EU.

Intergroups Often relatively informal groups of MEPs who share similar concerns and interests and periodically meet to discuss them. Altogether, there are more than a hundred of them. Of the much smaller number which regularly hold sessions, the Animal Welfare, AntiRacism and Diversity, Friends of Israel, Gay and Lesbian Rights, Media and Elderly People Intergroups are better-known examples. Much less prominent is the Friends of Tibet Intergroup.

Multi-level process The way the British political system operates in today's multiple layers of government. It is no longer the Westminster system of the past, with institutions and powers concentrated in London. There are various tiers of government, with the European Union at the top, then the UK government, the devolved bodies and local administration, plus a number of unelected **quangos** that also exercise considerable power.

New Social Movements Organisations that have emerged since the 1960s in order to influence public policy on broad issues such as the environment, nuclear energy, peace and women's rights. They have wider interests and are more loosely organised than most pressure groups, tend to have supporters rather than members and do not operate via detailed involvement with government. They are concerned to bring about fundamental change in society.

NGOs A term often applied to non-profit-making voluntary sector bodies to indicate that they are formally separate from government, even if their campaigning activities are directed at influencing ministerial policy. The nomenclature is favoured by many cause group representatives in the environmental and aid sectors in preference to 'pressure groups', which has overtones of intimidation or inappropriate influence.

Outsider groups Groups that either do not wish to have or cannot acquire consultative status with policy-makers. They tend to shun the political mainstream. Examples are Compassion in World Farming and the various human rights bodies.

Professional lobbyists Those who lobby on behalf of specialist organisations that offer to influence policy and effect high-level contracts, in exchange for payment. Often, the lobbyists use contacts made during an earlier career in Parliament or ministerial office as a bait with which to attract business. Many companies and large, well-resourced groups may employ a professional lobbying firm, in addition to conducting their own campaigning.

Quangos Formerly known in full as quasi-autonomous non-governmental organisations, quangos are now often referred to as quasi-governmental or non-departmental public bodies. They are financed by the government to perform some public service function but operate at arm's length from government, allowing management flexibility and political independence.

Think tanks Organisations formed to research and develop policy proposals, and campaign for their acceptance among opinion-formers and policy-makers. They are often ideologically based, their ideas sometimes being influential with the parties with which they share a broad affinity (e.g. the Institute of Public Policy Research and the Labour Party in the United Kingdom).

SECTION FOUR: POLICIES

Introduction

The European Union has evolved over time from a primarily economic community to an increasingly political one. This trend is highlighted by the increasing number of policy areas that fall within its competence: political power has tended to shift upwards from the member states to the EU.

EU policy areas cover a number of different forms of cooperation:

*   *Autonomous decision-making*: member states have granted the European Commission power to issue decisions in certain areas such as competition law, state aid control and liberalisation.
*   *Harmonisation*: member-state laws are harmonised through the EU legislative process, which involves the European Commission, European Parliament and Council of the European Union. As a result of this, European Union law is increasingly present in the systems of the member states.
*   *Co-operation*: member states, meeting as the Council of the European Union, agree to cooperate and coordinate their domestic policies.

All prospective members must enact legislation in order to bring them into line with the common European Union legal framework, the *acquis communautaire*.

What the Union does: past and present

The Treaty of Rome alludes to three areas of policy as 'common' ones: those involving agriculture (Article 43), commerce (Article 113) and transport (Article 74). In addition, there are other references to 'common policies', but it was in the later treaties that the term 'Community policy' began to appear. Initially, the emphasis on the Community was upon the development of a common market free of trading barriers and this aspect is still of fundamental importance. The common Commercial Policy, Competition Policy and the Single European Act are all related to the promotion of what used to be called the Common Market, a label some people still employ when they refer to the Union.

Today, the EU is much more than a common market, for it was always the intention that close cooperation would extend into other sectors. Some of these are economic policies related to tackling wider issues than those of tariffs and their elimination. Others go well beyond the economic and financial spheres, and deal with matters ranging from foreign policy to immigration, from broadcasting to combating crime. The Union has an impact on policies covering so many areas of governmental activity, from agriculture to the movement of goods and services, from justice and home affairs to issues of national security, that it is fair to say that it has a considerable impact on the lives of people across the twenty-seven states. Indeed, given the expansion that has occurred as a result of successive enlargements, its policies now directly affect the inhabitants of almost two-thirds of the European continent.

Level of Union involvement in policy areas

Just as the range of policies undertaken by the Union is a wide one, so is the degree to which the EU becomes involved in their management. In some areas, such as agriculture, industry and trade, many important decisions are now taken at European level, which is why national pressure groups spend so much of their time on European policy. In others, including some of those dealt with in the second and third (intergovernmental) pillars of the Maastricht Treaty, EU involvement is increasing. This is also the case with many aspects of social policy, particularly those relating to labour relations, working conditions and employment practices more generally. In a few areas, there is little or no Union involvement in national policy. This is true of issues relating to policy on education, health, pension and social welfare, as well as to some matters affecting the personal and moral outlook of Europe's citizens, such as policy on abortion and alcohol consumption.

Overall, there is scope for tension between EU and national (or subnational) competence. This has been an enduring feature of the development of the European Union. The position as regards responsibility for different policy areas is summarised in the table below.

The EU is not a giant superstate determining the outcome of all areas of policy. Rather, as is the experience in federal countries, its citizens have become used to the idea that different tiers of government exercise different functions. The responsibility for policy is shared between the Union and the nation states. However, the trend in recent years has been for Brussels to become more involved in many spheres, including some in which its role was once limited. Monetary policy has over the last decade assumed more importance in the lives of Europe's citizens, because decisions affect Europeans in thirteen countries who use the same currency. On defence, foreign policy and the environment too, the European machinery now has more of a role than was the case even in the 1990s, and many of the policies dealt with under the heading of Justice and Home Affairs had only very limited Community involvement pre-Maastricht. The extent to which adoption of the concept of subsidiarity involves any reversal of this broad trend has yet to become fully apparent, although so far few issues that have been within the competence of Brussels in recent years have ceased to be so.

The picture is then a patchy one, with the nature and extent of EU involvement in policy-making differing from issue to issue. In some areas, national

Table S4I.1 Level of EU involvement in a range of key policy areas

Policy area	Much involvement	Joint involvement	Little/no involvement
Agriculture	*		
Fishing	*		
Trade	*		
Drugs		*	
Environment		*	
Regions		*	
Working conditions		*	
Foreign affairs and security		*	
Education			*
Health			*
Housing			*
Welfare			*

NB Defence policy was not on the agenda a generation ago, but today there is limited involvement. In the whole area of foreign and security policy, the trend is towards greater EU interest.

governments have been more willing to relinquish some of their capacity to determine policy than in others. The representatives of any country inevitably have to ask themselves what benefits are to be derived from a common approach and to balance possible gains for Europe as a whole against pressing national considerations. They also have to bear in mind what public opinion at home will stand.

Eurobarometer has regularly polled people across the Union to ascertain their views about which policy areas are best decided in Brussels and which are better handled by national governments. The findings usually indicate that they prefer Europe-wide decision-making in those areas where the problems cross or go beyond national boundaries (the fight against drugs, the environment and overseas aid), and national action on issues where the decisions impact upon them more directly (education and health). Broadly, such findings are in line with the reality of existing practice, for the emphasis upon subsidiarity stresses that decisions are best taken at the most appropriate level. Those that require a cooperative approach tend to derive from Brussels; those which can be taken closer to the citizen are made by national or in some cases regional governments.

In *Eurobarometer* poll 61, conducted early in 2004, it was found that of those interviewed 61 per cent across the EU thought it desirable for the Union to have a common foreign policy, 72 per cent a common defence and security policy. Of the issues that mostly concerned voters in the run-up to the elections of that year, employment, immigration and the fight against crime were seen as the most important, with the environment, citizens' rights, agriculture, defence and foreign policy trailing after them.

Impact of Union involvement

The effectiveness of Union action also varies considerably. Even where there is a substantial degree of Brussels involvement, it does not follow that the best policy is promoted. Part of the difficulty lies in deciding what is best for the Union and what is best for individual nation states. Members have their own traditions and preferences, and the fight to maintain and protect national interests in particular policy areas can make it difficult to achieve a genuinely coordinated and consistent EU approach. Nugent[1] concludes that the pace, manner and effectiveness of advance depends on three factors:

1. '*The leadership given by the Commission*'. Some presidents, such as Walter Hallstein (1958–66), Roy Jenkins (1977–80) and Jacques Delors (1985–94), imparted their own enthusiasms and imposed a personal style on the Commission. They were particularly effective in galvanising the Community into action, taking up new initiatives and seeing them through to implementation.
2. '*The perceptions of the member states of what is desirable*'. Representatives of national governments have to be convinced that there are significant gains to be made from acting together, gains not just for the Union as a whole but that coincide with a substantial measure of national self-interest. With the introduction and increasing use of majority voting, it is not necessary for all states to perceive the advantages.
3. '*The individual and collective capacities of the member states to translate their perceptions into practice*'. Even if there is a sympathetic response to a particular initiative, the ministers of any country may feel unenthusiastic about supporting it in the Council of Ministers. Domestic political pressures can make it difficult for them, so that any French or German government is going to think twice

before it supports measures that could lessen the prosperity of its farmers, just as British ministers have been under enormous pressure from trawlermen over recent years to provide better protection for the domestic fishing fleet. Sometimes it is necessary for governments to concede, but negotiators need to show that they have earned some trophies in the negotiations before they yield to the pressure of other Council members.

CHAPTER 11

The Union Budget

Budgetary issues are highly relevant to the discussion of policies within the Union. It administers common laws between the member states and expenditure on common policies throughout the EU. To pay for this the Union has an agreed budget of €862 billion for the period 2007–13.

In this chapter, it is appropriate to cover EU revenue and expenditure and the contributions expected of member states before we move on to examine specific policy areas later in the section.

The EU's budget is in actual fact rather small. Most of its outlays are determined years in advance and the majority go on just two policies: support for farmers and support for poorer regions. Yet the negotiations over the budget invariably spark off acrimonious debate and a degree of scrutiny out of all proportion to their economic significance. Representatives of member states dig in their heels about who will pay and how much, and who will benefit during the next medium-term budget plan, known as the 'financial perspective'.

To put the figures into perspective, the EU's 2005 budget amounted to €106b euro or £73b, the equivalent of only 1 per cent of the member states' combined gross national income. National budgets in the EU typically amount to 45–50 per cent of national income, allocated between national, regional or local government. Again, the Union has a budget thirty times less than that of the US federal government, despite having a population which is more than 50 per cent larger than that of the United States.

Of the above amount, almost 95 per cent of the budget went directly to the beneficiaries of EU policies – i.e. to farmers' regions, third countries, research and so on. It is often alleged that too much money is spent on an inflated, unnecessarily large bureaucracy. But the running costs of the European Commission amount to little more than those of the London mayor. The total cost of running all EU institutions is less than the budget of the more powerful mayor of Paris.

In the enlarged Union of today, the battles over revenue and spending are perhaps inevitably bloody. But at an average of 1.15 per cent of GNI, it is still well within the established 1.24 per cent ceiling.

Revenue

Originally, the Community was financed by contributions levied on member states, but this was found to be unsatisfactory. In 1970, it was decided that in future EC finances would be based on its **own resources**, thus providing the

Community with a degree of financial autonomy. By 1978, this plan was fully implemented.

The components of these resources have changed over the years, but there are four principal forms of contribution made by member countries, as determined under the Delors budget package (Delors II) introduced post-Maastricht in 1992. (The first two are sometimes grouped together.) These components of Community revenue are:

- *75 per cent of the customs duties* charged on non-agricultural imports from non-member countries (member states keep the balance, to pay for the administrative costs involved in their collection)
- *75 per cent of the agricultural levies* charged on agricultural products from non-member countries
- *a proportion of national VAT revenue*, the one consumer tax common to all EC member states (0.5 per cent in 2004)
- *a direct charge on a country's gross national product* (GNP) as the best indication of what a country can afford to pay. This charge was fixed at 1.27 per cent for the period 2000–6, and 1.045 per cent for the following six years to 2013.

These components were first introduced in 1988 and the proportions of Community revenue then represented by the three were: VAT 59 per cent; customs duties, including agricultural levies 28 per cent; GNP charge 10 per cent (there was also about 3 per cent in miscellaneous revenue outside the three main headings). After 1993, the balance between the components was changed, because some of the poorer EC countries had a high consumption rate and therefore paid too much VAT in relation to the size of their economies. Accordingly, substantial reductions in the proportion represented by the VAT component were compensated for by increases in the GNP component. By 2002, the figures were respectively 35 per cent; 17.5 per cent; 45 per cent (and 2.5 per cent miscellaneous). Details of the 2005 budget are given in Table 11.1.

It is apparent that all the revenue of the Union comes from levies on the revenues of member states. The EU, unlike any other form of government, has no tax-raising powers of its own; there is no 'eurotax'. It is entirely at the mercy of the Council of Ministers, relying as it does on whatever levies the Council sees fit to grant. Out of this figure, the Union must meet the expenditure commitments also fixed by the Council. It should be noted that technically only the European Community has a budget, the other two pillars of the European Union created by Maastricht being directly paid for by national governments.

Table 11.1 EU budget, 2005

Source	€m	%
Agricultural duties	1,613	1.5
Customs duties	10,749	10.1
VAT-based revenue	15,313	14.4
GNP-based revenue	77,583	73.0
Miscellaneous	1,040	1.0

Figures taken from the budget statement issued by the European Commission.

NB Figures counted as 'miscellaneous' include any surplus carried forward from the previous year.

Box 11.1 Financing the Union: some differing ideas

'Own resources' have been in the limelight since the start of talks on the funding of the long-term spending plan of the Union, the so-called financial perspective. The system has not been reformed for almost twenty years and some commentators link this with the difficulty in agreeing a new perspective for the 2007–13 period.

In a Joint Parliamentary Meeting of the European and national parliaments (Brussels, 8–9 May 2006), there was broad agreement among participants that the existing 'own resources' system should be replaced by a scheme more understandable to the public. Whether it should be tax-based or built on existing instruments was the subject of a lively debate.

Various proposals were advanced, among them the suggestions that there might be:

- a tax on the profits of EU companies (oil profits were a target for Green MEPs)
- an energy tax to complement the own resources system
- a tax on flights
- a tax on short text messages sent by mobile phones.

There was general agreement that any tax would have to be comprehensible to the general public and that it would be necessary to link its introduction to an attempt to sell the benefits engendered by the EU. European citizens would need to recognise that there was 'added value' to the services they received, if they were asked to pay more. One of the main stumbling blocks in the way of any such taxes would be the need for unanimity between national governments in support of a thorough Europe-wide fiscal harmonisation. Several members doubted whether this could be achieved without a proper supranational fiscal regime. It was widely recognised by the committee that it would be difficult to persuade the European public of the need for any new tax in the foreseeable future.

Expenditure

The largest proportion of Community expenditure has always been devoted to the CAP, but reforms in the 1990s meant that this proportion was reduced to a figure below 50 per cent for the first time. This reduction, however, is balanced by a whole new range of expenditure created by the Maastricht agreement. This new spending is divided between three main areas:

- *increased aid to the Social and Regional Development Funds*, to provide help for the poorer regions of the EU and to assist convergence of economic standards prior to monetary union. After the CAP, these 'structural funds' are the largest recipient of EU expenditure, taking 36.4 per cent of the budget in 2005
- *money spent on increasing the competitiveness of European industry* to reap the full benefit of the single market
- *increased foreign aid to countries outside the EU*, especially to states in eastern and southern Europe that were formerly part of the Soviet bloc and which are now working towards making themselves acceptable for EU member-ship.

See p. 111 for figures on the current pattern of expenditure within the EU.

Who pays?

As we have seen, the Union budget is remarkably small in comparison with the budgets of even medium sized member states. However, the outgoings of the EU, especially on the Common Agricultural Policy, have always been heavy. That expenditure continues to increase, despite reforms to the CAP, to the dismay of net contributors such as Britain and, even more so, Germany.

Broadly speaking, countries contribute to the budget in line with their ability to pay, assessed on the basis of criteria including their level of economic development, population and per capita income. However, the net contribution may not reflect this, for payments made from Union funds are distorted in favour of countries with a large agricultural sector. Those countries that have few eligible poor regions and smaller agricultural sectors, but are broadly well off (Germany, the Netherlands, the UK and Sweden), end up paying much more into the budget than they get out. A further distortion is caused by the differing procedure in regard to the levying of VAT. Rates vary, so that the proportion of money collected from them differs across the member states. Moreover, some countries exempt certain items which others include (the UK exempts books, children's clothing and food; Belgium taxes books at 6 per cent instead of its usual 21 per cent).

The Fourth Enlargement was beneficial to the Union's funding. It was realised that countries such as Austria and Finland would make a useful addition to the

Table 11.2 Contributions to and payments from the European Union in 2002 by member states (in €)

Net contributors		Net recipients	
Germany	5,896.9	Finland	−18.0
UK	3,985.0	Luxembourg	−791.0
Italy	3,038.9	Belgium	−1,474.7
Netherlands	2,876.3	Ireland	−1,581.1
France	1,928.7	Portugal	−2,685.5
Sweden	840.9	Greece	−3,356.9
Austria	255.1	Spain	−8,665.6
Denmark	215.8		

NB There has been very little change in the countries to be found in either column over the last few years, other than the addition of new member states to the second one. The amounts, of course, are liable to fluctuate. The British figure allows for the rebate received via the Fontainebleau Agreement, June 1984 (see Box 11.2).

hard-pressed budget. On the other hand, the most recent members (including Bulgaria and Romania, the latest countries to join) are in a very different position. They are all net beneficiaries of the EU budget. Taken together, they employ four times as many people in agriculture as the rest of the EU. The financial implications of extending even the current, semi-reformed CAP to these countries have long been recognised by the major contributors.

Budgetary disputes

Budgetary disputes have been highly contentious, not least because of the domestic backlash liable to be suffered by the government of any member state that appears to be yielding to EU pressures. The British Budgetary Question and rebate (see Box 11.2) have periodically provoked enormous tensions, but so too has the attempt made by the Union to curb agricultural spending which has been at the heart of much of the debate. French statesmen have regularly objected to any change to the CAP, of which their country has been the greatest beneficiary. The linkage of the two questions of the budget and spending on agriculture has often made the task of reaching agreement extremely difficult and is likely to do so even more in the enlarged Union of twenty-seven states.

Box 11.2 The British rebate

The question of Britain's contribution to the European budget arose at Margaret Thatcher's first European Council meeting and dominated discussions in the Council for five years, much to the despair of Roy Jenkins, the president of the Commission, and the other member states. The issue was known in Brussels as 'the BBQ' which, according to Jenkins,[1] was often referred to in Brussels as 'the Bloody British Question'.

The problem
The problem was that, despite economic difficulties, Britain was making net contributions to Community funds as large as those being paid by Germany. Overall, it was paying into the EC vastly more than it got out of it. At the time, nearly three-quarters of the EC budget was being used to support agriculture. Britain did not greatly benefit from this, for its agricultural base was smaller and more efficient than that in most of Europe. Payments to Britain out of CAP funds were comparatively so low that efficient farmers in Britain were heavily subsidising inefficient farmers in France. To make matters worse, EEC rules forced Britain, which imported more food from outside the Community than the others, to pay a much higher import levy than they did. What would have helped Britain was assistance for its ailing regions and for the modernisation of traditional industries. But compared to the 74 per cent of the Community budget spent on farming, only 4 per cent was spent on the Regional Fund whose purpose was to make grants to areas of low income, chronic unemployment or declining population.

Soon after her election victory in 1979, the British prime minister set out to discover the exact size of Britain's contribution to the European budget and to estimate just how much Britain ought to be paying. As a result of her findings, she presented her first European Council in Dublin (November 1979) with the exact amount by which she wanted British contributions to be reduced – £1b. The Community offered a reduction of £350 million, which she rejected out of hand.

At this point Mrs Thatcher succeeded in shocking both her European colleagues and her own advisers. Repeated demands for what she called 'her money' made it clear that the sum she wanted was not negotiable and she would do no deals. She reportedly accused other European states of the outright theft of British money, an accusation that horrified Foreign Office advisers who knew the rules of the European game. Experienced negotiators were lost in what for them was an unprecedented situation. Among Britain's partners there were many who, while originally sympathetic, were subsequently alienated by such behaviour. The complete breakdown of the Council was only prevented by postponing a decision on the BBQ until the next year.

A solution: the British rebate
Matters dragged on over several more Council meetings, with constant behind-the-scenes negotiations taking place to find a compromise solution acceptable to the prime minister. Finally, at the Fontainebleau Summit of June 1984 there was an eleventh-hour agreement under which Britain would receive a permanent

rebate worth 66 per cent of the difference between what Britain paid into the Community and the amount Britain got back from the Community.

Recent developments: the rebate under attack
Subsequently the rebate has often been called into question at the time of any budget round and periodically there is strong pressure for its abolition. Not surprisingly, British ministers have been reluctant to yield on what they see as a good deal. They can accept being a relatively small net contributor to Union funds, but find it difficult to sell any erosion of the rebate to the British electorate.

During the Brussels talks in June 2004, British ministers were keen to see that the rebate was accepted for the foreseeable future. They thought that it would be preserved, but shortly after the talks ended the Commission put forward a plan to operate from 2007 to 2013 under which the rebate (then worth some £2b) should be shared among other more affluent member states. The effect of the proposal would have been for Britain to become the largest net contributor, paying 0.51 per cent of its GDP into the Union funds, compared with 0.35 per cent for Italy and 0.33 per cent for France, countries of similar size and wealth.

Some other states, including Finland publicly and others privately, called for the end of the rebate, which they saw as unfair, the more so as Britain was at the time markedly more prosperous than it had been at the time of the Fontainebleau settlement. The British continued to resist strongly, pointing out that the UK still received a low per capita share of EU receipts because of its relatively small agrarian sector. At Brussels (December 2005), the British negotiators were willing to make some concessions, in order to see progress on reform of the CAP. The outcome was a deal by which Britain would pay 63 per cent more by way of its contributions to the EU budget, thus forgoing €10,500 (effectively approximately £1,000m a year) from its rebate over the seven-year period. France, in particular, and other wealthier member states will also see their net contributions significantly increase.

Discussions over the budget for 2007–13 at the Brussels Council (December 2005) proved especially complex and controversial. In the event, the issue of agrarian spending was put back for fuller review in 2008.

See pp. 214–19 for discussion of CAP spending.

Conclusion

The European Union budget comprises revenues and expenditures for activities to be undertaken during the following twelve months. The revenues come mainly from member states' membership contributions. The expenditures are primarily directed towards EU policies, notably in the areas of agricultural and regional support. Money is also needed for the running of EU institutions.

The budget of the EU is modest compared to that of member states. Nonetheless, it has been a source of periodic dispute both between member states and between them, the Commission and the Parliament.

For details of the budgetary procedure, see pp. 111–12.

Glossary

Own resources The 'own resources' system, created in 1970 to finance the EU budget, comprises four main instruments: funds from VAT; customs duties; agricultural levies; and contributions from member states, the so-called 'Gross National Income resource', calculated according to their wealth. Over time, the GNI resource has grown to represent the main source of funding of the EU. Together, these sources provide the Union with a degree of autonomy which was lacking in the early days when the EC was financed by contributions made by member states.

CHAPTER 12

First-Pillar policies

The policies covered by the First Pillar are of two types. Some are designed to boost economic growth and prosperity. These are concerned with promoting economic efficiency, building markets and encouraging economic liberalisation. They are largely devised in and run from Brussels. Others are designed to cushion the impact of market forces. In these areas, policy is jointly decided by the Brussels machinery and the national governments, with the Commission playing a key role.

In this chapter, we will deal firstly with the market-building policies, then move on to those designed to mitigate the consequences of market forces.

Market-buliding policies

1. Creation of the single market

The Treaty of Rome provided for the creation of a 'common market' based on the free movement of food, persons, services and capital. To this end, it established deadlines for the removal of customs duties or taxes on imports. These were met within the allotted time, so that – in most cases – by the late 1960s goods bought in one member state could be exported free of duty to another. Member countries were banned from restricting imports from other member countries, unless they were able to gain exemption under limited powers granted by the Treaty.

But by the early 1980s there was concern that some fifteen years after the creation of the Community, it was still far from being the common or single market that had been envisaged. A range of barriers to trade had developed: fiscal, physical and technical. Some of the obstacles were associated with enlargement. But they had also come about because at a time of recession in the 1970s, member governments had introduced hidden barriers. In some cases, they had subsidised firms and introduced regulations ostensibly designed to promote safety or consumer protection but in fact protectionist devices intended to protect hard-pressed industrial sectors. Such obstacles prohibited the development of a genuinely free Community market. Its leaders concluded that it was failing to reap the benefits which a unified market should provide.

A further important factor that created a need for action to secure the internal market was a Court of Justice ruling in the Cassis de Dijon case. A German law prevented this French blackcurrant-based liqueur from being sold in Germany, because its alcohol content was below the minimum laid down by German law. To the Court, this was an unacceptable interference with trade. Their ruling to this effect secured the idea that goods which could be legally sold in one member country could be legally sold in all of them. This was an example of how the Court assumed a role in furthering the objects of the Community, in this case securing the removal of non-tariff barriers to trade between member states.

The creation of a single market following the passage of the SEA marked a major extension of the original idea of a common market. It planned for an area without internal frontiers within which the free movement of people, services, goods and capital (the four freedoms) would be assured. The Commission's 1985 White Paper *Completing the Internal Market* – devised by the British minister responsible for the internal market, Lord Cockfield – set a target date (1 January 1993) for the completion of the single market. Achievement of the programme required the enactment of some 300 measures which were later consolidated into 282 directives.

Box 12.1 Main barriers to the creation of the single market

The White Paper listed actions that would need to be taken if a genuine single market was to be achieved. They involved the removal of three categories of impediments:

Physical barriers were those that confronted people or goods as they crossed frontiers, involving customs and immigration. A symbol of division in the Community, they also imposed heavy costs on business. For instance, lorries had to wait clearance at the Community's internal frontiers, sometimes for hours, on occasion even for days. Their drivers had to fill up to seventy forms before they could cross internal borders. Moreover, the costs of frontier checks on consignments of goods varied from country to country. The Commission wished to see them all removed. The introduction of a Single Administrative Document (SAD) paved the way for easier and smoother transit.

Technical barriers included a range of regulations and standards. Regulations defined the specifications of a product to assure the consumer of its quality and safety, and standards were needed to ensure the compatibility of products. (Plug compatibility was thought to be particularly important in the areas of information technology.) The Commission urged the adoption of a system of mutual recognition of national standards, whilst EU standards were devised. Guarantees of safety were required not only for products ranging from the bodywork of cars to the tyres fitted upon them, but also for articles of capital equipment and services such as banking and life assurance.

Fiscal barriers concerned indirect taxation, mainly in the form of value added tax (VAT) and excise duties such as those on alcohol, petrol and tobacco. The Commission argued that wide variations in levels of taxation between the member states necessitated frontier controls to prevent tax evasion by individuals and firms importing goods from a state with a lower tax rate into one with a higher one. In this way, varying taxes represented a distortion to trade. The Commission favoured the introduction of approximation of VAT rates, preferably a complete harmonisation. But it did not see the issue as necessary for the completion of the single market and compromised on a minimum general rate of 15 per cent with lower rates for some specified items.

Some 258 of the measures planned by Lord Cockfield had been agreed by the set date of 1992, of which an overwhelming majority (79 per cent) were being implemented. The single market had a notable impact in moving forward the process of integration, providing as it did an enhanced regulatory role at the European level. Its importance was recognised in the Rome Treaty, Article 2 of which outlined the high expectations of the benefits that might accrue from its achievement:

> The Community shall have as its task, by establishing a common market and progressively approximating the economic policies of the Member States, to promote throughout the Community a harmonious development of economic activities, a continuous and balanced expansion, an increase in stability, an accelerated raising of the standard of living and closer relations between the States belonging to it.

The single-market programme was keenly supported by many business leaders, even though they were conscious of the intense competition that might derive from it. Governments were keen to make them aware of what was going to happen, so that '1992' was a date that received enormous recognition among those involved in enterprise, but also among the public. Surveys for *Eurobarometer* suggested that there was widespread public backing in all countries, those in favour outnumbering the doubters by some 3:1.

The initiative received enthusiastic support from both committed European federalists and economic liberals. In the United Kingdom, Margaret Thatcher – though distinctly unenthusiastic about most proposals aimed towards the further development of the Community – was a strong supporter of the 1992 programme which she viewed as a massive exercise in deregulation. Her government and subsequent administrations have been committed to the deregulation and liberalisation of the economy and have wished to see their policies entrenched at European level. The Blair administration was an enthusiastic supporter of the strategy agreed at the Lisbon Summit (March 2001) to create the most competitive and dynamic knowledge-based economy in the world by 2010, seeing this as the means of 'sustaining economic growth with more and better jobs, and greater social cohesion'. In pursuit of this modernising agenda, Blair was prepared to ally himself with right-of-centre governments in Italy and Spain in pursuit of the 'new economy' agenda, stressing the value of liberalisation for European firms and peoples.

2. Harmonisation and consumer protection

Although the bitterest arguments between eurosceptics and those in favour of European integration revolve around the issue of monetary union and the single currency, most misunderstandings about Union directives originate in the Single European Act and attempts that were made to apply the principles of the single market as from 1993. The problem initially was that each member country had its own national rules on health, safety and consumer standards. Because of this, products that satisfied the standards in one country might still offend the regulations of another. Similarly, products made in one country might not be accepted for sale in another, negating the principles of the single market.

In the Treaty of Rome, reference had been made to 'approximation' rather than 'harmonisation'. Originally the means of achieving approximation was seen to be the standardisation of rules, with the replacement of many different national regulations with a single set of rules common to the whole Community. But over the years a more realistic sense of what is practicable has meant that the emphasis has changed. Standardising or harmonisation has been replaced by a practice known as 'mutual recognition', meaning that whatever is legally produced in one member country is judged to be legally available for sale in any other member country.

Harmonisation was important in the area of consumer policy. It was evident that consumers would be resistant to EC initiatives, unless there was a serious attempt to enable them to make informed choices between competing products; to be able to use goods and services safely; to be in a position to claim redress in the event of not being satisfied; and to make the range of goods available to them as wide as possible by establishing common product standards.

Consumer policy was not mentioned in the original Treaty of Rome. The first Consumer Action Programme began in 1975, but it was accorded a low priority. However, Article 153 of the Amsterdam Treaty recognised the duty of the Community to 'contribute to protecting the health, safety and economic interest of consumers as well as to promoting their right to information, education and to organise themselves in order to safeguard their interests'. In addition, consumer interests were to be regarded as an important component of other EU policies. The aim was to empower consumers to exercise their rights to protection of health and safety, financial and legal interests, and to representation, participation, information and education. The most recent Action Plan, *Priorities for Consumer Policy 1996–1998*, was concerned with the implementation of these priorities. It was also concerned with environmental issues (what was called 'sustainable consumption') and consumer representation in applicant and developing countries.

Consumer interests are protected by stringent rules concerning labelling and consumer information, drawn up in accordance with certain fundamental rights:

* the protection of consumers' health and safety – banning the sale of products that may endanger the health or safety of the consumer
* protecting the consumer's economic interests – involving regulation of misleading advertising, unfair contractual agreements and unethical sales techniques such as those used in selling time-share

- granting the right to full information about goods and services offered, including all directives on the labelling of foodstuffs, textiles and medicines. Acceptable ingredients, additives and weights and measures are legitimised by e-numbers.
- the right to redress – involving the rapid and affordable settlement of complaints by consumers who feel they have been injured or damaged by using certain goods or services
- consumer representation in the decision-making process, usually meaning the Consumers Consultative Council, which is a committee made up of consumer associations from the various member states together with five EC advisory bodies: the European Bureau of Consumers Organisations (BEUC), the Confederation of Family Organisations in the EC (Coface), the EC Consumer Co-operatives (Eurocoop), the ETUC and the European Inter-regional Institute for Consumer Affairs (EIICA).

Despite the flood of regulations and directives emanating from the Commission, most legislation on consumer affairs is the responsibility of national governments. Community legislation either fills in gaps left by national laws, or covers areas where the consumer in one member state has a complaint concerning another member state. The guideline for Union legislation is: 'As little regulation as possible, but as much as is necessary to protect consumers'.[1]

Since the European Union's first consumer programme was issued in 1975 there have been directives requiring national action on many topics, ranging from the labelling of foodstuffs to advertising aimed at children, from the selling of financial services to the safety of toys and from the safety of building and gas-burning materials to the creation of an internal market in postal services.

3. Competition policy

Article 85 of the Treaty of Rome prohibited undertakings from entering into 'agreements . . . and concerted practices which may affect trade between Member States and which have as their object or effect the prevention, restriction or distortion of competition within the Common Market'. The terminology included such things as discriminatory contracts, market-sharing arrangements, price-fixing and production controls. Article 86 banned 'abuses of dominant position' by firms or groups of firms. Finally, Articles 92–4 forbade government subsidies that distorted or threatened to distort competition.

Competition policy is regarded as an important market-building feature of the European Union. It is one in which the Commission acts as an independent institution, the Council of Ministers not being involved in decision-making. Legislation on competition in industry and commerce has been in existence for some time but in the early years of the Community the Commission was rather lax in its application. The policy gained greater importance after the establishment of the single market, since when the Commission has been more active. Even now, however, the Commission is still concerned to assess the balance between the threat to competition and possible benefits to the public. It does not wish to impede cooperation between small- and medium-scale enterprises and takes into account the prevailing economic climate facing companies seeking particular exemptions. When there is a failure to observe competition requirements, the Commission may be tougher and impose fines on erring companies.

Relevant commissioners have often been keen to utilise the powers available to them. As one of them explained: 'The continuing integration of the Community and the ever-present need for the protection of the consumer from competitive abuses, ensures that competition policy will always play a vital role in Europe'.[2] In recent years, the Commission has ruled on several proposed acquisitions and mergers. It has become involved as an international player, particularly in relation to American companies which have gained a foothold in Europe. It can even veto mergers between US firms, if their joining together poses a threat to competition within the Union. To this effect, it has acted to prevent a merger between General Electric and Honeywell, even though this had gained the blessing of American anti-trust bodies.

The requirements of EU competition policy can be harsh on any member state, most especially those countries which have recently joined the Union. Former communist countries of Central and Eastern Europe had economies in which public ownership was predominant. Moving over to market-based economies was difficult for the new democracies in any case, but the requirement to prepare for entry into the EU made the transition harder to achieve.

4. The Common Transport Policy

A precondition for freedom of movement within a single market is provision for the efficient transportation of goods and persons. Article 3 of the Treaty of Rome had required 'a common policy in the sphere of transport' but few specifics were laid down. In the original form, Article 84 specified that the common policy was to apply to inland waterways, rail and road only, but via the SEA this was amended to extend its terms to cover air and sea transport. As preparations were made for the creation of the single market, so too there was greater movement on transport policy. A 1991 report, *Transport 2000 and Beyond*, established objectives for an integrated continent-wide transport system, involving Community assistance in linking national networks and establishing better links with Central and Eastern Europe.

The Common Transport Policy establishes common rules relating to the passing of international transport across one or more member states, as well as setting rules relating to the operation of carriage within member states. Any decisions in this area are – post the Amsterdam Treaty – made on the basis of co-decision.

Current policy

The European Union's role in transport policy is to ensure that people and goods have access to fast and reliable transport and that local public transport systems can interact with each other. Policy measures focus in particular on developing road and rail networks that can move goods and people from one side of the EU to the other quickly and cheaply.

The EU's Common Transport Policy was introduced in 2001 and aims to realise this goal by regulating those areas of transport that are overused, such as road, and switching demand towards underused means of transport such as rail, inland waterways and short sea shipping. The European Commission has developed a range of transport policies that will affect both freight and passenger transport, including:

- introducing road pricing for heavy goods vehicles (HGVs) and a single European road toll service
- making proposals for a sustainable urban transport plan to achieve a common standard across the EU
- reforming the state aids regime for public transport subsidies
- developing pan-European transport networks
- developing ports and 'motorways of the sea'
- promoting cleaner, greener fuels and new technologies in transport
- issuing proposals for a pan-European driving licence
- promoting road safety
- introducing new rights for passengers.

However, those involved in policy-making have found transport to be a difficult area in which to achieve a common policy for several reasons:

- Some countries have always had substantial state involvement in transport.
- There were many public and private entrenched interests to face down, not least because the number of people directly or indirectly involved in transport makes it one of the largest European industries.
- Transport costs have a significant impact on economic activity and competitiveness in member states, especially in the peripheral regions.
- There is an interaction between transport provision and energy use, so that any policy designed to maximise transport facilities has an environmental impact.

The EU's 2001 White Paper on transport was noted for a 'modal shift' target designed to halt the decline in freight transport by rail in favour of road transport. A revised strategy (2006) did not abandon this approach, but the specific target of increasing the level of rail freight to its 1998 level was dropped from the revised paper. A few days prior to its publication, European leaders had met to agree and publish a 'Sustainable Development Strategy' (SDS), which contained 'operational objectives and targets' for sustainable transport in eight areas including climate change, energy use, air and noise pollution. But the second document, which sets out European transport policy in detail, makes no reference to these objectives and targets, nor does it propose a strategy for how they should be achieved.

The conflicts between the two strategy papers are notable in three important aspects. The **Sustainable Development** Strategy defines objectives to break the link between economic growth and growth of transport; to reduce greenhouse gas emissions from transport; and to bring air and noise pollution down to levels that minimise the impact on human health and the environment. The new transport policy paper does not mention these objectives.

5. Economic and Monetary Union (EMU): the single currency

Economic and monetary union has been the most ambitious EU objective, yet it was not mentioned in any of the treaties signed prior to the Single European Act. The goal of EMU was first proclaimed at a meeting of the heads of government in The Hague (1969), with 1980 mentioned as a target date for its implementation. However, the adverse economic climate of the 1970s made its fulfilment an impossible dream.

EMU was again taken up towards the end of that decade, when the European Monetary System was introduced. But it was the commitment and enthusiasm of Jacques Delors which provided a real impetus to action and secured its inclusion in the SEA. The publication in 1989 of the Delors Report was a key breakthrough. It envisaged progress in three stages: first, the linking of the currencies together via a strengthening of existing procedures; secondly, integration between states through a new treaty; and finally the creation of a European Central Bank (ECB) resulting in the transfer of monetary policy from national authorities and the irrevocable locking of currencies.

European leaders meeting at the Madrid Council (June 1989) saw the Delors Plan as the basis for further work and decided that the first stage should begin in July 1990. At Maastricht, they agreed a strict timetable for achieving economic and monetary union. This was to include economic convergence on inflation, interest rates and currency stability, the introduction of a single currency and the setting up of a Central European Bank. Stage 2 was to begin in 1994, the project culminating in the final Stage 3 in 1999, when complete union was to be achieved.

Eleven states were deemed to have met the convergence criteria in 1999 and proceeded to adopt the euro as their common currency. From day one the ECB set a single interest rate for the entire eurozone. Four countries did not join: Britain, Denmark, Greece and Sweden. The British government had secured an opt-out at Maastricht and decided against immediate membership. The Scandinavian countries held referendums which resulted in rejection of the euro and Greece was not judged as having met the criteria. In 2001, it became the

Box 12.2 The UK position on the euro

Conservative ministers adopted a 'wait and see' approach to membership of the proposed single currency in the early to mid-1990s, some sceptical as to whether it would really happen. After the 1997 election, the Labour government advanced the position to 'prepare and decide'. As Chancellor of the Exchequer, Gordon Brown argued for Britain to wait until it was absolutely clear that Britain had satisfied the five criteria that he and his Treasury team had laid down as conditions for British entry. In October 1997, he told the House that he favoured entry in principle, but when he delivered his verdict in June 2003 he announced that only one of the five tests had been passed. Prime Minister Blair always seemed more enthusiastic about entry, but was aware of the lack of popular support for entry into the eurozone as well as the political opposition the issue aroused.

The nature and importance of the single-currency debate

The issue of the single currency is of massive importance, for to join euroland would have a key impact on the British economy and strike at the heart of the debate about national sovereignty. Not surprisingly, ministers in any recent administration have been reluctant to commit their country to an innovation in policy that could go seriously wrong, in the same way that British membership of the ERM (see p. 48) provoked havoc in the money markets and initiated a fundamental rethink about the handling of economic affairs. On that occasion, the Conservatives paid a heavy price for getting things wrong. They never recovered in the years before the 1997 election and continued to pay a political price thereafter because of the damage the episode caused to their reputation for economic competence.

twelfth country to join, Slovenia then being the first of the recent batch of new entrants to participate (2007), with Cyprus and Malta following a year later. Others intend to do so within ten years of entry, as the state of their economies permits. Euro banknotes and coins have been in circulation since 1 January 2002 and are now a part of daily life for over 300m Europeans living in the euro area.

Advantages and disadvantages of the single currency
Advocates of the single currency portrayed it as being an obvious accompaniment of the drive towards a single market more than a decade ago. In their view, there was a limit to how much market integration could be achieved, as long as national currencies and economic policies differed; a single market functions more efficiently if there is one system of coinage employed throughout the trading area. They believed that the combination of the single market and the euro would equip Europe as a solid and successful trading block, eventually covering the majority of the twenty-seven European countries and potentially a population of nearly 500m people.

More specifically, for private individuals and firms, there were a number of advantages in a single currency and monetary policy, namely:

- the lowering of costs involved in cross-border business, ending the conversion costs involved in currency exchanges and thereby easing transactions between countries. It would be easier to buy and sell in other euro-area countries, theoretically meaning more competition and pressure to drive down prices, the outcome being cheaper goods and services.
- greater certainty in the financial markets as sterling ceased to be vulnerable to exchange-rate fluctuations
- lower interest rates over a period of time.

Those who doubted the value of membership did so on either constitutional or political/economic grounds, or both. British Conservatives tended to stress the importance of the constitutional considerations, whereas politicians of the centre left were more influenced by the extent to which membership would adversely impact upon the British economy.

Opponents portrayed control of the currency as an indication of national sovereignty and disliked the idea of economic policy – and especially interest rates – being decided by a distant and unaccountable Central Bank in Frankfurt. They did not believe that what the Conservatives often described as a 'one size fits all' policy was in the interests of Britain, with its distinctive traditions and requirements. They emphasised the need for a country to retain flexibility to deal with national problems, such as balance of payments difficulties. If a country was locked into EMU, it possessed no options, for control over economic policy instruments was being ceded by individual countries. British politicians and voters would lose all say in the difficult decisions that inevitably have to be made about the short-term trade-offs between inflation and unemployment, ministers only retaining the power of persuasion over representatives of other member states.

Critics in Britain and elsewhere also questioned whether there can ever be genuine convergence between member states. Even where there does appear to be convergence, from a purely economic standpoint there are doubts about the timing of entry. Getting it wrong can prove costly, as Ireland found when it joined EMU at an exchange rate that was too weak. They additionally point out that Europe lags behind the flexible British economy in its pursuit of economic reform and that the European economy needs to come into line with the British, before the moment is appropriate.

More generally, for those who wish to resist the move towards an ever closer union, they saw membership of the eurozone as a move that would further enmesh their country into the process of integration. They feared that closer fiscal and economic ties might ultimately be associated with closer political ones, for in this way it is easier to make EMU function effectively.

The outcome in Europe

It is still early days to pass judgment on how well the eurozone has performed. Membership has caused difficulty in individual countries, some of which have struggled to meet the required constraints on budget deficits. Italy had to restructure its economy radically to meet the rules and other countries have found the rules on debt difficult to apply. Their governments have lost the flexibility to conduct an independent monetary policy, for no longer can they regulate their economies by adjusting their interest rates. In the past, they could attach priority to certain areas such as job creation or price stability, but now they have to behave in the way ordained by the increasingly powerful – but unelected and unaccountable – Central Bank.

Membership of the eurozone has either abolished or greatly restricted the freedom of manoeuvre of national governments, at a time when the EU in general has hovered on the brink of recession. Both France and Germany have had to defy the terms of the Growth and Stability Pact which makes the convergence criteria binding on member states. Faced with growing discontent at home at a time of dwindling economic growth and cuts in social spending, they found its requirements too onerous. The Pact had to be amended in 2003, in such a way as to retain the 3 per cent limit on deficits but grant individual countries more leeway in special circumstances. Here was an example of how two large states could flout EU requirements in their national interest, whereas smaller countries wished to see the Pact honoured in the way that had always been intended.

Market-mitigating policies

1. Agriculture: the Common Agricultural Policy (CAP)

In early postwar Europe, there were serious problems of hunger and even starvation in parts of Europe. People were accustomed to shortages. In the years which followed it was a guiding theme of agricultural policy to ensure that there was plenty of food available and at reasonable prices for the consumer. It was also important to ensure that the farming community received an appropriate reward for its efforts to produce more food. In some parts of the continent, it was difficult to ensure farm profitability, because geographical and climatic conditions were harsh.

If today the idea of shortages seems ridiculous, it was a very real concern in postwar Europe. Prices and production were important issues, but so too was maintaining the rural way of life and preserving the income of those who worked in agricultural regions. Rural protection is an issue which arouses strong feelings among those who live in hostile environments such as the Massif Central where, without some subsidy, small farmers would find it impossible to keep their enterprise going and would have to leave the region in search of work elsewhere. This might be seen as particularly unfortunate, because small farmers are more likely to use their land in an environmentally friendly way, involving 'natural' methods of production.

Agriculture is unlike other sectors of the economy. It is very price-sensitive. People spend much of their money on food but prices can rise or fall sharply depending on climatic or seasonal conditions. If prices go too high, the consumer suffers. If they fall too low, some farmers might suffer and be driven off the land. The availability of food at the right prices matters to everyone.

When a policy for agriculture was devised, it was recognised that it was sensitive for other reasons:

1. The agricultural workforce in a number of member states represented a significant electoral bloc. Any government which alienated the farming lobby could be in political trouble. In France, although agriculture now accounts for only 3.6 per cent of GDP, it accounts for 17 per cent of the votes.
2. More than any other section of the economy, it was protected by national subsidies and tariffs. Almost every country subsidised its farmers after the war and it made sense to do so.
3. Agriculture was more than a commodity. It reflected individual, social and cultural values that were of great significance, especially in France.

This is the background to the controversies surrounding the debate about the CAP, introduced in 1962.

Agreement on a Common Agricultural Policy
The Treaty of Rome committed the Six to a common policy on farming. Article 39 set out its main objectives:

1. to increase agricultural productivity
2. to ensure a fair standard of living for the agricultural community
3. to stabilise markets and to ensure that supplies were available to the consumer at reasonable prices.

The purpose was to provide guaranteed prices for farm produce, along with loans and grants for modernising farm procedures. The Common Agricultural Policy, agreed in 1962 after hard bargaining especially between France and Germany, aimed to give farmers a decent standard of living and to guarantee consumers a steady supply of produce at reasonable prices. The objectives were geared to the needs of producer and consumer, as they were then conceived.

The CAP is the oldest of the integrative policies of the European Union. To achieve a common policy, the debate had to accommodate various political concessions. The final package placated national concerns by safeguarding the position of Europe's rural population whilst at the same time providing German industry with the prospect of a customs union of goods, services and capital. Both France and Germany wanted to uphold the rights of the agricultural community in their respective countries, but whereas the Bavarian farmers were fully supportive of a protective agricultural policy other Germans were keener to see a common market for industrial goods. The French liked the ideal of a common market in agriculture, but one which ensured that the large farming interest in France would benefit. Each side got enough in the negotiations to satisfy the wishes of their many citizens.

Problems with the CAP
The principles underlying the CAP had been laid down in 1960:

- free trade within the Community in all agricultural products
- common guaranteed prices for most commodities
- protective heavy levies placed on all imported agricultural product
- purchase by the Community of all commodity surpluses.

In its conception, the CAP had the worthiest of aims and objectives in attempting to make the Community self-sufficient in food, while guaranteeing a good standard of living for those involved in agriculture. In the implementation of the CAP, however, some of the worthiness of purpose disappeared. Encouraged by the French, with an essentially peasant agricultural economy, the CAP provided a guaranteed intervention price for all agricultural products without any limit being put on production.

For critics of the European Community, the second and fourth points together came to represent all that was wrong with the Community. The fact that the Community would not only pay guaranteed prices but would itself guarantee the purchase of any unsold surplus produce would not have mattered if the Community had also laid down limits on production. But the French held out for the absence of any such limits and this represented an invitation for farmers to produce more than could be sold on the market, in the certain knowledge that the Community would buy any surplus at the full market rate. It is because of this that we began to hear about '**butter mountains**' and the '**wine lakes**'. It also led to two-thirds of the EC budget being swallowed up by the CAP and, in the 1980s, almost led to bankruptcy.

As a result the CAP could be claimed as both a success and a failure. By 1973 the Community had become self-sufficient in cereals, beef, dairy products, poultry and vegetables. In the years that followed, however, despite the increase in population brought about by enlargement, production increased into ever greater surpluses. By 1990 the countries of the Community were producing 20 per cent more cereals than they could consume, but continuing to pay the farmers more than the world price for all the cereal crops they could produce. The costs of the CAP increased at an even faster rate than production, since there was not only the cost of the support price to farmers but also the cost of storing the vast food surpluses.

By 1990 the cost of the CAP to the EC, in terms of the taxes and higher prices needed to pay for it, had reached around £92 billion.[3] There were also non-financial costs, both in terms of the dubious morality of that level of expenditure for the benefit of the relatively small percentage of the EC population actually engaged in agriculture, and in the righteous indignation of the rest of the world as it saw EC surplus production being sold off at rock-bottom prices with what amounted to a massive subsidy. The repercussions of this last point nearly destroyed settlement on the Uruguay round of talks on the international settlement that was due to replace **GATT**.

Reform
Reform of the CAP became inevitable in the 1980s as the Community repeatedly failed to agree a budget and teetered on the brink of bankruptcy. In 1991 reforms began under the then commissioner for agriculture, Ray MacSharry, and switched the whole emphasis of the CAP away from support payments for unlimited production towards topping-up payments for farmers who restricted their production within strict quotas. At the heart of this reform was a 'set-aside' policy by which farmers withdrew a percentage of their land from food production, a concession for which they were then compensated. For poorer farmers such as the hill farmers of Wales, Scotland and the Pennines, the emphasis of support moved out of the CAP and transferred to the programme of regional aid.

The reforms of 1992 were judged to be successful in that they cut the product surpluses held by the Community without jeopardising a 4.5 per cent increase in farmers' incomes. Further reform was, however, rendered necessary by the potential impact of the enlargement of the EU eastwards, which could mean an increase of 50 per cent in the extent of agricultural land, not to mention a doubling in the size of the agricultural workforce. There was general agreement, however, that the main thrust of reform should be to move away from subsidising overproduction and turn instead to selective aid programmes.

It was declared that reform was required in three areas:

1. cereals, where it was projected that surpluses could rise to 58m tonnes by 2005
2. beef, where – despite BSE – stocks of surplus meat were due to reach 1.5m tonnes by 2005 unless there was a change of policy
3. dairy prices.

These were the problems tackled by Franz Fischler, the new agriculture commissioner, as soon as he took office in January 1999. Under the German presidency of the Council of Ministers it was agreed that:

1. Intervention prices for cereals would be progressively reduced by 20 per cent, with farmers receiving compensation payments for about half the drop in prices.

2. Subsidies to beef farmers would be cut by 20 per cent in three stages over seven years.
3. There was to be a 15 per cent cut in support for dairy prices but implementation was delayed.

Agenda 2000 set out a programme for continued agricultural reform, the emphasis being on a new decentralised model that would allow countries to be more flexible in their application of CAP requirements, so that they could adjust implementation to suit sectoral and local conditions. Specific aims of the new programme were to promote:

• an agriculture which is competitive in world markets
• production methods which are environmentally friendly
• diversity in the forms of agriculture, product variety and rural development
• simplicity in agricultural policy and sharing of responsibilities with the member states
• greater food safety and quality.

Major reform was postponed, but a mid-term progress report pointed to the need to decouple direct payments to farmers from production, make payments more conditional on compliance with considerations such as environmental, food safety and animal-welfare standards and shift more money into rural development policy – all this, against a background of increased concern to satisfy the consumer's demand for safe food of high quality and an awareness of the need to achieve the environmental goals of sustainability and improved animal welfare.

One of the crops subsidised by the CAP is sugar produced from sugar beet. The EU is by far the largest sugar-beet producer in the world, with annual production at 17m metric tons. Sugar was not included in the 1992 MacSharry reform, or in the 1999 Agenda 2000 decisions. However, in early 2006, the EU decided on some reforms of sugar subsidies. The guaranteed price of sugar was cut by 36 per cent, with European production projected to fall sharply as a result of this. According to the EU, this was the first serious reform of sugar under the CAP for forty years.[4]

The difficulty of achieving reform
There is often discussion of further change, but fundamental departures from existing practice are hard to achieve, because governments of some states are determined to resist any innovations that threaten their electoral prospects. French sensibilities are a particular problem, for the country still has a strong agrarian lobby and a larger than average farming vote.

Inevitably, Britain is on the other side to the French in such discussions. As we have seen, agriculture is a much smaller sector of the economy than in all other

EU countries apart from Belgium. In both cases, only 1.4 per cent of the work-force are engaged in the agricultural, fisheries and forestry industries. In the United Kingdom, agriculture now accounts for only 0.8 per cent of the total UK economy, as opposed to 2.9 per cent at the time it joined the European Community. Moreover, unlike the situation in France or Germany, UK farmers – being relatively efficient – have needed the protection of guaranteed prices less than their European counterparts.

At the Brussels Council (December 2005), Britain agreed to some reduction in the rebate it was due to receive, in return for agreement that the issue of agricultural spending would be subjected to a more extensive review in 2008.

2. Common Fisheries Policy

Article 38 of the 1957 Treaty of Rome stated that there should be a common policy for fisheries. The Common Fisheries Policy (CFP) was created in 1973 to manage the industry for the benefit of both fishing communities and the consumer. The policy lays down regulations on fishermen's access to EU waters, quotas, measures for the conservation and management of resources of stocks of fish which swim in the waters of member states, programmes to improve production and the conclusion of fishing agreements with non-EC countries, plus long-term security for the fishermen who depend on the EU for protection.

At the heart of the common policy was the principle that fish stocks should be managed on the basis of scientific advice, so that viable stocks can be maintained and stocks that have been seriously reduced can be replenished. Hence the need for a total allowable catch (TAC). Each year, a decision is made on the total catch that may be taken of each species without damaging the future of the stock. This total is then broken down by fishing areas and divided into quotas for each country.

In 1992, the earlier agreement was amended and extended, the main point of the revision being to provide for the Council 'to set . . . objectives and detailed rules for restructuring the Community fisheries sector with a view to achieving a balance on a sustainable basis between resources and their exploitation, taking account of possible economic and social consequences and of the special characteristics of the various fishing regions'.

A comprehensive review was undertaken in early 2003, for it was thought that the original policy emphasis was not adequately coping with the task of conserving fish stocks, matching fleet size to supply and providing consumers with quality fish at affordable prices. The purpose of the reformed policy is to ensure that the Union has biologically, environmentally and economically sustainable fisheries. Conservation is a cornerstone of the CFP, with measures to regulate the amount of fish taken from the sea and to allow young fish to mature. It also protects other marine life, by requiring that fishing techniques minimise the number of dolphins and porpoises that get caught up in fishing nets. More and more, policy-makers examine the environmental implications of their decisions not only on fisheries and marine life, but on the whole marine ecosystem.

Impact of the CFP

Fishing remains an important economic activity within the EU. It contributes generally less than 1 per cent to gross national product, but employs 260,000 fishermen catching 8m tonnes of fish in 1995. It represents no more than 10 per cent of local employment in any region of the EU, but it is often in areas where other employment opportunities are limited. For this reason, community funds have been made available to fishing as a means of encouraging regional development.

The market for fish and fish products has changed in recent years. Supermarkets are now the main buyers of fish and expect steady supplies. Fresh fish sales have fallen, but demand for processed fish and prepared meals has grown. Despite this, employment in fish processing has been falling, with 60 per cent of fish consumed in the EU coming from outside. This is partly due to improvements in the ability to transport fresh fish internationally. Competitiveness of the EU fishing industry has been affected by overcapacity and shortages of fish to catch.

In the pursuit of its objectives, the Common Fisheries Policy has run into heavy criticism. Some of it derives from those who think that action has been delayed and ineffective. Much comes from within the fishing industry, for decisions about TACs and the ability of fleets to fish freely in British waters have had a serious impact on several fishing ports.

3. Environmental policy

Green politics did not get underway until the 1960s, so there was no mention of environmental policy in the Treaty of Rome. However, as concern developed about damage to the atmosphere, fauna, flora, habitats, health and landscape, various European organisations began to talk about such problems and to propose solutions. The Club of Rome, an early Green movement, argued for zero economic growth as a means of preventing further damage. The Council of Europe selected 1970 as European Conservation Year. In 1972, the United Nations staged the Stockholm Conference on the Human Environment. The European Community responded by launching its own initiatives.

In 1972, the six member countries and the applicant nations met in Paris at the European Summit and declared that special measures were needed to prevent environmental damage, for unchecked economic expansion could not be the basis for protection. Thereafter, in the 1970s and 1980s, the Community began to adopt a range of initiatives, even if the topic was still not a priority in its thinking. But these initiatives had to be justified as relevant to the achievement of a common market – so they were classified as 'economic policy'.

Growing importance of environmental policy
Above all, it was the passage of the Single European Act 1986 that marked the new departure in Community policy. The EC officially recognised that this was an area within its competence and obtained formal authority to legislate on the environment in its own right. It was recognised that the process of harmonisation required action to ensure that common standards were established across the Community. Article 130R.i made it clear that policy could not be compartmentalised, but was 'a component of the Community's other policies'. Three principles were put forward: prevention, the rectification of damage at source and 'polluter pays'. Preventative action was recognised as the guiding theme of any environmental policy. The 'polluter pays for damage done' principle is one that the Commission has subsequently pursued.

Between 1973 and 1992, the Community initiated five Action Programmes on a wide range of topics. The fifth one covered the period through until the turn of the century. The approach adopted was not to produce legally binding regulations, but rather to issue directives, which gave individual countries more freedom to devise policies in line with their national circumstances. The SEA accepted that Community action was only desirable on those issues where the objectives it embraced could be better fulfilled at the EC level rather than by member states acting on their own. But in a number of areas, it did lay down minimum standards.

By the time of the next Treaty revision, environmental thinking across Europe had moved on. Green movements were well established and making new demands of policy-makers. At Maastricht, in December 1991, the summit confirmed the new status of environmental policy within what was to become the European Union. Agreement was reached on four goals (the first had already been recognised):

1. to preserve, protect and improve the quality of the environment
2. to protect human health
3. to make prudent and rational use of natural resources
4. to promote international measures to tackle problems which have implications over an area wider than the Union itself.

A new theme was added to the three existing principles, namely that there should be 'sustainable and non-inflationary growth respecting the environment', as part of an attempt to reconcile economic progress with environmental concern. Sustainability has been defined as 'development that meets the needs of the present without compromising the ability of future generations to meet their own needs'.

The objectives were vague and this enabled them to command general assent. But their very inclusion in the Treaty was a further sign that the environment is now recognised as an area of growing significance. Among indications of the new importance attached to protecting our surroundings, encouragement was given to firms that launched products which were seen as environmentally friendly. They could be rewarded with an EU eco-label. In addition, a European Environment Agency was created in Copenhagen, to accumulate statistical data on many features of policy. This resource bank shares technical information and good practice.

The Treaty of Amsterdam 1997 gave further impetus to environmental policy, enshrining the principle of sustainable development. It affirmed that environmental protection affects all other Union policy and provided that states must maintain *or introduce* national measures. This was an attempt to 'beef up' environmental policy and reflected the impact of the new Scandinavian membership (Finland and Sweden). In future, even where there has been harmonisation already, states were encouraged to introduce their own measures, subject to the proviso that they notify the Commission which could arbitrate on whether the proposal would (illegally) restrict trade. In addition, all measures were subject to the simplified co-decision procedure which, given the green credentials of many MEPS, means that greening of all areas of policy is likely.

The Treaty of Nice 2000 was a big disappointment to environmental activists, for there was a broad shift in the balance of power towards the larger member states and the Council, away from the smaller – and generally greener – states and the Commission. Nice was associated with movement towards enlarging the Union. As yet, it is still early to comment on the impact of the Fifth Enlargement (Central and Eastern parts i and ii) on environmental policy, but there is at first sight a difficulty in reconciling the impetus to economic and political growth and transformation in the Central and Eastern European states with the requirement of sustainable development. It may not feature as a top priority in their thinking.

Meanwhile, the EU is operating under its Sixth Environmental Action Programme, *Environment 2010: Our Future, Our Choice*, covering the first decade of the new millennium. This builds upon and develops the previous programmes, but emphasises the continuing importance of integration of environmental considerations into other EU policies and focuses on the health-related aspects of environmental issues. It aims to maintain the EU's leadership role among international gatherings. Long-term targets for 2010 include benchmarks for the stabilisation of global temperature change and carbon dioxide concentrations; the gradual withdrawal of fossil fuel subsidies; reversing the loss of biodiversity; and the derivation of 12 per cent of total energy use from renewable energy sources.

Box 12.3 Environmental action programmes

Of the first five Action Programmes, it was the fifth (1993–2000) which was boldest and most far-reaching. Entitled *Towards Sustainability*, it stressed the causes of pollution and identified five areas where a strong EU approach is essential (agriculture, energy, industry, tourism and transport). The focus was on the way in which all EU policies must be made to conform to the needs of environmental policy and on the differing responsibilities of all tiers of government, from local to European, in ensuring that appropriate action was taken. Some 200 measures were adopted under the fifth Action Programme and the British presidency (1998) gave a notable push to them. They covered such things as:

- acoustic pollution (sound)
- air pollution, especially vehicle emissions
- chemical substances and standards in chemical plants
- eco-labelling
- habitat protection
- nuclear safety
- waste disposal and management
- water quality (for bathing and drinking).

Foremost among the measures adopted over the five programmes were the following:

- *Environmental Impact Assessment (EIA)*. Borrowing an American innovation, it was decided that the effects of any capital project for EU development should be assessed as early as possible. The directive appeared in 1988 and established standardised procedures for measuring the environmental impact of projects such as the construction of airport runways, long-distance railway lines and waste-disposal installations. In theory, it was easy for states to agree to such a procedure, but when their pet project had to be assessed (a time-consuming process) some were reluctant to carry out the directive in the way intended. The economic and political bonuses that governments hoped to derive from their policy initiatives could be delayed. Other than Denmark, all member states have at some stage fallen foul of the Commission, as it has tried to enforce EIA.
- *The European Environment Agency*. Its task is to monitor environmental issues and to provide objective information about the environment as a basis for policy decisions and to work with similar national bodies. The Agency lacks the teeth which Parliament originally envisaged; states have resisted ideas to expand its scope.
- *Vehicle emissions from small cars*. Other than Germany, states were opposed to tougher standards. Parliament wanted to see more rigorous, American-style regulations and the Commission eventually adopted them. Some car-producing EC countries were granted extra time in which to prepare for the introduction of new procedures.

As we have seen, the sixth Environmental Action Programme emphasised the need for environmental policy to be an integral part of all other EU policy-making.

> It wanted to ensure that business and consumer interests contribute to more sustainable production and consumption; enable individual citizens to have access to better information on environmental issues; and adopt more environmentally conscious attitudes towards land use.

Effectiveness of EU environmental policy

Amongst the issues on which the Union legislates are water pollution, including setting standards for drinking water as well as for bathing-water quality on beaches, air pollution from factories and cars, noise pollution, the packaging of chemicals and other products, plus the transport and disposal of waste. Some good work has been achieved, and substantial EU funding has been made available to tackle air and water quality, and the protection of habitats and species. Blots on the record so far include the facts that:

- Few – if any – states have fully implemented all the directives that have been introduced on the environment. The directive on Environment Impact Assessments ran into particular difficulty. The original document went through twenty-two drafts and the resulting one had to be radically amended within five years.
- The Commission has had to take proceedings against states which breached environmental laws; these amount to approximately one-fifth of all the proceedings it has launched.
- The Court of Justice has considered cases against every state for noncompliance with the directive on the protection of migratory birds (1979). In recent years, Britain has a much better record in this area.

4. Regional policy

The EU contains several advanced and affluent nations, some of the wealthiest in the world. Yet there are also economic and social disparities within the Union, a situation which has developed as a result of successive enlargements. The arrival of new states under the second and third expansion, allied to the need for all countries to prepare for the single market, meant that from the early 1980s there was a new emphasis on tackling regional problems.

Regional policy did not feature in the original Treaty of Rome, although its preamble did refer to the need to 'reduce the differences between the various regions and the backwardness of the less favoured regions'. The original impetus to the development of a regional policy was provided by the First Enlargement. One of the new British commissioners, George Thomson, was responsible for overseeing policy towards the regions, the stated goal being to improve the economic well being of certain parts of the Community. The SEA incorporated regional policy into the original treaty, formally recognising it as one of the means of strengthening the EC's economic and social cohesion.

Box 12.4 Pitfalls of environmental policy

All member states see the merits of safeguarding the environment and taking action on issues such as climate change. However, the actions required often involve short-term sacrifices for the sake of a long-term advantage. Governments – with elections to contest – are often looking for short-term benefits and become apprehensive about the cost of necessary measures, be they economic or political. In particular, they worry that necessary action might make their producers less competitive than those in other manufacturing states.

Environmental schemes are expensive and therefore tend to be unpopular with governments and industry. This is an area where disputes about non-compliance with Community directives are frequent. Although Britain has been involved in high-profile disputes over privatisation of the water supply, the standard of bathing water and the requirement for civil engineering projects to have regard to the environment, it is one of the nations most likely to implement directives.

Specific problems

Some of the main dilemmas of environmental policy are that:

1. National pressures can undermine policy. Environmental considerations take second place to the promotion of economic development. Uneven levels of prosperity in the EU also affect national attitudes and priorities.
2. Standards of implementation vary among member states; national pressures can undermine policies. Promoting environmental protection and economic growth at the same time can be difficult. Many companies are more aware of the costs of compliance with EU laws than of any benefits derived from controls. This casts doubt on the effectiveness of voluntary means of environmental protection.
3. Promotion of the single market can affect environmental standards. The search for high standards cannot be used as an excuse for protectionism within the EU. Some states may attempt to impose strict regulations as a means of keeping out goods from other countries that do not share the same standards. In the chemical and packaging industries, a few have introduced tough rules in order to protect home industries.
4. Even the most environmentally conscious countries in the EU, notably the Nordic states and Austria, are subject to pressures to adjust their priorities for reasons of economic necessity. They are still a potential force for good in the Union, although as less populous states their influence on decisions is relatively small-scale and this will reduce their ability to raise overall standards. Moreover, Norway, one of the pace-setters on environmental regulation, has stayed outside the EU.
5. The inclusion of Central and Eastern states in the future – with enlargement – will require additional resources to help them clean up the environment. The emphasis in the past has been on intensive production whatever the cost. Some states such as Poland and Slovakia used brown coal as the main energy supply and this is regarded as a heavy pollutant. Also, existing legislation in such countries has often been inadequately enforced.

Thomson found that there existed considerable disparities between the poorest and most prosperous regions, both within countries and within the Community as a whole. The less privileged areas fell into two principal groups:

- underdeveloped rural areas, whose economy mostly depended on agriculture. They often had low levels of income, high levels of unemployment and poorly developed infrastructures. Ireland was an obvious example.
- areas where prosperity was based on declining industries, leaving behind ageing plant and high unemployment. At the time, they were to be found in parts of Belgium, France and the United Kingdom.

Thomson set out three broad objectives of EU policy:

- to ensure that regional problems are taken into consideration in other Union policies
- to attempt to coordinate the regional bodies of the member states
- to provide a broad range of financial support for development of the Union's poorer regions.

Today, with around one-third of the EU's budget devoted to regional policy, the aim remains essentially the same – to remove the disparities in wealth across the EU, restructure declining industrial areas and diversify rural areas which have declining agriculture. Aid comes via the four structural funds:

- the European Regional Development Fund (ERDF) designed to provide infrastructure support for businesses and local development projects
- the European Social Fund (ESF) that was created to assist the return of unemployed and disadvantaged sections of society to the workforce
- the European Agricultural Guidance and Guarantee Fund (EAGGF) established to finance the CAP
- the Financial Instrument for Fisheries Guidance (FIFG), which was created to assist with the modernisation of the fishing industry.

These funds paid out about €213b, or roughly one-third of total EU spending, between 2000 and 2006. A further €18b was allocated to the Cohesion Fund, set up in 1993 to finance transport and environment infrastructure in member states with a GDP less than 90 per cent of the Union average at the time (Greece, Ireland, Spain and Portugal).

Unlike the Cohesion Fund, the four structural funds can benefit poor or disadvantaged regions in all EU countries according to certain criteria or objectives.

- A total of 70 per cent of funding goes to so-called Objective 1 regions where GDP is less than 75 per cent of the EU average. About 22 per cent of the Union population live in the fifty regions benefiting from these funds which go to improving basic infrastructure and encouraging business investment.

- Another 11.5 per cent of regional spending goes to Objective 2 regions (areas experiencing economic decline because of structural difficulties) to help with economic and social rehabilitation. Some 18 per cent of the EU population live in such areas.
- Objective 3 focuses on job-creation initiatives and programmes in all regions not covered by Objective 1. 12.3 per cent of funding goes towards the adaptation and modernisation of education and training systems and other initiatives to promote employment.

With the enlargements of the Union in May 2004 and January 2007, twelve new member states have entered the EU. Most of these countries are poorer than the existing members and the impact of their joining is that the EU's average GDP per capita has been reduced, leading to some regions in the fifteen nations that made up the Union prior to the early twenty-first century no longer qualifying for extra financial help. On the other hand, most regions in the new member states do qualify.

Impact of regional policy
Regional policy has had some notable successes. The whole of Ireland provides a good example, its GDP on accession being 63.8 per cent that of the EC, whereas today the figure is 162 per cent.[5] More specifically, an Objective 2 programme in Denmark which received €162m from the structural funds succeeded in improving transport and telecommunications in small islands and coastal communities with limited access by land and little local fresh water.

Yet many old inequalities in the Union remain to be eradicated and new ones have been added with the accession of the ten new member states from Eastern Europe and the Mediterranean. Their problems may be caused by longstanding handicaps imposed by geographical remoteness or by more recent economic and social change, or a combination of both. The Union tailored programmes of support for the period 2000–6, to assist them in taking advantage of EU membership. The goal is set out in Article 158 of the Amsterdam Treaty, namely to 'aim at reducing disparities between the development of various regions and the backwardness of the least favoured regions or islands, including rural areas'. To help achieve that target, the UK received more than £10b from the structural funds between 2000 and 2006.

5. Social policy
Most directives and regulations emanating from Brussels relate to economic issues and concern some aspect of the single market. The TEU introduced a comparatively new element in the emphasis it placed on social issues, specifically as they concerned employment policy. This was the so-called Social Chapter of the Maastricht Agreement which regulated matters such as workers' health and

safety, working hours and conditions, a minimum wage, rights to consultation through Works Councils and the rights of women in the workplace. It was a watered-down version of the original Social Charter proposed by Jacques Delors.

As a result of British objections, the Social Chapter was not integrated within the text agreed at Maastricht but was added as a protocol subscribed to, at the time, by eleven members, in other words by all members apart from the United Kingdom. The procedure demanded by this protocol meant that Commission proposals for social legislation would be vetoed by the UK but later reintroduced under the protocol as a measure applicable only to the Community minus Britain. This, for example, was the procedure adopted in September 1994 when Michael Portillo, the British employment secretary, vetoed a proposal before the Council of Ministers to permit men to take three months unpaid paternity leave on the birth or adoption of a child. At the same Council meeting, Portillo gave notice that Britain would treat proposed legislation on the rights of part-time workers in the same way.

Three years later the Labour government under Tony Blair accepted all the terms of the Social Chapter and agreed to implement the measures already adopted under it by the other fourteen member states – including the minimum wage, shorter working hours and paternity-leave provisions. At Amsterdam (1997) the Social Protocol was incorporated into the Treaty of Rome, so that there was a single framework for social policy. In addition, the promotion of jobs became an accepted goal of EU policy-makers, subject to its pursuit not being a threat to competitiveness.

By the time of the Amsterdam Treaty, there were six directives either passed or being negotiated:

- European works councils (1994)
- parental leave (1996)
- burden of proof in sex-discrimination cases (1997)
- part-time workers (1997)
- fixed-term work (1999)
- compulsory information and consultation procedures (national works councils) (2002).

Women's rights

Perhaps the greatest beneficiaries of European social legislation or judgments are women. In the words of one writer: 'All the most progressive legislation on women's rights is coming from Europe. The British government is continually being pushed to act by European directives and court decisions'.[6] The cases with the highest profiles were women who were dismissed from the armed services when they became pregnant. As a result of a ruling from Europe, the British courts had to award substantial damages to the 5,000 or so women affected.

These rulings over sexual equality have little to do with the Social Chapter of the TEU. Most are as a result of Article 119 of the Treaty of Rome, which states the principle that men and women should receive equal pay for equal work. In 1984 the European Court ordered the British government to amend the Equal Pay Act so as to read 'equal pay for work of equal value', which meant that employers could no longer justify inequalities in pay by claiming that men and women were doing different jobs. In one case a female speech therapist demanded equality with a much better-paid male pharmacist because they had a similar health-service grade.

European rules have also helped women in cases of equality of retirement, maternity benefits, compensation to pregnant women for unfair dismissal, invalid care allowances, sexual harassment in the workplace and so on. It is through actions such as these, from both the Commission and the European Court, that some measure of social legislation was forced on the UK government even during the years when it was hostile to the social dimension and before British acceptance of the Social Chapter.

Glossary

Agenda 2000 The title of a lengthy study presented by the then president of the European Commission, Jacques Santer, to the European Parliament in mid-1997. It was described in its introduction as a 'detailed strategy for strengthening and widening the Union in the early years of the twenty-first century'. Among other things, it included the Commission's assessment of the ten applicant states from Central and Eastern Europe; argued for an extension of QMV; and argued reform to the structural funds and the CAP.

Butter mountains/wine lakes The price guarantee and intervention system of the CAP resulted in overproduction of produce which then had to be stored. In the case of butter, the goods in storage were sold off at discounted prices – sometimes to the USSR.

GATT The General Agreement on Tariffs and Trade was created to promote international trade, by the reduction of tariff barriers, quantitative restrictions and subsidies on trade through a series of different agreements. Its functions were taken over by the World Trade Organisation which was established in the early 1990s.

Sustainable development/sustainability Development that meets the needs of the present without compromising the ability of future generations to meet their own needs.

CHAPTER 13

Second- and Third-Pillar policies

The policies covered under the Second and Third Pillars concern areas not related to the market. They encompass foreign and security issues, and justice and home affairs (referred to post-Amsterdam as 'police and judicial cooperation on criminal matters'). They are handled at the intergovernmental level, reserving a central role for the Council of Ministers. They are about the creation of a political community or **'polity'**. Had the Constitutional Treaty been ratified, the three pillars would have been merged together.

At Maastricht, the structure for the proposed European Union was created on the basis of three pillars. The First Pillar built upon the existing European Community and therefore allowed the Commission, Council and Parliament to exercise their full powers. The others were concerned with areas that had nothing to do with the market or the supranational institutions involved in its running. Foreign and security policy and justice and home affairs were placed under the primary jurisdiction of the Council of Ministers, although since the TEU was signed there have been changes to the handling of issues relating to the Third Pillar.

An indication of the desire to expand the Union's role in the lives of its inhabitants was to grant citizenship of the European Union to all people who held nationality of an EU member state. This conferred limited rights, including the right to move freely within the Union (without, as previously, having to prove that one was economically active or a close family member of someone who was); the right to use the embassy and consular services of any other member state if one's own country lacked diplomatic representation; the right of citizens residing in a member state to vote in that state in municipal and EP elections, or indeed to stand for election; and finally the right to petition the European Parliament and apply to the ombudsman.

The decisions to establish these new pillars at the Maastricht Summit reflected the wish of the majority of member states to advance beyond the old Community and create a new Union which would move into less familiar areas of cooperation and thereby create a new political community. Because it is concerned with domestic issues within the European Union with which we have been dealing so far, we turn first to the Third Pillar.

Internal security: police and judicial cooperation on criminal matters

At Maastricht, a new deal was reached on the policing of internal security through the Europol system, which would mean the abolition of border checks within the boundaries of the EU. The main advocate for the removal of internal borders was the Schengen Group of France, Germany and the Benelux countries, so called because of a meeting at the small Luxembourg town of Schengen in 1985. The five countries came to a formal agreement in 1990 and were joined by Italy (1990), Spain and Portugal (1991), Greece (1992) and Austria (1995). Occasionally the Scandinavian countries are reported to be thinking seriously about joining, but the United Kingdom and the Republic of Ireland resolutely remain outside the **Schengen Agreement**.

Migration

The reluctance of Britain and Ireland to agree to the removal of immigration controls for visitors entering one of the two countries from another EU country has a great deal to do with the problem of terrorism and the need to control the movement of terrorists and their weapons. But it has also a great deal to do with the insular nature of both the UK and Ireland and the two countries' lack of land frontiers. Both prefer to check entrants thoroughly at the point of entry and then allow visitors to move freely and unchecked within the country. In this way, the UK has in the past avoided the system of identity cards and residency permits demanded by most countries in the mainland EU, although discussion of ID cards is now firmly established upon the political agenda.

This drawing back from the removal of border controls is not unique to the British Isles. Many more states began to express doubts at the growing number of illegal immigrants, swollen by gypsies and others seeking political asylum. The influx reached new levels in 1999 and 2000. Estimates made in the summer of 1999 put the number of illegal immigrants smuggled into the EU every year at 400,000, with the EU already containing nearly a million displaced persons, the highest level of stateless migrants since the postwar diaspora of 1945.[1] The Amsterdam Treaty, which came into force in August 1999, took note of the growing concern and made dealing with immigration an EU-wide responsibility rather than leaving it to individual countries. In October 1999 a summit at Tampere in Finland established the first moves towards creating a system of fingerprinting immigrants and maintaining an EU-wide computer database, as well as proposing measures such as repatriation, which could lead to problems with civil rights groups.

In January 2000 the principle of the Schengen Agreement was undermined when both Belgium and Luxembourg reimposed border controls to counter an expected increase in the number of illegal immigrants. A clause of the Agreement allowed member countries to opt out for short periods in the light of special circumstances. For British eurosceptics, however, the actions of Belgium and Luxembourg were final proof that the Schengen policy of a common EU external border had failed to control illegal immigration at a time when the sheer number of immigrants and asylum seekers was causing major concern in the UK.[2]

As far as asylum seekers are concerned, however, the EU member countries do not have as much freedom of action as might be thought and adjustments to the Schengen Agreement are a very minor factor in the equation. A statement by a British government minister in February 2000 made it clear that Britain's response to the refugee crisis had very little to do with directives from Brussels, stating that, 'far from being a European treaty, it is the 1951 United Nations Convention on Refugees – signed by more than 120 countries – that obliges the United Kingdom to assess every asylum claim on its merits'.[3]

One other recent aspect of asylum and immigration policy has been a side effect of the Fifth Enlargement (Central and Eastern part i). Unlike some other EU countries, Britain imposed no transitional controls on the free movement of citizens from the new countries of Central and Eastern Europe. The Conservative opposition and elements in the tabloid press were urging action to prevent a mass influx of economic migrants seeking a better lifestyle in the more prosperous parts of the Union. Free movement of labour under EU rules is confined to people in search of jobs, not in search of benefits. Ministers did take late action to restrict benefits, but were prepared to argue their support for the open legal avenues available to economic migrants. The home secretary made it clear that blocking legal migration flows tends to encourage illegal migration and argued that any migrants from the accession countries would be welcome for the skills they could bring to a country with serious shortages of labour in the agriculture, construction, hotel and hospitality sectors. However, when Bulgaria and Romania were admitted in 2007, the UK government – in common with almost all others in the Union – imposed restrictions on working and claiming benefit, such was the pressure of opinion that had built up in Britain over the last few years about the extent of inward migration.

Personal liberty

The issues of personal mobility, asylum and immigration, management of frontiers and cross-border cooperation all have implications for individual liberty. From the beginning, the European Union has been based on respect for human rights and the rule of law. These values were enshrined in the Charter of Fundamental Rights (CFR) adopted by EU heads of government at Nice (December 2000). In a single document, the Charter sets out the personal, civil, political, economic and social rights enjoyed by inhabitants of the Union, as well as addressing new issues raised by technological progress such as bio-ethics and data protection. It was intended that this should become an integral part of the proposed constitution.

As it stands, the Charter is not a treaty of a constitutional or legal document. It has the ambiguous value of a 'solemn proclamation' by three of the Union's most important institutions (the Council, Commission and Parliament). Its text is mainly in harmony with the Universal Declaration of Human Rights and the

European Convention on Human Rights, and therefore can be taken as a confirmation of the pre-existing rights contained therein, while adding widely accepted principles such as the 'right' to good administration, workers' social rights and bioethics. It does not have the status of Community law. Therefore, cases cannot be brought solely on the ground of a contravention of the Charter.

Part II of the proposed European Constitution contained a version of the Charter. The intention was to enable the European Union to accede to the European Convention on Human Rights, thus enabling the European Court of Justice to rule on the basis of this Charter.

Defence and foreign policy

From the earliest days of postwar cooperation, there was always interest in the idea of developing Western security along the lines of the closest possible integration. The Preamble of the Treaty of Paris (1951) dwells less on the issues surrounding coal and steel and talks in more grandiose tones of setting aside the rivalries of the past and safeguarding peace in the future, via a merging of national interests.

The states of Europe were aware of their military weakness, and keen to put the situation right. Cooperation with the United States through NATO was the route chosen, for the Six (soon to become the original members of the EEC) were all signatories of the North Atlantic Treaty Organization. But the Americans were keen to see Europe strengthen its military capability, so that it would be a strong partner of the Atlantic Alliance.

With the failure of the attempt to form a European Defence Community in the early 1950s, Europe had no choice but to act as the junior partner of the NATO alliance. The only further attempt to create a European defence organisation was the development of the Western European Union, formed in 1955. But the scope of the organisation was quite unlike the Pleven initiative. The French proposal had embraced supranational thinking. The WEU proceeded on the basis that member states should act independently, but cooperate on an intergovernmental basis where this was feasible and desirable.

Progress towards the development of common policies

From the early 1970s, there was a greater attempt to harmonise foreign policies within the Community, the process then known as European Political Cooperation (EPC). On some issues this was relatively successful, for after failure to act together in response to the oil crisis of the early 1970s there was a greater appearance of agreement in dealing with events such as the Iran hostage crisis and the Soviet invasion of Afghanistan. But over the Falklands War, after initial consultation, the fragile unity began to crack as countries started to think about their own national interests. The agreement on modest economic sanctions was far short of a common foreign policy.

For several years, EPC was conducted on an intergovernmental basis outside the formal provisions of the Treaty of Rome. The passage of the Single European Act formalised the process of foreign policy consultation and cooperation between the member states, and brought it within the EC framework though not actually into the Treaty itself. For Holland,[4] this was 'the first step on the slippery slope to a common foreign policy and a federal Community'. It was certainly the case that the cooperation in foreign policy received a new impetus. Ginsberg[5] has drawn attention to the marked increase in foreign-policy initiatives in the five years after the SEA was implemented (188, compared with 121 in the previous five years). The trend towards developing a common and coherent approach to foreign policy was accelerating. Yet this was not the same as a common foreign policy, for it remained the case – and still does – that most member states intended to carry out their own external policy, with the backing of the Community if this could be obtained.

Dissatisfaction with Community policy was widespread within the EC by the late 1980s. Several states wanted to replace EPC with a more developed Common Foreign and Security Policy (CFSP). In the run-up to Maastricht, the issue of defence policy was hotly contested, being particularly difficult because it involved the wider question of relations with the United States. The British suspected that the French were using this issue as part of their long-standing Gaullist strategy of separating Europe from American power and influence. The French believed that Britain's approach to defence matters reflected a more general ambiguity about its attitude to the development of closer ties with the continent.

Britain distinguished defence policy from the more general issue of security. For British ministers, defence was not a matter for the EC, for it is primarily a question of how nations physically defend themselves when under attack. Besides, any new initiative might undermine NATO and prompt a US withdrawal from Europe. However, security policy involves a wider network of agreements to make war less likely, so that this could be an appropriate issue for Europe to handle – preferably at an intergovernmental level.

Pre-Maastricht, foreign policy again tested the ability of the Community to act on a common basis. Policy over the Middle East has long been an area on which a minority of members have had conflicting national interests with their EC partners. Over the Iraqi invasion of Kuwait (1990), it was not hard to agree that all EC citizens in that country should be protected and that sanctions should be imposed on Saddam Hussein. Beyond that, it was more difficult to move forward. It was left to the British and French to make their own individual approaches to avoid war breaking out. There was no effective Community approach in the run-up to and duration of the Gulf War.

Progress at Maastricht

At Maastricht, European Political Cooperation was taken further and placed within the wider conception of a 'Common Foreign and Security Policy'. The CFSP was the second of the 'three pillars' of the new European Union. At the Summit there was agreement that there should be closer cooperation on foreign and security policies to 'assert the Community's identity on the international scene'. Progress in these areas should build upon and develop existing forms of cooperation. National governments were still to be in the driving seat, though EC institutions such as the Commission and Parliament were able to express a view and have their recommendations taken into account.

The Treaty developed the position set out in the Single European Act. It was agreed that the new European Union should 'define and implement a common foreign and security policy . . . covering all areas'. This was to include 'all questions related to the security of the Union, including the eventual framing of a common defence policy, which might in time lead to a common defence'. The procedure laid down involved regular cooperation between the states on matters of general interest. Where appropriate, the Council would – on a unanimous basis – define common positions to which the policies of member countries would have to conform. Majority voting did not extend to defence policy.

The Western European Union was given the role of elaborating and implementing 'decisions and actions of the Union which have defence implications'. It was to be developed 'as the defence component of the European Union and as the means to strengthen the European pillar of the Atlantic Alliance'. Defence was therefore to remain a matter for NATO, but the European arm would be strengthened. The WEU was to become the bridge between the two other organisations.

Recent developments

One of the problems in articulating a coherent European foreign policy is the lack of a single voice. No one 'speaks for Europe'. Back in the 1970s, Henry Kissinger, the American secretary of state, was said to have asked: 'When I want to speak to Europe, whom do I call?' There is no one who can speak, let alone act, on Europe's behalf. Europe often seems to speak with different voices, and in response to issues such as the fighting in Bosnia in the 1990s or in Iraq more recently (see Box 13.1), there tends to be a lack of clear and agreed thinking. Alarmed at the dithering and squabbling in this field, Jacques Delors once spoke of 'organised schizophrenia'.

On occasion, the immediate handling of issues has been the responsibility of a troika of the foreign minister whose country holds the presidency, his predecessor and his likely successor. At other times, the president of the Commission and the prime minister of the government which holds the presidency of the Council have acted. It is because of this lack of an effective procedure that several calls have been made in recent years for a high-profile figure to represent the EU's

Box 13.1 The decision to invade Iraq in 2003

The decision to invade Iraq caused a major rift within the Union. Given its traditional role as a bridge between the EU and the USA, the UK was in a difficult position. Tony Blair would have desperately liked to get a second United Nations resolution in favour of action against Saddam Hussein, but when this proved impossible he backed the Americans, who had never fully shared his enthusiasm for the UN route. As de Gaulle had argued some four decades previously, when it came to the crunch Britain proved to be more Atlanticist than European.

In its approach to the Iraqi problem, Britain had some backing within the Union. On the Security Council, the Spaniards and the Bulgarians supported acting without a second resolution, but France and Russia were resolutely opposed to such action. Within the EU, France and Germany led the opposition to the war. Italy, Spain and some of the would-be members form Central and Eastern Europe were sympathetic to the British position. Yet again, as on so many earlier foreign policy issues, the Union found it difficult to reach agreement.

Box 13.2 Arrangements agreed in the Constitutional and Lisbon Treaties

The draft constitution made provision for the creation of an EU foreign minister and a team of assisting officials. The British government would have preferred the term 'EU external representative', but the title proposed by the Convention was accepted. In other respects, the draft treaty laid down that 'competence in matters of common foreign and security policy shall cover all areas of foreign policy and all questions relating to the union's security, including the progressive framing of a common defence policy, which might lead to a common defence'. It called on member states to 'actively and unreservedly' support EU policy in what is called a 'spirit of solidarity', refraining from actions 'contrary to the Union's interests' or effectiveness. It also provided for greater military cooperation and arms procurement systems, as well as a terrorist 'solidarity clause', if attacked.

The British government felt able to accept these provisions, as long as within the treaty it was made clear that member states and the Council of Ministers conduct foreign and security policy. It wished to ensure that NATO remained as the mutual defence organisation for the Western Alliance and resisted any inclusion of a defence structure that duplicated or weakened it. In the amending treaty signed at Lisbon in 2007, the foreign minister was re-named the High Representative of the Union for Foreign Affairs and Security Policy. The occupant of the new post will replace the European Commissioner for External Relations and the High Representative for CFSP and thereby give the Union a more distinctive international identity.

Box 13.3 Towards a European Army? The Rapid Reaction Force (RRF)

In 1998, France and the United Kingdom launched an initiative at St Malo to strengthen the EU's capacity to respond to international crises, on the premise that the Union could only play a coherent and effective political role if it was underpinned by a credible military capacity. Their plan was adopted at the Cologne Council in June 1999. By May of the following year, the Union had operational capability across the full range of tasks, albeit much limited and constrained by recognised shortfalls. By December 2003, it could – within 60 days – deploy some 60,000 troops with air and naval support, and sustain them in action for about a year. Of the troops, the UK was contributing some 12,500, in addition to 18 warships and 72 combat aircraft.

The crises that its creators had in mind included:

- humanitarian rescue work
- peacekeeping
- the tasks of combat forces in crisis management.

This military capacity is firmly rooted in NATO, which remains responsible for the collective defence of the West. NATO has and will retain the lead role in crisis management and the RRF will only act 'autonomously' when NATO chooses to do nothing. But there is a growing recognition in Europe that it should assume a greater share of its security burden and strengthen its military capability. The RRF is not a European army, even though it can be mobilised without NATO's approval, possesses a European command chain and draws primarily on European military resources. The troops are not members of a standing force and do not wear a common uniform; moreover, each country retains control over the number and deployment of its troops. Rather, the RRF represents a pooling of national armies that remain under sovereign national command. It is a useful tool for European Union policy-makers that can be called upon as any situation requires. It represents what Bomberg and Stubb[6] describe as a 'small but decisive step towards creating a European Security and Defence Policy'.

agreed foreign policy to the world. Sceptics were worried that such a supremo could easily become the master rather than a servant of the Union.

Difficulties in achieving a common foreign and security policy

Matters of defence, security and foreign policy go to the very heart of the debate on political union. Until now there has been only limited scope for joint decision-making on foreign-policy matters, but many members would like to see the development of common policies which would include the eventual framing of a common defence policy. In the eyes of many committed Europeans, the eventual goal of a common policy would be the creation of a European Army (see Box 13.3).

This is an area of contention. As the then Defence Secretary Michael Portillo told the Conservative Party Conference in 1996: 'We will not allow Brussels to control our defence policy. Britain will not be told when to fight . . . Britain is blessed with very brave soldiers, sailors and airmen, willing to give their lives – for Britain, not for Brussels'. Many British people would echo his suspicions of any Europeanisation of defence policy, for it is considered to be too basic to British national interests.

In defence and foreign affairs, the same problems that delayed the evolution of common policies in the past have still yet to be resolved. They include:

- the lack of any shared vision about what the nature and objectives of a CFSP should be like
- divergences of opinion about the role of the EU in European security and as to whether cooperation should follow an integrationist pattern or – as Britain favours – remain intergovernmental
- a lack of clarity about whether or not the enlargement of NATO or the WEU is a better route to developing European security in general and especially for the 'new democracies'.

The United States has been keen to see the Europeans develop a stronger role in looking after their own security, but in any burden-sharing it repeats its oft-stated position of 'three no's'. There should be no decoupling of the US from Europe, no duplication of American forces by the EU and no discrimination against the US, including in the area of arms purchases. Member states know the issues and are aware of the difficulties. As yet, they are unclear how to resolve them to the satisfaction of all members.

In some key parts of the world, the EU still does not count for very much. On paper, it is the largest block of the rich and free next to the US, its equal in every-thing but military power. In trade, aid and competition talks, it acts that way and is treated with respect. But not as yet in foreign policy. If its views are to be listened to in Washington, Beijing, New Delhi and the Middle East, it needs to speak with a clear voice and in such a way that the Kissinger question ceases to be relevant.

Glossary

Polity A politically organised unit; a political community.
Schengen Agreement An agreement working towards the gradual abolition of border controls was originally signed by five member states in 1985 (Belgium, France, Germany, Luxembourg and the Netherlands). Thirty countries are now signatories (including three non-member states: Iceland, Norway and Switzerland). Denmark, Ireland and the UK have Partially opted out. The Agreement also includes provisions for a common policy on the temporary entry of persons (including the Schengen Visa), the harmonisation of external border controls and cross-border police cooperation. It was incorporated into the Treaty of Amsterdam.

SECTION FIVE: ATTITUDES

Introduction

Eligibility for membership

Article 237 of the Treaty of Rome (1957) makes it clear that the Union is open to applicant countries whose economic and political situation are such as to make accession possible. Subject to that qualification, 'any European state may become a member'. In 1969, a communiqué from The Hague laid down the basis on which issues of enlargement were to be approached:

> In so far as the applicant States accept the Treaties and their political aims, the decisions taken since entry into force of the Treaties and the options adopted in the sphere of development.

These principles have remained in force ever since – acceptance of the Treaties, of the *acquis communautaire* and of the political aspirations of the members. However, they were updated in 1993, so that there were clear conditions for the entry of 'new democracies' in Central and Eastern Europe. The idea was that those countries with Europe Agreements 'that so desire shall become members of the [European] Union'.

Known as the Copenhagen Criteria, the revised guidelines required that applicant countries should have:

- stable institutions that guarantee democracy, the rule of law, human rights and respect for minority groups (the political criterion)
- a functioning market economy and the capacity to cope with competitive pressures and market forces within the EU (the economic criterion)
- the ability to take on the obligations of membership, including adherence to the aims of political, economic and monetary union (the criterion concerning the adoption of the *acquis communautaire*).

In every case of enlargement, new members have had to accept the existing EU institutions and arrangements, although they might be allowed a period of transition. As yet, only Morocco has ever been turned down as an applicant, on the grounds that it does not qualify as a European country. Turkey – a future candidate for entry – has been deemed to be a European Power.

The six nations that formed the European Economic Community became the Nine, the Ten and the Twelve. In 1989, Jacques Delors publicly aired the question in his mind: 'Is the time coming when we must start thinking about a twenty- or even a twenty-two-nation Community? Within a few years of his question, there were fifteen members. But the massive expansion in terms of number – if not size – of countries, came about in the present century. The recent enlargements have created an EU of almost 500m people. Since the

formation of the EEC, twenty-one additional applicant countries have therefore qualified for membership.

Attitudes among member states

The member states of the EU differ considerably in their approaches to the EU,
its institutions, policies, treaties and end-destination. Some are intergovernmentalist, some federalist; some want a looser Union, others one in which the bonds
are firmly cast; some are strongly committed and some are more lukewarm in
their enthusiasm. Whatever their differences, as member states they all have a
common interest in making the Union work. This is good for Europe, but it can
also serve their own national interests.

Member states applied to join for their own individual reasons. These were
based upon their perception of what was best for their country. They each had
their own concerns and interests, in the light of the circumstances of the day.
Many of those concerns and interests remain, even though the circumstances
may have changed since the time of their admission. These priorities continue
to affect the ways in which their politicians react when new initiatives are
advanced and when new issues and controversies arise.

The divergence of outlook between member states does not merely reflect the
time when they were admitted. There may be some differences between the groups
of nations that have joined in each of the enlargements, particularly in their
reasons for applying for membership. For instance, the original six were inspired
by some of the considerations mentioned in Section One in the early postwar
years, whereas the eight mainland countries that joined in 2004 shared some
common ideas about the need to advance peace and prosperity in their region and
ensure the safety and viability of their 'new democracies'. But more significantly
there have been differences between those who joined at the same time.

1. *There was and remains some divergence in outlook between the original Six*, although in
   their case they shared a similar sense of urgency about the need to build a
   new strong and peaceful Europe after 1945, as well as a commitment to the
   European Idea. The Benelux countries have always been in favour of
   European integration which enjoys cross-party support. Their politicians
   have assumed disproportionate importance in the institutions of the
   EC/EU. Brussels and Luxembourg have provided a base for its institutions,
   Maastricht the location for one of its key treaties. As far as possible, they
   support the Commission as the guardian of European interests and as a
   counterbalance to the dominant role inevitably played by the larger states.
   By contrast, in order to allay the fears of their national populations, France
   and Germany have had to demonstrate more clearly that their national
   interests and those of Europe are not in conflict.

2. *The differences were and are more evident between the countries which joined in the First Enlargement.* The British and the Danes have been less communautaire, retaining many of the attitudes which made them initially more doubtful about the desirability of membership. Both are firmly committed to an intergovernmental approach which enables them to fight strongly for national interests and seek to limit the scope of EU interference in national life. By contrast, the Irish saw evident advantages in joining the Community and thereby establishing more clearly their national distinctiveness from the countries that made up the United Kingdom. Aware of the benefits that membership has brought them, they remain broadly enthusiastic.

3. *Both of the two Iberian countries that joined in the Third Enlargement shared an aspiration to re-enter the European political and economic mainstream* after more than a generation of near-total isolation during their years of authoritarian rule. However, Spain is more Community-minded and committed to integration, identifying Europe with liberty, modernisation and prosperity. Portugal acknowledges the benefits that membership of such a community can offer, but also tends to support any scheme likely to reduce the role of Brussels in its national life.

4. *Of the two Scandinavian countries that joined eight years later, Finland has been more sympathetic to Union developments than Sweden.* Keen to throw off memories of Soviet involvement in the past, it has been willing to embrace policies such as the single currency and joined the eurozone at the earliest opportunity. Sweden lacked the same initial enthusiasm and has been a lukewarm member ever since. Swedes have been wary of Brussels interference and the country has still not signed up for membership of euroland. The Riksdag voted decisively against Swedish participation.

5. *Unsurprisingly, there are substantial differences between the ten new entrants admitted to the Union in 2005.* They are not solely based on the division between those countries which are new democracies in Central and Eastern Europe, and those two which are Mediterranean islands and have a very different background. There are differences too among the former Soviet satellites, some being broadly supportive of the UK and its negotiating positions, other more integrationist in their approach.

Factors that influence attitudes

Several factors help to determine the attitudes of individual countries towards membership of the European Union, how they behave as EU members and the stances they take in Brussels negotiations and over proposed new initiatives. Foremost among them are:

Table S5I.1 Varying attitudes towards membership in the member states in July 2006, pre the Fifth Enlargement part ii (%)

Country	Believe country has benefited from membership	Believe membership to be on balance a good thing	Have trust in EU and its institutions	Are satisfied with the way democracy works	Support a constitution for the EU	Believe in the process of further enlargement
Austria	39	34	43	45	44	27
Belgium	66	65	61	67	75	45
Cyprus	40	49	61	54	64	58
Czech Rep.	62	52	60	64	52	58
Denmark	75	65	55	65	45	51
Estonia	66	51	56	47	47	50
Finland	45	39	41	42	45	35
France	50	49	41	40	62	31
Germany	46	57	41	43	71	28
Greece	72	53	63	52	62	56
Hungary	52	49	70	60	78	59
Ireland	87	77	57	65	56	45

Italy	54	56	56	58	71	48
Latvia	55	37		53	52	54
Lithuania	72	59	57	47	58	60
Luxembourg	71	72	54	63	64	27
Malta	50	44	53	49	46	56
Netherlands	63	74	48	47	59	43
Poland	64	56	58	62	62	72
Portugal	56	47	57	39	53	47
Slovakia	70	55	60	43	55	58
Slovenia	68	54	63	65	71	73
Spain	71	72	50	60	63	55
Sweden	43	49	39	45	39	49
UK	42	42	31	40	42	44
EU average	**54**	**55**	**48**	**50**	**61**	**45**

Findings based on *Eurobarometer* polling, no. 65, published in July 2006

- the timing of their entry and the circumstances of their joining
- their location and size
- their level of prosperity
- their political and social characteristics
- their commitment to the causes of either integration or intergovernmentalism.

1. *Timing of entry and circumstances of joining* We have seen that there are differences in outlook between states that formed the original EEC and between those that joined in successive enlargements. However, the core six countries who together formed the ECSC and then created the common market had underlying similar experiences in World War Two, either being defeated or overrun and occupied. From the beginning, there was a desire to secure peace in Europe and – on the part of French and West German leaders – to lay aside the hostilities which had characterised relations between their two countries. Those ties have remained intact, whatever the differences over particular issues and developments. Often, they have been assisted by strong personal relationships, such as those between Mitterrand and Kohl in the 1980s and 1990s. The Franco-German axis has been fundamental to the development of the Community, later Union.

The Benelux countries and Italy have not had the same rivalries to overcome, but they regard themselves as part of that solid core. They are deeply attached to the Union, having played a key role in driving it forward and sustaining the momentum to integration.

2. *Location and size* Location has a number of consequences. The Scandinavian countries have proved less integrationist than the original core countries and some of the others, two of the three not opting to join the single currency. This may reflect that they are further from Brussels and therefore more reluctant to see it assume powers that they would prefer to keep to themselves. Geographically, they are on the periphery of the mainland, so that the seat of EU decision-making may seem remote. The same can be said of the UK, whose island position imposes a natural barrier between Britain and the continent.

So too geography affects the outlook of the Mediterranean countries. Greece, Italy (in Naples and Sicily) and Portugal have all been beneficiaries of the policy of cohesion which influences their attitude to budgetary issues and enlargement. Following the Fifth Enlargement parts i and ii, the inclusion of new states which have less developed economies now means that there is a rival area in need of EU spending.

Size is an important determinant of states' attitudes towards membership of the Union and their willingness cede powers to Brussels. The five large states with populations of 40m or more – in particular the 'big three' in terms of status

(France, Germany and the United Kingdom) – are keen to assert their national interests. In the negotiations at Nice and over the abortive proposal for an EU constitution, they were anxious to ensure that the weighting of the voting was in their favour. They have dominated the pace of development in the Union and at times have been resolute to the point of defiance in defending their position on issues that they regard as important to them.

Size affects the weighting of votes in the Council of Ministers and the scaled membership of national delegations in the European Parliament, Economic and Social Committee and Committee of the Regions. By virtue of its 82m inhabitants, Germany is inevitably in a strong bargaining position, the more so as it is the Union's main paymaster.

Small states such as Denmark, Finland, Ireland and Sweden do not have the same key interests to defend, but they are concerned to ensure that the big three do not ride roughshod over them and develop the Union according to their own priorities and preferences. Of course, there may be substantial differences in outlook between states with the same populations, as there are between Denmark and Finland, both of which have 5m people. In the future, as the EU continues to grow, it will have a considerably larger proportion of small states than in the past and the way they use their votes and become partners in coalitions in support of or opposition to new developments may well assume greater significance.

3. *Level of prosperity* The six mainland countries which pioneered European cooperation after World War Two were at the time battered and in need of reconstruction. But they recovered strongly and in the early years of the Community fared particularly well, their peoples benefiting from the expansion of Community trade. There were in those 'good years' few ailing regions. However, with the First Enlargement, regional variations became an important factor within the Community. There were areas of industrial decline in England, Scotland, Wales and Northern Ireland, and of course in the Irish Republic living standards were markedly less prosperous than in Europe as a whole.

The three states that joined in the Second and Third Enlargements were poor, giving a new impetus to discussion of the need for cohesion to ensure the harmonious development of their economies. So too, the economy and living standards of several of the new entrants in 2004 lagged well under the EU average. Inevitably, therefore, countries that are net contributors such as Germany (with its own economic problems in recent years) are concerned to limit the growth of Union spending, whereas poorer countries have joined in the expectation that they might benefit from the transfer of financial resources in their direction.

Again, some more affluent countries such as Austria and Sweden have placed considerable emphasis on environmental protection, both before and since joining the Union. They have argued for stringent regulations to make EU environmental policies more effective. Governments in poorer countries have not felt able to attach the same priority to clean air, conscious as they have been of the need for economic growth and the rapid development of their economies. They are unlikely to support restrictive policies that impose heavy burdens on their manufacturers.

4. *Political and economic character* Federalism and regionalism have had implications for EU development. They have created sub-national layers of government whose members have sought representation in EU bodies, the German Länder, the Scottish Parliaments and the Welsh Executive among them. They lobby for EU funding and monitor the way in which Union policies impact upon the areas they represent.

So too has the economic character of member states affected their attitudes. UK governments since 1979 have urged market-oriented solutions in economic and social policy. Nordic countries have also supported liberal economic policies, but they tend to stress the importance of the public sector and state provision as well. France, at the other extreme, has always been more concerned with the protection of workers, rights, its leaders often being critical of UK deregulatory initiatives.

5. *Commitment to the causes of either integration or intergovernmentalism* The UK has the reputation of being a reluctant European (see pp. 275–6), its politicians finding European issues particularly difficult to grapple with. Denmark and Sweden are usually less than communautaire, surveys suggesting that a significant element among their inhabitants have deep reservations about the benefits of membership and are wary of any move to closer integration.

By contrast, Greece, Italy, Luxembourg and Spain tend to be strong supporters of EU membership which they see as yielding decisive national benefits. Their leaders are often supporters of an enhanced role for the Union in national life and they accept that the loss of some national freedom of manoeuvre is more than offset by the benefits that integration can provide. In most countries, there is a discrepancy between politicians in office, who – with varying degrees of enthusiasm – see the desirability/necessity of membership, and the population at large, a growing number of whom in recent years have seen the Union as remote from and unhelpful in promoting their interests.

Of course, when it comes to negotiations, however fervent the pro-integrationist rhetoric employed by those involved, hard bargaining takes over. Whilst they may deploy the language of euro-enthusiasm, they may make a vigorous stand against the use of QMV on the policy issues which they regard as particularly sensitive.

The most effective way of seeing how far such considerations have influenced the attitudes of member states is by briefly examining each nation in turn. This will be done by grouping nations according to the stage at which they joined.

CHAPTER 14

Member states

Member states have joined the EU – with or without the expressed support of their national populations – in a bid for national advantage. National governments have concluded that, on balance, their countries would be better placed pooling their sovereignty and operating inside the Union rather than retaining nominal sovereignty and operating as free agents outside. The specific arguments for membership have varied among the twenty-seven states, as has the degree of enthusiasm among ministers and peoples about belonging to the EU.

In this chapter, we look at the experience of member states according to the stages at which they joined, ascertaining in the process perceived advantages from and popular reactions to membership.

The original core countries: the Six

Benelux countries: 1. Belgium

Along with Luxembourg and the Netherlands, Belgium had already had some experience of practical cooperation before it became a founder of the ECSC. The three Benelux countries had been involved in a customs union and this encouraged them to work towards wider economic and political harmonisation. In addition, the governments and peoples of each state knew that they could achieve more by working together than they could by acting on their own, particularly in the economic and political arena.

Belgium has been generally supportive of all moves to closer integration in Europe. Paul-Henri Spaak played a leading role in devising the draft treaties. Since then, the country has been responsible for urging the EC forward in many of its initiatives, not least in the run-up to Maastricht.

Lacking as strong a sense of national identity as some other member states, the Belgians have had no problems with federalist notions. They have seen benefits in advancing more swiftly in that direction. That Belgians favour a federal solution is not surprising, given the country's federal status. They see it as a means of catering for diversity, and of promoting decentralised and effective government. From this perspective, subsidiarity is an inevitable and desirable element of the federal idea.

Belgians have had few fears of EMU, CFSP and majority voting, seeing all of them as part of the general move towards closer integration, a goal which they warmly embrace. In the interpretation of that goal, Belgian governments have been flexible, accepting that it does not by definition mean that all states must proceed at the same pace or commit themselves to every policy initiative.

Politicians of all shades of opinion and people be they Flemish or Walloon all see benefits in European membership, making the relationship of Belgium and Europe what one writer has called 'a marriage of love and reason'.[1]

Benelux countries: 2. The Netherlands

The Dutch, like the Belgians and Luxembourgers, have always been in the fore-front of moves to closer integration in Europe. Like the other Benelux countries, they backed most of the policies discussed among the Twelve in the run-up to Maastricht, for the country had much to gain from its membership of a peace-ful and prosperous Community. On their own, the Dutch would play a much less significant role than they can do in a union, for size, geography and recent history have shown that they are vulnerable in times of continental upheaval. Yet as the host country at the 1991 summit, the Dutch representatives played an important role in brokering the agreement.

The Dutch are traditionally keen to see the Union move forward. They support the supranational over the intergovernmental model. Their priorities have been more majority voting, progress on CFSP (as long as it is compatible with NATO's primary role) and democratisation of the European institutions. They have long wanted to tackle the 'democratic deficit' by a strengthening of the European Parliament and welcomed the co-decision procedure as a useful step in the right direction. Above all, like the Belgians and Luxembourgers, they support a powerful Commission (which they portray as the driving force of inte-gration) and other supranational bodies such as the Court of Justice.

Like their Belgian counterparts, Dutch politicians can accept differentiated integration, though they tend to interpret this as states being permitted to move at different speeds but always towards the same goal. They dislike opt-outs and other devices designed to allow some states permanently to reject participation in particular Union activities.

For all of their pro-Europeanism, 65 per cent of Dutch voters rejected the proposed constitution in 2005, on a turnout of 63.3 per cent. Several reasons have been advanced for the rejection, which came soon after the French elec-torate had delivered a similar verdict.

- According to one poll,[2] 30 per cent of the Constitution's opponents used the referendum as an opportunity to demonstrate their dissatisfaction with the centre-right coalition government.
- Some voter anxieties were not strictly related to the provisions of the Constitution, having more to do with fears of an increase in immigration (particularly should Turkey be allowed to join); an outsourcing of jobs to some of the recently admitted member states; the rising cost of living of the euro; and a more general feeling that the political establishment had sought to advance European integration without sufficient consultation or a genuine attempt to engage the public.
- The majority of voters who voted 'no' did so for reasons that were concerned with the Constitution. The poll mentioned above found that 48 per cent of them thought the new Constitution was worse than the existing treaties and

44 per cent were worried about the declining influence of the Netherlands in the EU, which in their views the Treaty did nothing to arrest.

Benelux countries: 3. Luxembourg

Wedged between Germany, France and Belgium, Luxembourg (with a tiny population and a land area smaller than many English counties) has survived as an independent nation by a series of historical accidents. It was a founder member of the Community and retains the privileges of separate national status in the EU. In some circumstances it can veto measures which command the support of all the other member states. It seems hard to justify a situation in which it has two votes in the Council to represent under 400,000 people, when Germany has only twenty-nine to represent 80m.

Luxembourg clearly has much to gain from membership of the European Union, which accounts for its generally positive attitude to any proposals designed to bring about further integration. Membership has given Luxembourg far more of a say in European affairs than its size and resources would allow it to reasonably expect. Moreover, its former prime minister, Jacques Santer, was a president of the Commission and a powerful figure on the European stage.

On almost every economic indicator, Luxembourg is a very wealthy country. It carries little public debt and easily became the first member state to meet the Maastricht criteria. Its people are the best placed in Europe. GDP per capita amounts to $72,945, compared to the EU average of $28,477, a performance far outstripping that of other prosperous nations such as the Germans and Danes.[3]

France

The French commitment to the idea of unity in Europe is a long-standing one, for Frenchmen such as Monnet and Schuman were to a large extent responsible for moves to initiate the whole European project. Not all leaders have shared Monnet's enthusiasm for a ceding of sovereignty to supranational bodies in Europe. De Gaulle was particularly determined to preserve his country's independence and freedom of manoeuvre. Since his passing, however, other presidents from Pompidou onwards have been more willing to move the process of uniting Europe forward. The reunification of Germany in 1990 gave added urgency to this task. Mitterrand particularly was convinced of the need to cement ties within the Union to ensure that Germany was firmly anchored in Western Europe.

Yet Mitterrand and Chirac, along with many other French, have been committed to the pursuit of national self-interests. Whilst urging the need for the closest cooperation on some topics, they reserve other areas of policy for national solution. At Maastricht, Mitterrand firmly backed the intergovernmentalist approach used to handle the issues of immigration and law and order, and defence and foreign policy. Chirac has tended to avoid the rhetorical flourishes of his predecessor and is less of a euro-visionary. A United States of Europe is not on his agenda, but his approach differs little in essentials from that of earlier French presidents. Although fighting strongly to defend French interests, he believes in European cooperation and the importance of Union institutions. To his compatriots, this seems like sensible dualism, an acceptance of the need to divide and share political power in the modern world. History and geography have combined to place France in the forefront of the drive for closer coopera-tion. The attempt to achieve this has been backed by members of almost all parties for much of the postwar era.

French politicians have often sounded more committed than the French people. The referendum to ratify the Maastricht Agreement was only narrowly approved. In 2005, it was the French who effectively scuppered the likelihood of the Constitution ever being implemented even though Giscard d'Estaing and his team were the architects of its construction.

Some of the French reluctance has been based upon the country's status as a net contributor to the Union. Rightwingers such as Jean-Marie Le Pen of the Front Nationale actively campaigned against the EU, complaining – among other things – of its policies on employment, immigration and taxation. Many French like the Community, but have doubts about the way in which it has evolved.

Germany

Germany as a united entity has only existed since 1990. Before then, the gov-ernments of the Moscow-backed German Democratic Republic ruled in the five Eastern Länder, whereas the bulk of Germans lived in West Germany, which was a founder member of the ECSC and by the 1970s a leading Power in the Community. Unification has created a mighty German state of more than 80m people.

The Union has been good for Germany. The CAP has been beneficial to the agrarian community, which has received substantial subsidies. Although much of this money originally comes from the German economy (Germany is a heavy net contributor to the EU) such a method of reallocating the nation's resources has generally found favour with most German people.

The Germans have long prided themselves on being the most European of states. Along with President Mitterrand of France, Chancellor Kohl was a fore-most supporter of the idea of moving to ever closer integration. He held the view that whereas all European nations needed unification, Germany needed it more than the others, to ensure that his unified and powerful country was firmly locked into Europe. He understood the fears of some other nations about Germany's past record and also their anxieties about the potential strength of the German economy, actual and potential.

However, Kohl was acutely aware of some stirrings of a new national sense of self-awareness, following unification. The growth of strongly nationalist feeling in former Eastern Germany (with some ugly racial behaviour) in his view pointed to the need to anchor the country firmly in the West European camp. The 16m people in the East had their own preoccupations. The 62m in the West, denied a national debate on the implications of Maastricht for their political future and above all for their currency, increasingly grumbled about the cost. They also feared that their country, as the strongest on the continent, would be forever the milch-cow of a Europe eventually stretching from the Atlantic to the Urals.

From Maastricht onwards, there has been rising opposition within Germany to the European project. One writer even detected that by the end of the 1990s – a time when Germany was experiencing the costs associated with unification and higher unemployment – the country was turning from being 'a champion of federalism into an advocate of intergovernmentalism'.[4] Politicians at all levels began to talk more about national interests. In particular, the burden of being a net contributor weighed heavily in its attitudes, curbing its support for costly new initiatives.

Kohl's successor, Gerhard Schröder, continued his country's friendly relationship with Jacques Chirac, but in addition cultivated close ties with Russian president Vladimir Putin, in an attempt to strengthen the 'strategic partnership' between Berlin and Moscow. The three men were critical of US/UK policy over Iraq. In contrast, Angela Merkel has tried to improve relations with the United States and in her European policy has:

- sought a reduction of centralism in the EU management
- worked for a reduction of Germany's share in financing European projects
- supported the idea of beginning negotiations for admission of Croatia
- endeavoured to remove the Russian capital from the strategic axis of Paris–Berlin–Moscow created by Chancellor Schröder.

In the early twenty-first century, following the rejection of the constitution and anxieties among voters in some countries about enlargement, many observers of the EU were looking for a German lead, particularly during its presidency in the first half of 2007. At a time of weakened morale in the Union, there were hopes that 'Angela can fix it'. Her German presidency of the Union set itself three ambitious goals: progress towards a new European constitution or set of decision-making rules; beefing up the EU's common foreign policy, to show that Europe can be effective in tackling the world's most dangerous conflicts; and finding answers to the looming threat to Europe's energy security, as well as climate change and other long-term challenges.

Italy

Postwar Italy had no reason to look back on the history of the nation state with particular pride. In the years before Mussolini's rule, the country had been torn apart by internal schism. When he was in power, the Italian attachment to democratic government was abandoned and for several years he was an ally of Hitler. After the hostilities, many Italians felt a need to demonstrate their respectability by showing themselves loyal to other West European nations. In so doing, they hoped also to buttress their new democracy at home. Membership of the Six might prove economically and politically beneficial as well as desirable for these other reasons.

Nicoll and Salmon[5] have pointed to the twin approach of Italians to the Community and latterly to the Union, in their reference to the combination of 'pragmatism and idealism in Italian thinking'. They suggest that this accounts for the 'contradiction between the prevalence of pro-integrationist rhetoric in Italian political circles, and their marked inability or unwillingness to translate this into policy action'. Italians like and support the idea of Europe, but find that applying its rules can be inconvenient or even costly and disadvantageous. This is perhaps why they have a poorer record of implementation than other nations.

The Italians do not carry a heavy punch in Union affairs. Partly this may be because of their failure to show themselves as 'good Europeans' when it comes to carrying out EU policies. It also reflects the postwar weakness and instability of Italian politics, and of the national economy. This means that although they do not wish to be in the slow lane when new schemes are planned, they are rarely ready to join them. However, they are very concerned that the EU should not develop into a two-tier, two-speed Union. They tend to look with disfavour on opt-outs and exceptions.

Italian people tend to be strongly pro-European. They are keen to vote in European elections. Perhaps because they are unimpressed with their national political leadership, they have been more willing to embrace a European identity and support institutions such as the Parliament by voting for its elected representatives. Whilst not opposed to enlargement, they are wary of supporting any moves that might threaten the solidity of the core.

Countries of the First Enlargement

Denmark

Denmark applied to join the Community because a majority of its political leaders and people were aware of the perils of exclusion. The decision was determined by economic considerations. The Danes were never committed to federal ideas or the goal of wider integration. Subsequently, Denmark has been one of the few countries to stress national sovereignty in its approach to the EU. It still displays some resistance to political supranationality, its leaders preferring to work via intergovernmental cooperation, with a built-in right of national veto.

The Danes have had several chances to express their feelings about the European Community and their country's role within it. In direct elections to the

Parliament in Strasbourg, voter turnouts have generally been low by continental standards, although they were slightly above average in 1999 and 2004. However, by contrast, in the six referendums on membership of, and changes within, the Community, interest has been high, for in these there has been a keenly contested election with a real issue at stake. 82.3 per cent and 86.2 per cent respectively voted in the two referendums on the Maastricht Treaty.

Danish policy in the EU has always been pragmatic, based upon what seems beneficial to national interests. Accordingly, on certain issues the Danes have been more positive than Britain. They were supportive of the unreformed Common Agricultural Policy, for their competitive farming industry benefited from its generous subsidies. They also like the greater emphasis on environmental protection of recent years, but are less committed to the social dimension of the CAP.

Otherwise, Denmark has strongly supported free trade and the single market, and aspects of the EU's environmental, industrial, regional and social programmes. But it is wary of moves to harmonise taxes and tends to resist intrusions into the welfare arena which it sees as a national matter. On external matters, it has been sympathetic to enlargement of the Union, supporting the accession of its Nordic cousins in Finland and Sweden in the 1990s and towards the East (in particular, the applications from the three Baltic states of Estonia, Latvia and Lithuania) ten years later. This is in line with their view of the Union as a loose and open framework for cooperation.

In Denmark, there appears to be little popular support for further integration and the issue of Europe arouses excitement only when the future role of the country is under discussion. Even then, as we have seen, the voting is often finely balanced, suggesting that, like the British, the Danes are not natural euro-enthusiasts and tend to lag behind the pioneers of close integration. They have been particularly lukewarm over institutional change.

The explanation for Danish scepticism may well lie in the country's geographical location, for sandwiched between Scandinavia and Western Europe the Danes have an allegiance to their fellow Nordic peoples as much as to countries in the heart of Europe. They have not sought involvement in international politics. Neither have they been in the forefront in joining European organisations, unless their national interests have been obviously at stake.

Ireland

Membership has been good for Ireland, for it has offered something to almost everyone from farmers to feminists, and for many of them it remains a priority in their future thinking and plans. Discerning politicians have recognised that their country is such a beneficiary of the Union that, in the words of one former taoiseach, Garret FitzGerald, 'Ireland must seek to compensate for this by playing a positive and constructive role in the present running and future development of the Community'.[6]

Ireland supported monetary union for the same reason as the Greeks, in the hope that it would raise living standards. It similarly supports all policies which might help to bridge the gap between the richer and poorer nations of Europe, although Ireland is fast growing out of the latter category. Unsurprisingly, its leaders strongly backed the policy of cohesion, but recognise that with the programme of enlargement in recent years money has had to be steered away from traditional beneficiaries such as the Republic and directed towards the East.

The Irish have had a chance to express their pro-Europeanism in several referendums and have generally been one of the most supportive member states over moves towards further economic and political integration. They voted overwhelmingly in favour of membership in 1973; backed the Single European Act and the Maastricht and Amsterdam treaties by majorities of approximately two to one; but failed to ratify the Treaty of Nice at the first attempt in 2001, a decision subsequently overturned by a 'yes' vote in 2002.

Many Irish were attracted by the thought of EC membership, for it offered the country wider markets in which to export and the prospect of massive support for its agrarian way of life. EU Commission figures show just how much Ireland has benefited from its membership, receipts outstripping net contributions by €34b in the thirty years after joining. EU funding has been pumped into every imaginable aspect of Irish life, among them: building the economy; improving transport and communication networks; increasing trade; creating employment; promoting cultural diversity, peace and understanding; cleaning up the environment; restoring tourism amenities; and sustaining a country life and protecting human rights. Everywhere, there are visible signs of EU money – not least in the motorway programme, for those few which have been constructed have all been paid for with Brussels money.

Ireland has been marketed as the ideal European business location and Dublin headlined as the most youthful, vibrant European city. In the words of the present commissioner for regional policy, Danuta Hubner: 'It is an example of a society that knew how to use membership of the EU – in a way which is admired by everybody and probably envied by some'.[7] For the ten states that joined the EU in 2004, Ireland was a perfect example of a country that knew how to 'make maximum use of structural funds'.

Many Irish are sympathetic to Europe for a different reason, seeing it as an alternative to the fervent nationalism which has so much affected their own past history. Their involvement has helped the country to replace the inward-looking old-style national feeling with a new commitment to Europeanism and to the wider world. Moreover, it would place Ireland on a more equal footing with mainland Britain and enable it to establish a more distinctive approach to foreign affairs. Unlike many British people, the Irish seem to have no identity crisis about being Europeans.

United Kingdom
See the extended case study in Chapter 15.

Second Enlargement

Greece

Greece was not involved in the early stages of postwar European cooperation and the issue of membership of the EC was for many years hotly disputed. Accordingly, today's politicians feel that their country needs to show its commitment to integration, believing that unless it is a fully consenting member it still faces the prospect of being on the economic and political periphery of the Union. Fear of being marginalised and accorded less than equal respect is very strong in Greece. This is why the main political parties are unanimously in support of the EU and the public are pro-federalist. According to the opinion pollsters, Greece now commonly emerges as the most ardently pro-integrationist state in the Union. It was not always so, Greek attitudes having fluctuated over time.

Greek governments have recently shown strong support for the goal of political union, wanting to prove that they are 'good Europeans'. They have backed most of the leading initiatives, such as the Delors Plan and a single currency. Although the strict convergence criteria made Greece unready to join EMU in 1999, it was admitted in 2001. Its politicians dislike any notion of differentiated integration and are particularly keen to ensure that if any second division in a two-tier Europe does emerge, they do not belong to it.

Greek representatives are sympathetic to Germany's drive for more powers for the European Parliament, for as a country which itself gave birth to modern ideas of democracy they are conscious of the 'democratic deficit' in present EU institutions. Pro-European sentiment is particularly strong among the Greek people, who are traditionally critical of their own governments and often claim that if they were run from Brussels they might be better administered. They have also been notably supportive of those initiatives that have as their goal the promotion of rights, the ending of discrimination and the enhancing of democracy in Union decision-making. Whilst supporting enlargement (especially the entry of Cyprus and Malta), they have been keen to see that it is accompanied by sufficient funding from the EU's net contributors to ensure that Greece and other Mediterranean countries continue to benefit from EU largesse.

Third Enlargement

Portugal

Like Spain, Portugal was originally barred from membership of the European Community because of the authoritarian character of its ruling fascist regime. When democracy was finally re-established in 1976, it was keen to join for political reasons, largely bound up with consolidating freedom within the country.

Most Portuguese consider their country to have benefited from membership (particularly via payments made from the cohesion and structural funds) and are fully supportive of the idea of closer union in Europe. Whatever reservations they have about particular issues, they tend to view them in the context of the general drive to unity. Rarely in the forefront of moves towards integration, Portugal's politicians have tended to let other countries make the first move and then ensure that they get their fair share of the benefits. Portugal has recognised that to gain acceptance as a significant player it must sometimes accept political developments that it would not have been naturally inclined to support.

Portugal therefore tends to be among the more pragmatic member states, seeing compromise in one area as the key to gaining concessions in another. Its support for positive steps to further cooperation is an effective way of demonstrating its standing as a useful member of the Union. It supported the idea of EMU, like Greece being fearful of relegation to the slow lane if it did not join at an early opportunity. Although it carried excessive debt, it was judged to be moving satisfactorily towards resolving the problem and so was allowed membership of the eurozone when it began in 1999.

Broadly, Portugal has shown preference for intergovernmental cooperation, and its politicians are often more willing to examine the British viewpoint than those of some other member states.

Spain
Like Portugal, Spain was keen to re-enter the economic and political mainstream of Europe, after years of dictatorial rule under the Franco regime. It is, in principle, enthusiastic about union of all kinds, economic, military and political, although it tends to show some concern over the impact of questions of detail. At times, its governments have expressed concern over:

- its economic competitiveness in relation to Northern Europe and the costs of implementing the Social Chapter
- the need for national states to retain a right of veto in certain areas, notably on environmental policy, where its representatives were concerned that high EU standards might penalise Spanish producers
- the future allocation of funding from the EU budget. Spain has for several years been the greatest beneficiary of the structural funds.

Unlike Portugal, Spain has generally kept itself to the fore in the evolution of the Union, supporting initiatives such as the CFSP, EMU and the Constitutional Treaty, which was overwhelmingly approved in a referendum. It has not shown anxiety about an eventual federalist goal. The EU is generally popular, most Spaniards recognising the benefits that membership has brought to the country.

In 2004, the largest sum ever spent by the EU in one country within a year (€16.36b) went to Spain, which in 2005 again had the highest amount of Union spending (€14.82b).

For Spaniards, sovereignty is not an absolute concept which is possessed or relinquished. Rather, it is something that can be shared, so that in the Spanish view it is possible to pursue Spanish and European objectives at the same time – as long as due regard is paid to the details of what is being agreed as a Union priority.

Fourth Enlargement

Austria

Austria's traditional neutrality was at one time seen as a barrier to entry, for it seemed to conflict with the Maastricht aim of creating a common foreign and security policy. However, the Commission took the view that under Article 224 of the Rome Treaty a state can derogate from Treaty rules in the event of war or where they conflict with the 'obligations . . . accepted for the purpose of maintaining peace and international security'.

Austria was a welcome entrant to the club, for it was viewed as a prosperous country whose strong position as regards budgetary performance would help speed EMU on its way. Moreover its geographical position in the heart of the new Europe and its ties with Germany made it seem an ideal member. Austrians were initially enthusiastic for membership, as was evident in the referendum vote in which 66.4 per cent were in favour of entry, on a turnout of 81.3 per cent.

Austria quickly adapted to membership and soon began to play an active part in proceedings, joining the eurozone at the first opportunity and signing up for the Schengen Agreement. On policy matters, it has been in the forefront in discussion of environmental policy and in particular, the issue of sustainable development. In this area, the Austrians have supported the use of majority voting and co-decision. However, in general Austria has been wary of institutional change, particularly involving any significant extension of QMV or giving substantial additional powers to the European Parliament.

The formation of a new coalition government in 2000 created a new situation and led to a period of diplomatic isolation. It included members of the far-right Freedom Party which had performed well in the recent elections, an indication of a growing tide of anti-Europeanism among the Austrian people, whose appetite for membership cooled rapidly after the early enthusiasm.

Finland

Like Sweden, Finland was a long-standing neutral in global politics and, as such, it was for many years wary of forging alliances with the West. However, it saw in membership a chance to take one further step away from its former dependence on the USSR. Turning to Europe was an obvious move for a country which – following the breakdown of Soviet rule – had fears of an imperial revival in Russia or a chaotic breakdown in that country. Many Finns saw their physical security as being best protected via the Union, but they hoped for trade benefits as well via access to the single market. They also had a strong wish to strengthen ties with the three Baltic republics, whose early entry they championed after their own admission in 1995.

Yet there was no surge of enthusiasm for entry in Finland. As we have seen, Finns do not easily fit into any camp and are not by instinct convinced Europeans. In the referendum vote, 57 per cent were in favour of membership, on a high turnout of over 80 per cent. The result indicated that support was far from overwhelming. There needed to be early worthwhile gains, if that level of backing was to be increased.

Adaptation to membership was assisted by the help given to Finland via a new structural fund created to deal with problems of underpopulation and difficult living conditions in the areas affected. Within the Union, it was from an early stage a supporter of independent states working together for their mutual support, although it has been more sympathetic to federalism than the other Nordic countries. It also urges the causes of transparency in decision-making, human rights and anti-discrimination.

Sweden
For many years, Sweden was conscious of its position as a neutral nation, and as long as the EC was identified in people's minds with a blocking mechanism against the Soviet Union the Swedes they were not interested in joining it. Conscious of their national identity, they were reluctant converts and in opinion polls throughout the 1980s support for entry was low. What changed things was the fall of the Berlin Wall, and increasing doubts about Swedish national identity. By the early 1990s there was a strong wave of europhoria. In the ratification referendum, the vote in favour of the vote was a narrow 'yes' (52.2 per cent), after a late surge in which the pro-Europe campaign was backed by most of the political and business establishment. Many industrial companies, notably Volvo, saw benefits in access to the single market. They were also worried that a 'no' vote might jeopardise future investment in Sweden.

For all those who feared that Sweden was in danger of being isolated on the edge of Europe, there were those who felt that the country might end up losing itself within the Union. Doubts soon surfaced after 1995, many Swedes – naturally eurosceptic by inclination – feeling the need to see solid gains before they could be convinced that the effort was worthwhile. Some were concerned that closer integration might bring about a creeping Europeanisation.

Unsurprisingly, many prefer to see cooperation for mutual advantage, rather than any drift towards a federal future. They are conscious that, as a small state, it would be easy for Sweden and other less populated countries to lose out to the 'big three' member states.

Sweden did not join the eurozone and is unlikely to do so, not just because of economic considerations but also because they detect a threat to national sovereignty. However, in one area, environmental policy and sustainable development, Swedes are keen to see cooperation deepened. Having tighter controls than many countries to ensure clean air and water, they do not wish to see their policies undermined.

The impact of the Nordic states such as Finland and Sweden on the future of the Union is important, out of all proportion to their size. They have entered Europe with their traditional commitment to social and sexual equality and to the maintenance of national identity very much intact. The Nordic peoples are in an equivocal state of mind and will look to Europe to prove itself to Scandinavia, rather than the other way round.

Fifth Enlargement (Central and Eastern parts i and ii)

It is too early to assess the attitudes to, and benefits of, membership for the 2004 entrants in the Fifth Enlargement (part i). However, brief information on each of these is given in Table 14.1.

Table 14.1 Countries of the Fifth Enlargement (Central and Eastern part i)

Country	First applied	Commission attitudes and any problems re. entry
Czech Republic	1996	Czechoslovakia signed a Europe Agreement in 1991, but subsequent division into two countries made this obsolete. Commission found that it satisfied the Copenhagen Criteria and saw no significant problems to overcome, especially given its strong trade links with the EU. Work needed on ending discrimination towards Roma peoples and enhancing press freedom.
Cyprus	1990	Divided island since 1974, but Commission decided this was not a barrier to entry and welcomed its adaptation to Community policies under an Association Agreement. Only Greek-Cypriot controlled sector belongs to EU.

Table 14.1 (Continued)

Country	First applied	Commission attitudes and any problems re. entry
Estonia	1995	Commission saw no very significant problems, particularly as some 60 per cent of trade already with EU. Work needed on applying *acquis* re agriculture, consumerism and the environment, and to improve the administrative structure.
Hungary	1994	More liberal than most, the first former Soviet satellite to apply for membership. Strong trade links with EU and good cooperation under Europe Agreement. Need to improve judicial system and develop the ongoing process of modernisation – e.g. re. energy and environment.
Latvia	1995	Commission saw need to reform economy, despite much progress in 1990s: not withstand competition or apply all of the *acquis communautaire* re agriculture and environment. Also, doubts re weak administrative structure and treatment of minorities who account for more than 40 per cent of the population.
Lithuania	1995	Commission detected lack of economic preparedness. Possible problems in withstanding competition in areas of agriculture and banking, and in applying *acquis communautaire*. Weak administrative structure.
Malta	1990	Early application frozen in 1996, reactivated 1999. Commission detected economic, institutional and political problems, especially its heavily subsidised and large public sector and dependence on old and often unproductive industries. Smallest EU member.
Poland	1994	Commission noted impressive progress in restructuring economy and the extent of its trade with the EU. But low per capita income and backward agriculture, and also need to improve rights including press freedom. The largest of the 2004 entrants. population.

Country	First applied	Commission attitudes and any problems re. entry
Slovakia	1993	See Czech Republic. Lack of internal democracy in 1990s meant that it failed to meet political requirements of the Copenhagen Criteria. Also need to tackle corruption; improve its treatment of minorities; and undertake more structural reform of the economy on free market lines.
Slovenia	1996	The most prosperous part of the former Yugoslavia. Significant economic reforms in late 1990s made it a strong candidate, the more so as two-thirds of its foreign trade was with the EU. But difficulties over implementation of *acquis* re. agriculture, environment and justice. Also, a problem over Istria whose 350,000 ethnic Italians (who had fled after Yugoslavia had incorporated the territory) wanted to return and demanded compensation and restoration of property.

Table 14.1 (Continued)

As with the 'class of 2004', it is too early to assess the impact of the latest additions to membership in the Fifth Enlargement (Central and Eastern part ii). Brief details are included within Table 14.2.

Conclusion

The ability of governments in the member states to influence the conduct of Union affairs depends upon a number of factors, among them the size of the country; the ability of its leaders to establish good working relations with other national politicians, make deals and maximise their influence; the circumstances of their joining; their levels of development and prosperity; and their commitment to the causes of either integration or intergovernmentalism.

As for the peoples of member states, there is a wide range of attitudes both within and between individual countries, ranging from highly supportive countries (e.g. Ireland, Luxembourg and Spain) to the much less enthusiastic (e.g. Austria, Sweden and the United Kingdom). Across the Union as a whole, in 2006 *Eurobarometer* detected three broad strands of opinion on the issues of support for the Union and the cause of European integration:

Table 14.2 Countries of the Fifth Enlargement (Central and Eastern part ii)

Country	First applied	Commission attitudes and Any problems re. entry
Bulgaria		Need to enforce rule of law, tackle corruption and improve system of justice. Also, need for substantial improvements in application of *acquis* in areas such as agriculture, energy and the environment. Must develop private sector. Deemed not to meet Copenhagen Criteria in 1997. Lags well behind living standards of EU, having only 29 per cent of its average GDP per capita in 2003.
Romania		In 1997, the Commission saw a need to delay accession negotiations, noting significant problems re. administrative structure, democracy, economy and in society. Need for greater respect for rule of law and the protection of fundamental rights – especially those of Roma people. Also, need to restructure financial sector, remove rigidities in economy, implement key aspects of *acquis* such as agriculture, the environment and home affairs, and improve quality of administrative system.

1. About one in three citizens are strongly supportive.
2. Just over half range between uncertainty and grudging support.
3. Just over one-tenth are strongly opposed.

CHAPTER 15

Britain and Europe: a case study

Britain joined the EEC fifteen years after it began its operations, twenty years after the Six had pioneered the path to unity. Whereas other late entrants seem to have made the adjustments in attitude required to make a success of membership, this has not been the case for many British people and some of their elected representatives. They have found it hard to adapt, hence their reputation on the continent as 'reluctant Europeans'. Perhaps this reflects a national difficulty in coming to terms with Britain's reduced circumstances in the world. Since 1945, Britain's relatively declining industrial and military strength has meant that it has not been able to sustain the position it once held. Managing national decline is not a glorious role for politicians, for it arouses little popular enthusiasm.

In this chapter, we trace political attitudes to developments on the continent and note some of the facts that have made Britain seem like an 'awkward partner'.

A global power

In 1945, Britain was regarded as a major power, having just emerged victorious from the Second World War. Not surprisingly, the country which 'won the war' felt that with such a worldwide importance it could win the peace. In the following years, it did not need to tie itself in to any commitments with the countries which it had defeated or which had been overrun in the hostilities. Britons felt that they could afford to remain aloof from Europe. For a long while, their governments were not ready to recognise or admit the country's increasing weakness.

Hugo Young[1] has written perceptively about popular attitudes at the time:

> The island people were not only different but, mercifully separate, housed behind their moat . . . They were also inestimably superior, as was shown by history both ancient and modern: by the resonance of the Empire on which the sun never set, but equally by the immediate circumstances out of which the new Europe was born, the war itself. Her sense of national independence, enhanced by her unique empire, absorbed by all creeds and classes and spoken for by virtually very analyst, could not be fractured.

For years, Britain still attempted to preserve its global role. Churchill[2] expressed his view of the competing claims on British foreign policy when he spoke of relations with other Western European countries: 'we are with them, but not of them. We have our own Commonwealth and Empire'. In similar vein, Sir Anthony Eden spoke for many of his countrymen when he gave his reasons for not signing up for membership of the EDC. Speaking with the authority of a foreign secretary, he observed: 'Britain's story and her interests lie far beyond the continent of Europe. Our thoughts move across the seas to the many communities in which our people play their part, in every corner of the world . . . that is our life'.[3]

Such an attitude had deep roots in the British psyche and may be considered understandable in the circumstances of the time. However, it was combined with an inability to appreciate the enthusiasm and dedication of other nations to closer integration in pursuit of 'the European idea'. Consistently, British politicians then and in more recent years have underestimated the strength of this determination. They have assumed that carefully constructed measures of intergovernmental cooperation would be a substitute for the more visionary approach of the continental nations of Old Europe.

A change of direction

In 1963, Dean Acheson,[4] a former American secretary of state, observed: 'Britain has lost an empire, but not yet found a role'. The comment wounded British pride, but some politicians recognised that it contained more than a little truth. Among them, there was a growing belief that Europe might provide the theatre in which Britain would have the best chance of influencing events and opinions in the world at large. In the event, Prime Minister Macmillan found it expedient to apply for Britain to join the EEC in 1961, as it became clear that Britain's capacity to influence the outcome of events had been much curtailed. Neither the Commonwealth nor the American connection seemed to count for as much as had been assumed a decade or so before. But not until the retirement of General de Gaulle was British membership welcome to the whole Community.

When Britain joined the Community in 1973, it would be hard to detect evidence of any widespread enthusiasm. However, there was a fairly general feeling that changes on the world scene and the need for access to the large continental market made accession desirable, even necessary. When the chance came for the British people to express their view (in the referendum of 1975), they showed a strong backing for membership, for once the country had committed itself it was appreciated that it was probably wise and necessary for Britain to work with our new partners. The alternatives did not look very promising. The point was well made by FS Northedge:

> [The] important thing about British entry into Europe was that it had almost every appearance of being a policy of last resort, adopted, one might almost say, when all other expedients had failed. There was no suggestion of it being hailed as a brilliant success . . . the impression remained that it was brought about in humiliating circumstances, and when other options in foreign policy had lost their convincingness.[5]

Hugo Young[6] has written similarly of British motives: 'For the makers of the original "Europe", beginning to fulfil Victor Hugo's dream, their creation was a triumph. Out of defeat, they produced a new kind of victory. For Britain, by contrast, the entry into Europe was a defeat: a fate she had resisted, a necessity reluctantly accepted, the last resort of a once great power, never for one moment a climactic or triumphant engagement with the construction of Europe'. The point is a fair one. In many surveys in the first two decades of membership, *Eurobarometer*, the EC's polling organisation, consistently found that the majority of British respondents favoured closer cooperation in Europe in some form and recognised the inevitability of further steps along the route to unity, on the right terms. But they were unsure about any moves to further integration, a point noted by Geoffrey Martin,[7] one-time head of the European Commission office in London: 'The British have not seen Europe as an opportunity. They regard it as somewhere between an obligation and a mistake'.

Growing doubts: Conservative misgivings

The broad sympathy for British involvement began to change after the Maastricht Agreement had been signed. The public mood moved in a more eurosceptical direction. This may have been a reflection of the outcome of the Danish referendum and of other signs of growing doubt on the continent. It also reflected a popular feeling – fed by elements of the tabloid press – that after several years in the EC, membership was bringing difficulties rather than bene-fits and that Brussels was too fond of interfering in our national life. In an episode of the television comedy *Yes, Prime Minister*, Jim Hacker won much approval for his lament about the threat to our national way of life:

> The Europeans have gone too far. They are now threatening the British sausage. They want to standardise it – by which they mean they'll force the British people to eat salami and bratwurst and other garlic-ridden greasy foods that are totally alien to the British way of life. They've turned our pints into litres and our yards into metres, we gave up the tanner and the threepenny bit. But they cannot and will not destroy the British sausage!

The lack of a strong pro-European lead from British ministers was also a factor in this developing sense of disillusionment, there being a notable reluctance by those in office to challenge popular myths and misinformation about the Community. Indeed, throughout the period of British membership, public opinion has been very sensitive to the attitudes adopted by political leaders and the media, as well as to the turn of events.

British politicians – even ones who are seen as among the more pro-European – have often expressed a coolness towards their counterparts on the continent. It was the relatively pro-European Harold Macmillan[8] who expressed alarm that the Community would be 'dominated in fact by Germany and used as an instru-ment for the revival of German power through economic means', which amounted to 'really giving them on a plate what we fought two wars to prevent'. The author of *Using Europe, Abusing the Europeans*, Wolfram Kaiser,[9] shows that the

'British tradition of . . . abusing the Europeans [for failing to get its way] has a long history'. The tactic intensified during the era of Conservative rule after 1979. There was a developing scepticism in the government's approach to relations with Europe, at times a distinct frostiness. John Major, usually regarded as more sympathetic to Europe than his predecessor, nonetheless resorted to obstruction accompanied by accusations of bad faith, while the eurosceptic Lord Tebbit[10] was moved to describe the EU as 'a bunch of liars and cheats'.

Whilst Conservative leaders were concerned to stress and expand the role of the Community as a free-trade area, their continental partners often had a different long-term agenda. Their vision was of a Community in which the degree of union became ever closer, a goal which was written into the small print of the treaties. For several years, the full implications of membership were not realised in Britain. Even those who were involved in the negotiations and signed up for the next stage in the road to unity sometimes had an inadequate grasp of the detail contained therein. This was particularly the case with Margaret Thatcher, who by supporting the Single European Act committed Britain to what has been described[11] as 'a milestone on the federalist road'.

British ministers – especially during Mrs Thatcher's premiership – sought to fashion the Community along the lines set out in her Bruges Speech[12] in 1988. Rejecting any form of European superstate, she reminded her listeners of Britain's contribution to the liberation of Europe in 1944–5 and offered a description of how the Community might develop in the future. Her remarks cast her firmly in the Gaullist mould, for she made it clear that it was neither possible nor desirable to 'suppress nationhood and concentrate power at the centre of a European conglomerate'. She favoured 'willing and active cooperation between independent states', and wanted to see Europe speak with a more united voice. But this must be done in such a way that it 'preserves the different traditions, Parliamentary powers and sense of national pride in one's own country'. It was apparent that she had little or no sympathy with talk of a European Idea. No utopian, she took the view that Europe could be made to work to Britain's advantage – as long as British leaders made a firm stand against Community interference and regulation, and were determined to concentrate attention on developing a deregulated market in Europe.

In office (and subsequently), Margaret Thatcher was a strong exponent of intergovernmentalism. She shunned the integrationist road, her preference being for an enlarged Community, one that was broader and looser. She always remained a firm Atlanticist, seeing merit in the 'special relationship' that her government developed with President Reagan during the 1980s. Subsequent Conservative leaders have shared her broad euroscepticism.

In a thoughtful speech in Berlin, former leader Michael Howard[13] exhibited clear sympathy with the sentiments expressed in Bruges, even if his observations were modified by the development of events in the intervening decade and a half.

Like a number of other prominent British politicians in either party, he was willing to strike a markedly more pro-European tone when addressing a continental audience than when talking to the voters back home. Having assured his audience that he wanted Britain to 'remain a positive and influential member of the European Union', he went on to say that he did not want that Union to be

> a one-way street to closer integration to which all must subscribe . . . Forcing common standards upon them will mean that Europe as a whole falls further and further behind as each member state tries to put its own costs onto its neighbours . . . in areas which serve their own national interest, individual member states [should] be able to decide whether to retain wholly national control or whether to co-operate with others.

An about turn in British policy? Labour after the 1997 election

When Tony Blair entered 10 Downing Street, there were many optimists who hoped that the sometimes icy British relationship with Europe would thaw. There could be a fresh start, with an internationalist, pro-European government in office. The process of building support for the European Union might begin.

From the earliest days of the new administration, the rhetoric employed by ministers was generally more *communautaire* and there were signs that improvement of Britain's position in Europe was being accorded priority. In office, New Labour has been a broadly pro-European party. It has not been naively enthusiastic about the Union, recognising its faults such as the continued existence of the Common Agricultural Policy. Neither has it shared the interest of some continental socialists in creating a kind of federal Europe. The language used in the 1997 election had not been markedly different from that of the Conservatives, the stated preference being for 'an alliance of independent nations choosing to co-operate to achieve the goals they cannot achieve alone'.

As prime minister, Tony Blair argued for closer EU integration in some areas, but greater diversity in others such as education and health. In a speech in Paris[14] during the first British presidency of his premiership, he reassured the audience of his pro-European credentials: 'I happen to share the European idealism. I am by instinct internationalist . . . Britain's future lies in being full partners in Europe'. He spoke of the need to ensure that there was a political framework to match progress in other areas, and spelt out the need to make that framework more relevant and in touch with people's concerns across the Union. He also urged the need for decentralisation where possible, declaring 'Vive la subsidiarité!'.

The choice of Europe or America
Some continental leaders soon concluded that Tony Blair was unwilling to really try to sell the European cause – and particularly the single currency – to the

electorate. Also, when issues such as the handling of Saddam Hussein (Iraq) or Slobodan Milosevic (Serbia) emerged, the Blair reflex was to turn to the Americans rather than seek to consult with and rally European opinion. There may have been good reasons for acting as he did, but in continental eyes it sometimes seemed as though he should prove his European credentials in action as well as in words. Doubters noted that he regularly revealed a preference for Washington over Brussels and that his relationship with Bill Clinton seemed more important to him than his ties with European leaders.

By the time of the 2001 election certain themes were becoming evident. Like the administrations that preceded it, Labour preferred the intergovernmental approach; rejected integrationism; had an economic liberalisation agenda that stressed the value of flexible and dynamic labour markets, rather than the social welfare model preferred by some continental socialists; and was determined to retain a strong link with the United States.

A decade of dealing with the EU leaders was – perhaps inevitably – a chastening experience for the British prime minister. The Blair era illustrated the difficulty of trying to be a key player in Union affairs whilst at the same time firmly standing up for British interests on matters such as tax harmonisation, the euro and common policies on security and foreign affairs. Ministerial equivocation over the euro indicated that whilst the party wanted to stay ahead of the Conservatives by stressing its pro-Europeanism, Tony Blair recognised that he was operating in a country whose enthusiasm for the Union was muted and sometimes grudging, in which membership was often seen as a necessity rather than a cause for celebration.

Now that the Blair premiership is over, it is possible to detect broad threads in his attitude to our continental partners. Following the eighteen years of Conservative rule, there have been elements of continuity in some aspects of New Labour's approach. Tony Blair appeared to be more comfortable with other European heads of government than his Conservative predecessors and used the more obviously pro-European rhetoric which was always likely to win friends. But two strands – already apparent in 2001 – remain significant, namely the emphasis on intergovernmentalism and the value attached to the 'special relationship' within the Atlantic Alliance. The preference for mutually beneficial cooperation between nation states was reinforced by the latest EU enlargement, offering the prospect of support for the British outlook from new entrants in a wider and looser Union. As for the relationship with the White House, it was evident from the early days of the Blair premiership that Bill Clinton and the prime minister were personal as well as political friends. What was more surprising is that the special relationship survived the change of personnel in the Oval Office, with George Bush and Tony Blair working together over many areas of policy.

Beyond the underlying reasons for the 'special relationship', a series of events brought the two countries into active cooperation. Over the terrorist attacks on the World Trade Center of 11 September 2001, the formation of the 'coalition of the willing' to fight Al-Qaeda and other sources of terrorism and the decision to invade Iraq, Tony Blair was publicly very supportive of the American position. He took the view that it was preferable to seek to modify the president's views through quiet diplomacy rather than take a stand against his foreign-policy initiatives.

Tony Blair likes to use the 'bridge' metaphor to describe the British stance in foreign policy, portraying Britain as being an axis between a range of international relationships. According to this view, Britain has a unique position, one for which the country is well qualified by past history and circumstance. The thinking is that in this role Britain never has to make a choice between the USA and Europe; it is linked to, yet similarly distant from, both continents. Yet over Iraq, a serious rift began to develop and widen between Europe and the USA. Britain was unable to reconcile the two sides and had to make a choice. The divide could not be bridged by the prime minister's determined efforts to facilitate agreement. As de Gaulle had argued four decades previously, Britain ultimately proved itself to be more Atlanticist than European.

Britain was not without allies in Europe, particularly among the would-be entrants to the EU who were due to join within a year of the invasion of Iraq. Many of their peoples had had experience of living under a regime they viewed as tyrannous and they could understand the British and American position. But British influence in Brussels, Paris and Berlin was struck a damaging blow. By supporting Washington, the prime minister made it clear that when there is a potential conflict, British governments tend to see the special relationship as paramount. Speaking to the Foreign Office conference of British ambassadors, Tony Blair[15] outlined the British stance unambiguously: 'First, we should remain the closest ally of the US, and as allies influence them to continue broadening their agenda. We are the allies of the US not because they are powerful, but because we share their values'. But he continued:

> Britain must be at the centre of Europe . . . To separate ourselves from it would be madness. If we are in, we should be in wholeheartedly . . . For fifty years we have hesitated over Europe. It has never profited us . . . The [two] roles reinforce each other . . . We can indeed help to be a bridge between the US and Europe and such understanding is always needed. Europe should partner the US and not be its rival.

Whatever the difficulties over Iraq and other aspects of the Bushite approach in world affairs, Tony Blair would claim to have transformed British relations with Europe for the better. The main thrust of what he said in a speech in November 2000[16] was echoed in subsequent pronouncements. After extolling the virtues of 'enlightened patriotism', he stressed: 'If we want to stand up for Britain then we have to be in Europe, active, constructive, involved all the time. We have to negotiate tough and get our way, not stand aside and let other European countries make the decisions that matter to us'. Elaborating on the theme that Britain gains from closer European cooperation, he went on to say: 'It is patriotism, it is national self-interest, to argue for Britain's full engagement as a leading partner in Europe. It is a betrayal of our nation and our future constantly to obstruct every fresh opportunity for cooperation'.

That Tony Blair exhibited a greater enthusiasm for Europe than all of his predecessors other than Edward Heath is difficult to challenge, although the claim is not a particularly remarkable one. But as Geddes[17] observes, his dilemma [was] that 'whilst he [was] able to make the case for Britain in Europe . . . he [was] not able to make the case for Europe in Britain'. Of his successors' outlook, little is as yet known.

Box 15.1 Gordon Brown and Europe

The Brown approach to the future development of the European Union is as yet unclear. The pro-European rhetoric remains, albeit in a toned-down version, the Prime Minister being convinced of the necessity for Britain to be fully engaged in EU affairs. However, past performance indicates some re-shaping of British policy.

As Chancellor, Brown's reservations about membership of the eurozone became ever-more-apparent as the Blair administration progressed. But his doubts extended beyond the single currency. They were made evident in the month before he assumed the premiership when – in the discussion over the amended constitutional treaty – he argued that the outgoing premier must fend off a **Sarkozy**-led French attempt to remove the commitment to free and 'undistorted' competition as a key EU objective.

Both as Chancellor and Prime Minister, Brown exhibited scepticism about the European social model, arguing against 'labour market rigidity'. Whatever his unease about other aspects of US policy under the Bush administration, he seems to prefer the American economic model to that favoured by several European countries.

Political and popular reactions to Europe: a reflection

Europe has been a difficult area of policy for British politicians for many years. More recently, it has been something of a political football in the party battle, and those who exhibit signs of pro-European attitudes and policies tend to face a barrage of adverse media criticism in the tabloid press at home. David Butler and Simon Westlake[18] make the point that euroscepticism has a long history:

> If there is a European 'problem', it is not restricted to one British political party, but more generally diffused throughout the British political and administrative

establishment . . . In truth, virtually every post-war British Prime Minister has been in a similar position and played a similar role, from Attlee to Churchill and Eden, from Macmillan to Wilson, and from Callaghan to Thatcher and Major.

The difficulties of national leaders from Attlee to Blair relate to the problem of leading parties whose composition reflects the ambivalent attitudes of many British people to the postwar position. Britons are caught between the desire to hold on to country's past greatness and traditions (what former foreign secretary Douglas Hurd[19] has called 'punching above its weight'), and yet also to keep apace with the modern world. Although most MPs recognise that the country has a European future, a number of them do not enthuse about the prospect. Other countries, lacking the same attachments as Britain, do not experience the same feelings, or at least not to the same extent. As one former Conservative MP, Sir Anthony Meyer,[20] put it: 'For France, Europe offers a chance to extend its influence; for Britain, Europe is a damage-limitation exercise'. Similarly, a commentator in *Le Monde* stated[21] a common view in France that the two countries, France and Britain, start from different perspectives when they consider their place in Europe: 'For France, being at the heart of Europe remains a necessity. For Great Britain, it is just one option. Europe, seen from London, is not an end in itself, but a means of attaining specific objectives at particular times'.

The bonds between Britain and the USA as expressed in the Atlantic Alliance are in line with the broad preferences of many British people. Hugo Young[22] suggested that Britain needs to shed its 'Anglo Saxon' identity and its preference for things American and embrace more fully its membership of the European family. Yet for reasons of history, geography and language, the British do not naturally identify with Europe. As Geddes[23] remarks:

> A holiday in Tuscany or an appreciation of French wines does not necessarily translate into full-hearted enthusiasm for the Euro . . . they can enjoy a cappuccino, sip a glass of Chianti, book a holiday to Spain or cheer on the English or Scottish national football teams coached respectively at the time of writing [2003] by a Swede and a German. Yet these positive images of Europe can effortlessly be countered by the ubiquitous presence of American brands such as MTV, Starbucks, Nike and McDonalds . . . when the question 'Is Britain European?' is asked, then the answer must be 'Yes, but not only'.

Jacques Delors,[24] more of an admirer of things British than many people in this country ever thought possible back in the 1980s, has described the British aversion to many things European as 'a great mystery of history'. For him, it is not just about the special relationship with the US, although that is important. He claimed that 'there's just something in the people, the product as they are of a great and proud history'.

Are the British 'reluctant Europeans'?

Within Europe, Britain has long had a reputation as what Stephen George[25] describes as 'an awkward partner', semi-detached from the Union, its politicians and people never being fully willing to commit to a European road. A case for the 'awkwardness' of Britain from a continental point of view is easy to outline. It might start with the failure to join early supranational organisations such as the ECSC and the EEC; point to the early renegotiation of the terms of entry, once Britain was a member of the Community; note that the issue of European membership and the extent of British commitment to the Community/Union has caused division and strife within the main parties and provoked ministerial resignations; draw attention to the hostilities aroused over policy crises such as BSE and problems such as the CAP and CFP; mention the low degree of interest in European affairs among the British people and their reluctance to vote in European elections; and conclude by commenting on the preference shown for the American stance in the Iraq War and its aftermath, over that of Europe.

In fairness, there are other nations too that have expressed some reluctance to embrace the European Union and its works. The Swiss rejected membership of the EEA, the Norwegians did the same in regard to the EEC and later EU. The Danes have often shown a preference for intergovernmentalism over integration, and like the Swedes have decided against participation in the eurozone. Even the normally pro-European Irish at first rejected the Nice Treaty. And if critics of British administrations argue that they 'missed the European bus' after the Second World War and have consistently had a record of joining up with their continental partners too belatedly to influence the original negotiations, it can be said in their defence that perhaps this is not altogether surprising – given the country's unique global role and responsibilities. Moreover, there is an element of hindsight in such a viewpoint. It was not so obviously apparent in the 1950s that the ECSC and the EEC were going to be as successful as they turned out, nor that the supranational structures constructed at the time were destined to work as well as they did.

However, whatever the defence that can be mounted against 'the George thesis', few would dispute that for most of the post-1945 era Britain has been on the periphery of the broad thrust to European integration, at times more and at other times less willing to cooperate effectively with its European partners. In some areas, ministers have been willing to engage more fully; in others there has been a much greater degree of reluctance.

The implications of membership of the European Community, later Union, have become more apparent in recent years, in terms of their impact not just upon our constitutional arrangements but also upon the attitudes of parties and the fortunes of politicians. Many British people have been confirmed in their doubts about British membership; they may accept the fact of membership as inevitable, but they do not particularly like the experience. The lack of enthusiasm and commitment in Britain confirm our reputation on the continent as a country that always wants to slow down the pace of advance, that always says 'No, no, no!' In the eyes of many people in Britain and beyond its shores, British politicians and people remain 'reluctant Europeans'.

Concluding thoughts

The story of British relations with the continent is necessarily unfinished. The process of European integration is ongoing, and Britain's long-term approach over the coming years under a different set of ministers is difficult to foresee. On past performance, it has been resolutely pragmatic, the emphasis being on the search for national advantage. This has inevitably involved ministers in what one writer calls 'a more or less confrontational stance within a Community to which, it was [often] asserted, nothing significant had been surrendered'.[26]

Yet by signing the Treaty of Rome, Britain did bind itself to what was always a potentially federalist organisation. This was relatively unimportant when federalist feelings were kept 'under wraps' – for instance, in the 1970s when there were other preoccupations – but it is more important when the drive towards integration is back on the agenda. In dealing with European issues from the euro to tax harmonisation, from the stance on foreign policy to the drafting of a European constitution, British ministers have often found themselves forced onto the defensive as France and Germany seem to be racing ahead towards another distant euro-goal. That drive towards integration has been a consistent one ever since the two countries buried their national differences back in the 1950s, even if there have been periods when it has been placed on the back burner. As Young[27] expressed the situation: 'The integrationist thrust . . . is the likely long-term course of history. It has, with stops and starts, been the thrust of the last 20 years. The prophets of impasse have proved false, the prophets of evolution correct'.

Most British people recognise that Britain cannot separate itself from the European fold, but within Europe ministers seem to find it difficult to make the Union work to the national advantage. By seeming to resist the initiatives which other nations want in so many areas, it becomes harder to achieve those goals that really matter to Britain. Yet by going along with them, ministers risk having their actions savaged in the eurosceptic tabloid press. It is difficult for even a pro-European administration to be a constructive, if distinctive, actor on the continental stage.

Glossary

Sarkozy, Nicolas (1955–   ) Elected in May 2007, Sarkozy is the sixth and current president of the Fifth French Republic. He has expressed an interest in improving French relations with the United States.

Conclusion: the state of the Union, past and present

From the inception of the European Union, there have always been competing visions of its end-goal, as well as disputes as to the best means of getting there. The pioneering states have been in the vanguard of those urging a more federalist approach, although interpretations of what this implies differ considerably. Britain has usually been regarded as the staunchest supporter of intergovernmentalism.

In this chapter, we briefly review the history of the Community and its evolution into a Union, noting the nature, pace and direction of change. Finally, we consider some issues concerning the way ahead, following the failure to achieve ratification of the Constitutional Treaty in 2005.

Supporters of the European Union argue that its growth is a force for peace and democracy. They point out that the wars which were a periodic feature of the history of Western Europe have ceased since the formation of the European Economic Community in the 1950s. Others contend that peace in Europe since World War Two is the product of different causes, such as the moderating influence of the United States and NATO, the need for a unified response to the threat from the Soviet Union, the urgency of reconstruction after World War Two and a collective temporary tiring of waging war.

In more recent times, the European Union has been extending its influence to the East. It has accepted several new members that were previously behind the Iron Curtain, and has plans to accept several more in the medium term. It is hoped that in a similar fashion to the entry of Spain, Portugal and Greece in the 1980s, membership for these states will help cement economic and political stability.

The past reconsidered

The setting up of the European Coal and Steel Community in 1951 was an attempt to achieve unity in Europe by mutual consent rather than by force and because of its success the Six decided to further their experiment. The Treaty of Rome (1957) which brought about this development was a landmark in postwar Europe, for it created a common market in which the members were prepared to sacrifice some of their economic independence in the cause of closer economic and political harmonisation.

The Common Market was a means to an end, not the end in itself. The aim of the Rome Treaty was economic unity. It does not directly mention political unity, but it is quite impossible to divorce economics from politics in this context. Governments are by their nature political and decisions on economic matters cannot be made without taking political considerations into account. The founding fathers of the EEC were well aware of this, knowing that there were clear political implications in the treaty they had signed. Yet on this occasion their language was rather less grandiloquent than it was in the Treaty of Paris. There was no talk of 'merging interests' or 'sharing destiny', although the Six 'were determined to lay the foundations of an ever closer union among the peoples of Europe'.

A few years later, the president of the EEC Commission pointed the way forward, when he observed: 'The rest is for the future and by the rest I mean common foreign and defence policies and, in addition, the crowning of all our endeavours by a political arrangement that will embrace them all'.[1] The implementation of the customs union and the development of a Common Agricultural Policy were early signs of the success of the Common Market. Significant economic strides were being made, 'big business' flourished, statistics for industrial production were impressive and all in all the years through until the Western recession of the 1970s were good ones for the Community. It had become economically strong, but remained politically weak. Or, to use the quotation offered in some examination questions, it was an economic giant, a political minnow.

Following a difficult period in the early 1980s, the impetus was renewed with the passing of the Single European Act of 1986, the creation of a 'Europe without frontiers' and the transformation of the Community into a Union, of which all inhabitants of the member states became citizens. This marked a new phase in the history of European unification.

The process of unification within the Union has not been without its setbacks and crises. Each member country has inevitably been watchful of its own interests and anxious to preserve its best traditions; each step forward has had to be painfully negotiated. Yet, however slow at times the progress has been, the direction in which the six pioneering countries (now twenty-seven) have been moving has rarely been in doubt. One of the founding fathers of the Community, Robert Schuman,[2] shrewdly observed: 'Europe will not be created at a stroke or according to a single plan. It will be built through concrete achievements'.

Pace of change

Within the European Union, progress over fifty years has been in fits and starts. It has been characterised by what Nugent[3] refers to as 'an almost constant edging forwards, with advances followed by pressures for more advances'. Indeed, since the Community was formed in 1958 no treaty has reversed that flow, subsidiarity at Maastricht and Edinburgh having been included – to some extent, at least – as a concession to those anxious about the accretion of power in Brussels.

According to Wolfgang Wessels,[4] the integration process operates in a three-state cycle:

1. *National governments see the benefits of mutual cooperation with other EU countries in a particular policy area* and cooperate on a very loose intergovernmental basis, sometimes even outside the Union structure. This form of cooperation proves to be inadequate, so the governments move into the next phase.

2. *Member states give the policy areas treaty recognition which takes them within the structure of the Union.* This is still on an essentially intergovernmental basis, with Council decisions being taken on the basis of unanimity and the other key institutions having only a modest role.

3. *Finally, national governments realise that stronger decision-making processes are required if policy aims are to be achieved,* so that they proceed along a supranational route. This involves a larger role and more effective powers for the Commission, Parliament and Court of Justice. Within the Council, voting is decided on the basis of QMV.

Nugent quotes the example of justice and home affairs to illustrate the process Wessels describes:

> From modest beginnings in the mid-70s when, quite outside the framework of the treaties, governments began to cooperate with one another on such matters as cross-border crime and the fight against terrorism, the policy has steadily increased. Cooperation was stepped up in the 1980s through what became known as the Trevi process; justice and home affairs was given treaty status in pillar three of Maastricht, though very much on an intergovernmental basis; much of pillar three was transferred into pillar one by the Amsterdam Treaty; some provision was made for QMV, and new justice and home affairs issues – including provision for tighter and stronger police cooperation – were added to pillar three; and the Nice Treaty further extended QMV in the policy area.

As we saw at the beginning of this section, the pace of Community/Union development has varied considerably since its foundation. Since the mid-1990s, in some respects progress on integration has slowed down, if by integration we mean the intensification of cooperation between EU member states and the gradual centralising of power within European institutions. Yet the implementation of monetary union is a strong example of deepening bonds between the thirteen participants and if within the concept of integration we include the process of enlargement then there has been striking development.

What has been created?

The European Union is a distinctive creation. There have been several examples of countries that have joined with one another in ventures of mutual benefit, but in aim, method and achievement this arrangement has gone much further than the others. From the signing of the Treaty of Rome, the Community always aspired to be more than just a customs union. It aimed for an ever closer union of its peoples and developed supranational institutions with powers that were binding upon member states.

Today, the European Union is difficult to characterise. It is neither a state nor just another international organisation, but has elements of both. EU members have transferred considerable sovereignty to it, more than to any other non-sovereign regional organisation. But in legal terms, the states remain the masters, in as much as the Union does not have the power to transfer additional powers from states to itself without their agreement through further international treaties. Indeed in some key areas, member states have given up little national sovereignty, particularly in the matters of foreign relations and defence. Because of this unique structure most simply classify the European Union as *sui generis* (an entity *of its own kind*).

Character of the Union: intergovernmentalist or supranationalist?

Intergovernmentalism and integration have been two key forces at work in the evolution of the Community, now the Union. At different times over the last forty years, one set of ideas or another has gained the ascendancy, as different thinkers and statesmen have pressed their particular viewpoint. The dispute is still at the heart of the controversy within the Union about the way it has developed and the future direction it should take.

Some countries in European Union politics favour the intergovernmental approach, while others favour the supranational path. Supporters of inter-governmentalism argue that supranationalism is a threat to national sovereignty and democracy, claiming that only national governments can possess the neces-sary democratic legitimacy. Intergovernmentalism is favoured by the more eurosceptic nations such as the United Kingdom, Denmark and Sweden.

In many key areas from economic policy to defence, and from welfare to foreign affairs, key decisions are still taken by national governments, even if this is in some cases done after euro-level consultation. Where decisions are taken by the EU, it is usually by the European Council or Council of Ministers, so that the leading representatives of each country can mount a sturdy defence of national interests. Most of these decisions are still taken on the basis of unanimity and even where majority voting has been introduced there is always an initial search for agreement. The notion of intergovernmentalism has been remarkably resilient and at different moments has asserted itself strongly – whether in the failure of the EDC, the British fight over its budgetary contributions, the Thatcherite declarations in the Bruges speech or aspects of the New Labour approach. Yet in spite of these attempts to safeguard national interests, the Union has not only established itself but has moved more closely together.

In the search for new structures in Europe after World War Two, Monnet made clear his dislike of the intergovernmentalism of the OEEC, which he believed to be 'the opposite of the Community spirit'.[5] He rejected 'mere coop-eration' and urged the creation of 'new functional authorities that superseded the sovereignty of existing nation-states'. In his view, the sovereign nations of the past could no longer solve the problems of the day. They could not ensure their own progress or control their own future. Today, supporters of supranationalism argue that it allows integration to proceed at a faster pace than would otherwise be possible. Where decisions must be made by governments acting unanimously, the process can take years, if indeed it is ever successfully accomplished.

There are important supranational characteristics to the present Union. Decisions taken at European level have the force of law in member countries, European law being superior to domestic law. The Commission has the power to issue regulations and directives which are binding on member countries. Moreover, the growth of majority voting and the increasing powers of the European Parliament suggest that the element of supranationalism is on the increase. The more integrationist nations such as the Benelux countries, France, Germany and Italy have strongly backed such developments, seeing the supra-national approach as the way forward.

The process of integration has not always been easy, nor the path smooth. There have at times been difficulties between the member states, and the con-flict between national interest and the interests of Europe as a whole has posed particular difficulties for some countries. Yet the direction of movement has always been towards greater integration, a term which the *Oxford English Dictionary* describes as 'the harmonious combination of elements into a single whole'.

The European Union strikes a balance between the two approaches of inter-governmentalism and supranationalism. The dispute over their relative import-ance is closely related to the intergovernmentalism versus neofunctionalism debate, a debate about why the process of integration has taken place at all. Intergovernmentalists argue that the process of EU integration is a result of tough bargaining between states. Neofunctionalists, on the other hand, argue that the supranational institutions themselves have been the underlying driving force behind integration.

Towards a federal future?

One of the most contentious issues concerning the future of the Union is the extent to which it moves in a federal direction. Lady Thatcher[6] has expressed the fear that a creeping federal system is being achieved without it being fully appre-ciated, and urges the need to halt this 'conveyor-belt to federalism'. In the eyes of many rightwing British politicians the word 'federal' remains anathema, for they see ideas of federalism and national sovereignty as fundamentally incom-patible.

Most Europeans, including the Commission, wanted Maastricht to commit the EC to a federal European union. In itself, 'federal' is a harmless label, and is cited in the constitution of the European People's Party, the grouping to which the British Conservatives have been affiliated. Yet in Britain, the word has horrifying connotations to many Conservatives, for whom – when in office – stopping the drift in that direction has long been an object of policy. But Labour too has shunned federal rhetoric and remained wedded to the intergovernmentalism that has enabled it to defend British national interests and draw 'red lines' that it was not prepared to cross. Tony Blair was no federalist, preferring an enlarged and looser EU to the organisation envisaged by those who dreamed of European integration after World War Two. That preference for mutually beneficial cooperation between nation states has been reinforced by the latest EU enlargements.

Britain gave federal constitutions to Australia and Canada, and has used the system elsewhere in the Commonwealth. The latter experiments did not work well, as in the West Indies and Nigeria, but the former were much more successful. However, despite our willingness to use them elsewhere, federal solutions are clearly not seen as suitable for use by the mother country.

The *Oxford English Dictionary* describes the term 'federal' as applying to 'an association of units that are largely independent' and 'a system of government in which several states unite under a central authority but remain independent in internal affairs'. As such, federalism is designed to allow the maximum devolution of decision-making consistent with the needs of a workable union. In creating the Australian federation, no one wanted to see the Australians governed mainly from Canberra. Rather, those who devised the governing arrangements wished to provide the advantages of common action on major issues whilst fully satisfying and respecting local traditions.

The replacement term for 'federal' in the Maastricht Treaty was apparently more to the liking of the Major government. It was the 'ever closer union' formula to be found in the Treaty of Rome. Yet this seems to have more farreaching implications, for it implies a never-ending journey in which supporters seek ultimately to merge their identities. 'Federal' at least has an end in view, for it involves a division of functions between the centre and the individual member states. It also allows for the notion of 'subsidiarity', the idea that decisions should be taken at a local level wherever this is feasible.

The point was well made in a 1991 editorial of the *Agence Europe*.[7] It noted that the phrasing of the Treaty of Rome

> is far more menacing, to anyone concerned with preserving national sovereignty, than a 'federal union'. An ever closer union must mean, if it means anything, that no matter how far we have gone in linking the member states to each other we must strive to go further still. A federal union, by contrast, usually means one in which the respective spheres of competence of the Union and its component parts are defined in a manner intended to be permanent.

The difficulty is that the word federal has assumed a significance out of all relation to what it really means. The media in Britain, especially the popular press, have often used it in the way that some Conservatives do, as if it implied the removal of power from the nation state to some superstate. It is seen as denoting a move to centralisation and deeper integration, so that some British MPs pounce on any proposal from the Commission in the suspicion that it must bring the dreaded 'f' word ever nearer.

On the continent, the term arouses no such anxieties, for it implies quite the opposite. To a German, the notion of subsidiarity (which assumed so much importance in John Major's thinking in the months after agreeing the Maastricht Treaty) presupposes the idea of a federal European state. It is the very essence of federalism, with a division of power between the different layers of government: European, national and regional.

The word 'federal' has become a slogan for all those who fear the drift of events in the Union. In denying its use, they are rejecting not only the formal structure of a fully fledged federal European state, but all the moves such as the single currency, the stronger European institutions and the increasing search for a common approach to many matters of policy. As Hugo Young noted, 'to be a "fed" is merely to be on the pro-Union side of the argument. To be against the "federal", is to propose oneself as a valiant upholder of the unchanging nation-state'.[8]

The EU is a potentially federalist organisation. As Young went on to observe: 'The integrationist thrust . . . is the likely long-term course of history. It has, with stops and starts, been the thrust of the last 20 years. The prophets of impasse have proved false, the prophets of evolution correct'. Clearly, Maastricht and other recent developments have moved the Union in the direction of more common policies. The general flow of events is to allow the EU more power in fields as diverse as defence and foreign policy, monetary union and the environment, for the 'entire thrust is towards . . . consensual action on the basis of majority-voting'.

In a general sense, therefore, federalism is already with us, but in the exact meaning of the term, the creation of a new system of government, it is a long way off. No one is seriously proposing it as a practical possibility at the present time. Indeed, as Andrew Marr[9] has pointed out, 'Europe is a sprawling collection of states and cultures however economically close . . . some sort of settlement based on a loose federation is far likelier than the super-state feared by Germanophobes'.

Towards a giant superstate?

Several British parliamentarians, particularly but not exclusively Conservatives, have often expressed the fear that Britain is in danger of being dragged into some

European monstrosity, a form of superstate. In the Labour Party, such a view surfaces less frequently, although it was evident in the discussions over the desirability of a European constitution.

However, it was the then Conservative William Hague[10] who described those feelings in the most vivid terms, in the speech in which he outlined his 'elephant test'. Simplistically expressed, his view was that if it looks, smells and sounds like an elephant, then it is an elephant you're dealing with. Applying this test to the emerging shape of the European Union, he discerned the characteristics of a future superstate, among them a proposed president, a parliament, a court and a single currency. Recognising the possibility of such a state being created without remedial action, a *Mail on Sunday* writer[11] expressed the more extravagant view that this outcome would 'be worse than Stalin's Soviet Union'.

Elements of doubt

Again according to the *Oxford English Dictionary*, a state is 'the political organisation or management which forms the supreme civil rule and government of a country or nation . . . the sphere of supreme political administration . . . a community of people occupying a defined area and organised under one government: a commonwealth, a nation'.

Academics, constitutional experts, diplomats and European officials are divided in their views about what form the EU will eventually take, but the general view is that the Union will fall far short of being a superstate. For Julia Smith[12] of the Royal Institute of International Affairs, two key tests can be applied:

> *Will there be a single European defence force, a real European army?*
> *Will there be a single tax regime throughout Europe?*

They are in her view unlikely to happen and Britain's 'red lines' are all about ensuring that they will not do so.

Historian Eric Hobsbawm[13] points out that the idea of the nation state which is sovereign, independent and that no one interferes with – the nineteenth-century idea – no longer corresponds to the reality of the world today. There is one such state – the United States – and perhaps Japan and China also qualify. But in the rest of the world we are subject to the influence of the international markets, global corporations, bodies like the World Trade Organisation set up by treaty or convention that affect all our lives. We live in a world where more and more states are banding together – whether in Europe, the Americas or Asia – to make policies that benefit the member states. That does not mean new superstates are being created, rather that we are living in a world where layers of governance overlap in many different ways.

Another historian, Norman Davies,[14] points out that what is evolving is something of an in-between situation, rather than one on either of the extremes as they are sometimes presented. On the one hand, Europe is not going to be the

Common Market created by the Treaty of Rome, a free trading area designed to maximise economic advantage. Neither is it going to be a classic superstate 'which would have a head of state, an executive in permanent session, a legislative assembly to whom it is answerable and its own individual judiciary'. In his views, we are seeing a new kind of polity emerge, but still one in which the Council of Ministers, rather than the European Commission, has the final say: 'those ministers represent their national interests, not the interests of a superstate'.

At Nice, heads of government were keen to take control of the way in which decisions are taken and rather than expanding the power of the Commission or the EU itself, they wanted to limit it. They wished to retain their national identities within Europe. Again, whilst talks were proceeding in Brussels over the constitution, there was much discussion in the press and among eurosceptic politicians as to whether the act of devising a constitution was in itself an indication that a superstate was being created. Opposition foreign affairs spokesman Michael Ancram[15] saw it as 'a gateway to a country called Europe'. Others see the EU not as a country, but as a collection of nation states which choose to pool some of their sovereignty. The abortive constitution stated that countries confer competences upon the EU, not the other way round.

Finally, the point has been made by an Oxford don, Larry Siedentop,[16] that it is hard to imagine any superstate in which the size of the budget was limited by treaty to 1.27 per cent of the member states' GDP: 'No large state uses less than 30 per cent'.

Ways forward

The 'deepening and widening' debate

Unsurprisingly, different member states have at times taken different views about the admission of new countries. France has traditionally been less enthusiastic, fearing a setback to the process of strengthening links between present members. It has also been uneasy about the prospect of having first- and second-class applicants. Germany believes in enlargement, but has been more committed to the accession of economically advanced countries such as the Czech Republic and Slovenia. The British have long been supporters of enlargement. Under the Thatcher and Major governments, they liked the idea of extending deregulated trading areas and welcomed the fact that the new democracies saw free-market solutions as being British-driven. The Blair governments continued with the same policy. Above all, perhaps, the British have been attracted to the idea of enlargement to the East because ministers have felt that it might help to slow down the pace of integration in the West. To countries like Britain that are committed to closer economic rather than political union, enlargement makes sense. It caters for the first, whilst making the second less certain.

Under former president Mitterrand, France was alive to just that possibility. Mitterrand feared that the strength of the inner core might be sapped by too wide an expansion. The attitude has echoes today. The French are also aware that in a broader Europe, their influence could decline, hence their wish to deepen the existing integration before moving too quickly towards expansion. They recognise too that allowing too many poorer countries to enter might place some EU policies under heavy strain, not least the Common Agricultural Policy. Whereas acceptance of the Austrians, Finns and Swedes involved the membership of richer powers who could contribute to the Union, others were going to be a drain on funds. For instance, the application of Poland for membership had some positive strengths in its favour, such as its stable democratic institutions, observation of human rights and willingness to adapt its laws to EU standards. Yet it suffered from economic backwardness and low environmental standards. Above all, its large farming sector posed problems for the already overstretched EU agricultural and development budget. The scale of support necessary to put the new democracies on their feet was vast.

The widening or deepening question tended to emerge in any discussion of the merits of enlargement in the last years of the twentieth century. But it became irrelevant in the early twenty-first century, with the admission of ten and eventually twelve new member states. The expansion has had benefits. It has strengthened the EU by increasing its attraction as an export market for non-Union countries, has enabled the organisation to speak with a larger voice in world affairs and has helped to increase stability on the continent by promoting prosperity among the new states.

Continued expansion?

The enlargements of the Union to date have tended to take place in 'waves' of multiple entrants all joining at once. The only 'single-state' enlargement so far has been the admission of Greece in 1981. However, EU ministers have warned that, following the significant impact of the Fifth Enlargement parts i and ii, a more individual approach will be adopted in future, although the entry of pairs or small groups of countries may yet coincide. Croatia may be expected to join at an early date (possibly around 2010), with Albania, Bosnia and Herzegovina, the Republic of Macedonia, Montenegro, Serbia and Turkey following, either singly, together or in small groups.

A more flexible approach to integration?

In order to overcome the many problems associated with progress for the European Union, compounded on one side by the economic weakness of some new members and on the other by the reluctance of larger states such as Britain to surrender part of their sovereignty as represented by the national veto, the idea of *variable geometry* has re-emerged in recent years as a desirable possibility.

Sometimes today, it is known by the alternative name of 'enhanced cooperation' (*coopération renforcée*).

Originating in the plan for a series of concentric circles (see below), the term refers to models of European integration which allow member states the choice whether to participate in or stand aloof from new initiatives – accepting of course that there will always be a number of 'core activities' in which all states are involved. The approach allows for a greater flexibility in the evolution of the Union, involving as it does a tiered system whereby groups of countries at different levels of development would be enabled to move at different speeds within certain policy objectives.

The first reasoned argument for the variable approach was produced by the then French prime minister, Edouard Balladur,[17] in August 1994. Balladur called for a three-tier Europe that he described as three concentric circles. There would be:

1. a strong central core of France, Germany and perhaps the Benelux countries and Italy, united politically, economically and militarily
2. a middle tier made up of the other EU countries, unable or unwilling to join the political and economic union at the centre
3. an outer circle containing the other European countries which are not part of the EU but which have economic and security links.

Balladur claimed that only such an arrangement could prevent paralysis of the Union by the problems inherent in enlargement. Two days later, the German Christian Democratic Union published a policy document designed 'to strengthen the EU's capacity to act and to make its structures and procedures more democratic and federal'.[18] At the heart of this aim was the need to establish a form of constitution for the EU which would create a federal structure according to the principle of subsidiarity. Recognising that movement towards union would be impossible if all countries progressed at the speed of the slowest, the Germans repeated the Balladur suggestion that there should be a fast-track central core of countries, which they proposed should be France, Germany and the Benelux countries, since 'they (together with Denmark and Ireland) are the ones which come closest to meeting the convergence criteria stipulated in the Maastricht Treaty'. Two years later, the then German chancellor, Helmut Kohl, was insistent that the pace of European integration should not be set by those who wanted to advance more cautiously, or not at all. As he put it:

> The slowest ship in the convoy should not be allowed to determine its speed. If individual partners are not prepared or able to participate in certain steps towards integration, the others should not be denied the opportunity to move forward.[19]

John Major[20] was once dismissive of a 'multi-faceted, multi-speed, multi-layered' Europe, seeing a danger in there being 'an exclusive hard core either of countries or of policies'. He came to embrace the notion of variable geometry (see Box C.1 for its various forms), via which he envisaged different EU states cooperating on varying aspects of common interest. In his view, diversity was not a weakness to be suppressed, but rather a strength to be harnessed. The phrase sometimes used by British ministers of the 1990s was 'flexible integration', a more diplomatically worded variant of some prevailing ideas. Major took the view that there was a wide range of policies within the EU and member states should be allowed to adopt differentiated approaches to these policies, as Denmark and the UK had adopted a different approach to monetary union. The key word was flexibility, which was 'essential to get the best out of Europe'. Major concluded by attacking the idea of federalism and reasserting Britain's belief in the nation state, seeing the European Union as an association of nation states, cooperating but each at their own speed and in their own interest.

British Conservative ministers increasingly spoke of a Europe in which they could pick and choose the parts they favoured, a Europe 'à la carte' in which they sought allies with whom they could achieve those things that mattered to them. The difficulty was that when so many items on the agenda were unacceptable to London, leaders in other capitals were likely to hesitate before agreeing to such an approach. They feared that if one or more countries such as Britain opted out of nearly all major initiatives, the result would be a 'two-speed' or 'two-tier Europe' in which some countries moved ahead to integration at a rapid pace, whilst others who did not wish to go so far or so quickly trailed behind.

Since then, many suggestions have been put forward for a future based on some kind of 'variable geometry' model. The underlying idea in all of them is that all states would normally take part in a core of essential areas, but they would be free to move at a different pace on others.

Any model of 'concentric circles', with an inner circle committed to the fast track and an outer one to slower progress, has disadvantages, not least for Union solidarity. It would also call into question the rights of all member states to have equal status in decision-making, and could have budgetary implications as well; the inner few might be reluctant to finance those states which were unwilling to move ahead at the faster rate.

For British pro-Europeans, the danger of any approach based on different rates of progress is that it will be in the slow lane on all key issues. The fear is that if their country does not belong to the advance guard, it will be sidelined, and will lose any ability to influence events in Europe. Britain would not be 'at the heart of Europe'.

In its early years, the Blair government, not wishing to see Britain left behind, showed little enthusiasm for any version of variable geometry. Its rhetoric implied that the intention was to join the euro 'when the time is right' and that it would seek to cooperate in other fields unless essential interests were at stake. But as yet, in spite of its having two massive majorities and one comfortable one

Box C.1   Flexible forms of cooperation

The idea of a *two-speed Europe (Europe à deux vitesses)* has been around in EC/EU circles for more than two decades. It recognises that not all member states are able or willing to move towards integration at the same pace. Therefore, a means needs to be devised to allow the most committed states to fulfil their ambitions, without them being held back by those travelling in the slower lane.

The assumption is that all wish to reach the same destination and achieve the same degree of integration. It is understood that particular policies can be difficult for individual states for valid and acceptable reasons. Which countries proceed at which pace is a matter for discussion and agreement, and those involved in any new project may vary from case to case. The hope is that the more advanced countries will assist those who lag behind, as part of a recognition that whatever the problems all are aiming for the same federal goal.

Variable geometry is the term for a system of à la carte decisions to participate or not participate in particular EU policies. In practice, there may be a small number of core countries who are involved in all activities, and if there is such a group this could result in a two-speed Europe. To avoid this, the Union has usually chosen to move into only those policy areas where there is agreement on the desirability of an integrated approach; an exception would the double British opt-out negotiated at Maastricht.

The à la carte approach poses difficulties in what is meant to be a close Union. If a number of states join only in those actions which they perceive to be of direct benefit to their national interest, then the likelihood of cooperation over a broad front is reduced. However, in an enlarged EU it could be that such flexibility accords with reality. Variable geometry may be the only means by which the large Union can be made to work.

John Major supported the idea of a non-exclusive hard core as part of the flexible future he wished to encourage. He may or may not have understood the distinction between the two concepts here discussed. But it is a significant one. The idea of a two-speed or multi-speed approach is compatible with future integration, even if in practice some states never reach the ultimate destination. Variable geometry is not, unless the 'picking and choosing' is confined to a very few policy areas.

The British opt-outs, a two-speed Europe and variable geometry are all devices which points towards growing flexibility in the EU. They are an attempt to deal with a situation in which some members need to press ahead more quickly, but feel frustrated by those who move with greater caution. Former chancellor Kohl's remark (see p. 287) reflected the frustration of one committed European who wanted the Union to advance at a faster pace than that of the slowest ship in the convoy. His comment echoed prevailing thinking within his Christian Democrat Party, as expressed in a paper which drew attention to the existence of a 'hard core [of member states of the European Union] oriented to greater integration and closer co-operation'. The comment was a recognition of the obvious fact that the countries of Europe were beginning to move at different speeds.

in the House of Commons, 'the time has not been ripe' for the euro. Moreover, Britain has found itself resisting the thrust of integration in other areas favoured by the powerful Franco-German alliance that is usually in the vanguard of further progress.

After the talks over the constitution, the prime minister conceded that in order to preserve his red lines, it was necessary to agree that other states could be allowed to forge ahead with integration, including a common tax policy. Some states, particularly from the former Soviet block, shared his approach, indicating that what is beginning to emerge is a complex patchwork of alliances that form and reform over different issues, and come and go with changing governments. The outcome is likely to be a looser Union, in which the integrationists form a core group who will drive things forward, with other nations choosing how and when they will participate, as national interests and pressures permit.

Former Conservative leader Michael Howard[21] recognised how Europe has been developing in recent years, as we see in the speech to a German audience from which I have already quoted:

> So far, everyone has had to move forward together, with individual countries negotiating specific opt-outs. This has caused tremendous tension . . . But since 1998, there has been a new procedure within the treaties to allow some member states to go ahead with further integration in a specific area, without involving every other member state . . . known as enhanced co-operation. It means that, instead of individual member states having fraught negotiations to opt-out of a new initiative, those that support it can simply decide to opt-in . . . it suits the integrationists, it suits the non-integrationists . . . let's use it . . . it would [then] not be necessary for them to drag Britain and quite possibly some other member states kicking and screaming in their wake . . . I am not talking about a two-speed Europe. That implies that we are all agreed on the destination and differ only about the speed of the journey. I don't want to reach the destination that some our partners may aspire to.

Increasingly today, there is talk among some European politicians not committed to the older, integrationist model of a more flexible Europe in which member nations would in future be able to decide retain wholly national control or cooperate with others. In effect, this would create a series of overlapping circles, with different combinations of member states pooling their responsibilities in different areas of their own choosing.

What happens next?

At a crossroads

Some writers and politicians have argued that the entire existence of the European Community was based on the Cold War which began within a few years of the ending of the 'real war' in 1945. They suggest that a strongly united

Western Europe was highly relevant in the face of possible Soviet aggression, but that circumstances have changed following the downfall of communism and Soviet control. In the era of the Cold War a preoccupation with deepening the bonds between all of the member states was understandable and perhaps inevitable. It is not so self-evidently justifiable in a very different Europe which now embraces states at contrasting stages of development.

Martin Kettle[22] took up such a line of thought a few years ago. In a penetrating article, he discerned five 'big ideas' on which the new Union is being constructed:

- cooperation in foreign and security policy to allow Europe to play a coordinated role in world affairs
- convergence on a federalist political model based upon solidarity
- convergence on a deregulated free market governed by a stability orientated monetary policy
- convergence around a network of social benefits, largely to mitigate the effects of the tight money policy
- enlargement to take in all nations, of whatever size, west of Russia.

Kettle pointed out that – other than the tiny Benelux states – none of the fifteen members at that time was committed to all of these goals. Britain may have been particularly lukewarm, but others too lacked enthusiasm for some of them. In such a situation, 'in an internally unequal Europe, a variable geometry solution is not so much an option as an inevitability', and the 'push to the East is making it so'.

In varying degrees, the 'big ideas' have been implemented, some more than others. Just as the ending of the Cold War was a catalyst for change in the 1990s, causing a rethink of the European enterprise, so too enlargement and the impasse over the Constitutional Treaty have been the cause for reflection on the state of the Union today. Member states have to think again about the European project to equip it to cope with present realities and a new agenda. They face a situation in which the expansion of the EU and the growth of its competences in recent decades have made its capacity to manage its affairs more questionable. Moreover, these developments have been introduced on the basis of only limited support from EU citizens, there being a developing gap between those who have taken the decisions and those affected by them.

The failure of supporters of the Constitution Treaty to win popular support for their work in some member states (especially France and the Netherlands, where referendums were held) caused other countries to postpone or halt their ratification procedures and the Constitution now has an uncertain future. Had it been ratified, the treaty would have entered into force on 1 November 2006. However, as of January 2007, Austria, Belgium, Cyprus, Estonia, Finland, Germany, Greece, Hungary, Italy, Latvia, Lithuania, Luxembourg, Malta,

Slovakia, Slovenia and Spain had ratified the constitutional treaty. The two countries which joined the European Union in 2007, Bulgaria and Romania, had already accepted the Constitutional Treaty too, when ratifying their accession treaties.

Rejection has caused uncertainty about the future direction of Europe. A Europe of twenty-seven members cannot easily continue as it is at present. The difficulty is that in order to reach agreement on any initiative, the Commission has to seek the lowest common denominator among the different national positions. Together with the Union's slow economic growth, the failure of the Constitutional Treaty has cast doubt on whether the EU will be ready to accept new, far poorer members after 2007. (Ratification of the mini 'Lisbon' version (see p. 58 and p. 293) would, of course, enable the machinery of the Union to work more effectively.)

So far, the 'period of reflection' has not brought about a solution to current problems and a vision for the future that would satisfy all member states. But there are those within the Union who are pointing the way forward and seeking to create a new agenda for the increasingly globalised world in which we live. Trade is fast becoming one of the most important drivers of economic growth. And that growth is creating jobs, not only here in Europe, but across the developing and developed world. At the beginning of October 2006, the Commission set out a comprehensive agenda for strengthening the contribution of trade policy to Europe's competitiveness, entitled *Global Europe*. The *Global Europe* agenda argued very strongly that social justice at home and abroad is an integral part of the competitiveness agenda.

Peter Mandelson,[23] the EU's trade commissioner, has grappled with the theme of trade in the era of globalisation. Committed to creating a social dimension in trade policy, he argues that the competitive challenge of the global economy 'can be harnessed to strengthen both our economy and our social models':

> That means policies at home which equip Europe's citizens to take the best from globalisation and avoid becoming victims of the worst. And using our external trade policies to promote growth and sustainable development abroad. These are not distinct agendas. They are one and the same. We will not shape a sustainable globalisation unless we maintain the support of Europe's citizens; and we will not maintain a global dynamic in favour of openness, unless economic change can really be seen to bring greater opportunity for everyone . . . Of course, there are tough choices to be made if Europe is to reform and modernise. But the protectionist alternative, the attempt to put up barriers to trade and, therefore, to change, is an economic dead end.

Speaking to the European Parliament in January 2007, Chancellor Merkel[24] presented a working programme for the next eighteen months, under the German, Portuguese and Slovenian 'presidency trio'. She made her opinion clear: 'The period of reflection is over . . . we now have to come to new decisions'. She was keen to find an answer to the constitutional impasse and wanted to see the adoption of a constitution treaty in some form before the next European elections in 2009. Merkel warned that 'a failure would be a historical default'. She stressed that institutional changes should be made before any further enlargement.

Commission president José Manuel Barroso[25] similarly spoke of the need for some concrete proposals to lay out the path towards an institutional settlement and chart the way forward to 'the Europe we want for the next fifty years'. In particular, Barroso pointed to the issues of social and economic cohesion, energy and climate change, transparency and information, security and the spread of European values.

Agreement on a way forward was reached in June 2007. Ratification of the amending 'Reform' treaty is due to be completed early in 2009. Most states are likely to try to avoid holding a referendum and will aim to approve the Lisbon Treaty via their national parliaments. Only Ireland is obliged to stage such a vote, although there is pressure in Denmark and the UK to have one.

The challenge
The European Union has been more successful and long-lasting than any other rival organisations. Its steady enlargement – with other nations still queuing up to join – points to its relative health and vitality. It has already produced substantial benefits, primarily in keeping the peace in Western Europe, consolidating democracy and contributing to general prosperity. The challenges for the future are to continue to do those things, but also to create a Union which can win the wholehearted consent of its diverse peoples, one which is free, strong and united in its commitment to find a distinctive role in the twenty-first century.

Fifty years ago, at the time of the signing of the Rome Treaty, Europe had a powerful and resonating rationale. It signalled the end of European war, a pact that stopped Germany and France invading each other again. In unity lay strength to resist the threat of Soviet aggression. Half a century later, peace between France and Germany is taken for granted, the two countries having closely cooperated in recent decades; the threat from the East has seemingly disappeared; and Europe has transformed itself into the world's largest single market. In the eyes of many enthusiasts, what the Union lacks is an articulated rationale for the twenty-first century, something to inspire its inhabitants. It is now at the point where fundamental decisions have to be taken about its future development.

References

Introduction

1. N. Nugent, *The Government and Politics of the European Union*, Palgrave, 2006
2. J. Monnet, *Memoirs*, Doubleday and Co., 1978
3. W. Hallstein, *Europe in the Making*, Allen and Unwin, 1972

Section One: History

Introduction

1. S. Henig, *The Uniting of Europe: From Discord to Concord*, Routledge, 1997

Chapter 1

1. H. Macmillan, as quoted by A. Adonis, *Observer*, 17.11.1996
2. J. Monnet, *Memoirs*, Doubleday and Co., 1978
3. M. Holland, *European Integration: From Community to Union*, Pinter, 1994
4. W. Churchill, speech at the University of Zurich, 19.9.1946
5. J. Monnet, as in 2 above
6. J. Monnet, as in 2 above
7. M. Burgess, *Federalism and European Union*, Routledge, 1989
8. J.-P. Duroselle, 'General de Gaulle's Europe and Jean Monnet's Europe', in C. Cosgrove and K. Twitchett (eds), *The New International Actors: The UN and the EEC*, Macmillan, 1970
9. H. Truman, speech to US Congress, 12.3.1947
10. P. Hennessy, *The Prime Minister*, Allen Lane, 2001
11. J. Monnet, as quoted in 2 above
12. J. Monnet, as in 2 above
13. J. Monnet, as quoted in 2 above
14. R. Schuman, speech to French National Assembly, 9.5.1950
15. R. Schuman, as quoted in 2 above
16. K. Adenauer, as quoted in 3 above
17. K. Adenauer, as quoted in 3 above
18. J. Monnet, speech to French National Assembly, as quoted in 2 above
19. D. Acheson, speech at Military Academy, West Point, 5.12.1962
20. W. Churchill, as quoted in H. Young, *This Blessed Plot*, Macmillan, 1998
21. D. Dinan, 'How Did We Get Here?', in E. Bomberg and A. Stubb (eds), *The European Union: How Does it Work?*, Oxford University Press, 2003
22. F. Duchêne, 'More or Less European? Integration in Retrospect', in C. Crouch and D. Marquand (eds), *The Politics of 1992: beyond the Single European Market, Political Quarterly*, 107: 4, 1993

23. M. Holland, as in 3 above
24. J. Monnet, as in 2 above
25. S. Henig, *The Uniting of Europe: From Discord to Concord*, Routledge, 1997
26. C. de Gaulle, *Memoirs of Hope: Renewal and Endeavor*, trans. T. Kilmartin, Simon and Schuster, 1971

Chapter 2

1. P. Taylor, *The Limits of European Integration*, Croom Helm, 1983
2. *The Economist*, 13.3.1982
3. R. Jenkins, *European Diary 1977–1981*, Collins, 1989
4. R. Jenkins, as in 3 above
5. The view of the secretary-general of the EC, Emile Noel, as quoted in H. Young, *This Blessed Plot*, Macmillan, 1998
6. L. Tindemans, *The High Road to European Union* (report), 1975
7. E. Bomberg and A. Stubb (eds), *The European Union: How Does it Work?*, Oxford University Press, 2003
8. J. Delors, speech to TUC annual conference, 1988
9. As quoted in C. Pilkington, *Britain in the European Union Today*, Manchester University Press, 2001
10. D. Hurd, speech to House of Commons, 14.7.1992

Chapter 3

1. H. Young, *This Blessed Plot*, Macmillan, 1998
2. H. Grabbe, *New Designs for Europe*, Centre for European Reform, 2002
3. S. Henig, *The Uniting of Europe: From Discord to Concord*, Routledge, 1997
4. N. Nugent, *The Government and Politics of the European Union*, Palgrave, 2006

Chapter 4

1. A. Milward, *The Reconstruction of Western Europe*, University of California Press, 1984
2. A. Moravcsik, 'Preferences and Power in the European Community: A Liberal Interventionist Approach', *Journal of Common Market Studies*, 31:4, 1993
3. N. Nugent, *The Government and Politics of the European Union*, Palgrave, 2006
4. D. Mitrany, 'The Functional Approach to World Organisation', in C. Cosgrove and K. Twitchett (eds), *The New International Actors: the UN and the EEC*, 1970
5. M. Holland, *European Integration: From Community to Union*, Pinter, 1994
6. C. Pentland, *International Theory and European Integration*, The Free Press, 1973
7. E. Haas, *The Uniting of Europe: Political, Economic and Social Forces 1950–57*, Stanford University Press, 1958. See also *Beyond the Nation-State: Functionalism and International Organization*, Stanford University Press, 1964

8. L. Lindberg, *The Political Dynamics of European Economic Integration*, Stanford University Press, 1963
9. R. Harrison, 'Neo-functionalism', in A. Groom and P. Taylor, *Frameworks for International Cooperation*, Pinter, 1950
10. R. Keohane and S. Hoffman, 'Conclusions: Community Politics and Institutional Change', in W. Wallace (ed.), *The Dynamics of European Integration*, 1992. See also *The New European Community*, Westview Press, 1991, by the same authors
11. M. Holland, as in 6 above
12. A. Blair, *Companion to the European Union*, Routledge, 2006
13. A. Moravcsik, as in 2 above
14. J. Monnet, *Memoirs*, Doubleday and Co., 1978
15. K.-D. Borchardt, *European Integration: The Origins and Growth of the European Union*, European Commission, 1995
16. S. Henig, *The Uniting of Europe: From Discord to Concord*, Routledge, 1997
17. A. Moravcsik, as in 2 above

Section Two: Institutions

Chapter 5

1. TEU, Title 11 (amendments to the Treaty of Rome), Article 157, Clause 2
2. L. Brittan, as quoted by J. Palmer, *The Guardian*, 23.3.1994
3. J. Oman, 'Prodi lays foundations for "United States of Europe"', *Observer*, 11.7.1999
4. Books differ markedly in the figures they quote for the exact size of the Commission staff. The figure given here is the one mentioned on the Commission's own website. E. Bomberg and A. Stubb (eds), *The European Union: How Does It Work?* make the interesting point that within member states the average number of civil servants per 10,000 citizens is 322, whereas that for all EU institutions is 0.8
5. According to figures released in April 1998 the number of civil servants employed by the Department of the Environment, Transport and the Regions totalled 15,215, almost exactly the same as the numbers given for the Commission. Even the annual budget of €976 administered by the Commission is only half the budget spent by the British Department of Social Security. Figures given in C. Pilkington, *The Civil Service in Britain Today*, Manchester University Press, 1999
6. S. Mazey and J. Richardson, 'Pressure groups and the EC', *Politics Review*, September 1993
7. A. Geddes, *The European Union and British Politics*, Palgrave, 2004
8. A. Geddes, as in 7 above
9. M. Westlake, *The Council of the European Union*, John Harper, 1999

10. TEU, Article 151, Clause 1
11. As quoted in A. Keene in *Europa*, a discussion journal published by the European Commission, 1997
12. M. Westlake, as in 9 above

Chapter 6

1. E. Bomberg and A. Stubb (eds), *The European Union: How Does it Work?*, Oxford University Press, 2003
2. M. Holland, *European Integration: From Community to Union*, Pinter, 1994
3. E. Bomberg and A. Stubb , as in 1 above
4. The European Commission, *The ABC of Community Law*, European Documentation Series, 1991
5. The ABC of Community Law, as in 4 above
6. *New Statesman*, 10.6.1990
7. Lord Bridges, as quoted in A. Davies, *British Politics and Europe,* Hodder and Stoughton, 1998
8. Case 26/62, Van Gend & Loos [1963] ECR 1 (Nature of Community Law)
9. L. Lindberg and S. Scheingold, *Europe's Would-Be Polity*, Prentice Hall, 1970
10. Reflections Group, Publications of the European Community, 1996
11. W. Nicoll and T. Salmon, *Understanding the European Union*, Pearson, 2001
12. N. Nugent, *The Government and Politics of the European Union*, Palgrave, 2006

Chapter 7

1. L. Brittan, 'Making Law in the European Union', paper delivered to Centre for Legislative Studies, March 1994
2. G. d'Estaing, as quoted in W. Nicoll and T. Salmon, *Understanding the European Union*, Pearson, 2001
3. W. Newton-Dunn (MEP), who on his European Parliament website claims to have first used the phrase in a 1980s pamphlet
4. G. Majone, *Regulating Europe*, Routledge, 1996
5. A. Moravcsik, *The Choice for Europe*, Cornell University Press, 1998
6. A. Follesdal and S. Hix, 'Why There is a Democratic Deficit in the EU: A Response to Majone and Moravcsik', European Governance Paper (EUROGOV) no. C-05-02, 14.3.2005
7. J. Monnet, *Memoirs*, Doubleday and Co., 1978
8. M. Holland, *European Integration: From Community to Union*, Pinter, 1994
9. K. Reif and H. Schmitt, 'Nine Second-order National Elections: A Conceptual Framework for the Analysis of European Election Results', *European Journal of Political Research*, vol. 8:1, 1980
10. M. Kohnstamm, as quoted in 6 above

11. R. Holzhacker, 'National Parliamentary Scrutiny Over EU Issues: Comparing Goals and Methods', *European Union Politics* 3, 2002
12. P. Norton, *Talking Politics*, 7: 3, Spring 1995
13. L. Brittan, as in 1 above
14. R. Cook, interview in *New Statesman*, 13.8.1998
15. P. Norton, as in 12 above
16. A. Follesdal and S. Hix, as in 6 above
17. E. Bomberg and A. Stubb (eds), *The European Union: How Does it Work?*, Oxford University Press, 2003
18. R. Dahl, 'A Democratic Dilemma: System Effectiveness Versus Citizen Participation', *Political Science Quarterly*, 1994

Section Three: Representation

Introduction

1. A. Geddes, *The European Union and British Politics*, Palgrave, 2004

Chapter 8

1. J. Curtice and M. Steed, in D. Butler and M. Westlake, *British Politics and the European Union Elections of 1994*, Macmillan, 1995
2. A. Geddes, *The European Union and British Politics*, Palgrave, 2004
3. N. Nugent, *The Government and Politics of the European Union*, Palgrave, 2006
4. J. Straw, speech in House of Commons, 17.7.1997
5. R. Rose, 'Voter Turnout in Western Europe: a Regional Report', International Institute for Democracy and Electoral Assistance, 7.6.2004
6. W. Nicoll and T. Salmon, *Understanding the European Union*, Pearson, 2001
7. M. Engel, 'Parliament of Snoozers', *The Guardian*, 25.1.1994
8. *The Economist*, 5.6.2004. The database search was conducted by Factiva.com and based on a review of nine daily and Sunday quality papers in Britain, plus the *International Herald Tribune* and the *Wall Street Journal*

Chapter 9

1. Regulation on European Political Parties. No. 2004/2003, as adopted by the Council and EP, 2003
2. N. Nugent, *The Government and Politics of the European Union*, Palgrave, 2006
3. T. Jansen, 'The Emergence of a Transnational European Party System', *European View* 3, 2006
4. Tsatsos report on financing parties, 1996
5. T. Bale, *European Politics: A Comparative Introduction*, Palgrave, 2005
6. W. Martens, introduction to 3 above
7. N. Nugent, as in 2 above
8. S. Hix, A. Noury and G. Roland, 'Powers to the Parties: Cohesion and

Competition in the European Parliament: 1979–2001', *British Journal of Political Science*, 35:2, 2005

9. S. Hix and A. Noury, 'After Enlargement: Voting Behaviour in the Sixth European Parliament', paper on party cohesion presented to Federal Trust in London, 17.3.2006

10. E. Bomberg and A. Stubb, *The European Union: How Does it Work?*, Oxford University Press, 2003

11. T. Jansen, as in 3 above

Chapter 10

1. S. Mazey and J. Richardson (eds), *Lobbying in the European Community*, Oxford University Press, 1993

2. O. Gray, 'The Structure of Interest Group Representation in the EU: Some Observations of a Practitioner', in P.-H. Claeys et al, *Lobbying, Pluralism and European Integration*, European Interuniversity Press, 1998

3. W. Wessels, 'The Growth and Differentiation of Multi-Level Networks: A Corporatist Mega-Bureaucracy or an Open City?', in H. Wallace and A. Young, *Participation and Policy-Making in the European Union*, Clarendon Press, 1997

4. B. Coxall, *Pressure Groups in British Politics*, Pearson, 2001

5. E. Bomberg and A. Stubb, *The European Union: How Does it Work?*, Oxford University Press, 2003

6. W. Grant, *Pressure Groups, Politics and Democracy in Britain*, Harvester Wheatsheaf, 1999

7. R. Baggott, *Pressure Groups Today*, Manchester University Press, 1995

8. W. Grant, as in 6 above

9. A. Butt Philip, *Pressure Groups in the European Community*, Occasional Paper, University of Bath, 1985

10. E. Bomberg and A. Stubb, as in 5 above

11. J. Peterson, 'States, Societies and the European Union', *West European Politics*, 20:4, July 1997

12. E. Bomberg and A. Stubb, as in 5 above

13. M. Smith, *Pressure Politics*, Baseline Books, 1995

14. S. Mazey and J. Richardson, 'Pressure Groups and the EC', *Politics Review*, September 1993

15. M. Aspinwall, 'Collective Attraction – the New Political Game in Brussels', in J. Greenwood and M. Aspinwall (eds), *Collective Action in the European Union*, Routledge, 1998

16. S. McGiffen, *The European Union: A Critical Guide*, Pluto Press, 2005

17. H. Wallace and A. Young, *Participation and Policy-Making in the European Union*, Clarendon Press, 1997

18. J. Peterson, as in 11 above

Section Four: Policies

Introduction
1. N. Nugent, *The Government and Politics of the European Union*, Palgrave, 2006

Chapter 11
1. R. Jenkins, *European Diary, 1977–1981*, Collins, 1989

Chapter 12
1. C. Scrivener, Consumer Rights in the Single Market, *European File* series, European Commission, 1993
2. Sir Leon Brittan, then commissioner for competition policy, *Competition Policy in the European Community*, European File Series, European Commission, 1992
3. L. Elliott, 'Year of Living Dangerously', in V. Keegan and M. Kettle, *The New Europe*, Fourth Estate, 1993
4. Press release, 'EU ministers adopt groundbreaking sugar reform', European Commission, 20.2.2006
5. The on-line CIA World Factbook
6. J. Grant of the National Alliance of Women's Organisations, as reported by S. Rutherford, 'Europe, my Europe', *The Guardian*, 17.5.1994

Chapter 13
1. I. Black, 'Refugees in Britain: Special Report', *The Guardian*, 27.3.2000
2. E. MacAskill, 'Belgium Restores Frontier Curbs', *The Guardian*, 10.1.2000
3. B. Roche, then junior Home Office minister, as reported in *The Guardian*, 17.2.2000
4. M. Holland, *European Integration: From Community to Union*, Pinter, 1994
5. R. Ginsberg, *Foreign Policy Actions of the European Community*, Adamantine, 1989
6. E. Bomberg and A. Stubb, *The European Union: How Does it Work?*, Oxford University Press, 2003

Section Five: Attitudes

Chapter 14
1. A. Poole, in M. Van Meerhaeghe (ed.), *Belgium and EC Membership Evaluated*, Frances Pinter, 1992
2. M. De Hond, 'Dutch Say Devastating No to EU Constitution', *The Guardian*, 2.6.2005
3. OECD figures; see also its figures for purchasing power parities per head for the year 2002, based on information provided by *Eurostat*, 11.1.2005. Using a

base index of 100, these show 205 for Luxembourg, 103 for the 12 members of the eurozone and 96 for the 25 member states

4. A.-M. Le Gloannec, 'Germany and Europe's Foreign and Security Policy: Embracing the British Vision', in C. Lankowski (ed.), *Break Out, Break Down or Break In? Germany and the European Union after Amsterdam*, American Institute for Contemporary German Studies, 1998
5. W. Nicoll and T. Salmon, *Understanding the European Union*, Pearson, 2001
6. G. FitzGerald, speech to Irish Royal Academy, 10.11.1975
7. D. Hubner, conference speech on 'Regional Policy Responses to Demographic Challenges', Brussels, 25–6 January 2007

Chapter 15
1. H. Young, *This Blessed Plot*, Macmillan, 1998
2. W. Churchill, speech in House of Commons, May 1951
3. A. Eden, as quoted in S. Greenwood, *Britain and European Cooperation Since 1945*, Blackwell, 1992
4. D. Acheson, speech at the Military Academy, West Point, 5.12.1962
5. F. Northedge, *Descent From Power: British Foreign Policy 1945–1973*, Allen and Unwin, 1974
6. H. Young, as in 1 above
7. G. Martin, quoted in A. Davies, *British Politics and Europe*, Access series, Hodder and Stoughton, 1998
8. H. Macmillan, quoted by A. Adonis, *The Observer*, 17.11.1996
9. W. Kaiser, *Using Europe, Abusing the Europeans: Britain and European Integration 1945–1963*, St Martin's Press, 1996
10. N. Tebbit, as quoted in 8 above
11. M. Thatcher, as quoted in 8 above
12. M. Thatcher, speech to College of Europe in Bruges, September 1988
13. M. Howard, speech to Konrad Adenauer Stiftung, Berlin, 12.2.2004
14. Tony Blair, speech to French National Assembly, October 1998
15. Tony Blair, speech to Foreign Office Conference of Ambassadors, 7.1.2003
16. Tony Blair, as in 14 above
17. A. Geddes, *The European Union and British Politics*, Palgrave, 2004
18. D. Butler and M. Westlake, *British Politics and the European Elections 2004*, Macmillan, 2005
19. D. Hurd, as quoted in *Memoirs*, Little, Brown, 2003
20. Sir A. Meyer, as quoted in 1 above
21. *Le Monde*, as quoted by M. Kettle, *The Guardian*, 22.9.1995
22. H. Young, as in 1 above
23. A. Geddes, as in 17 above
24. J. Delors, *The Guardian*, 17.10.2004

25. S. George, *An Awkward Partner: Britain in the European Community*, Oxford University Press, 1998
26. S. McGiffen, *The European Union: A Critical Guide*, Pluto Press, 2005
27. H Young, as in 1 above

Conclusion

1. W. Hallstein, *Europe in the Making*, Allen and Unwin, 1972
2. R. Schuman, *The Schuman Declaration*, 9.5.1950
3. N. Nugent, *The Government and Politics of the European Union*, Palgrave, 2006
4. W. Wessels, 'The Growth and Differentiation of Multi-Level Networks', in H. Wallace and A. Young, *Policy-Making in the European Union*, Oxford University Press, 1997
5. J. Monnet, *Memoirs*, Doubleday and Co., 1978
6. M. Thatcher, *The Downing Street Years*, HarperCollins, 1993
7. *Agence Europe*, 1991, as quoted by H. Young, *The Guardian*, 10.9.1991
8. H. Young, *This Blessed Plot*, Macmillan, 1998
9. A. Marr, *The Observer*, 10.1.1999
10. W. Hague, speech to Conservative Party annual conference, 5.10.2000
11. *Mail on Sunday*, as quoted in a special report for *The Observer*, 10.12.2000
12. J. Smith, as quoted in 11 above
13. E. Hobsbawm, as quoted in 11 above
14. N. Davies, as quoted in 11 above
15. M. Ancram, as quoted in 11 above
16. L. Siedentop, as quoted in 11 above
17. E. Balladur, interview in *Le Figaro*, 30.8.1994
18. Reflections on European Policy, German Christian Democrat Study Paper, November 1994
19. H. Kohl, speech in Cologne, February 1996
20. J. Major, William and Mary Lecture, University of Leiden, the Netherlands, 6.9.1994
21. M. Howard, speech to Konrad Adenauer Stiftung, Berlin, 12.2.2004
22. M. Kettle, *The Guardian*, 5.11.1994
23. P. Mandelson, EU Decent Work Conference on Globalisation, Brussels, 5.12.2006
24. A. Merkel, speech to European Parliament, 17.1.2007
25. J. Barroso, European Conference, Frederiksdal, Denmark, 19.5.2006

Further reading

Books

EU in general

Much of the writing on the European Union is highly academic and specialised. The classic book is *The Government and Politics of the European Union*, by Neill Nugent, published by Palgrave (2006) and now in its sixth edition. It is part of an impressive series that is intended to provide an authoritative library on the European Union, some of the works being the definitive study of their chosen subject, others providing a fairly comprehensive guide and useful references. Nugent's volume is an excellent work of its type, but inevitably demanding, detailed and excessively lengthy for students tackling the subject for the first time. Desmond Dinan's *Ever Closer Union: An Introduction to European Integration* and Ben Rosamund's *Theories of European Integration* (Palgrave, 1999 and 2000 respectively) are important components of this series. Again, they are scholarly and immensely valuable.

In the same series is *Understanding the European Union: A Concise Introduction* (2005), by John McCormick, which is – as its title implies – much briefer. However, its very 'conciseness' means that it would not provide sufficient detail to meet the requirements of many candidates in examinations. The same author has also written a well-rated study, *European Union: Politics and Policies* (2004), for Westview Press. This is a worthy volume, well written, not overloaded with detail, and well geared to its potential audience. It covers history, institutions and policies, but not attitudes of the member states.

E. Bomberg and A. Stubb have co-authored a useful volume for Oxford University Press (2003), *The European Union: How Does it Work?* This is a very well-written study, good (although brief) on history and development and especially strong on institutions. It does not provide any or much coverage of areas such as elections and parties, and is cursory on policies, too. W. Nicoll and T. Salmon, *Understanding the European Union* (Pearson/Longman, 2001), is comprehensive and provides many helpful references, a book that acts as a useful follow-up on some key aspects of the EU. Much more manageable but less analytical is Dick Leonard's *The Economist Guide to the European Union* (Economist Books, 2005).

S. George and I. Bache, *Politics in the European Union* (Oxford University Press, 2001), covers its chosen ground effectively, but is not the text for someone seeking an overall view of the development of the Union. It is also now rather dated. Steven McGiffen's *The European Union: A Critical Guide* (Pluto Press, 2005) offers a critical and partisan perspective on the origins, development and current direction of the EU.

What is lacking is an up-to-date and comprehensive text covering key aspects – including history and developments, institutions, actors, policies and policy processes, and the role and attitudes of member states – in a way that meets the needs of a wide audience of teachers, students, practitioners and interested general readers. Two books which will be useful for any student of the subject are: Alasdair Blair's *Companion to the European Union* (Routledge, 2006), and Timothy Bainbridge's *The Penguin Companion to the European Union* (Penguin, 2002). Both are invaluable contributions to the available literature, providing information and some analysis of the key developments and policies of the EU.

More specialist books on aspects of policy development and the road to integration are mentioned in the text and included in the appropriate section of the References.

Britain and the European Union
Similarly, there have until recently been few accessible and authoritative accounts of Britain's place in the European Union, although in recent years a few have appeared that are more geared to the school and college market. There is also a growing recognition of the European perspective in general textbooks on British government and politics.

Useful general works include: A. Geddes, *The European Union and British Politics* (Palgrave, 2004), D. Watts and C. Pilkington, *Britain in the European Union Today* (Manchester University Press, 2005), S. George, *An Awkward Partner: Britain in the European Community* (Oxford University Press, 1998).

The most recent addition to the literature on Britain and Europe is the excellent study written for Edinburgh University Press by Alistair Jones, *Britain and the European Union*, published in the Politics Study Guides series in 2007.

More specialist in character are: H. Young, *This Blessed Plot* (Macmillan, 1998). This is a lengthy, informative and thought-provoking study of the relationship of Britain and the EU, from the early postwar days. Philip Giddings and Gavin Drewry, *Britain in the European Union: Law, Policy and Parliament* (Palgrave, 2004). It analyses the main developments in the relationship between Britain and the EU between the ratification of the Maastricht Treaty and the 2001 general election, focusing especially on the impact of the Union on parliamentary institutions and controversial areas of policy, such as asylum and immigration, and foreign and security policy.

On the Web

A vast amount of information is available on the Internet.

General sites
www.europa.eu.int
A truly massive site that is a valuable starting point for further reference, offering

in all languages of the EU direct access to the home pages of EU institutions, basic information about the EU and its policy areas, enlargement, official documents etc.

www.cec.org.uk
UK office of the European Commission

www.europarl.europa.eu
European Parliament. See in particular its introductory factsheets at www.europarl.eu.int/facts/default_rn.htm

www.uaces.org/
University Association for Contemporary European Studies

EU development and policies
Other than the europa site, current issues concerning EU development and policies are aired via several think tanks, notably:
www.ceps.be Centre for European Policy Studies
www.cer.org.uk Centre for European Reform
www.theepc.be/ European Policy Centre
www.eiop.or.at On-line research papers on European integration
www.fedtrust.co.uk Federal Trust
www.iiea.com/ Institute of European Affairs

Index

Bold denotes glossary entry